LINKING GLOBAL TRADE AND HUMAN RIGHTS

During the global economic crisis of 2008, countries around the world used national policy spaces to respond to the economic crisis in ways that shed new light on the possibilities for linkages between international trade and human rights. This book introduces the idea of policy space as an innovative way to reframe recent developments in global governance. It brings together a wide-ranging group of leading experts in international law, trade, human rights, political economy, international relations, and public policy, who have been asked to reflect on this important development in globalization. Their multidisciplinary contributions provide explanations for why the global landscape for national policy space has changed, clearly illustrate instances of this change, and project the future paths for policy development in social and economic policy spaces, especially with reference to linkages between international trade and human rights in countries from the global North as well as Brazil, China, and India.

Daniel Drache is Professor Emeritus of Political Science and Senior Research Scholar at the Robarts Centre for Canadian Studies, York University. He has been a research associate at the European University Institute, Florence; a professor invité at CEPREMAP-CNRS, Paris; a visiting scholar at Macquarrie University, the University of Western Sydney, and the Australian Graduate School of Management at the University of New South Wales; a guest lecturer at Universidad Nacional Autónoma de México; and a Ford Foundation visiting professor at JNU, New Delhi. His books include *Defiant Publics: The Unprecedented Reach of the Global Citizen* (2008), *The Continental Illusion: Borders and the Search for North America* (2006), *Borders Matter: Homeland Security and the Search for North America* (2004), and *The Market or the Public Domain: Global Governance and the Asymmetry of Power* (2001).

Lesley A. Jacobs is Professor of Law & Society and Political Science as well as acting Director of the Institute for Social Research at York University and Executive Director of the Canadian Forum on Civil Justice. He has held a range of visiting positions, including ones at Harvard Law School (Liberal Arts Fellow), Oxford University (Wolfson Fellow), Law Commission of Canada (Scholar in Residence); Waseda University Law School (International Law Visiting Professor); University of California, Berkeley; Emory University, and the University of British Columbia. He is the author of numerous books, including *Privacy Rights in the Global Digital Economy* (2013), *Balancing Competing Human Rights in a Diverse Society* (2012), *Pursuing Equal Opportunities* (2004), *The Democratic Vision of Politics* (1997), and *Rights and Deprivation* (1993).

Linking Global Trade and Human Rights

NEW POLICY SPACE IN HARD ECONOMIC TIMES

Edited by

DANIEL DRACHE

York University

LESLEY A. JACOBS

York University

CAMBRIDGE
UNIVERSITY PRESS

CAMBRIDGE
UNIVERSITY PRESS

32 Avenue of the Americas, New York NY 10013-2473, USA

Cambridge University Press is part of the University of Cambridge.

It furthers the University's mission by disseminating knowledge in the pursuit of education, learning and research at the highest international levels of excellence.

www.cambridge.org
Information on this title: www.cambridge.org/9781107633896

First published 2014
First paperback edition 2015

A catalogue record for this publication is available from the British Library

Library of Congress Cataloguing in Publication data
Linking global trade and human rights : new policy space in hard economic times / [edited by] Daniel Drache, York University; Lesley A. Jacobs, York University.
    pages cm
"This book has its origins in a major international workshop held at York University in Toronto in October 2011." – Acknowledgements.
Includes bibliographical references and index.
ISBN 978-1-107-04717-4 (hardback)
1. Foreign trade regulation – Congresses.   2. Human rights – Congresses.   3. Law and economic development – Congresses.   4. Law and globalization – Congresses.   I. Drache, Daniel, 1941– editor of compilation.   II. Jacobs, Lesley A., editor of compilation.
K3943.A6L56   2013
382'.3 – dc23   2013032182

ISBN 978-1-107-04717-4 Hardback
ISBN 978-1-107-63389-6 Paperback

Contents

Contributors

Saradindu Bhaduri is Assistant Professor at the Centre for Studies in Science Policy, Jawaharlal Nehru University, New Delhi. His research focuses on the interface of technology and policy institutions from the perspectives of evolutionary and institutional economics. He has published his research in journals such as *Oxford Development Studies*, *European Journal of Health Economics*, *Public Understanding of Science*, and *Mind and Society*, as well as in edited volumes and handbooks.

Sarah Biddulph is Reader in Law at the Melbourne Law School, specializing in the research and teaching of Chinese law. Her particular areas of research are contemporary Chinese administrative law, criminal procedure, labor, comparative law, and the law regulating social and economic rights. Her recent publications include *Legal Reform and Administrative Detention Powers in China* (2007) and, with Sean Cooney and Ying Zhu, *Law and Fair Work in China: Making and Enforcing Labour Standards in the PRC* (2013). She co-edited, with Pip Nicholson, *Examining Practice Interrogating Theory: Comparative Legal Studies in Asia* (2008).

Ljiljana Biuković is an Associate Professor in the Faculty of Law and Co-Director of the National Centre for Business Law at the University of British Columbia. Her research interests are European Union law, international trade law, international dispute resolution, e-commerce, and comparative law. She has published several books and papers on these topics including, with Pitman Potter, *Globalization and Local Adaptation in International Law* (2011).

Adelle Blackett is Associate Professor of Law and William Dawson Scholar at the University of McGill. She was a recipient of the 2010–2011 Bora Laskin Fellowship in Human Rights for her research on rethinking the relation between trade and labor law from a redistributive perspective.

Tomer Broude is the Sylvan M. Cohen Chair in Law, Faculty of Law and Department of International Relations, and Academic Director of the Minerva Center for Human Rights, Hebrew University of Jerusalem. His publications include *The Politics of International Economic Law* (2011), *Law and Development on International Trade* (2011), and *International Governance in the WTO: Judicial Boundaries and Political Capitulation* (2004).

Chang-Hee Lee works as a senior policy analyst at the International Labour Organization in Geneva. He has worked extensively on labor relations and collective bargaining in East Asia, with a particular focus on China. His publication include *A New Face of China: Dialogue with Leading Intellectuals of Modern China* (2005) and a major 2012 report for the ILO, *Measuring the Effects of the Collective Voice Mechanism and the Labour Contract Law*. He is currently leading an ILO research program on comparative studies of labor market institutions in BRICs.

Daniel Drache is Emeritus Professor of Political Science in the Faculty of Liberal Arts and Professional Studies at York University. He is the author and editor of many books, including *Borders Matter: Homeland Security and the Search for North America* (2004) and *Defiant Publics: The Unprecedented Reach of the Global Citizen* (2008). Additional information on his reports and studies can be found at http://www.yorku.ca/drache.

Jorge Heine is a Distinguished Fellow at the Center for International Governance Innovation at the University of Waterloo. At the Center he has been a co-editor of several major volumes focusing on trade in Latin America, including *The Dark Side of Globalization* (2011).

Kathryn Hochstetler is the Chair for the Americas at the Center for International Governance Innovation and a Professor at the Balsillie School of International Affairs at the University of Waterloo. She has published three books, including, with Margaret E. Keck, *Greening Brazil: Environmental Activism in State and Society* (2007).

Lesley A. Jacobs is Professor of Law & Society and Political Science at York University and Executive Director of the Canadian Forum on Civil Justice. His research focuses on human rights, health and welfare state polices, and the uses of legal institutions and mechanism to pursue social justice in both international and domestic law. He is the author of many books, including *Rights and Deprivation* (1993), *Pursuing Equal Opportunities* (2004), and *Balancing Competing Human Rights in a Diverse Society* (2012).

Ronald Labonté is the Canada Research Chair in Globalization & Health Equity, Institute of Population Health at the University of Ottawa; he is also a Professor in the Department of Epidemiology and Community Medicine there. His books include *Health for Some: Death, Disease and Disparity in a Globalizing Era* (2005) and *Fatal Indifference: The G8, Africa and Global Health* (2004).

Matias E. Margulis is Assistant Professor of International Studies at the University of Northern British Columbia. A former Canadian delegate to the WTO, OECD, and UN agencies, his recent publications include "The Regime Complex for Food Security: Implications for the Global Hunger Challenge" (*Global Governance*, 2013) and, with Tony Porter, "Governing the Global Land Grab: Multipolarity, Ideas and Complexity in Transnational Governance" (*Globalizations*, 2013). He also co-edited, with Nora McKeon and Saturnino Borras, Jr., *Land Grabbing and Global Governance* (2013).

Kuldeep Mathur has taught at Jawaharlal Nehru University and at the Indian Institute of Public Administration, New Delhi. He is a recipient of awards from the University Grants Commission and Indian Council of Social Science Research for his contributions in the field of political science and public administration. Mathur was a member of the United Nations Committee of Experts on Public Administration from 2003 to 2006. He is the former director of the National Institute of Education Planning and Administration and Rector of Jawaharlal Nehru University. Mathur has published extensively on subjects such as public policy processes, bureaucracy, decentralization, and state-society relations. His recent publications are *Public Policy and Politics in India: How Institutions Matter* (2013) and *Panchayati Raj* (2013).

Ernst-Ulrich Petersmann is Emeritus Professor in the Department of Law at the European University Institute. He is the author of many influential books, including, most recently, *International Economic Law in the 21st Century: Constitutional Pluralism and Multilevel Governance of Interdependent Public Goods* (2012).

Sol Picciotto is Emeritus Professor of Law at Lancaster University, United Kingdom, and served as Scientific Director of the Oñati International Institute for the Sociology of Law from 2009 to 2011. He is the author of *Regulating Global Corporate Capitalism* (2011), *International Business Taxation* (1992), and numerous edited books, chapters, and journal articles on law and capitalism, the state and economic regulation, and various aspects of international economic and business law, including international trade, investment, transnational corporations, corporate control and accountability, intellectual property rights, and financial market regulation.

Pitman B. Potter is the HSBC Chair Institute of Asian Research Professor of Law, UBC Law Faculty, University of British Columbia. His research interests include Chinese law and politics, international trade and investment law, human rights, comparative law, and globalization. His publications include, with Ljiljana Biuković, *A Guide to Business Law in Asia* (2012); *The Chinese Legal System and Legal Culture* (2011); and many publications in *Law & Social Inquiry, The China Quarterly,* and *The International Journal.*

Amit Shovon Ray is Professor of Economics at the Center for International Trade and Development at Jawaharlal Nehru University. He has been a consultant for various national and international bodies including the World Bank and the Indian Council for Research on International Economic Relations.

Joseph F. Turcotte is a PhD candidate and SSHRC Doctoral Fellow in the Communication and Culture (Politics & Policy) program at York University, Toronto, Canada. His research focuses on the ways in which emerging digital and networked technologies alter established institutions and practices, with a focus on the political economy of intellectual property rights, international trade, the global digital/knowledge economy, and the media and culture industries.

Acknowledgments

This book has its origins in a major international workshop held at York University in Toronto in October 2011 on the theme of international trade and human rights linkages on the new global landscape that emerged after the 2008 financial crisis. The workshop was organized by the directors of two research centres at York, Lesley A. Jacobs (York Centre for Public Policy and Law) and Daniel Drache (Robarts Centre for Canadian Studies), with valuable administrative support from Laura Taman (at York University) and Rozalia Mate (at the University of British Columbia). Our feeling when organizing the workshop was that the global financial crisis of 2008 presented opportunities for major policy initiatives on both the domestic and international levels, which were not possible for the most part in the previous decade. Contrary to conventional wisdom, hard economic times globally have fostered new policy spaces and not just shrunk them. Numerous workshop participants reinforced this observation with their contributions. Many of the chapters in this book stem from draft papers presented during that workshop, although a number of the contributors to this book were not present at the workshop. We also wish to acknowledge the valuable contributions to the workshop by individuals not represented in this book: Chantal Blouin, Lorne Foster, Milind Kandlikar, and Amy Kapczynski.

This book as well as the workshop received financial support from the Asia Pacific Dispute Resolution Project (APDR) housed at the Faculty of Law, University of British Columbia, funded through the Social Sciences and Humanities Research Council of Canada (SSHRC) MCRI program. Pitman B. Potter is the Principal Investigator for the APDR Project and has provided valuable input and insight on the themes around which this book is organized. We also benefited tremendously from the efforts of Matthew McManus (PhD student, Socio-Legal Studies) and Marco Quezada (Economics undergraduate student) in the editing of the various chapters that make up this book. Their time and commitment to seeing the book through to the finish played an important role in our being able to produce the book in a timely fashion. We also want to acknowledge John Berger, Senior Editor at Cambridge University Press, for strong support and enthusiasm for the book project, as well as the anonymous reviewers who offered insightful and constructive comments.

This book has taken an immense amount of our time over the past two years. The two of us have spent a great deal of time together identifying the central unifying concept for the book – new policy spaces for linking international trade and human rights – and constructing that theme in a bold and innovative way that sheds new light on globalization. The time spent together reinforced for both of us the immense value of collaborative research as a catalyst for new ideas.

Daniel Drache and Lesley A. Jacobs
Toronto, March 2013

Introduction: Emerging Policy Spaces During Global Economic Crises

Daniel Drache and Lesley A. Jacobs

POLICY SPACE: A CRITICAL ARENA FOR GOVERNANCE

The concept of policy space is critical to understanding the impact of globalization on public policy in the twenty-first century. For the purposes of this book, a policy space is an arena where national governments have the freedom and capacity to design and implement public policies of their own choosing (Grindle and Thomas, 1991; Koivusalo et al., 2010). In market economies, policy spaces reflect the insight that certain realms of public life should be governed by collective decision making designed to advance the public interest whereas in other realms markets reign (Drache, 2001). The spatial metaphor expresses, in other words, the claim that there are certain sites where government action has legitimacy. Ultimately, national policy spaces matter because they provide opportunities for governments to be innovative in the development of public policy on these sites, especially in terms of advancing social justice goals (Jacobs, 2004).

The unifying theme of this book is that there are major reconfigurations of social and economic policy spaces for national governments on the international landscape during the hard economic times that follow global financial crises. After the 2008 financial crisis, state action extended into new areas and was being deployed in new and innovative ways from the Cash for Clunkers program in the United States to successful anti-poverty programs in Brazil. In India the national Rural Employment Scheme to guarantee a minimum number of paid hours annually to hundreds of millions of its poorest is the largest social welfare scheme in the world. Obamacare pushes Washington into a new, albeit controversial, policy area requiring complex coordination between the federal government and the states that impacts significantly on the daily lives of Americans. The trillions of dollars invested in bailouts and infrastructure spending across the globe marks a departure from neoliberalism

1

pur et dur. In the EU, the establishment of the European Bank regulator is widely seen as the first step toward regaining economic health. Curbing financial private-sector compensation is also on the agenda in both Europe and the United States. State intervention in the economy has reemerged as a strategic option for policy makers. Even the International Monetary Fund (IMF) is relenting and bending. In a remarkable intellectual shift, some observers are of the view that a sea change has occurred and the IMF is embracing stimulus spending and just not espousing strict austerity in its junior troika role along with the European Commission and its Central Bank (Beattie, 2012).

These new policy spaces promise potential and, with the global slowdown deepening and the onset of dismal economic times, more innovative responses are likely on the way within global cities and countries. Pessimists look at these global events as evidence of the structural barriers further institutionalizing neoliberal practices. They see financial crises as constraining the maneuver room of states. We beg to disagree! As change speeds up, the most recent global meltdown has had many transformative progressive impacts on policy making. The new policy spaces created in the aftermath of the 2008 economic panic is enabling the building of mass public transportation systems in India, South Africa and Brazil, all of which suggest a new role for governments in these countries. In Los Angeles, its citizens recently voted to build a fully integrated subway and light rapid transit system funded by an increase in the sales tax in order to reduce cars on the freeways. These mega-projects are transformative for millions who inhabit the mega-cities of the globe. By far the most innovative new public arena has been the World Wide Web, social networking, and especially the mobile smart phones which have enabled massive participation across the globe in policy development. Governments have lost tight control over the agenda on public debate and discourse. The revalidation of the role of the state in the economy explains the powerful attraction of using policy space innovatively for many different pressing domestic goals.

The exact character of the new era for national policy space is, however, still contested. Moreover, it is not yet even clear that the new era is a decisive break from the neoliberal period that preceded it. Global labor remains under siege and in transition as workplace representation and the historical gains from collective bargaining continue to shrink. The pushback from workers is still in its early days as can be seen in the newfound labor militancy in South Africa's strategic mining sector around a national living wage. Influential American economists such as Krugman (2009, 2012) and Stiglitz (2012) argue for renewed stimulus spending and other forms of macroeconomic intervention in the economy of the United States but fear that the neoliberal perspective is once again prevailing in Washington. Nonetheless, despite being unsure about the future direction of the reconfiguration of policy space, what is undeniable is that the changing landscape for policy space is on a global scale and that making sense of the new era of policy space requires focusing on the impact that recent globalization and the expansion of international trade and human rights law has on the shape, size, and availability of policy shape for states.

Of course, policy space is nothing new in federal states. Federal states are configured around distinct policy spaces for national and state governments, although there are shared policy spaces in some instances between federal or national governments and state or provincial governments. In fact, many of the most important programs such as health care, education, industrial relations, and mass transit require cooperation between levels of government in countries like Canada, Germany, and the United States. Moreover, in a post-Westphalian age where sovereignty is more porous and less rigid, policy space has emerged a way to mediate those sites where local and national government action has legitimacy to address concerns of a global reach such as public health and financial regulation. What is new we are suggesting today is that the most important and challenging policy spaces are now being defined in this globalized context.

For popular democracy, this emerging global realm for policy spaces poses difficulties that are reflected in deep unease about the power of international institutions and the lack of representation and control by ordinary people in the decisions made by these institutions. At root, social movements from Seattle in 1999 to Occupy Wall Street in 2011 to student movements in London, Montreal, Santiago, and Madrid in 2012 can all be seen as galvanizing around the lack of visible democratic decision making in these policy spaces. The transition in the World Trade Organization (WTO) from being initially a club for the few to a coalition of the many is in a similar vein.

THE QUANDARY OVER LINKING TRADE AND HUMAN RIGHTS

Traditionally, international trade and human rights law have operated in separate spheres and had distinctive orientations toward policy space (Cottier et al., 2005; Hernndez-Truyol and Powell, 2009). The orientation of global trade law has been towards constraining governments in their uses of national policy spaces whereas the orientation of international human rights law is to provide aspiring manifestos for the uses of national policy spaces. International trade law has valued trade liberalization between countries where trade liberalization is understood to reflect a series of commitments including the reduction of tariffs, deepening market access, the removal of subsidies, greater transparency, anti-dumping and openness to foreign investment. The legal instruments for trade liberalization have been multilateral trade agreements between many countries such as the WTO or the EU and bilateral trade agreements between two countries such as, for example, the free trade agreement negotiated between the United States and Canada in 1987. Now there are hundreds of such agreements with the prospect of more jumbo deals between the United States and the EU and the EU and India, not to speak of the eleven-member Transpacific Partnership soon to be formalized with Washington. These agreements have aspired to so-called hard law in the sense that they ordinarily include dispute resolution and enforcement mechanisms (Abbott and Snidal, 2000). The point of trade agreements is in part to bind national governments in their uses of national policy spaces, in effect reaching over borders and preventing them from pursuing policies that hinder trade liberalization.

By contrast, international human rights law emphasizes in an even-handed way both civil and political rights as well as social and economic rights to well-being. The legal instruments for protecting international human rights have been multilateral declarations such as the 1948 United Nations Declaration on Human Rights, the International Covenant on Civil and Political Rights (1966) and the International Covenant on Social, Economic, and Cultural Rights (1966). The point of these legal instruments is to set international norms and performance standards for member states. Unlike in international trade law, however, violations of international human rights agreements are not constructed as disputes between member states but rather as assaults on individual citizens and peoples. Human rights declarations and conventions typically contain neither dispute mechanisms nor enforcement provisions, but do nonetheless ground legal and moral obligations for states. They are for this reason often described as soft law (Abbott and Snidal, 2000). International human rights law is oriented towards encouraging governments in their national policy spaces to embrace progressive policies that promote better access to health care or lower levels of child poverty or protections from arbitrary arrest and detention. The critical point of the current international human rights system is that enforcement and implementation norms are left to domestic authority, with a significant degree of flexibility (Jacobs, 2013).

Despite separate spheres of trade and human rights, over the past two decades since the end of the Cold War there has been growing sensitivity to the fact that international trade and human rights law share a similar intellectual lineage reflecting a liberal commitment to the importance of the rule of law, private property, economic markets, representative democracy, education, and limits on social inequality (Ruggie, 1982; Cottier et al., 2005; Petersmann, 2012). In the 1990s, international organizations like the World

Bank, which is a champion of trade liberalization, began to embrace the idea that accessible schools and health care as well as anti-poverty measures are fundamental to economic development and free trade (Sen, 1999). Although there is already a vibrant debate among international law scholars about what these changes mean, it suggests to us that it is worthwhile to better understand the prospects for coordination between free trade agreements and international human rights law from a much broader multidisciplinary perspective.

The impetus for this book is our observation that during the global economic crisis of 2008, countries around the world used national policy spaces to respond to the economic crisis in ways that shed new light on the possibilities for linkages between international trade and human rights. In response to an economic crisis that was created in large part by failures of government oversight in global financial markets and trade liberalization, countries globally seemed to be embracing policies that reflected the progressive social and economic agenda of international human rights law rather than treating policy spaces as constrained arenas where concerns about trade liberalization should reign. In the United States, we witnessed massive government spending designed to promote job security through measures like the bailout of the auto industry, public investment in green energy innovations and the cash for clunkers program, the extension of unemployment benefits to two years of eligibility, universal health care, and the nationalization of some financial institutions and insurance companies. In Germany, government spending was directed at ensuring that companies did not lay off workers. In India, the national government introduced its rural employment guarantee. China stimulated its economy by pouring new funds into schools and its decaying rural health care program. Brazil embraced new spending on anti-poverty programs. All of these national policy developments and others occurred in the shadow of a global economic crisis that revealed the failings of existing techniques of global governance and the need to reframe how international institutions and legal instruments interact. So far, however, governments have sought technical solutions to the failures of oversight of global financial markets and trade liberalization without seeming to address the underlying reasons for the structural crisis in global governance. Some of these new policy spaces are fragile and at risk, and indeed often by design temporary and fluid. Nonetheless they provide significant opportunities to address structural crises and global governance.

This book is designed to explore the reframing of global governance and the opening up of new and reconfigured policy spaces for linking human rights and trade. It brings together a wide-ranging group of leading experts in international law, trade, human rights, political economy, international relations and public policy who have been asked to reflect on this important development in globalization. Their multidisciplinary contributions provide explanations for why the global landscape for national policy space has evolved and illustrate clearly instances of this change and the failure to adapt to new social and economic circumstances. The book also projects future paths for development in social and economic policy spaces, especially with reference to linkages between international trade and human rights in major market countries like China and India.

DIVERGENT CONFIGURATIONS OF POLICY SPACE

The idea that governments operate in certain national policy spaces and that these spaces reflect beliefs about what governments can and should do gained currency only in the twentieth century. Influential economists and political theorists such as Polanyi (1944), Arendt (1958) and Habermas (1991) all maintained that contemporary capitalism has an impact on how we understand the importance of politics and the public sphere. Polanyi argued that in market societies such as the United Kingdom, the development of the modern state occurred in tandem with the development of modern market economies. The state and market function in market societies in a complementary fashion. The state has certain spheres in which it can operate and others in which it has no role. The configuration of those spheres is a reflection of what goods citizens in a capitalist society should share in common and that the state has the responsibility to pursue. Policy space emerged as a way to think about collective decision making by governments oriented towards certain public goods.

The initial watershed configuration of policy spaces occurred in the context of the Keynesian revolution in macroeconomic policy beginning in the 1930s in modern industrial countries. The Keynesian revolution was organized around an explicit commitment to full employment as a public good (Keynes, 1936). The logic of full employment as a public good is a policy space where governments have policy instruments and levers to intervene in the economy with the objective of promoting full employment. Instruments like money supply, deficit cycles, and lending rates emerged as familiar elements in a nation's policy toolkit. In the post–World War II period, the emergence of modern welfare states is largely tied to this vision of full-employment capitalism. This new industrial state, to use Galbraith's (1972) famous phrase, is oriented in its economic and industrial relations policy towards establishing stable market conditions that enable long-term planning by corporations and avoids the boom-bust unemployment cycle that characterized earlier stages of capitalism. Countries differed of course in how they governed their economies, despite the broad consensus on the public good of full employment (Hall, 1986). National governments also configured their welfare state programs in a wide variety of ways (Epp-Andersen, 1985, 1990; Ringen, 1987). The diversity in economic policy and welfare states should be seen as a reflection of the opportunities for innovation and freedom that the concept of national policy space attempts to capture. The establishment of welfare states after World War II was rarely, if ever, connected to the commitment to international human rights, which is a striking omission, one that is almost inconceivable from our current vantage point (Jacobs, 1993).

The national policy instruments of the Keynesian period were supported through the establishment at Bretton Woods in 1944 of a system of international organizations, most notably the IMF and the predecessor of the World Bank. The Bretton Woods system was oriented towards supporting governments in the pursuit of full employment and economic development by ensuring stability during economic downturns (Ruggie, 1982). This was followed in the postwar period by efforts to establish the International Trade Organization (ITO). The ITO was proposed by the United States at the United Nations Economic and Social Committee in 1946. The ITO Charter was successfully negotiated in Havana in 1948 at the United Nations Conference on Employment and Trade, along with the General Agreement on Tariffs and Trade (GATT). The ITO Charter emphasized trade liberalization but within the perimeters of international social and economic rights. It addressed, among other things, multinational corporate governance, labor standards, and the stability of food prices. The U.S. Senate never ratified the agreement, and the ITO collapsed in the early 1950s. GATT continued to regulate international trade until it was replaced by the WTO in 1994.

THE HAYEKIAN TURN AND NEOLIBERAL POLICY SPACE

The neoliberal reconfiguration of economic and social policy space has its origins in the work of hugely influentially economists such as Hayek (1944; 1960) and Friedman (1962), who argued against the Keynesian expansion of policy space that characterized the macroeconomic and welfare state policies of most advanced industrial countries in the post–World War II period. The neoliberal conceptual vision is one where markets, not governments, are the principal vehicle for advancing economic growth. Full employment is not a priority in this vision. In its most ideological form, only the private sector is said to create jobs, not the government. Neoliberal arguments gained considerable political currency in the 1980s and 1990s in many countries, leading to the election of governments that sought to cut government spending, lower taxes, reduce intervention in the economy and retrench welfare state programs. At its extreme, the neoliberal agenda can be seen to be promoting the disappearance of the state on the policy horizon. New institutions established during the Keynesian period were path dependent in the sense that once initial policy paths were chosen, they have been difficult to reverse (Hacker, 2002; Thelen, 2004).

Policy legacies express the idea that during periods of transformation, institutions remain in place but their underlying rationale or normative foundation is altered to align itself with the new public policy paradigm (Thelen, 2004; Jacobs, 2005). Still, the Keynesian-era institutions proved to be surprisingly resilient during the neoliberal period. Welfare state programs in particular have been exceedingly difficult to dismantle in most countries, although many of them have been downsized and benefits cut (Pierson, 1994, 2001, 2004). Moreover, because of the many varieties of state-market relations (Hall and Soskice, 2000), neoliberal efforts to transform policy space have not been standardized or uniformly effective. This effect led some to question the very idea of globalization and its impact on state power (Hirst and Thompson, 1999; Weiss, 1998).

However, despite the policy legacies of the Keynesian era, the underlying rationale or justification for certain institutions was transformed. The European Union is representative of this shift into a neoliberal institution, but like many institutions originating in the Keynesian era, this transition has not been seamless and Keynesian policy legacies remain highly visible. The most important illustration of this phenomenon is its social market covering 500 million people. An example of policy legacies in Canada and the United States concerns private pension funds, which during the Keynesian era were seen as a type of deferred compensation for workers and were largely organized around defined benefit plans, but during the neoliberal period were transformed into retirement savings plans organized around defined contributions with the level of benefits paid depending on the rate of return on the savings (Wooten, 2004).

The neoliberal reconfiguration of policy space required a realignment of international institutions. In the Keynesian period, the Bretton Woods system was seen as creating international institutions that enable national governments to exercise their policy options within newly established policy spaces oriented toward full employment. Although these institutions were preserved during the neoliberal era, their role and purpose was transformed from supporting national governments in their goal of sustaining full employment to advocating for wider reliance on market mechanisms to determine economic outcomes. What developed during the neoliberal era was the role of international economic organizations as constraints on policy choices for national governments and shrinking their policy space (Gallagher, 2005). These institutions pressured countries to enter into free trade agreements and other forms of international law that promote trade liberalization at the cost of a departure from full employment.

The establishment of the WTO in 1994 was for many the most powerful expression of this new relationship between international organizations and national policy space (Drache, 2010). The WTO sought to promote multilateral trade liberalization agreements based on the vision of a global market for goods and services. The increased globalization of norms in areas of tax policy, industrial relations, and financial markets reinforced the neoliberal approach to diminishing policy spaces for national governments. Domestic policy space simultaneously became internationalized through hard law and globalized by soft law norms and values. The Washington Consensus is ordinarily explained from this neoliberal prospective, providing that during financial crises, national policy space is restricted to monetary policy, and in other contexts allowing nations fiscal policy space only to the extent that the situation of the government is financially sustainable (Heller, 2005).

Both neoliberals and Keynesians share an outdated understanding of policy space in relation to the Westphalian state, a shorthand for the concentration of legal and political authority in the modern nation-state. International institutions were seen as a function of member states entering into contractual agreements to further their own self-interest. In our current dismal economic age, policy space is positioned differently in its relationship to the state and global institutions. The new global landscape requires an understanding of policy space beyond the Westphalian state model.

THE NEW GLOBAL APPETITE FOR POLICY SPACE

The 2008 global financial crisis made visible the likely end of the neoliberal era regarding policy space or at least a different configuration of what having that space means for individual countries. That crisis revealed the declining importance of the WTO and the failure of the Doha Round of negotiations to agree to lower trade barriers and reform trade rules. Prior to the crisis, certain outlier countries such as Brazil, China, and India resisted the Washington Consensus's capital deregulatory logic but supported the WTO. However, in response to the crisis, many more countries broke from the Washington Consensus and instead were innovative in their attempts to protect their own economies, institutions and citizens from the crisis. Many countries made protecting employment their highest priority. As noted earlier, the U.S. government in response to the 2008 economic crisis implemented an $800 billion economic stimulus plan, nationalized financial institutions, imposed regulations on executive compensation, extended unemployment benefits for two years, embraced Buy American provisions and bailed out the auto industry. Most countries in the EU, led by Germany and France, responded in a similar fashion. The agreed-on stability mechanism and the new role for the European Central Bank is a major step towards intergovernmental cooperation to stabilize the euro crisis. The ECB promised stunning Keyesnian-like measures to rein in European capital markets and so far they have quelled further financial panics. It would surprise few if the European Central Bank becomes the common supervisor of all EU banks.

Even countries such as Canada, with governments that expressed a lingering faith in the Washington Consensus, embraced stimulus plans and halted deregulation of the financial industry. In developing countries, the 2008 financial crisis engendered a wide range of policy innovations that would have been difficult to imagine a decade earlier when the neoliberal approach to policy space was so dominant. China and other countries on the Asia Pacific Rim provided massive public stimulus spending to prime their economies. From a broader policy perspective, what this break from the Washington Consensus showed is that despite significant globalization over the past three decades and increasing regulation via free trade agreements, governments still have national policy space to innovate in response to grassroots social movements and the human rights agenda.

The changing global landscape for policy space requires better understanding the dynamics between national policy space and international organizations and institutions. There is a need to correct our understanding of transnationality that shrunk the domestic realm of policy making and left it gasping for air. What makes the new era of policy space especially interesting, in our view, is the impact that recent globalization and the expansion of international law has on the shape, size and availability of policy shape for states. The chapters in this book explore three competing views on the dynamics between national policy space and the expansion of free trade agreements and international human rights conventions, with a view to better making sense of national policy space as the landscape for making linkages between international trade and human rights.

THE DYNAMICS OF INTERNATIONAL INSTITUTIONS AND DOMESTIC POLICY NEEDS: THREE CONTRASTING VIEWS

The dominant view, which stems from the neoliberal era, is that globalization and the expansion of international trade agreements results in the shrinkage of national policy space. The reasoning is that although most international trade and human rights agreements are premised on the formal sovereignty of nations to enter into these agreements, these instruments of international law are designed to bind national governments in ways that shrink their control over policy decisions. This viewpoint underlies, for example, Meyer's (2009) definition of national policy space as "the combination of de jure policy sovereignty and de facto national policy autonomy" (p. 376). Free trade agreements are often seen to be squeezing out national labor relations policies that emphasized fair collective bargaining and demanding employment standards. Likewise, social programs such as public health care and income security are frequently viewed as under threat when trade agreements shrink national policy space.

The second view represented in this book is that free trade agreements and international human rights conventions do not shrink national policy space but rather enrich existing national policy space or create new policy space. They are often the trigger for transnational cooperation between governments. The reasoning here is that these instruments of international law have the potential to be game changers in the setting of the national policy agenda, setting new priorities or allowing governments to question policy commitments that had in the past been untouchable. Free trade agreements that lead to scrutiny of agricultural subsidies, which disproportionately benefit farmers who own large tracts of farmland, may, for example, allow a national government to recalibrate its food security policies so that those policies are more sensitive to the most vulnerable in their society. Likewise, although the rapid spread of emerging infectious diseases such as SARS or H1N1 is often connected to increased global travel and other forms of expression of globalization, in practice breakdowns in communications between national and local governments often play a pivotal role in pandemics. New international agreements on infectious diseases and global health such as the 2005 International Sanitation Regulations adopted by the World Health Assembly may force cooperation in a multi-tiered state between the national government and local governments on a pandemic plan (Jacobs, 2013).

The third view represented in this book is the fragility of national policy space in an era of global governance. The dynamics between, on the one hand, free trade agreements and international human rights conventions and, on the other hand, national policy space is a fluid one that is constantly being negotiated and renegotiated in particular countries. This view reflects the fact that in part national policy space evolves in response to developments in civil society. Certainly, the most significant development has been in the emergence of social networking and internet online and offline social activism, often motivated by concerns about popular democracy. Protests and other expressions of dissent by civil society or social movements often are engendered by concerns about international organizations like the WTO. These social movements voice the fragility of national policy space because, in the words of Habermas (1991), the "refeudalization of the public sphere" is always imminent. They have become in our times the principal institution of modern society capable of mass mobilization across the globe. Yet, it is significant that national governments, especially since the 2008 financial crisis, have in some cases carved out innovative policies that protect their economics in responses to civil society protests and demands of social movements for social justice while remaining fully compliant with their obligations under international law. China of course continues to quell political expression on the internet. In India, despite being the world's largest democracy, in uneven and users face many obstacles open and free access to the World Wide Web.

This book is unique in its rich exploration of the second and third views on the dynamics between globalization and national policy space from a multidisciplinary perspective. The claim that universally national policy space necessarily shrinks when countries enter into free trade agreements or human rights conventions is difficult to defend in light of the analysis and illustrative case studies presented in this book. Instead, the new global landscape is one where instruments of international law often shrink national policy space, occasionally enrich national policy space, and sometimes affect the ongoing negotiation and transformation of national policy space.

CRITICAL FEATURES OF THE NEW GLOBAL LANDSCAPE: FACTORS THAT MAKE A DIFFERENCE

The analysis in this book suggests five important factors that are influencing the new global landscape for policy space. The first factor is the dialogue between policy space and global governance. This dialogue is rich and diverse, one where policy innovation is often encouraged and at times demanded. In the powerful language of castells these networks of "hope and rage" have not only educated the public about the need for a new policy agenda but also have succeeded in moving many issues like poverty eradication and environmental concerns from the margins to the mainstream. It is still early days, which makes it difficult to make predictions with confidence, but social movements like the Occupy Wall Street and the Quebec student movement have contributed to challenging the entitlements of the top 1 percent and the role of international institutions in defending an unsustainable status quo. Policy spaces in this dialogue are both an expression of the promise of global governance and an incentive to innovate in policy making. Developments in global governance force us to think about the shape and rigidity of policy spaces. These features of national policy space speak to the strengths and weaknesses of particular international institutions.

This certainly explains in part the decline of the WTO and the difficulties it has faced with the Doha Round of negotiations. The establishment of the WTO in 1994 brought to the forefront concerns about trade liberalization for national policy space and the scope for local democracy. This was a major theme during the 1999 protests at the WTO Ministerial Conference in Seattle. Concerns about the Agreement on Trade-Related Aspects of Intellectual Property Rights (TRIPS) curtailing national health policy, for example, lead in 2001 to a global backlash during the Doha Round to the Declaration on TRIPS and Public Health, which affirmed the right of countries to produce generic drugs as a public good, using compulsory licensing. What are the broader implications of the dialogue between global governance and the configuration of existing policy space?

Do new techniques in global governance require innovations and the creation of new national policy space? For example, does the adoption of new International Sanitation Regulations by the World Health Organization, which are oriented toward emerging infectious diseases, require new institutional capacity for its individual member states? To what extent do these kind of global agreements enlarge the margin of maneuver? The point is that global governance helps define policy space but at the same time issues of policy space reveal weaknesses of global governance, as the rise and fall of the WTO clearly illustrate. The new global landscape requires striking a balance between global norms and standard setting on the one hand and the particular goals and priorities of national governments on the other.

The second factor influencing global policy space is the emerging consensus on certain global public goods. These global public goods include poverty reduction, education, population health, food security, and personal security – the core ideas behind the Millennium Developmental Goals. The World Bank (2008) in its recent initiatives has tried to galvanize the consensus on these global pubic goods. From our perspective, it is notable that all of these public goods are a reflection of the international human rights agenda with respect to social and economic rights. These goods are driving social and economic policy agendas in countries all over the world, as well as global governance initiatives. Although it makes sense to characterize these public goods as global in character, collective decisions about how they are being realized is occurring in national policy space, which reinforces the strategic importance of national policy space as well as its dialogical relationship to global governance. No consensus exists at this point in time about the importance of job security or full employment, which makes for a marked contrast to the Keynesian era after World War II. It is also significant that some other goods such as environmental protection or gender equality are not yet part of the consensus on global public goods, but are slowly making their way from the margins to the mainstream.

The third factor is the reemergence of states and national governments as autonomous organizations capable of leadership in policy spaces. Although there are global public goods, the policy vehicles for pursuing those goods vary from country to country. There is no convergence on the uses of policy space, nor is there the lexical ordering of these global public goods. This was evident in the way in which, in response to the 2008 financial crisis, some countries prioritized jobs, others prioritized infrastructure and still others concentrated on subsidies for life's necessities such as food and medications. This is, of course, the broad insight of the varieties of capitalism approach (Hall and Soskice, 2000). Across the globe, health care, education, job security, environmental protection and social welfare are all delivered in different ways, reflecting the diversity in market-state relations. Many would argue further that in the developing world, governments never receded from a leadership role in national policy spaces. In fact, the state in India and China has acquired a more prominent role powering and steering the economy and society. This lesson is not lost on other countries in the global South, few of whom share the Anglo-American anti-state animus.

The fourth factor impacting global policy space is the increasing appreciation of the dynamics in which individual countries selectively adapt to international law and the regulations and demands of international organizations. All countries interpret the performance norms of international governance such as agricultural subsidies, food security and industrial policy in accordance with their own perceptions and policy needs, which are often less aspirational than those found in international law. This may mean that the United States complies with an international trade requirement like transparency in one way, reflecting its own democratic political culture, whereas China has a different understanding of that requirement. The point is that the relationship between international law and norms, on the one hand, and policy development at the national or sub-national level, on the other hand, is a complex one of interpretation and adaptation (Potter and Biukovic, 2011). This is reinforced by the observation that individual states have opportunities for innovation and leadership in policy spaces that allow them to pursue the aspirational goals of the international human rights agenda and enlarge their margin of policy maneuver. Few countries actually exercise this freedom, instead remaining constrained by local performance norms. In terms of policy making, these countries muddle through, innovating on a case-by-case basis.

The final factor is the growing presence of BRIC countries, especially Brazil, India, and China, in the global economy. In the past, developed countries led by the United States, EU, and Japan have been seen as the leaders in policy innovation, from advanced computer engineering to breakthrough medical science. Brazil, China and India are all now innovators in the uses of policy spaces and serve in mentoring roles for many other developing countries, despite immense challenges of corruption and administrative authoritarianism. Governments remain the prevalent agent for economic growth and development in all three countries, as we noted already. Examples abound from these BRIC countries in the fields of poverty reduction and health care delivery as well as their models for economic development. China's success at combating child poverty is well known. Likewise, India's innovations in neonatal health care reflect concrete commitments to gender equality in health care delivery. Brazil is a leader in both its treatment for persons with HIV/AIDS and in its comprehensive anti-poverty strategies. The new global landscape for policy spaces must, in our view, take into account the successes and failures of the BRIC countries. Many of the essays in this volume are grounded in research from three of these countries, Brazil, India and China.

CONTESTED POLICY LEGACIES SCENARIOS

In summary, the concept of national policy space offers critical insights into the new global landscape for international trade and human rights that has emerged since the 2008 global financial crisis. As we have seen, national policy spaces matter because they provide opportunities for governments to be innovative in the development of public policy on these sites. The unifying theme of this book is that there has been a major reconfiguration of social and economic policy spaces for national governments on the global landscape. The state is being extended into new areas and it is being deployed in novel and innovative ways.

Our claim in this book is that there has been a transformation in the policy spaces that provide for concrete linkages between trade and human rights. Although it is certainly too early to say definitively what the pattern is within those policy spaces that have been created, four things are worth highlighting. The first is that the novel policy spaces are a reality in the post-crisis world. European Central Bank's new role in pledging to defend the euro against market speculation is perhaps the most important policy innovation addressing the mind-numbing legacy costs of the 2008 financial panic and meltdown.

The second is that the uses of these policy spaces is highly divergent and context specific. What works in Brazil for fighting poverty will not have great currency in the United States or China. The third is that the uses of policy spaces are being influenced not just through traditional political channels but also through the formation of virtual communities of stakeholders who are operating in the digital world of social networking, the Internet, and mobile devices. They continue to surprise political elites, and defiant publics are exasperated with political systems that cannot deliver real change. The fourth thing worth highlighting is that these policy spaces are a valuable resource for national governments adapting to globalization in all of its different forms. This is why initially all the major governments of Europe except for the United Kingdom have adopted a Tobin-type tax on financial transactions designed to capture negative externalities and deter unconstrained flows of investment capital. This tax is predicted to generate between 15 billion and 30 billion euros annually to be spent by each country as it sees fit.

GLOBAL GOVERNANCE IN CRISIS

It is also significant that the 2008 crisis made visible the declining importance of the WTO and other international organizations associated with neoliberal global governance. This decline was reinforced by the complete breakdown of the Washington Consensus, as countries led by the United States choose to use policy instruments to protect their economies, institutions and citizens that were outside the realm of that consensus. Governments around the world are seeking to distance themselves from the policy options promoted by neoliberal international institutions. The reconfiguration of national policy spaces is occurring on a global scale and is being influenced by developments in global governance, which is in turn being shaped by the changing global landscape in national policy spaces. The complex and very dynamic links are global but the anchor is inevitably local.

It is, however, important to acknowledge the difficulty of achieving genuine policy transformation particularly with regard to social policy and human rights. Policy choices are, as we noted earlier, heavily path dependent. Policy decisions made years ago in the golden age of Keynesianism impact significantly the policy options we have today. Those early decisions have in many instances set us on policy paths from which it is difficult to veer because they have created institutions and vested interests that veto change.

Countries that in the 1950s and 1960s resisted committing to high levels of public spending on welfare state programs with a strong emphasis on redistributive policies have found it generally far more difficult to innovate today in the realm of human rights and social policy than countries that did invest heavily in high-standard social welfare systems. France, for example, has found it much easier to innovate in its health care system and adapt to the emerging global economy than the United States has. Labor relations may be one area where this trend has not proven to be the case.

The evidence is that industrial relations systems have been unable to adapt to new production technologies and the transfer of millions of jobs to the global South. Once robust institutions, collective bargaining and industrial democracy in the workplace saw their influence reach an all-time low. Path dependency has also influenced the evolution of international governance structures. New structures associated with the neoliberal era, such as the WTO, were layered onto the GATT infrastructure of the postwar Keynesian period. This sort of layering creates policy legacies that affect how policy spaces are used in the future. Anticipating new directions for the uses of policy spaces for linkages between trade and human rights requires recognition of policy legacies.

FOUR SCENARIOS FOR FUTURE POLICY SPACE

Although we do not yet know the ultimate shape of this new era for social and economic policy space, we can imagine four possible scenarios. The optimistic scenario is that national policy space will emerge as a vibrant progressive arena for linkages between international trade and human rights. In this arena, governments will tie their embrace of trade liberalization to the advancement of global goods like health care, education, poverty reduction or food security.

A more tempered scenario is that over the next decade we will witness experimentation with national policy spaces as an arena for linkages between international trade and human rights but without a discernible pattern emerging. This will involve governments in a piecemeal fashion using national policy spaces to coordinate their trade and human rights obligations, but not doing so on a consistent basis. There will be ad hoc breakthroughs in certain policy areas such as, for instance, the facilitation of generic drugs manufacturing through the adoption of compulsory licensing or the introduction of corporate social responsibility legislation.

A different, more pessimistic scenario is that during economic crises we will continue to see innovations in national policy spaces like what we witnessed in response to the 2008 global economic panic and crisis, but in more "normal" times national policy space will not be used boldly. In India, for instance, the government established its rural employment guarantee scheme after 2008 but is now following the global trend of opening its economy up to multinationals largely without conditions. In the United States, the adoption of a universal health care system grounded in an individual mandate enforced through the income tax system has been followed by a return to the more sterile debates over tax cuts. The most pessimistic scenario is that what we witnessed during the 2008 economic meltdown was a mirage and we have returned to the neoliberal period that preceded it. The austerity measures imposed by the EU on Greece, Spain and Ireland suggest this, even though there is also an emerging consensus around a single regulator of the banking sector. In the global North, collective bargaining is losing the high ground it once held. Organized labor's status is that of an embattled stakeholder, little different from a special interest group.

Whichever scenario for national policy spaces ultimately emerges, what is already evident is that its character and shape will be determined not just by global institutions and developed countries in the global North but also by the BRIC countries and likely also by grassroots social movements and the international human rights agenda on social and economic rights. We are still in the early days of experimentation with national policy space as a lever against the dark side of globalization. The challenge globally as well as for individual countries will be how to use this new opportunity to better advance the global economic goods tied to international trade and human rights law. The learning curve for how to do this is steep, and policy makers need to stay the course in their fundamental choices about which scenario they want to bring closure to in this dismal economic era.

STRUCTURE OF THE VOLUME

The contributions to this book are organized into six thematic parts. Part I examines recent developments in international trade and human rights governance structures and practices. It is designed to provide insight into how globalization is impacting the nature of policy space. The discussion shows that policy spaces require legal regulation and that the linkages between international trade and human rights have emerged unevenly. In Chapter 1, Sol Picciotto explores how international human rights law and discourse are affecting ideas of good global governance and regulation. In Chapter 2, Ernest-Ulrich Petersmann argues that developments over the past decade in international human rights law and the diverse forms of multilevel constitutionalism emerging in the EU indicate the growth of a novel form of global constitutionalism, which synergizes human rights and economic law. This new form of global constitutional justice can be seen as bounding the market activities of private actors and directing economic activity towards enhancing human dignity rather than just acquisition. Jorge Heine and Joseph Turcotte in Chapter 3 use the example of Chile to argue that there is an important place for bilateral free trade agreements in global governance because they can stimulate economic growth and development.

Part II of the book is organized around the theme of pushback and innovation from below directed at forms of global governance. This pushback is contributing to the refinement of the new policy spaces on the global landscape. Protest and social activism are effectively contributing to new ways to think about policy spaces for engaging enduring problems like poverty reduction, inequality, and public health, but ironically this pushback has been less effective in the context of the world of work. In Chapter 4, Tomer Broude shows how protest movements in different time periods are alike and how they differ and evolve in understanding. Broude discusses different periods in recent history marked by global protest around certain shared parameters of linkages: (1) conflict, (2) conditionality, (3) constitutionalism, (4) conformity, and (5) confluence. In Chapter 5, Daniel Drache argues that we are witnessing in countries like China, India, and the United States decisive shifts in state-market relations as evident from five interconnected issues that impact directly on their fragile national policy spaces for industrial relations: workplace democracy, labor-shedding technologies, new employment practices, the geoeconomic redistribution of power, and the fragmentation of the multilateral trading system. The expansion of workplace democracy to the global South has been slow and uneven, but even in China, hundreds of thousands of non-authorized work stoppages recently are suggestive of an incipient dynamic present despite the highly authoritarian setting of the communist regime. For instance, the pushback from below for a living wage at the world's leading manufacturer of electronics in China, Foxcomm with its workforce of more than 2 million, the factory occupations at Hyundai in Korea and the unrest at Tata automobile plants in India are evidence of the deep structural discontent with existing industrial relations in BRIC countries. In Chapter 6, Lesley Jacobs explores how the 2005 World Health Organization Framework Convention on Tobacco Control, which grew out of concerns about trade liberalization in the tobacco industry by public health activists, has enriched in new and innovative ways policy spaces in developing countries like China and India for health rights advocates to establish tobacco control measures.

Part III of the book is organized around paradigm shifts in national governance in response to globalization, focusing in particular on recent developments in India. National governments remain the principal actors in the uses of new policy spaces in terms of realizing the linkages between trade and human rights. In Chapter 7, Kuldeep Mathur argues that in recent decades business in India has gone from being mistrusted and regulated to being seen as a partner in development and well-being and thus unregulated and even championed. Mathur then discusses the results of this new relationship in the area of social policy spaces and finds the partnership a troubling model. Amit Ray and Saradindu Bhaduri in Chapter 8 argue that India's pharmaceutical industry has evolved considerably in the face of substantial changes in international and domestic policy, focusing on challenges to the efforts to develop the capabilities to independently research, develop and produce affordable drugs. Ray and Bhaduri also argue for changes in the international regulation of drugs to make Indian generics more affordable and available to populations around the world.

Part IV of the book explores contested policy spaces in social welfare that have evolved in the breakdown of the Washington Consensus and the 2008 global financial crisis. In areas like health care and food security, it remains unclear that the new policy spaces are uniformly expanding rather than shrinking. Significantly, as we noted previously, countries like Brazil, China and Venezuela had resisted the Washington Consensus long before 2008. Perhaps for this reason these countries have been bolder and more successful in their innovative uses of policy space after the financial crisis. In Chapter 9, Kathryn Hochstetler focuses on Brazil, which has recently experienced a period of impressive economic growth while managing to meet the challenge of redistributing this wealth to the poor in a sustainable and equitable fashion. Hochstetler argues that the Brazilian state played an important role in this success story through its various heterodox policies such as Bolsa Familia and the Brazilian National Development Bank. Hochstetler concludes by considering such policies applicability in other development contexts. Ron Labonté in Chapter 10 argues that although intellectual property rights and privatization receive the bulk of the attention in discussions of global governance and its consequences for global health, in fact liberalized investment policies, the impact of trade liberalization on poverty and the global diffusion of unhealthy "lifestyles" pose much greater threats to the international health agenda. In Chapter 11, Matias Margulis examines the new transnational policies surrounding food security and the role the WTO has played in abetting and exacerbating the series of food crises that have rocked the world since 2008. Margulis argues that the development and growing consensus around the "human right to food" and its intersection with international trade law is framing global policy spaces around food security.

Part V of the book illustrates other recent innovations in the dynamics between human rights and international policy spaces. These innovations reflect, in part, evolving understandings of precarious work as well as the growing leverage of China on the global stage. In Chapter 12, Adelle Blackett focuses on the International Labour Organization's adoption in 2011 of the Decent Work for Domestic Workers Convention (No. 189), arguing that this new convention reflects a new international policy space that balances the demands of the labor market against the need to develop fairer standards of decent work for female migrant care workers. Ljiljana Biuković in Chapter 13 argues that China's network of regional free trade agreements, which secures for China markets and resources with other trading nations and regional blocs, has been achieved through the exercise of soft power that contrasts with the methods championed by the IMF and the WTO.

Part VI of the book focuses on China's evolving industrial relations and labor policy and practices in light of international trade and human rights law. China is now seen as the workshop of the world. How it uses different policy spaces to regulate that workshop affects not just Chinese workers but consumers and workers around the globe. In Chapter 14, Pitman Potter argues that there is an important tension in China between issues of social justice, which are closely linked to economic development and growth, and demands that its labor regime adapt to the changing global landscape for labor rights and industrial relations policy. Potter finds that China has used national policy space to adapt selectively to the demands of international trade and human rights law while still pursuing a path of sustainable development. In Chapter 15, Sarah Biddulph argues that although China is frequently seen as setting itself apart from developments in international labor law that seek to empower laborers and give them a say in the production process, new developments in China suggest the policy space is opening to steps towards a new and more inclusive labor system, especially in the realm of collective bargaining, but these transformations remain beset with many challenges and barriers. Closing out the volume, Chang-Hee Lee in Chapter 16 argues that the role of the Chinese state in labor relations has evolved significantly over the past two decades, and that there are now new policy spaces for negotiating and advancing labor rights in China in areas like industrial relations and social protection.

A FINAL WORD

Our current economic age is a dismal one. Although in the wake of neoliberalism we would expect diminishing policy spaces and little innovation globally in the responses to these chaotic times, this book shows that in fact, since the 2008 financial crisis, new policy spaces have emerged that are taking on a character that suggests that the global dominance of neoliberalism is evolving in a new direction, with much greater room for flexibility and room for maneuver. The new and emerging landscape promises possibilities for vibrant linkages between international trade and human rights. The political imagination of policy elites has not yet caught up with the times and this is indeed cause for alarm.

REFERENCES

Abbott, K.W., and Snidal, D. (2000). 'Hard and soft law in international governance', *International Organization* 54(3): 421–456.

Arendt, H. (1958). *The Human Condition*. Chicago: The University of Chicago Press.

Beattie, Alan (2012). 'Troika a barrier to IMF's new fiscal faith', *Financial Times*, October 12.

Cottier, T., Pauwelyn J., and Burgi, E. (2005). 'Linking Trade Regulation and Human Rights in International Law', in T. Cottier, J. Pauwelyn and E. Burgi, Eds., *Human Rights and International Trade* (pp. 1–27). Oxford: Oxford University Press.

Drache, Daniel, Ed. (2001). *The Market or the Public Domain: Global Governance and the Asymmetry of Power*. London: Routledge.

Drache, Daniel. (2008). *Defiant Publics: The Unprecedented Reach of the Global Citizen*. London: Polity Press.

Drache, Daniel. (2010). 'The Nasty Business of Protection and New State Practices at a Time of System Disturbance: The Expectation for Global Demand Management.' New York: UN World Economic and Social Survey.

Epsing-Andersen, G. (1985). *Politics against Markets*. Princeton: Princeton University Press.

Epsing-Andersen, G. (1990). *The Three Worlds of Welfare Capitalism*. Princeton: Princeton University Press.

Friedman, M. (1962). *Capitalism and Freedom*. Chicago: University of Chicago Press.

Galbraith, J. (1972). *The New Industrial State*, Second edition. Harmondsworth, UK: Penguin.

Gallagher, K., Ed. (2005). *Putting Development First: The Importance of Policy Space in the WTO and IFIs*. London: Zed Books.

Grindle, T., and Thomas, J. (1991). *Public Choices and Policy Change*. Baltimore, MD: Johns Hopkins University Press.

Habermas, J. (1991). *The Structural Transformation of the Public Sphere*. Trans. T. Burger. Cambridge, MA: MIT Press.

Hacker, J. (2002). *The Divided Welfare State*. New York: Cambridge University Press.

Hall, P. (1986). *Governing the Economy: The Politics of State Intervention in Britain and France*. Oxford: Oxford University Press.

Hall, P., and Soskice, D., Eds. (2000). *Varieties of Capitalism: The Institutional Foundations of Comparative Advantage*. Cambridge: Cambridge University Press.

Hayek, F. (1944). *The Road to Serfdom*. London: Routledge.

Hayek, F. (1960). *The Constitution of Liberty*. Chicago: University of Chicago Press.

Heller, P. (2005). *Understanding Fiscal Space*. Washington, DC: International Monetary Fund.

Hernndez-Truyol, B., and Powell, S. (2009). *Just Trade: A New Covenant Linking Trade and Human Rights*. New York: New York University Press.

Hirst, P., and Thompson, G. (1999). *Globalization in Question: The International Economy and the Possibilities of Governance, Second Edition*. Cambridge: Polity Press.

Jacobs, L. (1993). *Rights and Deprivation*. Oxford: Oxford University Press.

Jacobs, L. (2004). *Pursuing Equal Opportunities*. New York: Cambridge University Press.

Jacobs, L. (2005). 'Universal hospital insurance and health care reform: Policy legacies and path dependency in the development of Canada's health care system', *Buffalo Law Review* 53: 635–661.

Jacobs, L. (2013). 'Adapting Locally to International Health and Human Rights Standards: An Alternative Theoretical Framework for Progressive Realization', in Mikael Rask Madsen and Gert Verschraegen, Eds., *Making Human Rights Intelligible: New Theoretical and Empirical* (pp. 233–246). Oxford: Hart Publishing.

Keynes, J. M. (1936). *A General Theory of Employment, Interest and Money*. London: Palgrave MacMillan.

Koivusalo, M., Schrecker, T., and Labonté, R. (2010). *Globalisation and Policy Space for Health and Social Determinants of Health*. Ottawa: Globalization and Health Knowledge Network.

Krugman, P. (2012). *End This Depression Now!* New York: W. W. Norton.

Krugman, P. (2009). *The Return of Depression Economics and the Crisis of 2008*. New York: Penguin.

Meyer, J. (2009). 'Policy Space: What, for What, and Where?' *Development Policy Review* 27(4): 373–395.

Petersmann, U. (2012). *International Economic Law in the 21st Century: Constitutional Pluralism and Multilevel Governance of Interdependent Public Goods*. Oxford: Hart Publishers.

Pierson, P. (1994). *Dismantling the Welfare State? Reagan, Thatcher and the Politics of Retrenchment*. Cambridge: Cambridge University Press.

Pierson, P., Ed. (2001). *The New Politics of the Welfare State*. Oxford: Oxford University Press.

Pierson, P. (2004). *Politics in Time: History, Institutions, and Social Analysis*. Princeton: Princeton University Press.

Polanyi, K. (1944). *The Great Transformation*. New York: Rinehart.

Potter, P., and Biukovic, L., Eds. (2011). *Globalization and Local Adaptation in International Trade Law*. Vancouver: University of British Columbia Press.

Ringen, S. (1987). *The Possibility of Politics*. Oxford: Oxford University Press.

Ruggie, J. (1982). 'International Regimes, Transactions, and Change: Embedded Liberalism in the Postwar Economic Order', *International Organization* 36(2): 379–415.

Sen, A. (1999). *Development as Freedom*. Oxford: Oxford University Press.

Stiglitz, J. (2012). *The Price of Inequality*. New York: Penguin.

Thelen, K. (2004). *How Institutions Evolve: The Political Economy of Skills in Germany, Britain, the United States, and Japan*. Cambridge: Cambridge University Press.

Weiss, L. (1998). *The Myth of the Powerless State*. Ithaca: Cornell University Press.

Wooten, J. (2004). *The Employee Retirement Income Security Act of 1974: A Political History*. Berkeley: University of California Press.

World Bank. (2008). *2008 Annual Report on Development Effectiveness*. Washington, DC: World Bank.

PART I

Trade Governance and Human Rights

1

Humanizing Global Economic Governance

Sol Picciotto

INTRODUCTION: THE SHAPING OF HUMAN RIGHTS AND NEW POLICY SPACES

Neoliberal ideologies have powered the international processes of liberalization since the 1980s, a time dominated by the so-called Washington Consensus. The opening of markets, privatization, deregulation, and minimal government were all characteristics of this period, each playing no small role in the shaping of human rights and social policy spaces. Impulses to resort to human rights ideas to counter neoliberal ideologies are thus easy to understand and even to sympathize with, but they also pose an important question: Can human rights discourses and law provide an adequate response to the challenges of the post-liberal order confronting us?

The neoliberal model was significantly modified from the mid-1990s and especially after the Asian financial crisis of 1997–1998, toward a post–Washington Consensus paradigm stressing the importance of good governance and regulation. This shift involved not only reform of the public sphere (politics and government) but also of the apparently private sphere of economic activity, the latter taking the form of pressures for greater corporate accountability and responsibility. These pressures sparked the renewal of the various types of corporate codes and guidelines which first originated in the 1960s, as well as the relaunching of attempts to construct an overarching framework for responsible global business under the auspices of the United Nations (Picciotto, 2011, ch. 5.2.2.1). Significantly, the recent initiatives are founded on human rights obligations as opposed to the earlier movement for a UN Code of Conduct for Transnational Corporations (TNCs), and are focused on strengthening new policy spaces for national and international regulation.

SOFT LAW VERSUS HARD LAW

The new obligations were first expressed in the UN Global Compact and more recently in the 'Protect, Respect and Remedy' approach put forward in the Ruggie report for the UN Human Rights Council (Ruggie, 2008). A major weakness of these counterbalancing attempts has been that formulations of principles regarding business responsibility have usually taken "soft law" forms, usually expressed as voluntary codes and guidelines and generally having weak compliance procedures. This is in sharp contrast with market liberalization rules, which have been entrenched as "hard law" and backed by powerful enforcement mechanisms and sanctions. Indeed, states which needed to draw on the resources of the International Monetary Fund (IMF) and World Bank have been obliged to comply with "conditionalities" reflecting the Washington Consensus policy prescriptions.

An even more powerful and formalized system of obligations and "disciplines" on states has been embodied in the extensive and complex framework of treaties that have come to form the "single undertaking" of the World Trade Organization (WTO). These treaties have established what can be described as a world economic constitution, complete with its own adjudication system and backed by uniquely stringent sanctions (Picciotto, 2011, ch. 8). In practice, corporations themselves have been given direct supranational legal rights to challenge state regulation through the investor-state arbitration procedures of bilateral and multilateral investment treaties, enforced by awards of monetary damages, strong remedies often running into the millions of dollars US (Picciotto, 2011, ch. 5.2.1.3). These have increasingly been used by corporations to challenge public policy decisions of states and consequently diminish states' policy spaces. Environmental protection or tobacco labeling are just two of many contested spaces.

CORPORATE RIGHTS AND HUMAN RIGHTS IN
INTERNATIONAL LAW

As stated in the preceding section, corporate rights, as well as state obligations toward business, have been entrenched as hard law, either supranational or international. In sharp contrast, attempts to establish standards of corporate responsibility generally take a soft-law form. Even where corporate obligations are formulated in binding rather than voluntaristic terms,[1] only rarely is an independent adjudication mechanism established to consider complaints, and sanctions are generally limited to "naming and shaming." Thus, corporate power has been strongly entrenched in international law through hard-law rights enforceable by adjudication in tribunals dominated by free market ideologies and backed by monetary penalties. All the while corporate responsibilities at the global level are expressed in essentially hortatory forms.

Not surprisingly, this has led many who are concerned with humanizing global governance to look for ways to strengthen corporate responsibility. It should first be noted that soft and hard law are far from mutually exclusive, and there are many ways in which soft regulation can be and has been embedded into hard law.[2] Furthermore, human rights advocates have been as inventive as corporate lawyers have in conceiving legal bases for corporate accountability; a notable example was the activation of the Alien Torts Claims Act – a long-dormant U.S. statute. Class-action negligence claims have also been devised in order to establish the liability of transnational corporations (TNCs) for harmful activities such as asbestos mining (Picciotto, 2011, ch. 5.1.3.2). It is important, however, not to take an instrumentalist or functionalist view of the law, and to recognize that it is not necessarily an effective means of changing behavior; its effectiveness generally depends on political support and the ideological climate.

A strong advocate of the rule of law and human rights has been Ernst-Ulrich Petersmann, who aims to broaden out the neoliberal global economic constitution along ordo-liberal lines by incorporating human rights principles into the WTO policy spaces (Petersmann, 2005). Perhaps surprisingly to some, these proposals met with suspicion and even hostility from leading proponents of human rights, and were denounced as an attempt to "hijack . . . international human rights law in a way which would fundamentally redefine its contours" (Alston, 2002, p. 816).

HUMAN RIGHTS IN THE NEOLIBERAL MODEL

Clearly, much depends on which human rights are incorporated into institutions such as the WTO, and in what form (Picciotto, 2011, ch. 8.3.3.2). Human rights principles can be compatible with neoliberal policies, and indeed may reinforce them. The classical liberal individual human rights were aimed at restricting state powers while establishing and preserving economic activity as a realm of private markets; it is notable that the only economic human right was that of private property. Seeking to carry forward this liberal tradition, Petersmann urges an expansive view of property rights to encompass "private rights to supply or demand one's goods in private markets," and argues that markets can be "justified not only on grounds of economic efficiency but also as preconditions for individual autonomy and for a free, informed and accountable society" (Petersmann, 2005, pp. 48–49).

A very different view is propounded by contemporary human rights specialists, stressing the more recently formulated socioeconomic rights such as those to education, health care, food, and shelter. These are not individual, legally enforceable rights, however, but at most obligations on states to develop appropriate socioeconomic policies (Jacobs, 1993). Nevertheless, despite not being entitlements, they could operate to counterbalance the liberalization obligations that inevitably restrict states' powers of regulation, if not their "right to regulate" and with it a diminution of their social policy spaces. This type of balancing is actually inscribed in the very structure of the WTO, inherited from the General Agreement on Tariffs and Trade (GATT). In both organizations, broad nondiscrimination and market access principles are generally counterbalanced by "exceptions" preserving individual states' rights to regulate and thus effectively leave the state (often in a weakened position compared to transnational capital) to be the sole protector of "human, animal and plant life or health" (GATT article XX (b)). It would also be technically possible to insert a similar balancing "exception" into the WTO Agreements to safeguard human rights, as well as environmental protection, although the political feasibility of such a proposal remains highly doubtful.

What might be gained by including such a provision to counterbalance liberalization with human rights obligations into global governance regimes such as the WTO? A real possibility is that the neoliberal market-opening obligations of contemporary trade and investment law could simply be reinforced and legitimized if they were complemented by classical liberal versions of human rights principles (Picciotto, 2007). Even if the reference were to the broader socioeconomic human rights principles, which many such as Petersmann would presumably oppose, the effect would be only symbolic. As Andrew Lang has pointed out, it is difficult to generate "at least in any simple or direct way, alternative visions of the global trading order from human rights norms," but perhaps such a move might help open up the closed policy communities to alternative perspectives (Lang, 2007, p. 87).

Some practice already exists of linking trade rights to human rights obligations, but these are expressed as separate issues, although involving a quid pro quo. Thus, the European Union's policy in negotiating "association agreements" is to offer preferential market access to partner states, complemented by acceptance of a broad obligation to respect human rights, together with institutional arrangements for "political dialogue and cooperation." For example, such an agreement has been in place with Israel since 2000, including the standard provision in article two that it "shall be based on respect for human rights and democratic principles, which . . . constitutes an essential element" of the agreement. Yet attempts by campaigners to press for suspension of the market access benefits in response to Israel's violation of the human rights of Palestinians in the Occupied Territories have so far met with very little success, and the "political dialogue" has yielded to realpolitik.[3]

Thus, it does not seem that any formal linkage of human rights to trade and investment regimes could have much impact in changing the dominant neoliberal perspectives of social and economic development. I suggest that any alternative vision for global economic governance needs to start from a more cogent critique of neoliberalism and a more profound understanding of the historical trajectory and contemporary characteristics of corporate capitalism.

CORPORATE CAPITALISM AND THE REGULATORY STATE

The most lasting and damaging legacy of the neoliberal revival of the 1980s has been its fostering of a series of myths and misconceptions that have clouded the perceptions of analysts and commentators from all points of the political spectrum. Neoliberal ideology posits a radical separation between the market and the state and envisages the market ahistorically, as a system based simply on exchange. This entirely overlooks the enormous transformations of capitalism in the past 150 years. The period between 1885 and 1914, in particular, saw a decisive shift, with the emergence of the corporation as the primary business model, as well as the growth of these first TNCs to their eventual domination of the world political economy during the twentieth century. State forms have undergone equally major changes, resulting in total transformation of the state-firm-market triad from what it was in the first heyday of liberalism in the late eighteenth century.

Certainly, the past three decades have seen a further widespread process of renegotiation and redefinition of the nature of the state, market and firm, and the forms of their interrelations. Most visibly, there has been a reduction in the scope of direct provision by state or public bodies of goods and especially services such as energy, transport, and prisons, as well as the introduction of extensive elements of contractualization into many areas of publicly administered provision such as health care, low-cost housing, and education.[4] This has been accompanied by a significant liberalization, in the sense of the reduction of barriers between markets (both within and between states) and the ending of many types of structural controls.

Although these processes have been generally described as privatization and deregulation, this is a serious misconception. What has occurred is the reconfiguration of relationships between state and corporate bureaucracies, coupled with the creation of new types of public-private interaction and hybrid forms of state-corporate entities. In fact, there has been a major *growth* in regulation, introducing extensive governance of economic activity through formalized laws and administrative oversight by various public bodies. These public bodies define markets, specify firms' investment obligations and hence influence profit rates, delimit the terms of competition, adjudicate between rivals, monitor quality, and generally supervise business activity.

Much of this entails an international transplantation of a type of "regulated corporatism," which emerged in the United States during the Progressive Era of 1890–1920 (Sklar, 1988; Weinstein, 1968; Law and Kim, 2010)[5] and was consolidated in the 1930s during the Franklin D. Roosevelt's administrations. However, also in the United States, many of the earlier regulatory structures have been undermined and further transformed through changes in the character, strategies, and control of large enterprises, molded by shifts in state regulation (Fligstein, 1990). Thus, far from seeing the reign of "free markets," the current period has witnessed the emergence of a "new regulatory state," characterized by new forms and interactions between the public and private spheres, raising fundamental issues of accountability and bureaucratic responsibility in the new policy spaces that have emerged (Picciotto, 2001; Jacobs, 2004). Democratic accountability through liberal representative democracy has thus been drastically undermined, not in the least by the delegation of public functions to autonomous technocratic bodies, and sometimes even the privatization of such functions, at both the sub-state and supranational levels (Buthe and Mattli, 2011).

THE INTERTWINING OF CORPORATE AND PRIVATE BUREAUCRACIES

The illusory conception of the corporation as a private entity has been reinforced by politicized reforms of corporate governance and the strengthening of shareholder rights to cultivate the support of the financial sector, fostering an increasingly unstable, financially driven economic order (Cioffi, 2011). The key feature of corporate capitalism is that economic activity and its organization have become increasingly *socialized*, yet within a framework of private ownership and control. This is seen in particular in the dominance of the corporate form, which enables the coordination of labor and assets on an enormous social scale, with protections and privileges granted by state law, although the corporation is considered a private entity. The oligopolistic corporations that came to dominate the key global industries of the twentieth century, first in oil, minerals, chemicals, engineering, automobiles, food, and agribusiness and then in pharmaceuticals, computing, media, and the Internet, can generate extraordinary profits. At the same time, their dominant positions have depended in many ways on state support.

Consequently we see a close intertwining of corporate and public bureaucracies on many levels. Many business activities require concessions, autho-
rizations, or licenses from public authorities, including natural resource firms
such as oil, mining, and logging, telecommunications and broadcasting firms,
construction and property development firms, as well as those providing a
wide range of professional services. Others depend on public financing of
infrastructure, such as roads, railways, telecommunications, and energy networks; the terms of access to such networks remain crucial. For many, such
as pharmaceutical, aircraft, and electronics manufacturers, the state is the
major customer. At the same time, the enormous growth of state expendi-
ture has made taxation – or, more specifically, tax exemptions, subsidies, and
incentives – a major element in profitability, especially in sectors such as oil,
minerals, banking and finance, and cultural industries such as film-making.
As a result, tax planning has become routinized, and TNCs in particular can
take advantage both of attracting investment by offering tax incentives and of
opportunities to avoid paying taxes. Increased state regulation in fields such as
consumer and environmental protection also has a direct impact on profitability. In basic infrastructure and utilities industries such as telecommunications,
broadcasting, gas, electricity, and water, decisions on the often very high levels
of fixed investment and on financing via higher costs to consumers or general
taxation are of major social importance. It has been, to a great extent, the difficulty of managing these decisions through state bureaucracies and financing
them via taxation that led to privatization, although generally under public
supervision. This has resulted in experiments with various forms of regulation
and public-private partnerships. Finally, as we have seen only too starkly in the
crisis of 2008–2009, the entire financial system and hence the world economy
depend directly on state support.

None of this looks remotely like the market economy envisaged by Adam
Smith or the other great liberal political economists or philosophers. Instead,
the key feature of regulatory capitalism is the close relationships and tight
interactions between the public and the private, the state and the market,
government and corporations. Paradoxically, however, we have seen a parallel process of the functional fragmentation of the state, as well as increased
decentralization of business, and the consequent emergence of both corporate
networks and multilevel governance.

THE POWER OF LAW IN THE CREATION OF
CORPORATE CAPITALISM

Law has not been peripheral to these historical processes – far from it –
although not as an external check on the inherent logic of market-driven

economic processes. Lawyers have played a central role in designing and shaping the institutional forms of corporate capitalism and its regulation. Law, therefore, is integral to the creation and shaping of the corporate entity and policy spaces.[6]

Not only have specific legal forms helped construct social institutions and relationships; law affects the particular ways in which power is exercised. This also entails consideration of the *power of law itself* as a form of legitimation. In general terms the power of the "rule of law" lies in the claims of classical liberal or bourgeois legality to provide justice based on universal principles granting equal rights to all legal subjects. The central critique of these claims to legal justice is that enforcing formal equality between those who are unequal in material terms (economically, physically, socially, and politically) reproduces inequality (Jacobs, 2004; Miéville, 2005). However, this again implies that inequality and power are somehow external to law, and that law's neutrality merely provides a cloak for extralegal forms of power.

This is a serious mistake, especially in the realm of economic law. To focus on law only as a balancing of rights is to restrict attention to economic exchange and to ignore the fact that it is indeed all obligations that ensure the enforcement of apparently equal rights. The ideologies of both classical liberalism and contemporary neoliberalism consider the role of law as simply to enforce contracts and protect property rights. Against this, welfare liberalism argues that there is a need for greater intervention to correct market failures, remedy asymmetries between parties to contracts, and perhaps even initiate some redistribution to correct excessive social inequalities. Thus, principles of equal treatment may sometimes be modified by permitting differential treatment, though usually without affecting the basic structures.

What is generally overlooked is the role of law in shaping and defining the property rights on which exchange depends, as well as the extensive state interventions affecting pricing and profit rates, which take place through legal regulation. Basic theory tells us that markets require property rights. Beyond that, academic theory has told us surprisingly little useful about property rights. This seems to stem largely from equating property with private property. A human rights perspective reinforces this fetishization given that, as has already been noted, the only individual economic right is that of property, generally understood as private property.

In fact, the basic legal forms of property and contract are infinitely mal-leable. In particular, the concept of exclusive private property rights has been extended to intangible or "fictitious" property. Thus, a legal claim on assets such as a share in a company came to be treated as a private property right, so that the corporation is conceived as a private legal person, governed by contract and "owned" by its shareholders. Not only shares but all manner of financial instruments have been formulated in terms of increasingly ingenious combinations of property and contract. The concept of intellectual property enabled the complex and contentious interactions of science with nature, on the one hand, and commerce and business, on the other, to be articulated in terms of proprietorial control over new technologies. Literature, the arts, and cultural life generally have also become molded by proprietorial principles, and hence dominated by the media industries. Similarly, contracts have been transformed from simple bargains between individuals and adapted to serve all kinds of administrative and regulatory purposes, otherwise thought of as the domain of public law (Campbell, 1999).

The skilful use and adaptation of these private law forms have enabled continued private appropriation, even though, as already pointed out, economic activity and its organization have become increasingly socialized. The enduring ability of private law forms to be adapted and reformulated to provide the institutional forms of corporate capitalism perhaps helps explain the enduring myths of the market economy.

Law's key role and importance is attributable to the techniques that lawyers have developed as creative ideologists of the texts that define the institutions and terrains through which economic activity is conducted. The key element of these techniques is the ability to assert authoritative interpretations of texts which are nevertheless inherently indeterminate and highly malleable. These techniques provide great advantages in managing the interactions between the different areas of lawmaking, adjudication, application, and enforcement as well as between different jurisdictions and arenas. In that sense, law is what Halliday and Carruthers (2007) have described as a recursive process. Social changes and political pressures are mediated through the formulation of legislative or administrative measures that create a new potential legal field. Such a field may be left neglected and barren if there is little incentive to cultivate it, but if it offers opportunities to build legal capital or exploit lucrative possibilities of representation, the work of cultivation will be intensive. This helps explain the sudden rise of investor-state arbitration after North American Free Trade Agreement (NAFTA), although similar provisions had been in force in bilateral treaties for several decades, largely unused. On the other side of the coin, it was activist lawyers who revived the long-dormant ATCA in the United States to bring human rights claims against corporations, and others in the United Kingdom and elsewhere who devised creative uses for tort litigation strategies against TNCs.

Lawyers are able to move both between the private and the public spheres, and also between different public or semipublic arenas: they lobby legislatures and help draft statutes, then devise legal forms to comply with, adapt to, or evade the measures; they make representations to executive bodies and administrative agencies charged with implementation; and they represent their clients before courts and tribunals that deliver adjudicative interpretations of the texts. Such processes have created and shaped the key legal institutions of corporate capitalism and have played key roles in determining the extent of a state's policy spaces.

Lawyers have therefore played a central part from the end of the nineteenth century in constructing the institutions of the corporatist economy. Notably, the debates over corporate concentration in the United States between 1880 and 1915 were mediated by lawyers devising legal forms (agreements, trusts, mergers), lobbying legislatures (New Jersey and Delaware as well as the U.S. Congress), and debating interpretations of the Sherman Act with the executive and in the courts. The outcome was the creation and legitimation of the oligopolistic firm, organized as a corporate group, able to spread its tentacles around the world as a TNC.

The 1880–1930 period also saw the emergence of new forms of regulatory law. This was strongest in the United States, with its antitrust law and sectoral regulatory commissions, while in Europe and elsewhere, governments took a more direct role in economic management, at least at the national level. The interstate rivalries and conflicts of the first half of the twentieth century offered solid ground for international politics and public international law, so the first lawyer-diplomats began to fashion forms of international economic regulation based on private law. Major firms in key industries used cartels to manage international trade and pool knowledge of new technologies; international shipping was registered under the privately managed system of "flags of convenience"; conflicts and overlaps of national claims to tax international business were eliminated by devising international tax avoidance structures using the flexibilities offered by the corporate form and other legal entities such as trusts.

In the second half of the twentieth century, regulatory law became transnationalized. To a great extent U.S. lawyers took the lead, shaping the legal forms as agents of the increasingly powerful U.S. corporations. Indeed, they invented the TNC, by exploiting the freedom of incorporation (overcoming some initial opposition) to create complex corporate group structures, taking advantage jurisdictional regulatory differences. They extended the reach of U.S. regulatory law itself through expansive doctrines of jurisdiction and theorized "transnational law" as a mixture of national and international, public and private law. American ideas, concepts, and institutions were transplanted into other countries, often with the help of local lawyers, some of whom had absorbed such perspectives by pursuing postgraduate studies in the United States. However, such transplants were also in some cases adapted by local acolytes to their own ideas and conditions, influenced by different legal cultures, producing hybrids. These developments further liberated transnational capital from each country's social policy space, effectively adding to the latter's diminution.

For example, the export of the U.S. antitrust philosophy to Europe and Japan resulted in significant adaptations; the European Commission indeed became an enthusiastic convert to the competition law gospel, although U.S. lawyers have complained that Europe applies a perverted version of the doctrine. In some arenas, non-U.S. lawyers made their own contributions. For example, techniques to avoid perceived regulatory burdens such as double taxation, by exploiting jurisdictional interactions and the legal personality of companies and trusts, were developed also in the United Kingdom, France, and the Netherlands (which became the home of the influential International Bureau for Fiscal Documentation). The strengthening of banking secrecy to develop a financial entrepôt and a system of discreet private banking was pioneered in Switzerland from the early 1930s. Lawyers and bankers in London took advantage of the Bank of England's relaxation of exchange controls to use dollar deposits for sterling-dollar swaps, and create the Eurodollar market. The field of IPRs has been dominated by continental European lawyers, especially from Germany and France, who have been at the forefront of developing the international framework and expanding intellectual property rights to ensure corporate control of new technologies. This has involved expansive interpretations of general principles such as the right of reproduction in copyright or the isolation from nature for patents, as well as devising new concepts such as plant variety protection.

SUPRANATIONAL CONSTITUTIONALISM

A particular contribution of European lawyers has been forms of supranational constitutionalism. Indeed, Europeans going back to Vitoria and Grotius first devised the notion of the *jus gentium* to manage and legitimize the complexities of conquest and colonialism. Liberal internationalism from the last part of the nineteenth century also created the first wave of international institutions, whether private (e.g., the International Chamber of Commerce), quasi-public (e.g., the International Committee of the Red Cross), or intergovernmental but with a strong private input (e.g., the international Unions governing copyright and industrial property). Europeans also originated and sustained the organizations for international legal harmonization (the Hague Conference

on Private International Law, and UNIDROIT), launched in the early twentieth century, which took on a new life in the second half of the century.
Also in the second half of the twentieth century came first the building of
international human rights institutions (more recently strengthened by the
Rome Statute for the International Criminal Court), the Council of Europe,
and then the great project for an ever-wider European union (Madsen and
Vauchez, 2004). As the EU became transformed from a proto-confederation
to a system of multilevel governance using a variety of modes of coordination,
its development interacted with the emerging networks of global economic
governance, especially through the WTO.

Although the models of supranational constitutionalism and transnational-
ism appeared to be very different, there has been an increasing convergence.
This suggests that the processes of their construction have shared a similar
dynamic. Indeed, it seems that the actual practices of lawyers, acting both
on behalf and sometimes as critics of corporate capital, have significant sim-
ilarities, even if the contexts in which they operate involve different legal
cultures. Lawyers are also influenced by their clients: the economic and military dominance of the United States since the mid-twentieth century has
meant that various U.S. administrations have veered between asserting unilateral power and supporting multilateral frameworks. Since the United States
would inevitably dominate these, they are more likely to be proposed by the
friendly rivals of the United States, such as Canada or the Europeans. With
the formation of the EU as a major economic bloc, projects such as the WTO
are increasingly multilateral, especially with the recent emergence of China
and a wider group of important developing countries (Brazil, India, and South
Africa). In some ways this seems to make multilateralism more difficult, as
seen with the stalling of the WTO's Doha Round and the response to the
financial crisis.

The emergence of global governance, although dominated by the United
States, is not just a process of Americanization, but perhaps a new form of
empire. It has involved contributions from not only characteristically American
styles, but also European, Latin American, and Asian "ways of law" (Dezalay
and Garth 2001, 2010; Kagan, 2001; Gessner and Nelken, 2007). This indeed
is a central element in the power of law: the ability of its general principles,
norms and institutions to offer universal prescriptions, while being capable of
adaptation by interpretation to suit local circumstances and cultures.

Furthermore, contributions can be made to the construction of the legal
edifice from many hands and in different styles. Legal principles can be sufficiently flexible both to allow and to absorb radical departures. The "open
source" movement, for example, has overturned the exclusive private rights

paradigm of IPRs by asserting authors' rights. A wide variety of creative-commons-style licenses provide the flexibility to explore different methods of both organizing and commercializing creativity and innovation, based on a kind of commons. The issues raised by transnational liability litigation, seen most dramatically in the Bhopal case, cannot be described simply as an imperialist attempt to export American law or legal culture, but they do put into question the "uncertain promise" of law both in managing hazardous activities and compensating victims (Cassels, 1993). Law is not neutral; it shapes and legitimizes social relations of power, but the directions of change depend not only or even mainly on law but on more general social processes of which law is but a part.

LAW, TECHNOCRACY, AND DEMOCRACY

These questions about the role of law are also part of a broader debate about technocratic governance. The moves to legalization represent not only a failure to resolve issues politically but also a concern that they should not be left solely to a specialized technocracy. Many issues and areas of global concern are indeed now governed by delegated experts; indeed, technocracy has come to constitute the main form of global governance. This results not only from the difficulties of reaching international agreement but also from the more fundamental social changes that have led to the transformations of the state, its functional fragmentation, and the emergence of regulatory governance.

There are clearly fundamental questions about the legitimacy of technocratic decision making. Within nation-states, these have been dealt with mainly through Weberian models of bureaucracy, according to which specialist technocrats must take decisions on the basis of an objectivist and instrumental rationality, within a framework of values decided by political processes, to which they are accountable. However, these models have come under increasing pressure, as a variety of factors has led to a growing public mistrust of expertise and science. Expertise is important and indeed necessary, especially in today's complex world. However, it needs to operate within new structures to ensure that specialist knowledge is developed and deployed responsibly and accountably.

Taking a wider perspective, some political theorists have argued that the effects of liberalization and globalization have been to unleash socially destructive behavior based on the competitive pursuit of self-interest, as existing normative and institutional restraints are undermined or dismantled. They argue that this necessitates the reconstitution of democracy based on principles adapted to the emerging forms of the new public sphere, but which explicitly aim to structure it to ensure the most effective forms of popular participation (Jacobs, 1997). Indeed, new forms of active citizenship and political action have been developing, often around the local and national impact of regional or global policies. Some have also been institutionalized, for example, the system of participatory budgeting pioneered in Porto Alegre and other parts of Brazil, which have also spread worldwide, although too often in forms that reinforce existing systems of political patronage (Shah, 2007; Van Zyl, 2010).

The recognition that the public sphere has become fragmented into multiple intersecting networks and overlapping jurisdictional spheres emphasizes the importance of building democratic participation through new political principles, institutions, and practices. These should recognize the diversity of political sites in which public policies are developed and implemented, also involving processes of reflexive interaction between these sites.

Jürgen Habermas in particular has argued that such principles must attempt to transcend the two main traditional constitutional models, which are increasingly proving inadequate for the contemporary phase of globalization (Habermas, 1996, 2001). On the one hand, liberal conceptions, based on a view of society as composed of individuals pursuing their self-interest or preformed "preferences," see the role of the polity as complementing the market, and as aiming to identify a collective interest either by authoritarian means or via majoritarian representative democracy. Postindustrial capitalism, with its integrated global production and marketing networks, raises a wide range of social, environmental, and moral issues that cannot be adequately resolved by aggregating individual preferences, using either authoritarian or democratic methods.

The alternative model of civic republicanism rejects the narrow view of citizenship based on weighing and balancing competing private interests. However, its stress on an ethical politics based on visions of the common good implies a communitarianism requiring shared values, which in today's culturally fractured world takes reactionary forms and may generate conflict rather than consensus. Habermas has suggested that, whereas both these views tend to see the state as the center, deliberative politics can be adapted to a decentered society:

> This concept of democracy no longer needs to operate with the notion of a social whole centered in the state and imagined as a goal-oriented subject writ large. Just as little does it represent the whole in a system of constitutional norms mechanically regulating the interplay of powers and interests in accordance with the market model. (Habermas, 1996, p. 27)

Others also have stressed the attractiveness of a direct, deliberative form of participatory democracy for solving problems in ways unavailable to representative systems:

> Collective decisions are made through public deliberation in arenas open to citizens who use public services, or who are otherwise regulated by public decisions. But in deciding, those citizens must examine their own choices in the light of the relevant deliberations and experiences of others facing similar problems in comparable jurisdictions or subdivisions of government. (Cohen and Sabel 1997, pp. 313–314)

DELIBERATIVE DEMOCRACY IN NEW POLICY SPACES

In this perspective, decision making in relevant policy spaces, especially by public bodies, should result as much as possible from active democratic participation based on discourse or deliberation rather than on instrumental reasoning. Instead of the pursuit of individual interests based on the assumption of fixed preferences, the aim is to go beyond an objectivist rationality (in which choices are considered to be made by reference to absolute and objective standards), without falling into the trap of relativism (Dryzek, 1990). Thus, while accepting that there is no single objective standard of truth, because perspectives are always subjective (and hence epistemology is to that extent relativist), truth can be said to be an emergent property of the deliberative interaction between perspectives (and hence its ontology is objective). In other words, there is an objective truth, even if we can only know it through subjective interactions. From this perspective, decisions taken by democratic deliberation are superior because they are *better*.

Deliberative democracy accepts the existence of a diversity of perspectives and aims to facilitate interactive deliberation about values through which preferences may change or be accommodated to each other. An emphasis on process may help overcome the weaknesses of this model if conceived as a political ideal, or as relying on the generation of consensus purely through the public use of reason. Crucially, account must also be taken of inequalities of power, which generate conflicting interests as well as imbalances in capacities to participate in a politics based on reasoning.

A key element, therefore, is the fostering of informed participation in deliberative decision making, rather than merely elite or expert deliberation. There is a certain tension between the two, because the deliberative evaluation of specialized knowledge or data entails a degree of insulation or autonomy from

private interests and other pressures.7 However, this may result in an unjus-
tified authority being claimed by or given to the judgments of specialists or
experts. Thus a key element in democratic deliberation is to ensure a fruitful
interaction between various sites of deliberation and awareness by specialists of
the conditional or contingent nature of their expert knowledge and judgments
(Wynne, 1992). Thus, experts should be more explicit about the assumptions
behind the abstract models underpinning their evaluations, and allow input
into their deliberations from both other specialists and alternative perspectives
and social values.

This has important implications for lawyers, given that law generally structures regulatory arenas and interactions, as well as mediating social conflicts
and interactions. A significant weakness of international legalization is that
it has reinforced formalism and instrumental rationality. Notably, international adjudicators have tended to rely on a closed epistemology, based on
an objectivism that treats the abstract concepts in the texts through an instrumental rationality, resulting in decisions expressed in legalistic terms. This
closure tends to exclude debate about the values involved in the interpretive
choices made by the adjudicator, which would entail acceptance of a more
extended and direct accountability to a broader political constituency, rather
than through national governments. It is also technicist (taking its specialist part
for the whole), because its closed rationality excludes reflexive dialogue with
those outside its specialist epistemological sphere. For example, the formal-
ist reasoning shown in the decisions of the WTO's Appellate Body reflects its
accountability dilemma; hence they are generally expressed in legalistic terms,
but astutely tread a difficult political line aimed at ensuring their acceptability
to its various constituencies (Picciotto, 2005).

NEW ARENAS OF GOVERNANCE

It is clearly illusory to consider that law alone can provide adequate legitimacy
for global governance. It is nevertheless equally clearly important that the law
and lawyers should play their part. This includes helping construct forms and
arenas of governance that are insulated from undue influence from private
interests, and which foster democratic participation and deliberation based on
explicitly articulated values and aims in the new policy spaces that link trade
and human rights. Lawyers play a crucial role in accommodating public concerns to private interests. Lawyering entails interpretive practices that mediate
between the public standards and values expressed in the wide variety of
norms and the particular activities and operations of economic actors, offering
the hope that economic power ultimately might be exercised for the general

good. However, this aspiration is illusory unless law operates within a broader democratic framework, in which legal practices themselves are also subject to high standards of transparency, accountability, and responsibility. Rethinking the lines between public and private in policy making is fundamental during structural change and financial crises when market institutions have been weakened and new policy spaces are emerging. An important dimension of this rethinking includes the responsibility of each individual to reflect on their own practice and methodology, and when putting forward either analyses or prescriptions to do so on the basis of clearly articulated assumptions, taking due account of the perspectives of others, even if within a critical evaluation. International trade and human rights law function in this vision of global governance as a regulative ideal on the uses of the policy spaces that are emerging on the new landscape of the global economy.

REFERENCES

Alston, P. (2002) 'Resisting the Merger and Acquisition of Human Rights by Trade Law: A Reply to Petersmann', 13 *European Journal of International Law*, 13, 815–50.

Buthe, T. and Mattli, W. (2011) *The New Global Rulers: The Privatization of Regulation in the World Economy*, Princeton University Press, Princeton, NJ.

Campbell, D. I. (1999) 'The "Hybrid Contract" and the Merging of the Public and Private Law of the Allocation of Economic Goods', in N. D. Lewis and D. I. Campbell (eds.), *Promoting Participation: Law or Politics?* 45–73. Cavendish, London.

Cassels, J. (1993) *The Uncertain Promise of Law. Lessons from Bhopal*, Toronto University Press, Toronto.

Cioffi, J. W. (2011) *Public Law and Private Power*, Cornell University Press, Ithaca, NY.

Cohen, J. and Sabel, C. (1997) 'Directly-Deliberative Polyarchy', *European Law Journal*, 3, 313–42.

Collins, H. (1999) *Regulating Contracts*, Oxford University Press, Oxford.

Dezalay, Y. and Garth, B. (2001) *The Internationalization of Palace Wars: Lawyers, Economists, and the Contest to Transform Latin American States*, University of Chicago Press, Chicago.

Dezalay, Y. and Garth, B. G. (2010) *Asian Legal Revivals: Lawyers in the Shadow of Empire*, Chicago University Press, Chicago.

Dryzek, J. S. (1990) *Discursive Democracy*, Cambridge University Press, Cambridge.

Fligstein, N. (1990) *The Transformation of Corporate Control*, Harvard University Press, Cambridge, MA.

Freeman, J. (2000) 'The Contracting State', *Florida State University Law Review*, 28, 155–214.

Gessner, V. and Nelken, D. (Eds.) (2007) *European Ways of Law: Towards a European Sociology of Law*, Hart, Oxford.

Habermas, J. (1996) 'Three Normative Models of Democracy', in S. Benhabib (ed.), *Democracy and Difference: Contesting the Boundaries of the Political.* 21–30. Cambridge University Press, Cambridge.

Habermas, J. (2001) *The Postnational Constellation*, Polity, Cambridge.

Halliday, T. C. and Carruthers, B. G. (2007) 'The Recursivity of Law: Global Norm-Making and National Law-Making in the Globalization of Corporate Insolvency Regimes', *American Journal of Sociology*, 112, 1135–1202.

Jacobs, L. (1997) *The Democratic Vision of Politics*. Prentice-Hall, Upper Saddle River, NJ.

Jacobs, L. (2004) *Pursuing Equal Opportunities*. Cambridge University Press, New York.

Joerges, C. (1999) 'Bureaucratic Nightmare, Technocratic Regime and the Dream of Good Transnational Governance', in C. Joerges and E. Vos (eds.), *EU Committees: Social Regulation, Law and Politics*. 3–47. Hart Publishing, Oxford.

Joerges, C. and Neyer, J. (1997) 'From Intergovernmental Bargaining to Deliberative Political Processes: The Constitutionalisation of Comitology', *European Law Journal*, 3, 273–99.

Kagan, R. A. (2001) *Adversarial Legalism: The American Way of Law*, Harvard University Press, Cambridge, MA: London.

Landfried, C. (1999) 'The European Regulation of Biotechnology by Polycratic Governance', in C. Joerges and E. Vos (eds.), *EU Committees: Social Regulation, Law and Politics*. 173–94. Hart, Oxford.

Lang, A. (2007) 'The Role of the Human Rights Movement in Trade Policy-Making: Human Rights as a Trigger for Social Learning', *New Zealand Journal of Public and International Law*, 5, 77–102.

Law, M. T. and Kim, S. (2010) 'The Rise of the American Regulatory State: A View from the Progressive Era', in *Jerusalem Papers in Regulation & Governance* 6.

Madsen, M. R. and Vauchez, A. (2004) 'European Constitutionalism at the Cradle. Law and Lawyers in the Construction of a European Political Order (1920–1960)', in A. Jettinghoff and H. Schepel (eds.), *In Lawyers' Circles: Lawyers and European Legal Integration*. Elsevier, The Hague, 15–34.

Miéville, C. (2005) *Between Equal Rights: A Marxist Theory of International Law*, Brill, Leiden; Boston.

Petersmann, E. U. (2005) 'Human Rights and International Trade Law: Defining & Connecting the Two Fields', in T. Cottier, J. Paulwelyn, and E. Bürgi Bonanomi (eds.), *Human Rights and International Trade*. 29–94. Oxford University Press, Oxford.

Picciotto, S. (2001) 'Democratizing Globalism', in D. Drache (ed.), *The Market or the Public Domain? Global Governance and the Asymmetry of Power*. 335–59. Routledge, London.

Picciotto, S. (2005) 'The WTO's Appellate Body: Formalism as a Legitimation of Global Governance', *Governance*, 18, 477–503.

Picciotto, S. (2007) 'The WTO as a Node of Global Governance: Economic Regulation and Human Rights Discourses', *Law, Social Justice and Global Development Journal*, vol 10, issue 1. No page numbers.

Picciotto, S. (2011) *Regulating Global Corporate Capitalism*, Cambridge University Press, Cambridge.

Ruggie, J. (2008) *Protect, Respect and Remedy: a Framework for Business and Human Rights*, Report of the Special Representative of the Secretary-General on the issue of Human Rights and Transnational Corporations and other business enterprises. United Nations Human Rights Council.

Shah, A. (ed.) (2007) *Participatory Budgeting*, The World Bank, Washington, DC.

Sklar, M. J. (1988) *The Corporate Reconstruction of American Capitalism 1890–1916. The Market, Law and Politics*, Cambridge University Press, Cambridge.

Stern, J. (2012) 'The Relationship between Regulation and Contracts in Infrastructure Industries: Regulation as Ordered Renegotiation', *Regulation and Governance*, 6(4), 474–98.

Van Zyl, A. (2010) *What Is Wrong with the Constituency Development Funds?* International Budget Partnership, Washington, DC.

Vincent-Jones, P. (1999) 'The Regulation of Contractualisation in Quasi-Markets for Public Services', *Public Law*, 1–31.

Vos, E. (1999) *Institutional Frameworks of Community Health and Safety Legislation. Committees, Agencies and Private Bodies*, Hart Publishing, Oxford.

Weinstein, A. J. (1968) *The Corporate Ideal in the Liberal State 1900–1918*, Beacon, Boston.

Wynne, B. (1992) 'Risk and Social Learning', in S. Krimsky and D. Golding (eds.), *Social Theories of Risk*. 275–97. Praeger, Westport, CT.

2

The Promise of Linking Trade and Human Rights

Ernst-Ulrich Petersmann

Law and governance need justification in order to be accepted by citizens and democratic parliaments as legitimate. In contrast to the natural sciences, law is not about discovering "scientific truth out there"; rather it is about "institutionalizing public reason," enabling individuals to cooperate peacefully in order to realize their individual, social, and democratic self-development. The international financial crisis since 2008, the unnecessary poverty crises in many less-developed countries and overindebted developed countries, and the failure of United Nations (UN) and World Trade Organization (WTO) institutions to protect international public goods effectively – like transnational rule of law protecting human rights, prevention of harmful climate change, and a liberal world trading system enabling each country to increase consumer welfare through division of labor – have revealed multilevel governance failures challenging the legitimacy of both UN law and international economic law.

RECOGNIZING HUMAN DIGNITY: A FUNDAMENTAL PRINCIPLE

From a human dignity perspective on constitutionalism and international law, reasonableness, autonomy, constitutionally agreed-on principles of justice, and the human rights of citizens are all instruments designed to realize the ultimate goals of individual and democratic self-development. However, over the past ten years the need for promoting synergies between human rights and trade by interpreting international economic law to conform with human rights has been recognized by ever-more international economic organizations and courts as well as many nongovernmental organizations (NGOs) (Petersmann, 2009, pp. 69–90). The customary rules of treaty interpretation and the recognition by all UN member states – in numerous UN and other human rights instruments – of civil, political, economic, and social human rights, and of their interdependence and indivisibility, requires interpreting and developing international economic law to conform with the human rights obligations of UN member states. Even though states appreciate the requirement that international economic law conform with their respective human rights obligations, a purely utilitarian conception of trade risks undermining the human rights dimensions of international economic law.

This chapter examines the complex interactions between human rights law, international economic law, and trade over the past ten years. The central argument is that the diverse forms of multilevel constitutionalism in the European Union (EU), the European Economic Area (EEA), and the European Court of Human Rights (ECHR) illustrate that a multilevel constitutionalism that synergizes international human rights and international economic law has become a politically feasible and realistic conception of constitutional justice and is no longer only a cosmopolitan dream. Policy space is a new, perhaps elusive idea for international law, but it reflects the importance of diversity and room for maneuver by national actors within transnational constitutional frameworks. The new multilevel constitutionalism I describe here creates new policy space to be used in diverse and innovative ways while at the same time allows for multilevel judicial protection of human rights in international commerce, trade, investment, and regional integration.

The belief that there are tangible synergies between human rights and trade dates to the 1980s. It was evident in the decisions of the European courts as well as my academic work. The judicial balancing of human and economic rights in European courts is now cited and emulated in regional economic courts globally.[1] And even investor-state arbitral tribunals acknowledge the need for interpreting international economic law in conformity with human rights.[2]

UN human rights bodies increasingly admit the need for strengthening human rights in international economic law, as illustrated by the UN Human Rights Council's endorsement on June 16, 2011, of the "Guiding Principles on Business and Human Rights: Implementing the UN *'Protect, Respect and Remedy'* Framework" proposed by the UN Special Representative J. Ruggie,[3] and the *Human Rights Impact Assessments for Trade and Investment Agreements* elaborated by the UN Special Rapporteur for the Right to Food in cooperation with UN bodies and NGOs (de Schutter, 2011). UN human rights bodies increasingly recognize the crucial role of trade and international economic law for poverty reduction, and no longer discredit the WTO (ECOSOC, 2011, para. 15). Westphalian interpretations of UN human rights law and international economic law, with the traditionally one-sided focus on the rights and obligations of states without acknowledging citizens as the primary sources of legitimacy for international law, are increasingly challenged by civil society, human rights courts, and economic courts. These bodies invoke human rights and other principles of justice as justifications and relevant context for cosmopolitan interpretations of certain international legal rules to the benefit of citizens.

STRENGTHENING THE CONSTITUTIONALIZATION OF INTERNATIONAL LAW

At the turn of the century I published a series of articles calling for mainstreaming human rights into the law of worldwide organizations to strengthen the constitutional functions of international economic law. I argued this would contribute to poverty reduction and protecting, respecting, and fulfilling the human rights of citizens. The two constitutional principles underlying this proposition – (1) the customary law requirement of interpreting international treaties in conformity with principles of justice and human rights, and (2) the need for a four-stage-sequence of constitutional, legislative, executive, and judicial institutionalization of public reason to protect human rights effectively – were consistent with the successful merger of human rights, economic law, and constitutional law in European international law (Petersmann, 1987, pp. 621–650).

However, my proposal for mainstreaming human rights was challenged by several leading international lawyers who argued that we should keep human rights law and international economic law separate because of the lack of human rights expertise in most economic organizations, and reject judicial balancing of human, economic, and social rights as practiced by Courts throughout Europe (Petersmann, 2002, pp. 845–851). More than ten years on, I think the case for mainstreaming human rights is even stronger, as evident from the developing trends, which I identify throughout the chapter, that show the promise of multilevel constitutionalism.

COSMOPOLITAN RIGHTS AND DUTIES TO PROTECT MORE EFFECTIVE IN HUMAN RIGHTS LAW AND INTERNATIONAL ECONOMIC LAW

The customary law requirement of interpreting international treaties in conformity with principles of justice and with the human rights obligations of states reflects a broader constitutional insight emphasized, among other examples, by John Rawls in his classic book, *Theory of Justice*. This insight implies that the welfare of citizens and their adequate access to essential goods and services depend on reasonable rules and institutions rather than domestic resources. Hence, the 2011 World Development Report rightly identifies the "absence of legitimate institutions that provide citizens security, justice and jobs" as the main cause of mass violence and unnecessary poverty in many countries. If the protection and fulfillment of human rights depends on developing responsible policy, then cosmopolitan rights are a precondition for empowering citizens to govern themselves (e.g., by engaging in mutually beneficial trade) and ensuring the accountability of all delegated policy capabilities.

Constitutional democracies, European international law, and international economic law recognize that the legal task of institutionalizing public reason depends on a four-stage sequence of constitutional, legislative, administrative, and judicial safeguards of human rights with due respect for reasonable disagreements about particular conceptions of the good life. Civil society increasingly challenges the obvious failures of both UN human rights law and worldwide international economic law to institutionalize public reason in international relations. This is especially true given that they are confronted with ever-more crises in international monetary, trade, financial, environmental relations, and poverty reduction. Westphalian intergovernmentalism reflects discursive failures because of its propensity toward authoritarian treatment of citizens as mere objects of international law and its neglect of human rights as reasonable restrictions on government policy. The common constitutional problem of the crises in human rights law and international economic law is that regulatory discretion and rent-seeking by powerful interest groups are inadequately constitutionally constrained by rights, judicial checks and balances, and democratic public reason.

SILO EFFECTS IN INTERNATIONAL ECONOMIC LAW

International economic law and international human rights law evolved as separate regimes until their successful merger in European international law. In contrast to the hierarchical nature of domestic constitutional systems, UN human rights law remains essentially a horizontal legal system respecting state's sovereign right to apply *higher* standards of national and regional human rights law compared with those of the UN. This respect for legitimate constitutional pluralism entails that the content, legal protection, and balancing of civil, political, economic, social, and cultural human rights, and their contextual relevance for international economic law, often remain contested. The unnecessary poverty and inadequate access to water, food, health protection, education, and the rule of law experienced by 1–2 billion people illustrate that neither UN human rights law nor worldwide international economic law treaties have succeeded in realizing the declared objective of states "that human rights should be protected by the rule of law" so as to promote "universal respect for and observance of human rights and fundamental freedoms for all" as put forward in the Preamble to the Universal Declaration of Human Rights (UDHR). As human rights do not enforce themselves and the lack of any references to human rights in the IMF, World Bank, GATT, and WTO agreements impedes protection of human rights in international economic law, mainstreaming human rights into this medium remains a central challenge in the twenty-first century. The increasing legal and judicial protection of cosmopolitan rights empowering citizens to challenge welfare-reducing abuses of public and private power by invoking access to justice and other human rights, trading rights, investor rights, intellectual property rights, environmental, labor, and social rights, and the corresponding obligations of governments is among the most important changes to international economic law over the past ten years.

THE COMPLEXITIES OF INTERNATIONAL ECONOMIC AND HUMAN RIGHTS LAW

Many national constitutions, regional human rights conventions, and all UN human rights instruments philosophically derive human rights from respect for the dignity of human beings who "are endowed with reason and conscience and should act towards one another in a spirit of brotherhood." Since 1945, all UN member states have regularly reaffirmed their "commitment towards the full realization of all human rights for all, which are universal, indivisible, interrelated, interdependent and mutually reinforcing."[4] The statement in the Preamble of the UDHR is a critical recognition of human rights law: "It is essential, if man is not to be compelled to have recourse, as a last resort, to rebellion against tyranny and oppression, that human rights should be protected by the rule of law." This confirms the moral entitlement of every individual to "inalienable" human rights and to struggles for rights. This has been illustrated by the Arab human rights revolutions in North Africa and the Middle East in 2011 and by increasing civil society calls for better protection of human rights, including access to essential food, medicines, and health services in international economic law so as to fulfill everyone's right to "a social and international order in which the rights and freedoms set forth in this Declaration can be fully realized" under Article 28 of the Declaration. Today, the dual nature of human rights as moral rights and integral parts of positive national and international law is universally recognized by all 192 UN member states and prompts citizens, some governments, and courts to increasingly insist on stronger protection of human rights (Petersmann, 2011, chapter 2).

ANOTHER MILESTONE

The 1966 UN *Covenant on Economic, Social and Cultural Rights* focuses on "the right to work," the "right of everyone to the enjoyment of just and favorable conditions of work," labor rights and trade union rights, the "right of everybody to social security," protection of the family, mothers, and children, the "right of everyone to an adequate standard of living," and the human rights to health and to education. Yet, apart from a brief reference to "safeguarding fundamental political and economic freedoms to the individual" in Article 6.2, the CESCR does not refer to the economic freedoms of profession, trade, and private property, which are recognized as fundamental rights in many European constitutions, as well as the 2009 Lisbon Treaty and the EU Charter of Fundamental Rights, which conform with the constitutional traditions of EU member states. The disagreement on economic liberties reflects, inter alia, the tradition in many common law countries of protecting freedom of contract, freedom of profession, and other economic freedoms as common law guarantees rather than as constitutional and human rights. Democracy is conceived in terms of parliamentary freedom rather than the equal constitutional rights of citizens. The related disagreement on human rights law and its multilevel implementation in international economic law may justify claims for additional human rights – like "freedoms of the internet" and the "right to safe and clean drinking water and sanitation" as human rights that are essential for the full enjoyment of life and all other human rights. This interpretation has in fact been recognized in UN General Assembly Resolution A/64/L.63 of July 28, 2010, as well as in Resolution A/HRC/Res/15/9 of the UN Human Rights Council.

Protection of human rights by UN bodies and courts of justice may delegitimize authoritarian claims that governments have not conceded such rights to their citizens. Advocates increasingly claim that, from a human rights perspective, international economic law should be conceived as an instrument for protecting, respecting, and fulfilling human rights. Comparative legal and institutional research suggests that constitutional and judicial protection of cosmopolitan conceptions of international economic law, which empower citizens to challenge and influence public reason, have proven more effective and more legitimate than state-centered "Westphalian conceptions" of international economic law, which treat citizens as mere objects of intergovernmental regulation (Petersmann, 2012).

CONSTITUTIONAL JUSTICE AND THE CHANGING NATURE
OF THE "RULES OF RECOGNITION"

Legal positivists in the tradition of H. L. A Hart tend to define law not only by "primary rules of conduct" but also by legal practices recognizing, developing, and enforcing rules in conformity with "secondary rules" of recognition, change, and adjudication. The universal recognition of inalienable human rights by all UN member states has also contributed to the recognition of principles of justice (e.g., in the UN Charter, human rights conventions, and national constitutions) as integral parts of national and international legal systems. The ancient symbol of the independent, impartial judge administering justice by "weighing" the arguments of both sides (*justitia* holding the scales) and enforcing the existing law (*justitia* holding the sword) recalls much older traditions of recognizing justice as the main objective of law.

Arguably, the legitimacy of law, governance, and adjudication derives from constitutional justice no less than from democracy. John Rawls's theory of justice and the related priority of "public reason" explain why, in democracies with constitutional adjudication, courts of justice may be more principled "exemplars of public reason" than are political institutions based on majority decisions by organized interest groups. Hence, many lawyers and judges define law by, in the words of Justice O.W. Holmes, "prophecies of what courts will do in fact" and by how Courts will apply legal rules (e.g. "general principles of law" in the terms of Article 38 ICJ Statute). Economic courts in Europe[5] and also investor-state arbitral awards[6] increasingly recognize that rules, including international economic law, which violate human rights may not be a valid part of positive law. As human rights law recognizes the need for limiting "rule by law" through the "rule of law," the human right of access to justice and judicial protection of the rule of law acquires constitutional importance for both human rights law and international economic law.

The constitutional guarantees of democratic participation, individual "access to justice," and judicial protection of the rule of law enables citizens, their democratic representatives, and courts of justice to increasingly challenge power-oriented, intergovernmental economic regulation. This is true even in the case of EU regulations implementing legally binding sanctions approved by the UN Security Council.[7] Arguably, the emerging multilevel human rights constitution changes the "rules of recognition" of international law by constitutionally limiting the Westphalian monopolies of diplomats to interpret and define the scope of international rules, general principles of law, and human rights.

Human rights law may justify legal claims that human rights universally recognized in UN Resolutions may be relevant context for interpreting international economic law "in conformity with principles of justice." Also in less-developed countries such as such as India and South Africa, courts of justice increasingly insist on their constitutional mandate to interpret and apply economic law in conformity with human rights so as to protect citizens against abuses of public and private power (Petersmann, 2008, pp. 769–798). The changing structures of human rights, transnational commercial, trade, investment, and European economic integration law are illustrated by the fact that multilevel judicial interpretation and clarification of rules through thousands of dispute settlement findings by national and international courts and other dispute settlement bodies have become no less important for the progressive development of law and protection of individual rights than intergovernmental agreements are.

LEGAL AND JUDICIAL BALANCING AS THE ULTIMATE RULE OF LAW

Law as an instrument of governance needs justification. Economists tend to justify economic rules in terms of promoting economic efficiency, "individual utility," and consumer or "total welfare." Yet, mere promotion of market equilibrium through supply and demand, or price-setting by monopolistic suppliers (e.g., of tap water and patented medicines), may be inconsistent with human rights and the corresponding obligations of governments to fulfill the basic needs of their citizens (e.g., in terms of human rights of access to water, food, and essential medicines at affordable prices). A utilitarian focus on output legitimacy cannot avoid questions of input legitimacy, for example regarding the frequent producer bias in international economic law resulting from inadequate regulation of market failures and private-public partnerships that favor special producer interests over general consumer welfare.

Similarly, positivist legal claims, which are based on authoritative issuance of rules and their social efficacy, justifying the "rule of men" and their "rule by law," continue to be challenged, as they have been since antiquity, by invoking principles of justice as the legal conditions of the validity of rules and the rule of law. Whereas conservative conceptions of justice emphasize the need for rule-following and upholding legality, reformative conceptions of justice acknowledge the additional function of law and courts of justice to ensure equity with due regard to the particular circumstances of disputes and the inevitably incomplete nature of rule-making. Hence, there are long-standing traditions of complementing universal conceptions of formal justice (e.g., as defined by equal human rights and the sovereign equality of states) with particular conceptions of substantive justice. An example of this complementarity might be interpreting international economic law in terms of "equity" and "difference principles" justifying rectification of formally equal treatment so as to render to every human his or her due. As long as constitutional and legal protection of economic and social rights remains weak in so many countries, effective protection of "freedom from poverty" (Pogge, 2007) and of the transnational rule of law for the benefit of citizens requires overcoming the utilitarian and mercantilist traditions of separating human rights law and international economic law. Constitutional theory explains why national and intergovernmental power politics in international economic law can be constitutionalized only by legal and judicial protection of countervailing rights ensuring general consumer welfare, nondiscriminatory conditions of competition, human rights, and other reasonable long-term interests.

THE JUDICIAL NEED FOR COUNTERVAILING RIGHTS

Similar to Article 1 of the UN Charter, customary law prescribes that "disputes concerning treaties, like other international disputes, should be settled by peaceful means and in conformity with the principles of justice and international law." The Agreement establishing the WTO, like many other international economic treaties, recognizes the "basic principles and objectives . . . underlying this multilateral trading system." Some of these principles are specified in WTO provisions, for instance in the GATT and other WTO agreements on trade in goods, services, and trade-related intellectual property rights. Other principles are incorporated into WTO law by reference to other international law rules, for example in the WTO Dispute Settlement Understanding, which requires interpreting WTO law according to Article 3, "in accordance with customary rules of interpretation of public international law." These customary rules include rules and principles for textual, contextual, and teleological interpretation of treaties aimed at mutually coherent interpretations premised on the belief states will behave lawfully, on the systemic character of international law, and the mutual coherence of international rules and principles.

The customary law requirement of interpreting treaties "in conformity with principles of justice," including "universal respect for, and observance of, human rights and fundamental freedoms for all" as stated in the Vienna Convention on the Law of Treaties, also calls for clarifying the substantive principles of justice underlying international economic law, like freedom, nondiscrimination, the rule of law, independent third-party adjudication, and preferential treatment of less-developed countries. Rules and adjudication that are perceived as unjust by governments, citizens, and courts of justice are unlikely to be effective over time (Petersmann, 2009, pp. 137–194).

THE LINK BETWEEN INTERNATIONAL ECONOMIC LAW AND SOCIAL JUSTICE

Hence, international economic law needs to be justified and evaluated in terms of justice and human rights even if human rights are not specifically incorporated into the law of worldwide economic organizations. Legal and judicial interpretation of WTO rules in conformity with human rights may also be more appropriate for promoting legal coherence among international economic law and human rights law in worldwide governance institutions than incorporating UN human rights obligations into WTO law following the model of the incorporation of intellectual property treaty obligations into the WTO Agreement on Trade-Related Intellectual Property Rights.[8] The need for reconciling civil, political, economic, social, and cultural human rights, like the need for reconciling legal market access commitments under GATT and GATS with a state's need to develop independent policy to protect noneconomic public interests pursuant to Articles XIX–XXI of GATT, and XIV of GATS, requires legal and judicial balancing to optimize the protection of competing rights and obligations.

Outside Europe, most governments need to accept that they can protect public goods only in cooperation with international law and institutions. National constitutions have become partial constitutions. This stems from the globalization of ever-more public goods like the rule of law, protection of human rights, and efficient trade, financial, and environmental protection systems. The necessary demystification of the state and international limitation of welfare-reducing legal nationalism require new cosmopolitan and constitutional conceptions of international law as an ever-more indispensable instrument for limiting governance failures at home and abroad to the benefit of citizens.

As in European economic and legal integration, independent and impartial courts of justice, with their multilevel judicial protection of constitutional and human rights across frontiers on the basis of judicial comity and proportionality balancing as the "ultimate rule of law" (Beatty, 2004), must often take the lead in protecting citizens and their human rights. Whereas judicial review of a restriction and whether it is "suitable" and "necessary" for realizing specific public policy interests focuses on the rationality and efficiency between the means and the end, the *proportionality stricto sensu* test reviews the reasonableness of governmental balancing of competing values.

THE PRINCIPLE OF PROPORTIONALITY

In contrast to Ronald Dworkin's claim that in "hard cases" involving conflicts between constitutional rights and other public interests individual rights should "trump" public policies, proportionality balancing by European courts tends to perceive both constitutional rights and public policies as reflecting constitutional principles subject to weighting to promote their mutual coherence on a case-by-case basis. Judicial proportionality review of legislative and administrative restrictions on fundamental rights contributes to participatory and deliberative democracy across frontiers. It is a necessary compensation for the deficits of national parliamentary democracy and other forms of majority politics in a globally integrating world. Human rights and their multilevel judicial protection are also of crucial importance in international economic law for protecting citizens and democratic principles against abuses of power by governments and corporations. This is critical given that multilevel economic regulation all too often undermines the general consumer welfare and constitutional rights of citizens.

RESPECT FOR REASONABLE DISAGREEMENTS WITHIN NATIONAL POLICY SPACES

Human rights and democracy also protect diversity and reasonable disagreement within national policy spaces. International human rights conventions recognize that human rights "shall be subject only to such limitations as are prescribed by law and are necessary in a democratic society in the interests of public safety, for the protection of public order, health or morals, or for the protection of the rights and freedoms of others."[9] Hence, human rights – and economic courts – tend to recognize governmental "margins of appreciation" regarding the domestic implementation and legitimate "balancing" of human rights obligations and fundamental freedoms. Intergovernmental recognition by UN bodies of "derived human rights," like the diverse legal methods of protecting the human right to water inside national legal systems by means of constitutional, legislative, administrative and/or judicial rights (Thielbörger, 2013), may be protected by such legitimate "margins of appreciation" regarding optimal legal design and the protection of human rights.

Depending on the respective constitutional context, legislative and judicial interpretations and legal clarifications may lead to institutionalized public dialogues progressively developing "public reason" supported by citizens. For instance, in response to various disputes over the compulsory licensing of medicines, WTO members adopted a waiver in August 2003, as well as a subsequent amendment of Article 31*bis* of the TRIPS Agreement, authorizing compulsory licensing of medicines for export to countries with insufficient or no productive capacity in the pharmaceutical sector. Yet, the fact that Canada's license for exports to Rwanda has remained the single compulsory license to date, and only Zambia among Sub-Saharan African countries ratified the TRIPS Amendment, supports the view that access to essential medicines may also be secured by interpreting the TRIPS Agreement in conformity with the human rights obligations of WTO Members (Hestermeyer, 2007).

COMPETING CONCEPTIONS OF HUMAN AND CONSTITUTIONAL RIGHTS TO LIBERTY

Anglo-Saxon jurisdictions tend to interpret the human right to liberty narrowly in terms of freedom of bodily movement. Some other constitutional democracies protect comparable freedoms as first principles of justice not only through specific liberty rights but also through a general constitutional right to liberty to offer additional constitutional and judicial protection to the legal autonomy of citizens against arbitrary, public, and private interference in their liberties. This also includes protection against the restriction of individual freedom of action resulting from multilevel policy, for instance, if intergovernmental restrictions adopted in distant international organizations lack a constitutional foundation or sufficient justification in the national legal system (Alexy, 2002, chapter 7).

The multilevel constitutional guarantees of "free movement of persons, services, goods and capital, and freedom of establishment" as "fundamental freedoms" across the thirty member countries of the EEA are explicitly based on "the values of respect for human dignity, freedom, democracy, equality, the rule of law and respect for human rights." There is also increasing recognition that constitutional commitment to respect for human dignity and market freedoms (e.g. free movement of workers and their families) may require legal protection of positive liberties through social rights to effectively empower individuals to develop their "human capabilities" autonomously.[10] The diversity of provisions and institutional safeguards for social rights in national and regional laws, UN, and ILO conventions reflects not only diverse legal conceptions for designing social rights as indivisible parts of human rights. Constitutional agreement on how to reconcile and institutionalize civil, political, economic, and social rights is also inevitably influenced by democratic preferences and the scarcity of resources.

Legal and judicial remedies for enforcing civil, political, economic, and social rights continue to differ enormously between countries and jurisdictions, which is a reflection of the flexibility of national policy space. Constitutional and judicial protection of a general right to liberty and of common market freedoms can strengthen the reasonableness of international economic law, for instance, by conducting a judicial review of the necessity (rationality) and proportionality (reasonableness) of government restrictions on the basis of equal constitutional rights and the judicial administration of justice.

In common law countries, by contrast, law tends to protect specific liberties without constitutional protection of a general right to liberty.[11] Given that a major function of constitutional guarantees of maximum equal freedoms is to protect rights to justification and to judicial remedies vis-à-vis governmental restrictions, judicial review of economic regulation tends to be less comprehensive in common law countries than in European economic law. For instance, since the abandonment of substantive due process reviews of economic legislation in the 1930s, U.S. constitutional law protects individual economic freedom and a common market mainly by democratic legislation based on the constitutional requirement that there be a "rational basis" for government to restrict economic liberty (Hudec and Morrison, 1993, pp. 91–133). Because U.S. courts defer to Congress on economic issues, most lawyers see no need for U.S. courts to engage in the kind of strict judicial scrutiny of governmental restrictions of economic freedom that is practiced by German courts, European courts, WTO dispute settlement bodies, and investor-state arbitral tribunals. Even if national constitutional traditions legitimately differ from country to country, there are important arguments for basing legal and judicial remedies against abuses of multilevel governance powers on the cosmopolitan principle that multilevel governance restrictions of individual freedom require constitutional justification and judicial remedies.

THE PROMISE OF MULTILEVEL CONSTITUTIONALISM

The diverse forms of multilevel constitutionalism in the EU, like the multilevel judicial protection of cosmopolitan rights in international commercial, trade, investment, regional integration, and human rights law outside Europe, illustrate that multilevel constitutionalism has become a politically feasible and realistic conception of constitutional justice and is no longer only a "cosmopolitan dream." The legitimacy of "cosmopolitan international economic law" and of the additional multilevel constitutional restraints of worldwide economic organizations derives from protecting human rights, other principles of justice, and national democracies promise of the self-governance of citizens limited by rule of law. The needed institutional innovation must be based on the principle of subsidiarity, e.g. strengthening the involvement of national parliaments, courts, and self-interested citizens in reviewing and enforcing international rules protecting human rights and public goods. The inevitable legal fragmentation among national and functionally limited transnational legal regimes must be mitigated by multilevel legal and judicial cooperation in protecting the transnational rule of law and the cosmopolitan rights of citizens. This is required by the human rights obligations of all UN member states and the customary law requirement of interpreting international treaties, and settling international disputes, "in conformity with the principles of justice" and the human rights obligations of governments.

National and international courts continue to agree on only a few "core elements" of human dignity (McCrudden, 2008, pp. 655–724). This includes the requirements that (1) every human being possesses an intrinsic worth and moral entitlement to human rights, merely by being human; (2) this moral worth and entitlement must be recognized and respected by others; and (3) that the state exists for the sake of the individual human being, and not vice versa. Beyond these core elements, the transformation of moral principles of "dignity" and human rights into positive law may legitimately vary across jurisdictions depending on their respective traditions, resources, and democratic preferences.

The needed limitation of the "animal spirits" and rational egoism of economic actors by means of institutionalizing "public reason" in the worldwide division of labor must be based on stronger constitutional, legislative, administrative, and judicial protection of cosmopolitan rights empowering self-interested citizens and public-private partnerships to defend their rights vis-à-vis abuses of public and private power also in transnational economic cooperation. Even though human rights and constitutional principles say little about the optimal design of legal institutions (such as independent regulatory agencies), comparative institutional analysis suggests that rights-based cosmopolitan regimes in transnational commercial, trade, investment, and regional economic and environmental law have proven more effective and legitimate than state-centered Westphalian regimes. Yet, as illustrated by the current banking, financial, and sovereign debt crises in the EU and the United States addressing market failures, as well as of policy failures remains a perennial task in international economic law. Bottom-up strengthening of constitutional and cosmopolitan safeguards is necessary to protect self-interested citizens and their democratic representatives against abuses of intergovernmental "Westphalian governance" and against the rational egoism of private economic actors.

THE ELUSIVE GLOBAL CONSENSUS

The failures of the Doha Round negotiations in the WTO since 2001 illustrate that waiting for a global consensus on protecting global public goods is an unreasonable strategy. Bilateral and regional agreements on carbon emission reductions and unilateral safeguard measures such as border tax adjustments are usually necessary building blocks for worldwide consensus building. Proposals for coordinating hundreds of fragmented international and national legal regimes by using the formal "conflict rules" codified in the Vienna Convention on the Law of Treaties (such as *lex specialis*, *lex posterior*, and *lex superior*) are based on "Westphalian principles" such as the sovereign equality of states, which may neglect to protect human rights. A regular example is when corrupt rulers abuse their "lending privilege" and "resource privilege" for appropriating and transferring wealth abroad to the detriment of domestic citizens. The diverse forms of European international law in the EU, the EEA, and ECHR illustrate how, by interpreting state's policy space, popular sovereignty, and individual sovereignty in mutually coherent ways and subjecting multilevel economic governance to multilevel constitutional restraints, international economic law can be transformed bottom up into an instrument for promoting consumer welfare, the rule of law, and human rights across international borders (Petersmann, 2008, pp. 27–60). Constitutional pluralism, as applied by national and international courts throughout Europe, implies that interdependent national and international legal regimes need to be interpreted in mutually coherent ways on the basis of universalizable principles of justice and human rights. The plurality of legitimate yet potentially conflicting claims based on diverse national and international constitutional systems must be reconciled by legal and judicial balancing of competing constitutional principles, human rights, and deliberative democracy, especially in mutually beneficial cooperation among citizens across frontiers.

Similar to the private and public, national, and international regulation of international economic cooperation, human rights are regulated and protected at local, national, and international levels. Human rights can be interpreted as fundamental freedoms protecting "human capabilities" and legal autonomy (Jacobs, 1993). As UN human rights law tends to prescribe only minimum standards of protection with due respect for national "margins of appreciation" in regulating, prioritizing, and mutually balancing civil, political, economic, social and cultural rights, human rights require respecting legitimate constitutional pluralism in the multilevel protection of human rights and of international economic cooperation among citizens. The UN High Commissioner for Human Rights has argued for a "human rights approach" to multilevel economic regulation to limit the often one-sided focus on producer interests by promoting synergies between economic regulation and human rights.

The High Commissioner differentiates between obligations to respect human rights, to protect human rights, and to fulfill human rights. Given that recourse to trade sanctions for promoting respect for human rights abroad can aggravate the problems of people adversely affected by trade sanctions, the UN Commissioner's reports emphasize both potential synergies as well as potential conflicts between human rights and economic rules in the context of trade liberalization, trade restrictions, and other economic regulation. Arguably, modern international human rights law requires going beyond the prevailing "Rawlsian conception of international law between sovereign peoples" and respecting, protecting, and fulfilling human rights across frontiers as "the foundation of freedom, justice and peace in the world" (UDHR Preamble).

GOING BEYOND RAWLS'S CONSTITUTIONALISM

The Rawlsian argument – that it is "the fact that in a democratic regime political power is regarded as the power of free and equal citizens as a collective body" which requires that the democratic exercise of coercive power over one another be recognized as democratically legitimate only when "political power . . . is exercised in accordance with a constitution (written or unwritten) the essentials of which all citizens, as reasonable and rational, can endorse in the light of their common human reason" – also applies to the multilevel regulation of mutually beneficial economic cooperation among citizens in the worldwide division of labor (Rawls, 2001, p. 41). The less national parliaments control intergovernmental rule-making, the more the deficit in parliamentary and deliberative democracy must be compensated for by rights-based constitutionalism and multilevel judicial protection of constitutional rights and "participatory democracy" across frontiers.

As explained by Rawls (1993, p. 231), "[I]n a constitutional regime with judicial review, public reason is the reason of its Supreme Court." Transparent, rules-based, and impartial judicial reasoning, subject to procedural guarantees of due process of law, makes independent courts less politicized "fora of principle" that are of constitutional importance for developing an "overlapping, constitutional consensus." Such a consensus is necessary for legally stable and just relations among free, equal, and rational citizens who tend to remain deeply divided by conflicting moral, religious, and philosophical doctrines. The various EU courts such as the ECHR, the EFTA Court, and national courts have successfully transformed the international EC and EEA treaties and the ECHR into constitutional orders founded on respect for human rights, enabling new policy spaces as evidenced by innovative policy making across Europe in the wake of the 2008 global financial crisis. The new multilevel constitutionalism that the courts enforce has designed these policy spaces to be used in ways that allow national governments to be innovative in fiscal and social policy, provided that they do so within the parameters of human rights law.

REFERENCES

Alexy, R. *A Theory of Fundamental Rights*. Oxford University Press, Oxford, 2002.

Allan, T.T.S. *Law, Liberty and Justice*, Oxford University Press, Oxford, 1993.

Beatty, D.M. *The Ultimate Rule of Law*. Oxford University Press, Oxford, 2004.

Cass, D.Z. *The Constitutionalization of the WTO*. Oxford University Press, Oxford, 2005.

De Schutter, O. "Draft Guiding Principles on Human Rights Impact Assessments of Trade and Investment Agreements." United Nations, 1 July 2011. Available at: http://www.srfood.org.

ECOSOC. "Globalization and its Impact on the Full Enjoyment of Human Rights." United Nations Economic and Social Council, Geneva, 15 June 2000. Available at: http://www.unhchr.ch/huridocda/huridoca.nsf/%28Symbol%29/E.CN.4.Sub.2.2000.13.En.

Hestermeyer, H. *Human Rights and the WTO: The Case of Patents and Access to Medicine*. Oxford University Press, Oxford, 2007.

Hudec, Robert and Morrison, Fred. "The Role of Judicial Review in Preserving Liberal Foreign Trade Policies." In Hilf, Meinhard and Petersmann, Ernst-Ulrich (eds.), *National Constitutions and International Economic Law*. Berlin: Kluwer Law and Taxation Publishers, 1993.

Jacobs, L. *Rights and Deprivation*. Oxford University Press, Oxford, 1993.

Lixinski, L. "Human Rights in MERCOSUR." In Filho, M.T.F., Lixinski, L., and Giupponi, M.B.O (eds.), *The Law of MERCOSUR*. Hart Publishing, Oxford, 2010.

McCrudden, C. "Human Dignity and Judicial Interpretation of Human Rights." *European Journal of International Law* 19 (2008), 655–724.

Merten D. and Papier, H.J. (eds.). *Handbuch der Grundrechte, Vol. II*. Heidelberg: Müller Verlag, Heidelberg, 2006.

Nussbaum, Martha. *Frontiers of Justice: Disability, Nationality, Species Membership* Belknap Press of Harvard University Press, Cambridge, MA, 2006.

Petersmann, E.U. "Constitutional Functions of Public International Economic Law." In Van Themaat, V. (ed.), *Restructuring the International Economic Order. The Role of Law and Lawyers*. Colloquium on the occasion of the 350th anniversary of the University of Utrecht, 1987.

Petersmann, E.U. "Constitutional Theories of International Economic Adjudication and Investor-State Arbitration." In Dupuy, P.M., Francioni, F., and Petersmann, E.U. (eds.), *Human Rights in International Investment Law and Arbitration*. Oxford University Press, Oxford, 2009.

Petersmann, E.U. "Human Rights, International Economic Law and 'Constitutional Justice'." *The European Journal of International Law* 19, no. 4 (2008), 769–798.

Petersmann, E.U. "Human Rights and International Economic Law." In Linarelli, J. (ed.), *Research Handbook on Global Justice and International Economic Law*. Edward Elgar, Cheltenham, UK, 2011.

Petersmann, E.U. *International Economic Law in the 21st Century: Constitutional Pluralism and Multilevel Governance of Interdependent Public Goods*. Hart Publishing, Oxford, 2012.

Petersmann, E.U. "International Trade Law, Human Rights and the Customary International Law Rules on Treaty Interpretation." In Joseph, S., Kinley, D., and Waincymer, J. (eds.), *The WTO and Human Rights*. Edward Elgar, Cheltenham, 2009.

Petersmann, E.U. "State Sovereignty, Popular Sovereignty and Individual Sovereignty: From Constitutional Nationalism to Multilevel Constitutionalism in International Economic Law?" In Shan, W., Simons, P., and Singh, D. (eds.), *Redefining Sovereignty in International Economic Law*. Hart Publishing, Oxford, 2008.

Petersmann, E.U. "Taking Human Dignity, Poverty and Empowerment of Individuals More Seriously: Rejoinder to Alston." *European Journal of International Law* 13 (2002), 845–851.

Petersmann, E.U. "Time for a United Nations 'Global Compact' for Integrating Human Rights into the Law of Worldwide Organizations: Lessons from European Integration." *European Journal of International Law* 13 (2002), 621–650.

Pogge, Thomas. *Freedom from Poverty as a Human Right: Who Owes What to Whom?* Oxford University Press, Oxford, 2007.

Rawls, John. *Political Liberalism*. Columbia University Press, New York, 1993.

Rawls, John. *Justice as Fairness: A Restatement*. Harvard University Press, Cambridge, MA, 2001.

Thielbörger, Pierre. *The Right(s) to Water: The Multi-Level Governance of a Unique Human Right*. Springer Publishers, Munich, 2013.

Thomas, C. "The WTO and Labor Rights: Strategies of Linkage." In Joseph, S., Kinley, D., and Waincymer, J. (eds.), *The WTO and Human Rights*. Edward Elgar, Cheltenham, 2009.

CASES

AWG v Argentina
Case C-402/05P
Case C-415/05P, *Kadi*
Phoenix Action Ltd v Czech Republic, ICSID Arbitration Award of 15 April
   2009 (Case No ARB/06/5)

3

Free Trade Agreements and Global Policy Space after the Great Recession

Jorge Heine and Joseph F. Turcotte

INTRODUCTION: THE CRISIS AND CHALLENGE OF TRADE MULTILATERALISM

Bilateral and plurilateral free trade agreements (FTAs) have emerged as the policy tools of choice for states to assert their trade interests and further the project of global free trade and financial harmonization. In the wake of the Great Recession of 2008, global trade initiatives are questioned for their effectiveness and legitimacy as rising states and emerging economies assert their own interests and claim to represent the cause of the global South. FTAs are seen as a key instrument to assert domestic interests at the bilateral level and secure mutually beneficial results. Rather than viewing these agreements as barriers to optimizing conditions for a global trade regime, we argue that FTAs can be used as a way of asserting domestic interests and promoting growth within existing policy spaces while waiting for a multilateral breakthrough.

First, we discuss the international trade context in the post–Great Financial Crisis climate and explore the calls for protectionism that emerged following the crisis to determine what impacts this has had on the international trade regime. We then analyze the stalled Doha Round and the current state of FTAs. Finally we conduct a case study of Chile as it is the leading champion of FTAs.

INTERNATIONAL TRADE IN THE POST–GREAT FINANCIAL CRISIS CLIMATE

Following the massive stimulus packages applied after the London G20 summit in April 2009, many felt that the most serious threat facing the global economy since the Great Depression had been averted. Yet, although economic stimulus packages helped avert a financial collapse, they were unable

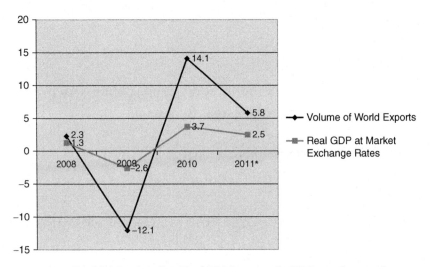

FIGURE 3.1. World Merchandise Trade Volume and GDP, 2008–2011. *Source*: WTO Secretariat for exports, consensus estimates for GDP (WTO Press Release, 2011).
*2011 Projections

to kick-start global economic growth. Prior to the financial crisis, global trade grew quickly, at an average annual rate of 14 percent between 2000 and 2008 (UNCTAD, 2010). However, with the onset of the financial crisis, this growth was dramatically reduced, and in 2008 trade declined. Most worrying for the global trade environment were fears that the financial crisis might result in across-the-board tariff increases or other protectionist measures.

When the Great Financial Crisis first broke, there were concerns about a contraction in global trade. Initially these concerns proved true. In the immediate aftermath of the crisis, total world merchandise trade fell from US$16.52 trillion in 2008 to US$12.71 trillion in 2009, a 12.1 percent drop for trade with a 2.6 percent drop in global gross domestic product (GDP) (see Figure 3.1). This dramatic decrease of US$3.802 trillion was an abrupt departure from the previous decade, which saw a steady increase in global trade (see Figure 3.2). However, as we discuss later in the chapter, because of coordinated global efforts to avert the contraction of international trade and the rejection of protectionist measures, global trade has rebounded. In 2010, total world merchandise trade, at US$15.376 trillion, eclipsed 2007 levels but remained below the 2008 peak (see Figures 3.3 and 3.4). The WTO remained conservatively optimistic about global trade growth, forecasting an annual increase of 5.8 percent for 2011 (WTO Press Release, 2011).

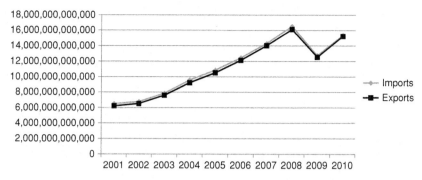

FIGURE 3.2. Total World Merchandise Trade (2001–2010), US$ Constant Prices. *Source*: World Trade Organization, Statistics Database (stat.wto.org).

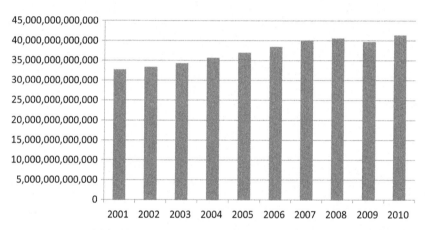

FIGURE 3.3. World Economic Growth (2001–2010), GDP in constant 2000 US$. *Source*: The World Bank Data Group, Database (databank.worldbank.org).

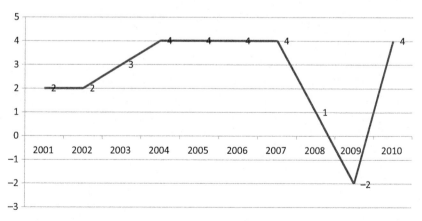

FIGURE 3.4. World Economic Growth (2001–2010), GDP growth (annual %). *Source*: The World Bank Data Group, Database (databank.worldbank.org).

This decline in global trade and economic output resulted from the contraction in accessible credit and financial liquidity that followed the crisis, and was not the product of protectionist trade measures. To prevent a collapse of the global economy, governments "used an array of fiscal and monetary measures to boost their economies. These efforts mitigated the ferocity of the [2007–08] crisis . . . avoiding an economic collapse on the magnitude witnessed during the 1930s Great Depression" (Aggarwal and Evenett, 2010, p. 221). Most significantly for the international trade environment, these measures did not include significant increases in across-the-board tariffs (Evenett, 2010). Coordinated global responses, including domestic government interventions, helped prevent a collapse of the financial system. By maintaining and promoting policies that were in line with the international trade agenda, these coordinated responses buttressed the existing economic system. These efforts also demonstrated the necessity of having developed and developing countries work together to solve global problems.

MURKY PROTECTIONISM, POST-CRISIS

Past experiences with financial crises, most noticeably during the Great Depression, show that trade protectionism in individual countries or allies can stifle of global trade and attendant economic activity. As Eichengreen and Irwin (1995) argued, protectionist policies during the Great Depression led to the breakdown of the multilateral trading system. These measures resulted from ill-advised macroeconomic policies designed to safeguard domestic and allied interests to the detriment of the multilateral system. As Eichengreen and Irwin show, trade protectionism differed greatly from country to country throughout the Depression, but the overall impact on the multilateral trade environment was similar. It led to a severe contraction in international trade.

The Great Recession did not result in anything comparable to that. International institutions such as the G20, the WTO, and the OECD reaffirmed their commitments to the multilateral trading system and the principles set out by the WTO agreements. However, as Aggarwal and Evenett (2010) have shown, this commitment to WTO principles has been accompanied by various forms of "murky protectionism." One of the major responses to the Great Recession were pseudo-protectionist measures designed to safeguard domestic industries. Baldwin and Evenett (2009) have argued that subsidies and bailouts to help domestic firms and national interests were used in nontransparent and discriminatory ways. For Aggarwal and Evenett (2010, p. 224), "it is in this context that the suspicion that [the financial] crisis has created 'murky protectionism' is important, because it forces any evaluation of discriminatory state action to go beyond transparent state interventions, such as tariff increases." This is especially true given that the measures taken in response to the crisis may not be breaking multilateral trade obligations set out in the WTO rules (Aggarwal and Evenett, 2010).

Trade protectionism following the crisis has emerged slowly in subtle ways, not with a vengeance (Sally, 2010). While less acute, this form of "murky protectionism" is no less real. The onset of the Great Recession demonstrated that "despite nearly 25 years of the Washington Consensus, widespread membership of the WTO and numerous trade agreements being signed, governments were not prepared to stand back and let market forces unfold" (Aggarwal and Evenett, 2010, p. 239). Aggarwal and Evenett suggest: "[T]he crisis has led to a revival of industrial policies, implemented using subsidies, biased government procurement policies, and some traditional trade policy instruments" (p. 240). Domestic political and economic considerations shaped these responses to the crisis, demonstrating that despite the existence of a multilateral trade environment, internal realities remain the prime motivator for individual governments when using new policy spaces.

Yet, this is the way it should be. As Rodrik (2011) has underlined, part of the reason multilateral trade liberalization efforts, from the Free Trade of the Americas (FTAA) project to the Doha Round, have come to a halt in the last decade is because we have entered the phase of what he calls "hyperglobalization." This is best embodied in the much more intrusive and extended powers of the WTO, as opposed to those of the GATT. Far from limiting themselves to negotiating issues pertaining to trade, which is what trade agreements are ostensibly about, developed countries suddenly began to put a vast array of additional issues on the table in a classic case of self-defeating overreach. The list of now-fashionable issues included intellectual property rights (IPRs), government procurement, competition policy, and export subsidies. All of these reached deeply into domestic politics and policies. Unsurprisingly, this has elicited a considerable backlash, as countries found themselves in the extraordinary position of having to dismantle decades-old programs designed to enhance their productive capacity for the sake of abstract rules favoring ever-deeper globalization. Moreover, in practice these rules seem to benefit primarily large multinational corporations mostly based in the global North.

Still, the overarching ideal about international trade has restrained individual impulses from straying too far from the trade agenda. As Chia (2010, p. 245) points out, "new antidumping, safeguards, and countervailing duty investigations have increased, but still affect only a small share of world trade and are concentrated on China." WTO data shows that the new anti-trade measures instituted as a result of the Great Financial Crisis affect approximately 1 percent of overall trade (Sally, 2010). While Aggarwal and Evenett's data show some 350 new forms of trade protectionism (Chia, 2010, p. 245), this appears to be minor and associated with specific domestic policies. These practices adhere to the WTO system, and in the Asia-Pacific region does not appear to be thoroughly serious (Kimura, 2010).

CAN THE WTO CONTAIN THIS "MURKY PROTECTIONISM"?

Global trade responses to the Great Recession of 2008 show that there is room for optimism regarding the continued evolution of the WTO system. Trade protectionism on the scale of the Great Depression did not materialize. The very existence of the WTO and buy-in from individual state governments to the tenets of free and open trade acted as disincentives to open protectionism. In a globally integrated trade environment, where domestic and international concerns and growth are highly intertwined, this is a significant advance. The Great Recession has demonstrated the willingness of international actors to look toward new tools for economic stabilization and growth. Multilateral and open trade is but one means of ensuring this. In times of crisis, "murky protectionism" has maintained important domestic industries and invaluable international trade opportunities. As Drache (2010, p. 48) noted elsewhere, "Fundamental changes in the world economy ... require policy makers to accept the fact that governance requires a new agenda of global policy co-operation." What is more concerning is the applicability and effectiveness of the WTO system in an increasingly dynamic trade environment. WTO rules are ill-suited for the realities of an accelerating and interrelated global economic situation that includes new actors and issues, which were not concerns when the WTO was established (UNCTAD, 2010, p. xi). In light of domestic responses to the global financial crisis and the emergence of "murky protectionism," it is important to evaluate how the WTO system and its rules encourage and discourage forms of protectionism as well as maintaining domestic and international stabilization. This becomes especially urgent with the latest round of WTO talks – the Doha Round – at an impasse.

IS THERE LIFE AFTER DOHA?

Since its creation in 1994, the WTO has only had successful rounds of multilateral trade talks. This track record is now under threat. Much has changed in the international environment since the WTO was first established. The apparently universal acceptance of capitalist principles as necessary conditions for global economic growth and stability has generated a multilateral trading environment based on market-based principles and objectives. Even the remaining holdouts to domestic capitalist economics – most noticeably China – have accepted and integrated minimum standards and characteristics (see Arrighi, 2007, 2009). With the end of the Cold War and the breakup of the Soviet Union, the times seemed ripe for establishing and extending market-based principles and free trade orthodoxies across the world.

Yet, in the early twenty-first century, discontent with economic and trade liberalization began to grow. The rejection of the Free Trade Area of the Americas (FTAA) in the mid-2000s signaled a shift away from the neoliberal approach. It also showed the growing assertiveness of developing countries as well as civil society (see von Bülow, 2010) in matters of global economic governance. The rise of the BRIC countries – Brazil, Russia, India, and China – and economic difficulties in the United States and Europe evidenced the emergence of a new international power distribution. The onset of the financial crisis has exacerbated this shift. Amid these changing conditions, global economic and trade discussions have become increasingly complex and contested.

A FAILED DEVELOPMENTAL ROUND

The history of the Doha Round trade talks illustrates this point. The Fifth Ministerial Conference, held in Cancún in 2003, showed an increasingly serious "north-south divide" (UNCTAD, 2010, p. 35, box 1) on a number of trade-related issues. As Sungjoon (2009, p. 1) argues, Doha's "negotiational stalemate is symptomatic of the diametrically opposed beliefs on the nature of the Round between developed and developing countries." Envisioned as a "development" round of trade talks, the North-South/developed-developing divide is best exemplified by the respective responses to it. From the perspective of developed countries, development is a matter of opening local markets to foreign investment and trade and leveraging this increased economic activity for development-related purposes. Developing countries – the BRIC countries and others – contend that a development focus must also take into account the specific domestic circumstances of various countries, as well as that policy flexibilities and exceptions should be granted accordingly. These divergent positions have complicated matters, with both sides reluctant to sign a "bad deal." Because of this, "WTO members are split between two diametrically opposed Worlds. This stark philosophical divergence on the nature of the Doha Round is the main culprit for the negotiational deadlock" (Sungjoon, 2009, p. 2).

The perceptions of developing countries who view past WTO negotiations and decisions as having been implemented in an asymmetrical manner have contributed to this deadlock. Among developing countries, there is a belief that the current WTO system is designed to serve the interests of developed countries. During the Uruguay Round, developing countries "raised a *substantive* concern that the Uruguay Round Agreements favored developed nations at their expense" (Dunoff, 2001, p. 981; emphasis in the original). This concern has remained throughout subsequent negotiations and contributes to an environment where one group of parties is reluctant to agree to terms that it deems unfavorable. Under these circumstances, the credibility of WTO trade talks as an effective means of addressing the domestic concerns of developing countries is undermined. Negotiating parties do not feel there is adequate space to assert their individual or collective interests.

TOWARD A MORE INCLUSIVE FORM OF GOVERNANCE

In recent years, the concerns of developing countries as well as of various domestic constituents have been picked up by nongovernmental and civil society actors favoring more inclusive and representative forms of trade-based governance. These nonstate actors are not necessarily aligned with developing countries but share the desire to create more accountable and responsive forms of trade and development (see Bradlow, 2001). While progress has been made in this regard, these actors remain on the margins of talks on these issues and, in turn, complicate their successful completion. Nonstate actors, which often seek to highlight and address human rights and other socioeconomic issues, have increased standing at WTO discussions but remain shut out of official proceedings. It is a challenge for an international organization in a state-based multilateral system such as the WTO to include nonstate actors. However, facilitating debate and input from these groups remains essential for fostering consensus.

Developing countries and nonstate actors have used various methods to advance their respective agendas. During the initial phases of the Doha Round, the divisive issues threatened progress; however, as a result of pressure from developing countries, the most contentious of these issues were dropped and negotiations continued (UNCTAD, 2010, p. 35, box 1). The ability to influence the WTO agenda and trade talks at a multilateral level remains a benefit of this form of diplomatic engagement and helps assuage concerns that these negotiations are one-sided. However, despite these advances, the Doha Round remains stalled. Concerns from developing countries have not dissipated.

KNOWLEDGE-BASED PROPERTY RIGHTS

The ways in which intellectual property rights are treated within the trade-based agenda of the WTO demonstrates this. The late twentieth and early twenty-first centuries have been a time of increased focus on the ways that information and intangible aspects of the global economy are regulated and traded. With the rise of the "knowledge based economy" (OECD, 1996), intellectual property rights have risen in prominence in international trade, and global economic regulation and are now regarded as one of the most important issues around globalization (Stiglitz, 2008). Asserting trade-based aspects and implications of intellectual property rights, developed countries – led by the United States, EU members, and Japan – sought to insert intellectual property provisions into WTO negotiations. Alongside the establishment of the WTO in 1995 came the Trade Related Aspects of Intellectual Property (TRIPS) agreement, which linked intellectual property rights with the global trade agenda for the first time. Through the WTO, then, "TRIPS effectively globalizes the set of intellectual property principles it contains, because most states of the world are members of the WTO" (Drahos, 2005, p. 147).

Inserting intellectual property rights into the trade-based agenda of the WTO has been controversial. A number of economic, social, developmental, and cultural concerns are implicated within debates over IPRs. Because of the complex and dynamic nature of international intellectual property law, domestic industries are rarely satisfied with international intellectual property provisions and increasingly lobby their governments to enact policies that align with their business models and needs (Duttfield, 2006, p. 4). Domestic and business concerns vary from country to country, making global agreement and coordination a daunting prospect. This complexity adds another level of contestation to WTO negotiations as various stakeholders have differing opinions about appropriate levels of protection for intellectual property rights. In particular, developed and developing countries have markedly different perspectives on the protection of intellectual property and access to knowledge. Developing states that do not adhere to Western notions and systems of intellectual property protection, as well as states with development needs that contradict the values and methods espoused through the TRIPS agreement, can run into conflict with developed states – as was the case during the lead-up to the Doha Declaration on TRIPS and Public Health (see Abbott, 2002).

PUBLIC HEALTH NEEDS AND THE HISTORIC DOHA DECLARATION

The case of the Doha Declaration on TRIPS and Public Health serves to highlight the differing perspectives found within the Doha Round in general. From the perspective of developing countries, the creation of the TRIPS

Agreement has greatly restricted the ways domestic governments can approach the use and regulation of intellectual property rights–protected goods to address developmental concerns (Sell, 2003). Furthermore, the then-developing WTO seemed ill-suited for dealing with the myriad concerns over intellectual property rights (Drahos and Braithwaite, 2002, p. 84).

For these and other reasons, developing countries initially resisted plans to create the TRIPS Agreement within the WTO. However, facing trade sanctions and other measures, they eventually relented (Sell, 2003, p. 123). With the Doha Round, developing country concerns were again foregrounded. The issue of public health and access to affordable medicine became a focal point of disagreement during the negotiations. Developing countries argued that the TRIPS Agreement did not provide enough flexibility for cost-efficient forms of pharmaceuticals because of associated intellectual property reasons.

Stemming from this opposition, at the November 14, 2001 Ministerial meetings, participants adopted the Doha Declaration on the TRIPS Agreement and Public Health, which affirmed:

> We agree that the TRIPS Agreement does not and should not prevent Members from taking measures to protect public health. Accordingly, while reiterating our commitment to the TRIPS Agreement, we affirm that the Agreement can and should be interpreted and implemented in a manner supportive of WTO Members' right to protect public health and, in particular, to promote access to medicines for all. (WTO Ministerial Conference, 2001)

The success of developing countries in getting the Doha Declaration affirmed demonstrates the flexibilities built into the TRIPS Agreement as well as the WTO system more generally. The stalled Doha Round is troubling in that it prevents deliberation over, and creation of, further mechanisms that might be used to address specific concerns in the trading system. At the same time, there are some who argue that the WTO system is being undermined by increased attention to FTAs and other non-multilateral trade initiatives.

THE STATE OF FTAS TODAY: CHALLENGE OR OPPORTUNITY FOR THE WTO?

The recent global financial crisis and the turn toward "murky protectionism" demonstrates the need for a coherent set of international trade rules. Divergent perspectives and competing blocs over controversial issues such as IPRs highlight the tensions within today's international trade regime. To this we must add an increasing shift toward free trade and other agreements.

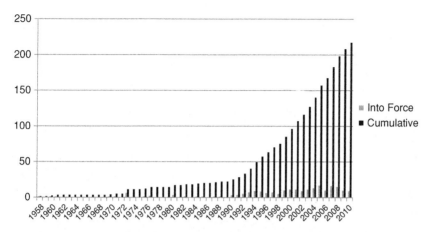

FIGURE 3.5. Number of Trade Agreements,* by Year (of entry into force). *Source:* World Trade Organization, RTA-IS Database (rtais.wto.org).
* List includes: CUs, FTAs, EIAs, and PSAs. Agreements with multiple Agreements are shown as one.

With the latest round of WTO trade talks permanently stalled, "the number of regional and bilateral FTAs – all of which are termed regional trade agreements in the WTO – has significantly increased particularly in the last five years. According to the WTO, as of February 2010, 271 regional trade agreements (which include bilateral FTAs) were in force. That trend suggests that the business sector is increasingly looking to FTAs as a more effective means of market opening than multilateral trade negotiations" (UNCTAD, 2010, p. 36; see also Figure 3.5).

While a more effective and expedient form of forging trade agreements, this turn to FTAs raises a number of concerns. One concern is that the proliferation of such agreements could undermine the international trade system. These issues hark back to the 1980s, when the United States and the European Community were expanding their own trading blocs (UNCTAD, 2010, p. 38). The creation of the North American Free Trade Agreement (NAFTA) as well as the European Union (EU) raised the specter of exclusionary trade practices between these groups. However, this shift toward regionalism "did not undermine the multilateral trading system" (UNCTAD, 2010, p. 38). On the contrary, it has been argued that these regional trade movements helped initiate and accelerate calls for the Uruguay Round of trade talks, as excluded countries looked toward multilateral forms of trade regulation as a means of overcoming or counteracting these initiatives (Baldwin & Evenett, 2009). These comparisons, however, overlook the very different ways these non-multilateral trade initiatives have taken place. Whereas the creation of NAFTA and the EU represented a form of regionalism, today's scenario is one where there are "a large number of bilateral FTAs rather than between trading blocks (regional FTAs)" (UNCTAD, 2010, p. 38).

THE SPAGHETTI BOWL EFFECT

A more eloquent argument against the proliferation of FTAs is offered by Bhagwati (2008). A long-time critic of proliferating bilateral FTAs (Bhagwati, 1993), Bhagwati (2008, p. xii) argues that, "acting like termites, PTAs [his preferred term for FTAs] are eating away at the multilateral trading system relentlessly and progressively."

Bhagwati (2008, p. 61) also argued against FTAs proliferation because of the resulting "spaghetti bowl" that is formed of the international trading environment. This systemic issue creates distortions in the international trading system as commodities are subjected to various tariff levels in different markets and "rules of origin" and relationships between trading partners are privileged.

Larger market and trading actors are able to assert their preferences and agendas through the international trade system. In particular, it is argued that countries such as the United States and the EU member states have used FTAs "as means of transferring the regulatory regimes of the EC and the US to other countries" (Horn et al., 2009). The inclusion of so-called WTO-plus is a way for larger countries to include controversial provisions from WTO negotiations in more amenable negotiating scenarios. So-called TRIPS-plus provisions, which extend the base levels of the TRIPS Agreement beyond the multilaterally agreed-on norms, are a growing concern for developing countries (see Sell, 2010; Drahos, 2007). This type of "hegemonic multilateralization" occurs when an economic power is able to disproportionately assert its own interests and models because of its size, and then extends these interests through subsequent bilateral or plurilateral agreements (Hoekman and Winters, 2007; see also Hoekman, 2008). As a result, developing countries are encouraged to enter into bilateral or plurilateral trade agreements to access other markets but may do so in ways that the broader terms of the agreements do not fully accord with their distinct domestic needs. By relying on FTAs beyond the scope of the WTO trade talks, the free and open nature of the WTO arena is systemically undermined and smaller actors are disadvantaged.

It is necessary to move beyond the false dualism created by debates over multilateralism versus FTAs. Dani Rodrik reminds us that there is "one economics [and] many recipes." This remains a valuable lesson for proceeding throughout the wake of the Great Financial Crisis. Just as domestically "the right way of thinking about industrial policy is as a discovery process – one where firms and the government learn about underlying costs and opportunities engage in strategic coordination" (Rodrik, 2007, p. 101), in the international arena domestic and international actors must coordinate strategically to ensure that policies are designed effectively. This requires recognizing the varied strategic and domestic interests of individual countries as well as the overall evolution of the global economy and international development. Policies designed in one country or from one perspective may not be universalizable. International trade systems should appreciate domestic specificity so that global coordination does not become a zero-sum game.

MEXICO AND FTAs: AN UNBALANCED TRADE
LIBERALIZATION STRATEGY

Mexico's experience using FTAs as a means of gaining access to international markets underlines areas of concern. Since the 1970s, Mexico has tried several strategies for export-led growth. Various stages of trade liberalization, including both multilateral trade through the GATTs and preferential FTAs (most noticeably the NAFTA with the United States and Canada), have given Mexican exports access to a number of foreign markets. Currently, Mexico has signed 30 FTAs with 80 countries (WTO, 2011). However, "Mexico's various policies of opening and liberalization have made the country's growth highly vulnerable to certain external constraints or 'shocks' since the late 1970s" (Blecker, 2009, p. 1274). Despite Mexico's pursuit of FTAs, its exports remain highly skewed toward the United States, where more than 80 percent of exports are traded (Villarreal, 2010). Unbalanced liberalization policies have been unable to spur substantial long-term economic growth and development.

While successive Mexican governments have looked to trade liberalization as a means of alleviating chronic underdevelopment, the FTAs that the country has entered into have hindered substantive economic growth. While other countries in the global South have used trade liberalization as an effective means of development, the Mexican case demonstrates how opening a domestic market to unbalanced external trade measures can be counterproductive and detrimental to domestic policy initiatives. Under NAFTA, Mexico has experienced a trade ratio that is highly skewed to U.S. markets. Despite the country's attempts to broaden its markets through subsequent non-U.S. trade agreements, Mexico's export market remains highly skewed toward its regional neighbor. In the post-NAFTA environment, Mexican exports in terms of GDP grew substantially; however, at the same time the country's annual GDP growth per capita remained relatively consistent and was prone to external shocks resulting from U.S. economic pressures (Zepeda et al., 2009). In part, this scenario results from Mexico's uneven distribution of external market orientations. While Mexico remained dependent on its partnership with the United States, the Americans began to explore and establish other trading partnerships with markets across the world. The United States' willingness to enter trade agreements under the WTO system with rising states such as China has weakened Mexico's comparative advantage and brought about further competition. In turn, Mexico has suffered from a detrimental trade imbalance, weak foreign investments, macroeconomic vulnerabilities, and slow job growth.

Adherence to the Washington Consensus has been a disappointment for domestic economic and development performance in Mexico. Policies to open Mexico's domestic markets to external actors and trade have proven inefficient in that they are overly dependent on the country's NAFTA trading partners. By becoming overly dependent on the United States and Canada as primary trading partners, Mexico has become vulnerable to situations where its NAFTA partners have opened their own domestic markets to further international trade liberalization. This sort of unbalanced approach has weakened the country's economic standing and made it susceptible to losses resulting from trade policies enacted by countries competing for their market share.

IN DEFENSE OF FTAs

The case of Mexico's unbalanced free trade initiatives demonstrates the pitfalls associated with an uncoordinated free trade regime. Despite the Mexican experience and the concerns identified by Bhagwati and others, FTAs remain an important tool for advancing the objectives of the WTO system and need not undermine it. An analysis of the rise of FTAs in the absence of successful multilateral talks highlights the various beneficial aspects of fostering bilateral and plurilateral relationships. While it is hard to argue against Bhagwati's assertion that FTAs are discriminatory and preferential in nature, they are also carried out within the confines of the broader multilateral trading system and create benefits for the parties involved without leading to larger negative externalities for the rest of the world (Brown and Stern, 2011, p. 337). The creation of a complex and interdependent system of FTAs means that there is little room for various trading partners to exclude other partners, as the multilateral nature of the world trade system entails shared responsibilities and constraints amongst its actors. Therefore,

> what generates conflict between the multilateral system and these preferential agreements is not the trade liberalisation that occurs but is rather the instances of trade diversion. However, as noted, countries have often responded to the threat of diversion with their own offsetting countermeasures. But this is not to deny that trade diversion exists and can be very damaging for individual firms or industries in particular instances. More might be done therefore to lessen the possible conflict on this score between the multilateral system and FTAs. (Brown and Stern, 2011, p. 338)

The proliferation of FTAs has created broader adherence to the overarching free and open trade agenda among negotiating parties and within the world system.

MESSY MULTILATERALISM: A STEP FORWARD?

When compared to the "messy multilateralism" (Haas, 2010) found within WTO round trade talks, the relative ease at which FTAs can be negotiated and enacted allows the world trade system to progress while multilateral negotiations remain stalled. With fewer actors at the table, FTAs may "provide an easier framework within which the countries can find ways of accommodating their differences in the aims and purposes of the regulations relating to specific services" (Brown and Stern, 2011, p. 339). FTAs need not detract from the broader multilateral environment and can be used as a means for advancing these purposes while disagreements within the multilateral system are negotiated.

The use of FTAs also enables more concentrated negotiations between trading partners. As opposed to sensitive multilateral negotiations, FTAs can be used as a means of tailoring and addressing specific needs and circumstances. The restrictive nature of FTAs also means that "market opening by a partner or partners is more tangible and immediate than multilateral liberalization, especially when big markets like China and India are involved" (UNCTAD, 2010, p. 37). For this reason many developing countries – such as Mexico, Singapore and, as we will discuss later, Chile – have looked to FTAs as a means of creating greater trade access and "as a route towards the realisation of a universal free trade policy" (Brown and Stern, 2011, p. 334). FTAs are therefore a way of normalizing international trade between partners and within the global system while awaiting consolidation at the multilateral level.

THE CASE OF CHILE: EXPANDING ACCESS DESPITE
STALLED MULTILATERALISM

Increased access to global markets provides opportunities for economic growth that can assist socioeconomic development. The rise of FTAs may be an area of concern for this multilateral agenda, but it need not be. From an economic perspective, which often approaches the world through abstract models and lenses that are removed from the realities on the ground, FTAs are messy, confusing, and suboptimal solutions. From this view, relying on FTAs is inferior to a case where countries, or at least the WTO member states, have a multilateral agreement to coordinate international trade measures. It is not surprising, then, that many economists are opposed to expanding FTAs. However, the real world (as opposed to the ideal projected by economists' models) is complex, messy, and imperfect – meaning that global agreements and coordination are hard to achieve. An incrementalist, iterative approach like the one followed by Chile in terms of FTAs shows that these agreements can be deployed to gain market access and foster domestic growth in the context of globalization.[1]

Chile's internal market, with its population of 17 million, is relatively small, and its economy is therefore highly dependent on foreign trade. Moreover, the country's development strategy since opening the economy in the 1970s and 1980s has been based on export-led development. In the past twenty years, Chile's growth rate has averaged 5 percent a year, making it the fastest-growing economy outside Asia, and the fourth-fastest in the world. To achieve an overall sustained 5 percent annual growth rate over time, an export-led approach requires export growth of 7–8 percent a year. For a country such as Chile, this is not easy considering its exports are largely made up of mineral and agricultural commodities whose prices are highly dependent on the business cycle.

THE CHILEAN FREE TRADE STRATEGY

In 1990, with the return of democracy, Chile faced a number of challenges to its international trade policy. With its economy growing fast but highly dependent on exports, it was crucial to maintain open access to foreign markets. This situation entails a constant search for new markets by expanding current ones and creating new ones. It also necessitates export promotion policies at home, raising productivity to stay competitive, aggressive phytosanitary policies to protect the agricultural environment, and the cultivation of an export-oriented culture and mentality even among medium and small-size enterprises. However, crucial to all of this is access to foreign markets.

This question generated a wide-ranging policy debate at the time. One position was that the way forward was to unilaterally lower tariffs to zero. This is very much how Ricardo (1971) put it: liberalization is good per se, and the very idea of mutual trade concessions is meaningless. The theoretical simplicity of this view has made it especially attractive to the neoliberal economists of the Chicago School. It started from the premise that the reduction of tariffs and other barriers to trade was a matter of domestic policy, not diplomacy. Yet, attractive as this notion may be, it fails to take into account the harsh realities of international relations. For example, what would happen if other countries, unaware of the principles of neoclassical economics, did not follow Chile in applying this "optimal" solution? What if they did not also lower their tariffs to zero and simply took advantage of Chile's newly opened market? Such a naïve economic opening could be a costly experiment.

A second approach, very popular on the political left, has been to argue that Chile has to rejoin the various multilateral Latin American initiatives from which the military regime had withdrawn, and pursue greater integration with the region. However, this was by no means easy, or even viable. When it was founded in 1991, MERCOSUR had made special provisions for Chile's access that ran counter to this push. Yet, to join MERCOSUR, Chile would have had to raise its external tariff from 6 percent to 14 percent, cancel all ongoing free trade negotiations, and eventually repudiate the bilateral agreements it had in place. This was not feasible, and Chile declined to join. However, Chile did become an associate member in 1996, and in 2000, the Lagos government attempted to have Chile become a full member, albeit to no avail (BN Americas, 2000).

Finally, a third approach has been, so to say, "multilateral is best." This would mean engaging proactively in the ongoing multilateral negotiations, hoping that this would result in lower tariffs more or less universally. Yet, no one expected a quick breakthrough on this front, given that negotiations can take decades. What would Chile do in the meantime?

CHILE'S PREFERENTIAL ACCESS TO MARKETS ORIENTATION: BUILDING TRANSNATIONAL POLICY SPACES

In the end, Chile rejected all of these alternatives and came up with its own distinct response: a "lateral" approach to international trade policy. Acknowledging that some components of each of these alternatives were needed – some unilateral tariff reductions, some formal relations with the

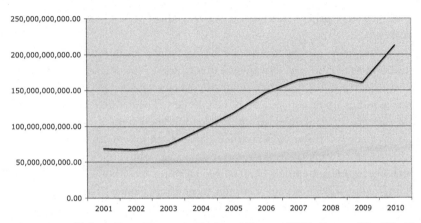

FIGURE 3.6. Chile – Gross Domestic Product (Current US$). *Source*: The World Bank Data Group, Database (databank.worldbank.org).

various regional integration schemes, and a constructive role in the multilateral trade talks (all of which were undertaken), Chile needed something else: preferential access to its main markets. It pursued this relentlessly for twenty years.

As part of its bid for economic growth and greater market access, Chile has been an active player in the proliferation of FTAs. To date, Chile has signed agreements with fifty-eight countries, accounting for 90.3 percent of its total trade (ProChile, 2011). The expansion of FTAs has been an integral part of Chile's economic development. Since 2001, Chile's GDP has steadily risen to US$212.7 billion in 2010 (see Figure 3.6), with exports amounting to US$69.622 billion. Most tellingly, during the financial crisis, Chile experienced only a modest reduction of growth and continued to outperform larger trading countries. This growth has been based mainly on exporting commodities. Chile is the largest producer of copper in the world, the second-largest producer of fish meal, the largest exporter of fresh fruit in Southern Hemisphere, and also extensively exports wood and wood products, as well as wine (Heine, 2009). This growth and a demonstrated commitment to free trade and open markets made Chile the first South American country to join the OECD in January 2010.

Today, Chile is the country with the largest number of FTAs anywhere, its latest being with Turkey in March 2011. Its exports increased 7.5 times from 1990 to 2008 (from US$9 billion to US$68 billion), and its current FDI-stock-to-GDP ratio is 65 percent, one of the highest in the world (Heine, 2009; see also, ProChile, 2011). This long-term commitment to FTAs, and Chile's extensive experience negotiating them over two decades, facilitates our understanding of two key points:

- An incrementalist approach like the one followed by Chile ("one free trade agreement at a time"), with the aforementioned results, is demonstrably a fruitful way of gaining market access and fostering sustained economic growth.
- Extensive negotiating capacity. In the early 2000s, Chile was simultaneously negotiating FTAs with the United States and with the EU. According to theories of negotiating fatigue between North-South actors, this was not a wise thing to do. If one compares the number of expert negotiators Santiago has on any given product with those that Washington or Brussels can bring to the negotiating table, Chile would be vastly outnumbered. This could lead to a severe asymmetry during negotiations. Yet, even though this was by no means easy, simultaneous rather than sequential negotiations turned out to be the best way to proceed. Chile signed an FTA with the EU in July 2002. This became something of an embarrassment for a U.S. administration ostensibly committed to finalizing a Free Trade Area of the Americas (FTAA) by 2005, but on which little progress was being made. The pressure for a U.S.-Chile FTA was thus ratcheted up, and a year later it was signed. Tellingly, something similar happened a few years later in the negotiations on trade agreements between China and India.

SURVIVING THE GREAT RECESSION, DEFENDING SOCIAL PROGRAMS

Chile's experience with FTAs demonstrates the practical application and success these agreements can generate. By devising a domestic policy goal that is in line with the country's specific needs and desires, Chile was able to negotiate successive FTAs that increased its trade access and exports (see Figure 3.6). In doing so, its export markets flourished, helping raise GDP at a constant rate (see Figure 3.7). This economic stability, even in the face of the Great Financial Crisis, has allowed Chile to retain various social and development programs domestically and abroad. With a strategic commitment to FTAs and free trade more generally, Chile has created a situation in which it can benefit from international trade while waiting for multilateral negotiations to catch up to its own success.

Hand in hand with its international trade policy, Chile has developed a number of social policies that have allowed it to make considerable progress

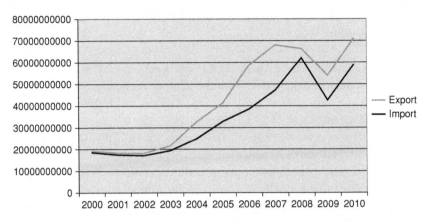

FIGURE 3.7. Chile – Total Merchandise Trade, 2001–2010 (US$ millions, current prices). *Source*: World Trade Organization, Statistics Database (stat.wto.org).

in poverty alleviation. An aggressive social housing program, another one targeting the eradication of informal settlements, the introduction of unemployment insurance, and ambitious pension reform legislation have not necessarily made much progress in diminishing Chile's considerable income inequality, but they have dramatically cut the poverty rate. The latter went down from 39 percent in 1990 to 13 percent in 2006 – a remarkable achievement by any account. This is also reflected in the Human Development Index (HDI) calculated on a yearly basis by the United Nations Development Program (UNDP), which regularly puts Chile at the very top in Latin America.

That said, Chile's relatively small internal market makes it difficult for the country to develop the sort of domestic manufacturing industry that could be competitive abroad in contrast to larger countries in the same region, such as Argentina, Brazil, or Mexico. Therefore, Chile has not been in a position to aim for legislation stipulating, say, "domestic content" for foreign direct investment in manufacturing or otherwise attract large-scale manufacturing investment. It has therefore mostly counted on foreign markets to spur internal growth.

EXPORT-LED GROWTH AND BILATERAL DIPLOMACY

On the other hand, in its position as one of the leading mining countries in the world, as well as a significant agricultural producer, Chile is not seen as threatening established industries in the North or in other emerging economies, but rather as a provider of needed raw materials or out-of-season products (in the case of fresh fruit, for example). Moreover, given the radical restructuring that the Chilean economy went through after the neoliberal reforms imposed by the military regime from 1973 to 1990, the country was ideally situated to make the most of FTAs. Many domestic market reforms, like those often demanded by United States Trade Representative negotiators for an FTA with the United States, were already in place.

In sum, Chile's "lateral" international trade policy, based on signing as many FTAs as possible, served it well, but it is not necessarily a panacea. It provided Chile with expanded market access and with a clear goal for its "diplomacy for development" for some two decades. The main lesson to be drawn relates to the degree to which international trade policy, particularly in the case of countries from the developing world, needs to be crafted in a way that responds to local realities. Rather than just opening the floodgates to the waves of globalization, as in the cases of Ecuador and El Salvador, when they internationalized their monetary policy and adopted the U.S. dollar as the national currency, or aiming for a self-defeating policy of autarky like North Korea, in almost all areas of the economy, what is needed is an approach that calibrates the economy's specific needs and proceeds accordingly. As in other areas of public policy – from telecom to infrastructure development, from public-private partnerships to FDI promotion – one reason Chile has done so well is because it came up with its own, tailor-made response to its international trade challenges.

CONCLUSION: FTAs AS A NEW POLICY SPACE

As we have argued throughout this chapter, FTAs play an important role in advancing the cause of multilateral international trade while awaiting progress at the Doha Round of trade talks. As a system built on the policy spaces of individual nation-states, the expansion of FTAs in recent years should not necessarily be seen as a negative development. Indeed, this expansion can be seen in countries like Chile as an opportunity to both fortify existing policy space and create conditions for new emerging policy space. This is significant because, while broader WTO negotiations remain stalled, the turn to FTAs demonstrates the buy-in that has occurred at the global level about the potential value of trade liberalization. Yet, to remain beneficial from the perspective of policy spaces, the expansion of FTAs must follow three basic principles.

First, FTAs must be conducted in accordance with WTO principles and the goals of more liberalized trade to foster economic as well as respect human rights. Second, smaller market actors must not be coerced into accepting trade-related measures that run counter to their domestic needs. Increased trade should be a means of furthering development, not a constraint on social and economic development. Thirdly, increased engagement with bilateral and plurilateral processes should not distract from multilateral negotiations. The agreements and commonalities fostered during the negotiation of FTAs must then be addressed at the multilateral level to foster further economic growth and trade access. In doing so, the proliferation of FTAs in the global trading environment can become an opportunity for fostering like-mindedness and the adoption of multilateral norms for effective and efficient world trade that addresses the distinct needs of domestic development as well as global connectivity around human rights.

REFERENCES

Abbott, Frederick M. (2002) "The Doha Agreement on TRIPS and Public Health: Lighting a Dark Corner at the WTO." *Journal of International Economic Law*, 5(2): 469–505.

Aggarwal, Vinod K. and Simon J. Evenett (2010) "Financial Crises, 'New' Industrial Policy, and the Bite of Multilateral Trade Rules." *Asian Economic Policy Review*, 5(2): 221–244.

Arrighi, Giovanni (2007) *Adam Smith in Beijing: Lineages of the Twenty First Century*. New York: Verso Books.

Arrighi, Giovanni (2009) *The Long Twentieth Century: Money, Power, and the Origins of Our Times*. New York: Verso Books.

Baldwin, Richard and Simon J. Evenett (eds.) (2009) *The Collapse of Global Trade, Murky Protectionism, and the Crisis: Recommendations for the G20*. London: Centre for Economic Policy Research.

Bhagwati, Jagdish (1993) "Regionalism and Multilateralism: An Overview," in Jamie Del Melo and Arvind Panagariya (eds.), *New Dimensions in Regional Integration*. Cambridge: Cambridge University Press and the Centre for Economic Policy Research, pp. 22–50.

Bhagwati, Jagdish (2008) *Termites in the Trading System: How Preferential Agreements Undermine Free Trade*. Oxford: Oxford University Press.

Blecker, Robert A. (2009) "External Shocks, Structural Change, and Economic Growth in Mexico, 1979–2007." *World Development*, 37(7): 1274–1284.

BN Americas (2000) "Lagos: Infrastructure Fundamental to Mercosur." *Business News America*, July 20.

Bradlow, Daniel D. (2001) "'The Times They Are A-Changing': Some Preliminary Thoughts on Developing Countries, NGOs and the Reform of the WTO." *George Washington International Law Review*, 33: 503–535.

Brown, Andrew G. and Robert M. Stern (2011) "Free Trade Agreements and Governance of the Global Trading System." *The World Economy*, 34: 331–354.

Chia, Siow Yu (2010) "Comment on 'Financial Crises, "New" Industrial Policy, and the Bite of Multilateral Trade Rules'." *Asian Economic Policy Review*, 5(2): 245–246.

Drache, Daniel (2010) "New State Practices at a Time of Disturbance and the Nasty Business of Protectionism: The Expectation for Global Demand Management."

A background paper prepared for the UN World Economic and Social Survey, April 8.

Drahos, Peter (2005) "Intellectual Property in the Knowledge Economy," in David Rooney, Greg Hearn, Abraham Ninan (eds.), *Handbook on the Knowledge Economy*. Cheltenham, UK: Edward Elgar Publishing, pp. 139–151.

Drahos, Peter (2007) "Four Lessons for Developing Countries from the Trade Negotiations Over Access to Medicines." *Liverpool Law Review*, 28(11): 11–39.

Drahos, Peter with John Braithwaite (2002) *Information Feudalism: Who Owns the Knowledge Economy?* London: Earthscan Publications.

Dunoff, Jeffrey L. (2001) "The WTO in Transition: Of Constituents, Competence and Coherence." *George Washington International Law Review*, 33: 979–1013.

Dutfield, Graham (2006) "'To Copy Is to Steal': TRIPS, (Un)free Trade Agreements and the New Intellectual Property Fundamentalism." *The Journal of Information and Technology Law*, Special Issue.

Eichengreen, Barry and Douglas A. Irwin (1995) "Trade Blocs, Currency Blocs, and the Reorientation of World Trade in the 1930s." *Journal of International Economics*, 38: 1–24.

Evenett Simon J. (ed.) (2010) *Unequal Compliance: The Sixth GTA Report*. London: CEPR.

Haas, Richard N. (2010) "The Case for Messy Multilateraiilsm." *Financial Times*, January 5.

Heine, Jorge (2009) "Chile's International Trade Policy." *World Focus* (New Delhi), 350, Special Issue, "Chile: Democracy and Development."

Hoekman, Bernard (2008) "The General Agreement on Trade in Services: Doomed to Fail? Does It Matter?" *Journal of Industry, Competition and Trade*, 8: 295–318.

Hoekman, Bernard and L. Alan Winters (2007) "Multilateralizing 'Deep Regional Integration': A Developing Country Perspective." Paper presented at the Conference on Multilateralising Regionalism Sponsored and organized by WTO – HEI Co-organized by the Centre for Economic Policy Research (CEPR), September 10–12, Geneva, Switzerland.

Horn, Henrik, Petros C. Mavroidis, and André Sapir (2009) "Beyond the WTO? An Anatomy of EU and US Preferential Trade Agreements." Discussion Paper Series No. 7317, Centre for Economic Policy Research, UK.

Kimura, Fukunari (2010) "Comment on 'Financial Crises, "New" Industrial Policy, and the Bite of Multilateral Trade Rules'." *Asian Economic Policy Review*, 5(2): 247–248.

Organization for Economic Cooperation and Development (1996) "The Knowledge Based Economy." OCDE/GD(96)102, Paris.

ProChile (2011) "Existing Agreements." *ProChile*.

Ricardo, David (1971) *The Principles of Political Economy and Taxation*. London: Watson and Viney.

Rodrik, Dani (2007) *One Economics, Many Recipes: Globalization, Institutions, and Economic Growth*. Princeton: Princeton University Press.

Rodrik, Dani (2011) *The Globalization Paradox: Why Global Markets, States and Democracy Can't Coexist*. Oxford and New York: Oxford University Press.

Sally, Razeen (2010) "International Trade and Emerging Protectionism since the Crisis." *East Asia Forum*, February 17.

Sell, Susan K. (2003) *Private Power, Public Law: The Globalization of Intellectual Property Rights*. Cambridge: Cambridge University Press.

Sell, Susan K. (2010) "The Global IP Upward Ratchet, Anti-Counterfeiting and Piracy Enforcement Efforts: The State of Play." *PIJIP Research Paper No. 15*. Washington, DC: American University Washington College of Law.

Stiglitz, Joseph E. (2008) "Economic Foundations of Intellectual Property Rights." *Duke Law Journal*, 57: 1693–1724.

Sungjoon, Cho (2009) "A Long and Winding Road: The Doha Round Negotiation in the World Trade Organization." Unpublished paper. Available at: http://works.bepress.com/sungjoon_cho/52.

United Nations Conference on Trade and Development (2010) *International Trade After The Economic Crisis: Challenges and New Opportunities*. New York: UNCTAD.

Villarreal, M. Angeles (2010) "Mexico's Free Trade Agreements." Congressional Research Service Report, R40784, July 12.

von Bulow, Marisa (2010) *Building Transnational Networks: Civil Society and the Politics of Trade in the Americas*. Cambridge: Cambridge University Press.

World Trade Organization (2011) WTO Regional Trade Agreement Database.

WTO Ministerial Conference (2001) *Doha Declaration on TRIPS and Public Health*. Ministerial Conference, Fourth Session, Doha, November 9–14, (WT/MIN(01)/DEC/2), November 20.

WTO Press Release (2011) "WTO Scales Back Its Trade Forecast to 5.8% as Downside Risk Builds." World Trade Organization, September 23.

Zepeda, Eduardo, Timothy A. Wise, and Kevin P. Gallagher (2009) "Rethinking Trade Policy for Development: Lessons from Mexico under NAFTA." *Carnegie Endowment for International Peace: Policy Outlook*, December.

PART II

Pushback and Global Protest

4

From Seattle to Occupy: The Shifting Focus of Social Protest

Tomer Broude

INTRODUCTION: TRADE LIBERALIZATION AND POLICY SPACE

This essay takes impressionistic stock of the changes in the linkages between international trade liberalization and human rights. To be more precise, it discusses changes in the perceived linkages between the two through the stylized lens of global social protest over approximately the past two decades.[1]

The World Trade Organization (WTO) – the international institutional "persona" of trade liberalization – was established in 1995. The first few years after its inception were accompanied by vocal and highly publicized international social protest. The time of this writing, nearly twenty years later, is also marked by significant expressions of social unrest around the world. While the existing elements of the WTO appear to be functioning at full swing, or at least muddling through, they are not progressing forcefully toward new horizons of international economic regulation, to say the least.[2] Much of the discontent expressed by the protesters, then and now, relates to the impact of trade liberalization on economic and social policy spaces.

Have there been changing perspectives on the relationship between trade liberalization and policy spaces? What *has* changed between the street protests of the 1990s and early 2000s and those of the 2010s? Have the anti-globalist prophets of rage from the 1999 "Battle in Seattle"[3] been vindicated by ensuing developments in the international economic scene and perhaps even by the 2011 "Occupiers"[4] of Wall Street? Or were the earlier generation of protesters rather misguided and mistaken, to the extent that the alarms they raised relating to the potential restrictions of human rights by trade liberalization were false? Is the face of the social battle now different, the contours of dissatisfaction fundamentally removed from those of the protests at the end of the previous century? I contend that there has indeed been a fundamental shift in the substance of protest, reflecting a change in the popular understanding of the trade liberalization–human rights linkage.

In the 1990s, protesters marched against "globalization" in defense of the disempowered state. Today's protesters have a more sophisticated understanding. They may share the concern of the erosion of social rights in the face of economic liberalization and corporate power and greed, but they understand that the focal point of their remonstration should be directed not at the international level of diffuse decision making (be it Geneva, Washington, DC, or wherever the next G8, G20, or WTO summit might be held) but rather toward their own political and economic state capital(s) and government(s). This shift in focus is reasonable on the grounds that the protests of 2011–2012 have reclaimed the state as the main addressee of political accountability for economic and social human rights conditions.

In the next section I evoke some of the main tenets of the social protests of the 1990s and early 2000s, in particular their anti-globalist nature. In the third section I will more analytically discuss the interactions between trade liberalization law and human rights, presenting both the fears that lay under the earlier protests in the areas of human rights and the ways in which these interactions have played out in practice since the establishment of the WTO in 1995. These sections provide a backdrop to an analysis of the current wave of worldwide social protest, which I undertake in the fourth section, followed by concluding comments in the last section.

THE "OLD" SOCIAL PROTEST OF THE 1990s–2000s: WHAT WAS IT ABOUT?

In some ways, the global social protest of the early 2010s can be seen as the continuation of similar public, anticapitalist protests going back even to 1985[5] – well before the fall of the Iron Curtain – and in particular to the demonstrations aimed at the World Bank (WB)/International Monetary Fund (IMF) joint conference in West Berlin in the fall of 1988.[6] The dynamics of mobilization and of mass expressions of dissent, now most familiar and well facilitated by the Internet and its social networks, were already evident at that event (Gerhards and Rucht, 1992). However, it is important to recall the globalizing nature of the targets of these demonstrations. They (the G7, WB, IMF) were not national governments but state groupings and international institutions (heavily tilted toward Western domination) acting at the international and global levels.

The main wave of global social protest really kicked off in 1999, with the "Global Carnival against Capital" at the G8 meeting in Cologne in June – a festive demonstration that is still considered a model for protest in the global justice movement and beyond (Bogad, 2010). It was here that the slogan "our resistance is as transnational as capital" was launched, a rallying cry for what evolved into diffuse elements of the anti-globalist movement; one of these elements was the People's Global Action Network.[7]

This was followed by the better-known mass demonstration and disruption of the WTO's Third Ministerial Conference in Seattle, in November–December 1999. Seattle was a significant development for several reasons. One was its scale (between 40,000 and 100,000 people on the streets). This factor contributed to its perhaps misguided impression of its impact on the summit, for the talks were largely bound to fail regardless of the street action.[8] The riots also succeeded in making "anti-globalization" a household term.[9] No less important was the fringe anarchist violence (trashing, literally, corporatist targets such as Starbucks) and the stiff police response,[10] unusual in the United States in events where no "important" and contentious national issues such as civil rights or war were concerned. All of this was of course aimed at the WTO, the emerging lightening rod of anti-globalization attacks.

Below is a short, by no means exhaustive, list of subsequent protests at global economic events:

- September 11, 2000: demonstrations in Melbourne against the World Economic Forum (Craig, 2002);
- November 2000: protests against the G20 in Montreal;
- April 2001: Quebec City protests against the Summit of the Americas (King and Waddington, 2005);
- July 2001: huge protests in Genoa against the G20 (which resulted in the death of 1 demonstrator and some 200 injured);[11]
- September 2003: demonstrations in Cancun against the WTO's Fifth Ministerial Conference where one South Korean protester Lee Kyang Hae went so far as to stab himself to death at the picket lines (Vidal, 2003).

The list goes on, the protests becoming increasingly routine until this day; the November 2011 demonstrations against the G20 summit in Cannes is one example of many (Chrisafis, 2011).

It was at the early protests in 1999–2000 that the arcane shorthand dated codes for protest events, increasingly used today, became standardized practice. "J18" was the code for the Cologne demonstrations, "N30" for Seattle, "S11" for Melbourne, and so on. This is but one superficial expression of the palpable relationship of continuity between the social protests of the 1990s–2000s and the demonstration of discontent witnessed since 2011. More substantively, the political thread running from then until now is also quite evident; the earlier protests were unabashedly of an anticapitalist, anti-corporatist, "leftist," even anarchist streak, and the current protests are similarly colored. This link between the earlier wave of protest and the current one is undeniable and important. However, here I would like to highlight one significant element of the earlier protests that is generally subdued in the dissent of today: the assault on international institutions such as the WTO, WB, and IMF, driven by the fear that these institutions will encroach on human rights, especially economic and social rights.

Quite simply, the older protests were blatantly anti-*globalist*, and their targets were *international* economic institutions, especially the WTO. This can be concluded from the locations of the demonstrations, each aimed at an international conference or summit. The object of the protests is also apparent in the public agendas of the protesters. The old genre of demonstrations initiated in the 1990s and continued in the 2000s was characterized by the chants of "WTO – No!" "WTO – Shrink or Sink!" and "Our World Is Not for Sale!"

MANIFESTOES: BLUEPRINTS OF DISSENT

Here are selected passages from what was perhaps the most coherent manifesto of the period – the "Turnaround Agenda International Civil Society Sign-On Letter." It reads:

> It's time to turn trade around. In November 1999, the World Trade Organization's (WTO) Third Ministerial Meeting in Seattle collapsed in spectacular fashion, in the face of unprecedented protest from people and governments around the world. We believe it is essential to use this moment as an opportunity to change course and develop an alternative, humane, democratically accountable and sustainable system of commerce that benefits all. This process entails rolling back the power and authority of the WTO.
>
> The GATT Uruguay Round Agreements and the establishment of the WTO were proclaimed as a means of enhancing the creation of global wealth and prosperity and promoting the well-being of all people in all member states. In reality, however, the WTO has contributed to the concentration of wealth in the hands of the rich few; increasing poverty for the majority of the world's peoples, especially in third world countries; and unsustainable patterns of production and consumption.[12]

In this relatively influential popular document, the WTO is clearly depicted as the manifestation of globalized capitalist evil, if not its root. The call is to decimate those international, global institutions that are inhumane and undemocratic and that contribute to global inequality and poverty. The manifesto goes on:

> The WTO and GATT Uruguay Round Agreements have functioned principally to pry open markets for the benefit of transnational corporations at the expense of national and local economies; workers, farmers, indigenous peoples, women and other social groups; health and safety; the environment; and animal welfare. In addition, the WTO system, rules and procedures are undemocratic, un-transparent and non-accountable and have operated to marginalize the majority of the world's people.

In short, the WTO is depicted as a central impediment to the achievement of social rights at a global scale, doing so by circumventing the civil and political rights of "the majority of the world's people." The fears of the manifesto's authors are vivid:

> It is inappropriate and unacceptable for social rights and basic needs to be constrained by WTO rules. Thus WTO Agreements must not apply to issues critical to human or planetary welfare, such as food and water, basic social services, health and safety, and animal protection. Inappropriate encroachment by trade rules in such areas has already resulted in campaigns on genetically modified organisms, old growth forests, domestically prohibited goods and predatory tobacco marketing. . . . In particular, areas such as health, education, energy and other basic human services must not be subject to international free trade rules. . . . The trading system must not undermine the livelihood of peasants, small farmers, artisan fishers and indigenous peoples. . . . Actions taken to implement multilateral agreements dealing with the environment, health, development, human rights, safety, indigenous peoples' rights, food security, women's rights, workers' rights and animal welfare cannot be challenged at or undermined by the WTO.[13]

These statements reflect the apprehensions both of the WTO as an institution and of international trade liberalization as a regulatory yet political trend. The implementation of trade liberalization by the WTO will lead to an erosion of human rights. In the realm of civil and political rights, erosion will occur as the WTO bypasses the democratic decision-making processes of national constituencies. In the fields of social and economic rights, erosion will occur as national policy spaces are constrained by supranational actors.

In other related contexts, it was not the WTO itself that was depicted or perceived as the nemesis of human rights, but trade liberalization, even when practiced at the regional level. An interesting source for this general sentiment is the 2006 "Cochabamba Manifesto," aimed at opposing international economic integration in the Americas, doing so very much in the vernacular of human rights:[14]

> The peoples of America have suffered from the application of an economic model which is based on market fundamentalism, privatization and free trade, which has led to a growth in inequality, the deterioration of labour conditions, unemployment, the spread of informal-sector work, degradation of the environment, deepening discrimination against women, poverty, marginalisation of indigenous and rural communities and the loss of State capacity to promote development and economic policies.

> With the aim of widening and deepening these policies, there were attempts to create the Free Trade Agreement of America (FTAA) and regional Free Trade Agreements, by which Governments abandoned any attempt at autonomous development based on the internal market which respects all human, social, economic, cultural and environmental rights.

The "old" social protests characteristic of the late 1990s and early 2000s therefore displayed – as they continue to display in their regular manifestations – not only a strong element of anticapitalism but also of anti-internationalism, referred to more usually as anti-globalism or anti-globalization.[15] These manifestoes portray international economic law and institutions – the WTO, free trade agreements, and more – as the principal threats to civil, political, and surely social and economic human rights.

Furthermore, under this reading, it is the globalized economy, promoted by politically driven international institutions, that eviscerates the state, weakening and disabling it. It is the international level of regulation that needs to be dismantled and removed; the national orders would then be able to support the rights that people want and deserve. As I argue in what follows, this vision has proven false in more ways than one, and the "new" social protests of the 2010s reflect a shift in focus from the global to the local.

MUCH ADO ABOUT NOTHING: HAVE THE ANTI-GLOBALIST HUMAN RIGHTS FEARS MATERIALIZED?

The WTO is now more than fifteen years old. Even though its membership has grown, it has failed to expand significantly in its substantive scope and coverage; but surely it has neither shrunk nor sunk. As the WTO has grown more mature, the debate over the impact of international trade law on human rights has also entered adolescence. Keeping in mind the characteristics of the original anti-globalist social protest reviewed in the preceding section, it seems apposite to take stock of the extent to which the potentially wholesale infringements on human rights feared by the protesters of the 1990s–2000s have materialized. How has the relationship between international trade liberalization and human rights played out in practice over the last decade or so? To what extent have international economic institutions – the WTO *primus inter pares* among them – constrained, developed, or otherwise made an impact on human rights? In this section I deal with these questions.

Analytically, there are five types of trade law–human rights linkages that have been contemplated and discussed throughout this period: (1) *conflict*, (2) *conditionality*, (3) *constitutionalism*, (4) *conformity*, and (5) *confluence*. This is clearly a much more expansive palette of interactions than envisioned by the anti-globalist movement, whose concerns focused largely on conflict, the first and most obvious type of interface. Let me now discuss the significance of each of these types of interactions in practice.

CONFLICT LINKAGES

In terms of regime *conflict*, the general debate revolves around the question of whether international economic liberalization furthers human rights or conflicts with them. The GATT and the WTO Agreements were drafted under the premise that trade liberalization stimulates economic growth and creates wealth, thus enhancing humanity and its welfare. That view is reflected in the Preambles to the GATT 1947[16] and the 1994 WTO Agreement,[17] both of which state that the Agreements are concluded "with a view to raising standards of living, ensuring full employment and a large and steadily growing volume of real income."

The line of thinking embodied in these texts argues that wealth generation ultimately enables governments and societies to better fulfill their human rights objectives (and obligations). This thesis is hotly contested, however, with significant research indicating that the mere growth in trade and even of gross domestic product (GDP) does not necessarily mean that the populace at large profits equitably or that human rights conditions are automatically improved.[18] Critics argue that trade liberalization conflicts with human rights by eroding the ability of states to provide social rights protections or by creating economic and social disparities whose maintenance drives governments and interest groups to wholesale violations of civil and political rights.[19]

Concerns over specific legal conflicts between trade disciplines and international human rights laws and policies have also been raised and analyzed, an example being the case of patent protection for pharmaceuticals. This protection was required by the WTO agreement on Trade Related Aspects of Intellectual Property (TRIPS),[20] even though it went against the right to health (Hestermeyer, 2007).[21,22] Indeed, in many circles – not least among the anti-globalization protesters of the early 2000s – there exists a general perception that trade law "trumps" human rights, or as Walden Bello, the leading Filipino anti-globalist thinker, put it soon after Seattle:

> By setting up the WTO, countries and governments discovered that they had set up a legal system that enshrined the priority of free trade above every other good–above the environment, justice, equity, and community. They finally got the significance of consumer advocate Ralph Nader's warning a few years earlier that the WTO, was a system of "trade uber alles."[23]

Almost a decade later, this perception is still prevalent, as echoed in a rhetorical question posed by WTO Director-General, Pascal Lamy in 2009: "Is not the World Trade Organization for many the symbol of a globalization in which mercantile pursuits have precedence over human beings, the market over individuals, and might over right?"[24]

But in the face of this long-standing alarmism, how much international trade–human rights conflict have we actually witnessed since the establishment of the WTO? Ask social activists, and they are hard-pressed to find specific concrete examples of cases in which social policies or civil and political rights have run into a brick wall, or any wall at all, of international trade law. It is more often the brick wall of domestic policy, unbridled by international law dictates, that they encounter. Yes, international legal obligations in the WTO and in regional trade agreements must be taken into account in regulatory fields relating to human rights, such as public health, access to food, social services and more, but no real conflicts constraining human rights have arisen – or, to err on the side of caution, at least surprisingly few. This is a key point in the assessment of the shifts in social protest and dissent with respect to the role of economic policy in infringing on, limiting, or promoting human rights. Quite simply, despite the concerns of anti-globalists, the action in this area has not been in the WTO, WB, or G20, but in national spheres of authority.

CONDITIONALITY LINKAGES

Conditionality is the second strand of the "trade and human rights" debate over the last two decades. This debate has focused on the creating of explicit, formal linkages between the economic benefits of trade agreements and preference programs while seeking to keep them compliant with international human rights norms. This has been attempted through international agreements or by unilateral measures.[25] Conditionality as a means of promoting international human rights has its proponents, yet empirical research casts doubt both on the real motivations for the establishment of human rights conditionality and on the extent of its effectiveness, given the low degree of willingness and capability to enforce it (Hafner-Burton, 2009). Here too, it seems tenuous to claim that international trade law has had any significant (positive) impact on human rights.

CONSTITUTIONALISM AND MARKET FREEDOMS

The third strand of the "trade and human rights" debate, *constitutionalism*, is perhaps the most controversial.[26] It contemplates the recognition of "market freedoms" as human rights in and of themselves. Whereas supporters of this approach envisage it as a bridge between trade liberalization and human rights, critics have vociferously argued that this approach misconstrues the foundations of modern international human rights law and threatens to erode them.[27] As such, it represents a certain normative understanding of the global social order, in which market-oriented rules are elevated to the level of human rights. This idea remains interesting at the theoretical level, though unsubstantiated at the level of practice and experience over the last twenty years.

CONFORMITY AND HUMAN RIGHTS LAW

Conformity is the idea that international trade law should be interpreted in light of human rights law, in particular through light of the right to development.[28] This is a very attractive approach, both normatively and doctrinally. However, looking back to the establishment of the WTO, and the more than 400 disputes that have reached the WTO roster ever since, one wonders what impact this view has actually had. In earnest I can think of only two cases in which such a harmonious interpretation could or should have been considered by the judicial decision makers: the first was the *China Intellectual Property Rights Enforcement* case (WTO, 2009) and the second the *China Audiovisual Services* case (WTO, 2010). Both of these cases involved a potential contribution of international freedom-of-speech considerations to the interpretation of WTO member obligations under the GATT. However the parties and adjudicators in these cases were essentially oblivious to any such potential. This is not to say that a human rights–sensitive interpretation and application of international trade law is not impossible, or undesirable, nor does it mean that there have not been practical effects outside of the courts such as in government agencies, academic debates, and so on. Still very little of it has taken place during the last two decades.

CONFLUENCE AND INTERNATIONAL TRADE LAW TO PROMOTE HUMAN RIGHTS

Finally, there is the rarely mentioned idea of *confluence*: that in at least some cases, the promotion of trade liberalization rules can seamlessly promote protections for human rights, as a legal technical matter. Here too, there is little evidence to work with, in the legal sphere, beyond the vague and general propositions. These include that international trade law promotes transparency and hence human rights, and that prying open markets for Internet services would promote freedom of speech. Again, reference can be made to the China intellectual property enforcement and audiovisual services cases mentioned earlier (Broude, 2010).

The practical effects of international trade law on international human rights as it regards the WTO are quite clear. The concerns raised by the anti-globalists of the 1990s – that international trade agreements and institutions would firmly encroach upon human rights – have proven less than certain. The responses by proponents of trade liberalization that said international trade law would in a variety of ways promote human rights have also largely proved to be disappointing red herrings.

THE "NEW" SOCIAL PROTEST: WHAT IS IT AND WHY IS IT DIFFERENT?

Throughout the world, the years 2010–2012 have been marked by a wave of social protest of dramatic proportions. The demonstrations that have taken place in dozens of countries and hundreds of cities each have their different contexts, causes, and coalitions; it is thus difficult not to acknowledge the importance of the general phenomenon of mass social protest at this time. Indeed, *Time Magazine*'s 2011 Person of the Year was "The Protester," with profiles of individual protesters and activists from the Americas, Europe, the Middle East, and Asia.[29] Without undertaking a comprehensive survey, what follows is a short summary of the major "new" protests to date, from which I will try to glean some observations on their commonalities and how they are different from the anti-globalist protests of the 1990s–2000s.

The precursors of the 2011–2012 global protests were generally direct results of the economic effects the 2008 global financial crisis as felt in precariously situated economies. These 2009 protests occurred in Bulgaria, Lithuania, Greece, and – most famously – Iceland. In Iceland, a particularly large and unregulated banking bubble collapsed, leading to high prices and increased unemployment. "Waking up to reality" entailed nationwide protests demanding full accountability from the national government (Danielson, 2009), leading to its resignation and to constitutional reform. The implications of the Icelandic "revolution" for other countries were not lost on some observers. Notably, Robert Wade of the London School of Economics was quoted as predicting that "large-scale civil unrest" was on the way:

> It will be caused by the rise of general awareness throughout Europe, America and Asia that hundreds and millions of people in rich and poor countries are experiencing rapidly falling consumption standards; that the crisis is getting worse, not better, and that it has escaped the control of public authorities, national and international.[30]

In Europe, similar public expressions of dissent were launched, sustained, and increased during 2010 and through the summer of 2011 in Greece, Portugal, the United Kingdom, Spain, Chile, and Israel. These were marked by indignation against austerity measures, tax hikes, and more generally against corruption and the overall sense of lack of democratic participation and influence over the future of most of society, perhaps most astutely described by the name given to the Portuguese variant of protest, the *Geração à Rasca* or "lost generation."

In the United States, post–financial crisis protesting was first expressed in 2009 by the Tea Party – a conservative-oriented nationwide popular movement with a broad range of economic concerns, from health care reform to financial bailout (Zernike 2010). A major development occurred with the launch of the Occupy Wall Street movement that began with street protests and campouts in Manhattan in September 2011 but mushroomed into a nationwide Occupy phenomenon in dozens of U.S. cities.[31] Occupy conjoined with the existing national protests and new locations, going truly global on October 15, 2011 – the "Global Day of Action," with demonstrations of varying sizes reported in dozens of countries, highlighted by hundreds of thousands on the streets in Italy, Spain, the United States, and Portugal.

THE ARAB SPRING: THE TRANSFORMATIVE REVOLT

In parallel with these developments in OECD countries, the so-called Arab Spring erupted at the end of 2010. It was characterized by a string of very large-scale civil unrest and uprisings in Arab states from Morocco to Oman, leading to government overthrow in Tunisia, Egypt, Yemen, and Libya (at the time of this writing, the severe situation in Syria has not yet been resolved), with significant social and political repercussions in other jurisdictions. The Arab Spring is a hugely complex, it's-too-soon-to-tell development, with many important differences between its national expressions (Anderson, 2011) all clearly different from popular protest in other countries. A key difference is that the Arab peoples' first challenge has been the very assertion of basic civil and political rights against repressive regimes, while in the OECD countries the focus has been social and economic. Popular protest in the Middle East and in the West has nevertheless been interlinked, in methods and mutual inspiration.[32]

NEW PROTEST AND OLD PROTEST CONTRASTED: SOME DEFINING DIFFERENCES

Is this global wave of social protest a forceful continuation of the anti-globalist demonstrations of the 1990s–2000s, or is it a new, different animal? I would say the latter; today's social protest is dissimilar in a variety of noteworthy ways.

First, the very scale of protest – quantitative, geographical, and temporal – is different, much larger and grander. The "old" anti-globalist protests mustered at most a few tens of thousands of protesters in limited locations, for a single event – usually an international summit of one institution or another – lasting only a few hours or days at most. In contrast, social protest in 2011–2012 included many mega-protest events, in which hundreds of thousands gathered in a single locale of domestic rather than international importance – whether in Tel Aviv, Madrid, Rome, or New York. Benefiting from Internet, mobile communications, and social media, large-scale protests have also taken place in coordination in many such places in the world simultaneously, most notably the October 15, 2011 protests. The protests have also been extended over time in visible public spheres, characterized by entrenched tent cities or otherwise long-term "occupations" – in Zuccotti Park, Rothschild Boulevard, Tahrir Square, and Puerta del Sol – lasting first weeks, then months, and now years.

Second, there are differences in the identity and representativeness of the protesters. Whereas in the past protest was strongly associated with particular political groups, "-ists" of various kinds – trade unionists, anarchists, environmentalists – protesters in 2011–2012 drew from a much broader public, including masses who have no structured agenda beyond their own discontent. Yes, there is no doubt that the protest is driven by similarly profiled people – students and unions in particular,[33] as well as anarchists[34] – but the extent of its mobilization is much broader, reaching deep into the middle class, building on the general public's antipathy toward big business and financial institutions. This has been enabled by rallying cries that appeal to virtually all of society, Such as "we are the 99 percent." So far these movements have avoided capture by institutionalized political parties. By emphasizing inclusiveness they are able to sidestep contentious political divides while focusing on the common denominators of social discontent.[36] The Manifesto of the Spanish *Indignados* begins with the words:

> We are ordinary people. We are like you: people, who get up every morning to study, work or find a job, people who have family and friends. People, who work hard every day to provide a better future for those around us.[37]

WHO IS THE ENEMY? WHAT DO THEY WANT?

Third, and perhaps most important, is the answer to the question: What are the "new" social protests against? In contrast to the protests of the 1990s–2000s, today's demonstrations are not especially aimed against the WTO, the WB, the IMF, or the G20. The difference between Seattle and Genoa, on one hand, and the *Indignados*, Rothschild Boulevard, Tahrir Square, and the Occupy Movement, on the other, is that the earlier protests were against global governance, against globalization. They targeted free trade as a source of social injustices and decried the disempowerment of local government by international institutions.

In contrast, the current wave of social protest seems not to care too much about the environment or international rules, and instead focuses on the domestic: national-level democracy and decision making. It no longer considers the sources of economic and social woes to be the result of international governance, but adroitly directs its criticism toward national governance rather than international commitments and international institutions. Global civil society that once directed resources to picketing outside grand international summits has recognized the truism whereby "all politics is local," and social movements are acting on it. The slogans are very concrete and localized: Take the square! *Toma la Calle!* In contrast, the Seventh and Eighth WTO Ministerial Conferences in Geneva, in 2009 and 2011, respectively, drew only a few dozen protesters and sparse media attention.

Compare the anti-globalist manifestos of the "old" protests, discussed earlier in the chapter, with those of the "new" protest, such as the 2011 manifesto of the Spanish *indignados*. It says not a word about international institutions, free trade agreements, or global forces:

The priorities of any advanced society must be equality, progress, solidarity, freedom of culture, sustainability and development, welfare and people's happiness. . . . These are inalienable truths that we should abide by in our society: the right to housing, employment, culture, health, education, political participation, free personal development, and consumer rights for a healthy and happy life. . . . The current status of our government and economic system does not take care of these rights, and in many ways is an obstacle to human progress. . . . Democracy belongs to the people (demos = people, krátos = government) which means that government is made of every one of us. However, in Spain most of the political class does not even listen to us.

In other words, the call is to prioritize the attainment of social and economic rights over the prevailing capitalist economic model, but the outrage is directed toward the Spanish and economic political system, not toward abstracted images of bogeymen in Geneva or Washington, DC. It is a call to change the system from below and from within instead of "sinking" the WTO.

THE FOCUS ON THE LOCAL ACTIVISM: ISRAEL AND THE INTERNET

In Israel, too, the calls to change the economic system have been distinctly localized. The protesters in the tent city of Rothschild Avenue adopted the rhythmic Arabic chant from Tahrir Square – *El shaab yureed isqat el nizam!* (the People demand the fall of the regime!) – and adjusted it to their concerns in Hebrew – *Ha'am doresh Tsedek Hevrati!* (the People demand social justice!). The protest is not against the international level of governance, but against the national economic system, with people asking themselves: What kind of state do we want to live in?[38] As if to emphasize the non-anti-globalist character of the Israeli social protest, the only recommendation of the government expert committee on social and economic reform, headed by economist Prof. Manuel Trajtenberg, which was widely embraced by both the Ministry of Finance and the informal leaders of the protest, was the recommendation to abolish all customs duties on imported goods. Moreover, importantly, in Israel the chants were not directed at toppling the regime, as they were in Egypt and Iceland. Indeed, polls during and after the 2011 protest showed no significant change in voting patterns that would erode the ruling Likud Party's hold on power.

One can detect similar trends in the North American Occupy movement, with its simple statement, "What is our one demand?" referring to social and economic justice, not to the dismantling of international institutions.

The closest to a manifesto held by the Occupy movement is the "Declaration of the Occupation of New York City" adopted by the movement's "New York City General Assembly" on September 29, 2011.[39] It is clearly anti-corporatist: "We come to you at a time when corporations, which place profit over people, self-interest over justice and oppression over equality, run our governments." However, it is not anti-globalist. International institutions are not even mentioned in the declaration. The targets of protest are banks, corporations and the "1 percent," and the call is for accountability from the government.

CONCLUSION: A NEW ERA OF NETWORKED ACTIVISM AND BUILDING POLICY SPACE FROM THE GROUND UP

The focus of social protest has shifted, therefore, significantly, from Seattle, 1999 to New York City, 2011. Contemporary protesters for the enhancement of social and economic rights are no longer anti-globalist in the old sense of the term. In an article written before the 2011–2012 social protest, Robert Howse expressed the view that "the anti-globalizers have themselves gone global,"[40] in the sense that they have found room for their social activism in spaces that transcend the state, in which they can advocate sets of values and causes at the global level. The preceding analysis of the current wave of social protest in comparison with the "old" anti-globalist protests suggests this is indeed at least part of the story. Civil society has matured, and international institutions, the WTO in particular, have been responsive by increasing transparency and public consultation. Moreover (as discussed in the third section of this chapter), the threats of conflict between trade liberalization and human rights perceived by anti-globalists have not materialized. However, global economic governance has not gained much credit for positively addressing economic inequality and social rights (whether through conditionality, constitutionalization, conformity, or confluence) – quite the contrary.

Civil society has understood both sides of the coin and diverted its energies from the international levels of governance back to the local, fueled by the very real discontent felt by large segments of national societies in the aftermath of the financial crisis. The demands for democracy, human rights, social justice, and accountability in the face of economic change are no longer directed at the WTO, but rather at national governments. At the same time, the protest is surely transnational and globalized in its core causes. In other words, the shift has been from anti-globalism to globalized national protest. Furthermore, the "new" protests are not necessarily *against* government. In fact, they can be seen as demonstrations *for* government, or rather as a participatory effort in reshaping and reforming it. Whereas in the past, "[t]he anti-globalization movement understood itself as defending the traditional (progressive regulatory and social welfare) state against 'globalization,'"[41] today's activists understand that the main threats to social rights and welfare are to be found within the state system of governance.

All this is not to say that international economic governance has entirely lost its relevance to human rights, and especially economic and social policy spaces. Trade agreements and international institutions remain central instruments to the achievement of national economic and social policies. The debate has returned, rightfully, to focus on just what those policies should be.

REFERENCES

Anderson, Lisa. (2011) Demystifying the Arab Spring: Parsing the Differences between Tunisia, Egypt and Libya. *Foreign Affairs*, May–June, at http://www.foreignaffairs.com/articles/67693/lisa-anderson/demystifying-the-arab-spring.

Bogad, Lawrence M. (2010) Carnivals against Capital: Radical Clowning and the Global Justice Movement. *Social Identities: Journal for the Study of Race, Nation and Culture* 16(4), 537.

Broude, Tomer. (2010) It's Easily Done: The *China – Intellectual Property Rights Enforcement* Dispute and the Freedom of Expression. *Journal of World Intellectual Property* 13(5), 660.

Chrisafis, Angelique. (2011) Anti-G20 Protests Confined to Nice as Police Seal Off "Fortress Cannes". *The Guardian*, 1 November 2011, at http://www.guardian.co.uk/world/2011/nov/01/anti-g20-protests-confined-nice.

CNN. (2000) Montreal G20 Meeting Greeted by Angry Protesters, October 23.

Craig, Geoffrey. (2002) The Spectacle of the Street: An Analysis of the Media Coverage of Protests at the 2000 Melbourne World Economic Forum. *Australian Journal of Communication* 29(1), 39.

Danielsson, Jon. (2009) Waking up to Reality in Iceland. *BBC News*, 26 January, at http://news.bbc.co.uk/2/hi/europe/7852275.stm.

Gerhards, Jürgen and Rucht, Dieter. (1992) Mesomobilization: Organizing and Framing in Two Protest Campaigns in West Germany. *American Journal of Sociology* 98(3), 555.

Hafner-Burton, Emilie M. (2009) Forced to Be Good: Why Trade Agreements Boost Human Rights. Cornell: Cornell University Press.

Hestermeyer, Holger P. (2007) *Human Rights and the WTO: The Case of Patents and Access to Medicines*. Oxford: Oxford University Press.

King, Mike and Waddington, David (2005) Flashpoints Revisited: A Critical Application to the Policing of Anti-Globalization Protest. *Policing and Society* 15(3), 255.

Vidal, John (2003). Farmer Commits Suicide at Protests. *The Guardian*, 11 September, at http://www.guardian.co.uk/world/2003/sep/11/wto.johnvidal.

World Trade Organization. (2009) Panel Report, China – Measures Affecting the Protection and Enforcement of Intellectual Property Rights, WT/DS362/R, 26 January.

World Trade Organization. (2010) Appellate Body Report, China – Measures Affecting Trading Rights and Distribution Services for Certain Publications and Audiovisual Entertainment Products, WT/DS363/AB/R, 19 January.

Zernike, Kate. (2010) *Boiling Mad: Inside Tea Party America*. New York: Times Books.

5

What's Next for Global Labor? Power Dynamics and Industrial Relations Systems in a Hyperglobalized World

Daniel Drache

A TURBULENT TIME FOR LABOR GLOBALLY

The dismantling of long-established collective bargaining arrangements globally is without precedent, and collective bargaining coverage has shrunk across the advanced industrial world to levels not seen since the 1950s. Everywhere, fewer workers are involved in collective bargaining, an institution that once gave workers new power and status (ILO, 2010). Nowadays in France, the United Kingdom, and the United States, private-sector union membership has fallen to record lows, representing less than 10 percent of the workforce. For Canada, the corresponding number is about 15 percent, which is trending down more slowly than in the United States where contracting out and deindustrialization have hollowed out its collective bargaining system. In the Organization for Economic Development and Cooperation (OECD) countries, union density levels have dropped from a high of 60 percent of the workforce in the 1980s to just around 30 percent (OECD, 2011). The retreat of labor at the negotiating table appears to be structural and long term, with large-scale consequences for employers who have profited from the pro-market environment. Once thought to be off limits, the EU's prized social market has begun to lose ground, and state workers' public pensions, previously declared untouchable in any labor negotiations, now are threatened by the global fiscal crisis (Standing, 2012).

The latest evidence from the OECD is that wages have trended downward in many member states as unions have lost their leverage at the bargaining table. The most extreme case is that between 2000 and 2010, wage increases in the majority of U.S. collective bargaining agreements have been negative or less than 1 percent. The benchmark standard is labor's share of national income, and it has been trailing the top income earners for at least two decades. Robert Reich has documented that U.S. median income has fallen every year since 2007 (Reich, 2012). Fifty-seven percent of the post-recession American jobs are low wage, paying between $7.70 and $13.85 an hour. Middle-income jobs are no longer there and are not coming back. However, the share going to capital has grown over the last two decades as investment income has produced deeply rooted income inequalities between the median paid worker and the take-home pay of the corporate elite. In the global South, for millions the picture is stark (Reich, 2012).

Millions are working in labor-intensive occupations from goods production to agrarian day labor without basic rights to a decent wage and proper working conditions. In emerging market economies, industrial relations and industrial democracy are in a turbulent state of transition as they respond to bottom-up pressure from restive workforces demanding a more equitable share of the greatest growth decades in human history. This is not just a story about the entry of more than 2 billion Indian and Chinese consumers into global markets, but about new institutional arrangements, new mechanisms of adjustment, new power dynamics, and a recalibration of state policy in leading jurisdictions in the global North and South. From Korea to India, work and employment are at the center of these renewed global processes, however different they are from country to country.

This essay looks at four interconnected issues that impact directly on the fragility of bottom-up policy spaces for the future of work and employment: labor-shedding technologies, new employment practices, the geoeconomic redistribution of power, and the fragmentation of the multilateral trading system. Importantly, it examines the collapse of the Anglo-American Keynesian model of industrial relations that predicted a bottom-up policy space to protect wage and salaried workers' social and economic rights in Canada and the United States. Surprisingly, despite North American market integration, the Canadian and American models are highly divergent. Thus the enormous transformations of capitalism have seen decisive shifts in state-market relations with the emergence of industrial relations systems. It concludes that more turbulent change is underway and that the Anglo-American model of industrial relations cannot be exported to China or other countries, although some fascinating points of convergence are visible.

OLD AND NEW POLICY SPACES: THE UNIVERSALIZATION LOGIC OF LABOR ADJUSTMENT

The challenge to researchers is to analyze how the "old pieces" of the global landscape are being reshaped by the global financial crisis that creates room for new practices and norms. It is not so simple as to blame globalization as a job killer; in fact, it is a mistake to do so. The universalizing logic is that global labor adjustment is more intense, complex, and dangerous for industrial relations practices both for the global North and South as each tries to increase their share of global markets in tough head-to-head competition at the expense of the other (Rodrik, 2011).

It is necessary to recall that modern industrial relations systems carved out a unique policy space to limit the reach of markets into the workplace, which in turn was achieved through protecting job security and limiting management's traditional right to fire without cause (Drache and Glasbeek, 1992, p. 208). The extension of industrial democracy into the factory system created a bottom-up policy space for millions of workers after World War II. Experts acknowledged it as a step toward industrial democracy, the capstone of embedded liberalism's attempt to reconcile social equity goals with international competitiveness (Arthurs, 2007).

The structural effects of privatization and deregulation have changed the balance of power between management and labor and have led to a widespread top-down process redefining public-private industrial relations systems. What can be observed is that labor shedding is widespread, outstripping the existing public policies to manage technological change effectively. It is driven by a matrix of forces motivated by the lure of export markets and the promise of productivity gains by labor-saving technologies. In the advanced capitalist jurisdictions, labor's traditional policy space is shrinking fast.

Paradoxically the trajectory in China is likely to move in the opposite direction: a gradual filling in of China's industrial relations practices from a model of tight state and party control to one of gradual autonomy and independence in the middle to long term. The hypothesis is that formalization of work and employment rights in China is likely to trend up rather than down (see Figure 5.3). The 2010 dramatic illegal work stoppages and strikes in southern China's manufacturing belt are the tip of an industrial-relations-sized iceberg, which are likely to be repeated in other jurisdictions in its dense industrial assembly zones. As this process unfolds, Chinese industrial relations will arguably share more in common with the European model of labor relations, where labor is recognized as a social partner on the national and provincial levels. In early 2013, it was announced that Foxconn workers are going to elect their own union representatives. The company's treatment of its own workforce has attracted intense scrutiny from Apple and Samsung. Its industrial relations system is about to change, and workers will vote to choose their union, but whether this will be the step toward an autonomous system of workplace representation remains to be seen.

STRATEGIC LONG-TERM STRUCTURAL CHANGE
AS A JOB KILLER

In the past, strongly focused Keynesian labor market strategies acted as a buffer to mediate the worst effects of the global business cycle. Now labor markets are in turmoil for a very specific reason. Labor-shedding technology leads to fewer hires in many mass production industries and large-scale resource-based sectors. This is attributable to a variety of factors, but the most important is the relentless search for "smarter" and "tougher" cost-cutting strategies at the firm and global levels, eroding the take-home pay of skilled workers and undermining labor's share of national income in many jurisdictions. In its 2012 report, the International Monetary Fund (IMF) showed that national income going to labor has plunged while the share going to the corporate sector is at a forty-five-year high. A decade ago, 64 percent of U.S. national income went to labor; today it is only 54 percent. In Europe, too, there is convergence as labor's share of the pie continues to shrink (International Monetary Fund, 2012). To make matters more difficult, collective bargaining in many jurisdictions throughout the advanced capitalist world has accepted close to zero percent increases in collective bargaining agreements in recent times. Wage and benefit cutting is widespread as transnational firms want to cut wages for full-time employees; this was the trigger to the highly publicized six-month Caterpillar strike in London, Ontario in 2012. Caterpillar, a U.S.-based multinational, demanded a 50 percent cut from its employees making complex train engines and alleged that the plant was unprofitable. After a massive public campaign, the U.S. owners closed the plant and all work was to be transferred to the U.S. operation. In many similar situations worldwide, the story is much the same. Weakness at the bargaining table has left labor in deregulated market economies highly exposed and vulnerable (Standing, 2011). There are other labor-shedding strategies that have proved to be job killers. Notably, the opening up of economies to international competition provides firms with a powerful incentive to capture economies of scale by becoming global exporters. The drive to realize highly profitable efficiency gains has shrunk payrolls and has made employers wary of more permanent new hires in many industries. In the United States alone, more than 10 million production-related jobs have been lost since 2000. Many of the old jobs are being replaced by robots or other labor saving technology. Productivity growth and job creation are moving in opposite direction. The effects of robotized production methods are being felt everywhere. While this phenomenon is not new by any means, the scale of the phenomenon is. Fewer workers are producing more goods than ever. In North American auto production (in the once Big Three), the workforce has fallen by almost 50 percent since the 1990s (Stanford, 2010). Finally the shift to a disposable workforce comprised of contractual and semi-temporary workers has become standard practice in many, if not most, of the newly emerging economies as well as in the Rust Belt industries in the global North. Global labor is more vulnerable and part time – hired by third parties to work full time in factories and many industries. It is estimated that as much as 25 percent of workers in emerging market economies have no contractual relationship with their actual employer. They are dependent on the contractor for wages, benefits, and protection. Industrial relations systems have not found a way to address this inherently explosive situation (Canada Watch, 2012).

A SYSTEMIC TURNING POINT FOR INDUSTRIAL RELATIONS SYSTEMS

It is important to know the reasons the vast army of human labor is not sharing the productivity growth that economically has transformed the global South. In these difficult circumstances, what institutions are needed to level the playing field? Secondly, it is critical to identify the institutions that provide workers the policy space for voice and workplace representation in the new global economy, three of which are the most important. The first is collective bargaining between employees and the employer, which enables workers to share in the productivity gains and bargain for a higher standard of living. The second is workplace representation to give employees the capacity to negotiate new rights against wrongful dismissal and arbitrary layoff, as well as to provide an adequate social wage as one of the goals of collective bargaining. Finally an effective system of industrial relations codifies all these employment rights with the state and the employer and optimally provides workers with a package of rights that underpin a workplace culture of industrial democracy (Murray and Yates, 2011). In the post-crisis world, a lot of stock-taking is in order as labor's standing is being redefined by innovative technologies that are often seen as job killers, as well as by new state policies aimed to reshape the labor market in competitive new directions with less protection against dismissal without cause.

Two startling interconnected pieces of evidence impact directly on the future of labor and human rights. First, in 2005, the *Economist* published what would become an iconic table showing that the BRICS had overtaken the global North's share of GDP at purchasing power parity (see Figure 5.1) The global pie suddenly had gotten bigger and incredibly – mainly because no one had foreseen it – the global South's share had grown faster than that

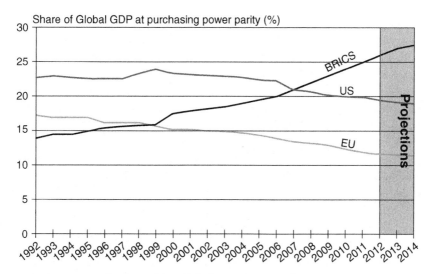

FIGURE 5.1. The Rise of the Global Rest. *Source: The Economist* (2005).

of the global North. The emerging economies not only had caught up but had overtaken the advanced capitalist ones that once held the commanding position in the global economy. This seismic shift has many implications on workplace representation as a general feature between late and emerging capitalist economies. Stiglitz (2010) and others are quite right to label this structural change as being long term, consequential, and irreversible. In a way that no economist of the right or left had predicted, India, Brazil, China, and South Africa, have not only caught up with but challenged the U.S. dominance as the epicenter of the world capitalist system. With the BRIC countries going head to head with the advanced capitalist world for dominance of global markets, the everyday practice of collective bargaining faces unprecedented competitive pressures. Further and equally important, hundreds of millions of agricultural workers remain largely outside any effective system of representational rights and are subject to widespread exploitative practices of labor contractors, particularly in India and China.

Second, in 2011, the *Financial Times* carried a small article of portentous importance, with the headline, "US hegemony of the world order had been challenged and overtaken by China." It presented new data that showed China had become the top manufacturing country in the globe, ending 110 years of U.S. dominance. Historians remind us that China used to be the world leader between 1700 and 1850, and that today we are living again through a dramatic period of unprecedented regime change. If history is any guide, China will find itself cast in a new global role as restless workers increasingly are acting outside the official state-sponsored system of industrial relations to fight for their collective bargaining rights – an intrinsically political goal. In 2010, there were more than 100,000 non-authorized work stoppages. Put differently, there were 100,000 spontaneous strikes for better wages and working conditions, the classic demand of workers left out from record-level growth. Economically they are trying to get a larger share of the national income or productivity bonus from two decades of double-digit growth. Wages have risen but not enough and for too few of the industrial workforce. We do not know how these events will play out in China, but their impact on wages and working conditions for emerging bottom-up spaces for industrial democracy is likely to be far-reaching in two aspects.

MULTILATERALISM IS AT ITS LOWEST POINT EVER

The first aspect is that the moral victory of the WTO legalists has imploded with the collapse of the Washington Consensus and the stalling of the WTO's Doha Round in 2011. Despite so much change in the international environment, it is noteworthy that the WTO has barely evolved beyond a narrow-gauge organization to promote the mercantilist interests of its members. It is now deadlocked, divided, and exhausted after more than ten years of fruitless negotiations. Without the metaphoric knife at its throat to transform its culture, the WTO will continue to be trapped by its existing architecture in the short term. The long-awaited denouement came on April 29, 2010, when Director General Pascal Lamy finally admitted that the Doha Round had failed and there were no prospects of a "grand" bargain. The WTO is out of gas and has shown no capacity to downsize its "bigger than big trade" agenda (Drache, 2011).

Multilateralism is at its weakest point in seven decades, and given the seismic shocks to the world trading system since the 2008 financial crisis, protectionism is in large measure amazingly absent (less than 1 percent of world trade), demonstrating – if any such demonstration is necessary – that the world trading order has learned the costly lessons of the 1930s, when mountain-sized tariff walls brought global trade to a standstill. In 2011, export growth is much lower than the halcyon days of Alan Greenspan's low interest rates responsible for fueling double-digit annual export growth. Even China has not escaped the chill of the 2008 global financial crisis, with growth now averaging around 8 percent annually. For the industrial powerhouses of the advanced capitalist countries such as the United States and the EU, export growth hovers around 4–5 percent annually, a marked slowdown compared to the pre-2008 period. The reality is that the global economy is stuck in a vicious cycle, according to the Bank for International Settlements (BIS 2012, quoted in

Cohen 2012). The world is no closer to finding a sustainable economic model to end the destructive interaction between the financial sector, consumers, and deleveraging. The struggle to contain spending and recoup tax revenue lost to output collapse means that so far there "is not a return to a balanced growth path."

Trade politics for the twenty-first century require a very different trading system – one capable of handling complex and challenging issues. With its narrow-cast rules, the current system has not been able to evolve into an institution of the twenty-first century with an emphasis on institution-building and the need for linkages between trade and non-trade issues. The deadlocked Doha Round raises many questions about the inability of the WTO to renew itself and move beyond the present boundaries set by laissez-faire free trade dynamics. Disappointingly it has not demonstrated any ability to correct organizational imbalances in its formalistic rules, decision-making procedures, and a bloated trade agenda. The Doha Round was to be a development round charged with responsibility to increase pro-poor policies to correct the legacy costs of the Uruguay Round. The promised but never concluded agreement was that the advanced economies had to contribute to poverty eradication and deploy trade as a critical policy tool for that broader social purpose and provide new standards to protect labor's rights and the future of work and employment in highly contrasted settings.

LABOR'S NEW CONDITIONALITY

The second aspect is that the new conditionality of labor in the global south needs to be mapped and analyzed. New forms of labor, especially contractual, part-time, rural, service, and casual, now comprise a major part of labor markets, not the once dominant blue-collar worker. Industrial workers are a rising power in China, Brazil, and India, all of whom are part of the new international division of labor. The question is: In what ways, if any, are the advanced industrial economies a model for the global south? Or should the global south be experimenting with building systems of workplace representation that are part of a larger globalization movement to protect workers' rights as found in ILO conventions, international human rights law, and in the European Court of Justice (ECJ)?

It is no longer evident for public authority how to define a high standard of workplace representation in a highly diverse world with competing centers of power. Every country needs to develop its own labor standards that reflect their values and policies within a general global governance framework. From a public law perspective, the ILO's core conventions with respect to freedom of association, the right to organize, the right to strike, and the elimination of child labor, among others, represent the core ideas and goals and objectives for a new global labor regime. Still, global governance institutions have shown their limitation to effect a consensual agreement to adopt a single global model. Faced with this impasse, the responsibility for best-practice work and employment standards in all likelihood needs to be addressed by national authorities that are best equipped to initiate national problem-solving and rebalancing the social agenda, and have the legal authority to effect strong regulatory policies to protect labor from the volatility of global financial markets.

The competitive alternative to contemporary neoliberal market driven policies are state-centric ones. For this reason, among others, countries are looking at new frames to pursue their interests. They require a whole range of institutions to protect labor, enforce contracts, deal with externalities and informational incompleteness, and establish national legitimizing institutions for social protection and insurance, redistributive policies, institutions of conflict management, and social partnerships. All of these *acquis sociaux* provide a contractual basis for different forms of labor security that define one's industrial citizenship. Guy Standing (2011) has compiled a useful list of different kinds of security for policy makers. Work security provides protection against accidents and illness at work. Job security affords the opportunity to retain an employment niche. Income security delivers an adequate stable income with public policies to reduce inequality. Representation security brings workers a collective voice in labor markets and the workplace. The interstate shifting of power from the global North to the global South highlights the absence of adequate trade and human rights linkages in emerging market economies.

Many experts such as Dani Rodrik (2011) and Robert Wade (2009) have shown in their detailed empirical studies that the open market strategy of the contemporary phase of globalization has not translated into higher employment levels, better wages, and working conditions as the theory of free trade and global integration postulates. In his earlier work, Rodrik (1997) has shown that there is most certainly a link, one that is not always positive, between trade and employment. For the effective functioning of the global economic system, the governance gap between mechanisms that favor economic globalization and those aiming to protect and improve workers' rights and living conditions domestically must be bridged, especially in the context of the current phase of the economic global crisis, with a stalled recovery and heightened market instability. But the world is no closer to finding a sustainable growth path because the major economies have been unable to come to terms with the daunting challenges facing the U.S. economy and the feeble recovery globally.

THE CONSEQUENCE OF THE INSTITUTIONAL DELINKING OF WAGES

As late as the 1980s the United States has been a relatively closed economy, enabling it to protect the good jobs in the mass production industries from overseas assembly operations. In the last two decades, however, U.S. companies have rushed to send jobs overseas and establish branch-plants throughout the global South. The hollowing-out effects of U.S. multinationals' relentless drive to cut jobs and labor costs have destabilized quite dramatically its industrial relations system, once the high standard for industrial relations practices at a time of global capitalism.

The hollowing out of the American Fordist model of industrial relations, anchored in its once-unchallengeable factory system of production, is a key development and, as such, must be given special attention (Piore and Sabel, 1984). The Fordist model of workplace production functioned as the gold standard of industrial relations practices in the postwar world for more than three decades, but the model has collapsed, pushed over the edge by the free market policies of the Reagan, Clinton, and Bush presidencies. For example, the structural delinking of the trade job growth and income linkage in North America has led to dramatic changes in the organization of the workplace. Collective bargaining in the United States now covers less than 7 percent of the workforce in the private sector and only 30 percent in the public sector. Twenty-three states have powerful employer-friendly right-to-work legislation, which further depresses wage levels. We have seen the flattening of the wage pyramid with an explosion in the number of minimum-wage jobs at $7.25 per-hour, the federal minimum wage in 2011. Post-recession minimum-wage jobs accounted for 58 percent of new jobs, according to the National Employment Law Project. Wage settlements hover around 1 percent or less, and 99 percent of all contracts are settled without a strike. Many contracts include wage cuts for new hires and a reduction of existing pension and health benefits.

NAFTA promised competitive industries, more employment, better-paying jobs, and a higher standard of living for U.S. workers (Drache, 2011). These promises were only promises and when American interest rates were under three percent. The boom years saw the hollowing out of U.S. industry as hundreds of thousands of once thought to be secure industrial jobs in the U.S. heartland went to Mexico, China, and other third-world assembly operations. It is estimated that more than 10 million better-paying industrial jobs have been lost by the U.S. economy in the last fifteen years (Blinder 2010). Presently, U.S. industrial jobs as a percentage of all employment account for about 7 percent of the workforce from its peak of more than 20 percent in the 1970s.

Job creation is weak, with only 150,000 monthly jobs created on average in
2012. According to the International Monetary Fund (2011), the U.S. economy
needs to add about 300,000 jobs monthly to bring unemployment down to
pre-recession levels. With its modest growth, the US economy is not out of
the employment crisis zone. Overall, the polarization of incomes has reached
levels not seen since the 1920s, a decade of unparalleled inequality. Stiglitz
(2011) has summarized the trend well: "In the US one percent of the people
take nearly one-quarter of the wealth of the nation's incomes every year. In
terms of wealth they control 40 percent. Twenty five years ago, the figures
were 12 percent and 33 percent." For Canada, the same skewing of income is
visible and pronounced. Armine Yalnizyan (2010) writes:

> The lesson of the decade prior to the global economic crisis – the *richest
> one per cent took one third of the income gains* from economic growth in that
> time. They took eight per cent in the 1960s, a comparable period of sustained
> and robust growth. They'll take it in wages, they'll take it in dividends, they'll
> take it in stock options. But they'll take most it. (Emphasis on the original.)

Global neoliberalism has triggered other changes as well, most notably
the replacement of the secure jobs of the salariat with the part-time, highly
insecure work of the precariat. The latter has emerged in the labor market as
a distinctive socioeconomic group most of whom do not have access to social
income like earlier generations of blue collar workers did.

BREACHING THE POSTWAR ACCORD: LINKING WAGES AND PRODUCTIVITY GROWTH

According to many experts, the growth of income inequality has several contributing factors. At its core lies a single relationship that, possibly more than
any other, explains the collapse of income redistribution through the dominant
postwar industrial relations model. In the postwar world, the universalization of
the U.S.-styled mass consumption model represented a distinct and innovative
feature that created an upward pressure on wages and profits. In economic jar-
gon, wages were sticky downward because the U.S. standard of living was tied
to the collective bargaining cycle in core industries anchored in U.S. prosperity. The model was founded on the principal idea that in the standard-setting
mass production industries wages were tied to a 3 percent productivity increase
to base plus a cost-of-living adjustment. It also provided pension, health care,
and other long-term benefits. In 1948, Charlie Wilson, then-president of GM,
accepted the automatic 3 percent productivity increase to the base and higher

wages as the model of collective bargaining with the then – president of the United Auto Workers union, Walter Reuther. This pact became the standard practice not only for this historic agreement; it also established a pattern for all American mass production industrial sectors including steel, tire manufacturing, meat-packing, and mining, among others. It was not a perfect system but it was as close to a national standard for labor as it was going to get, with the idea of industrial citizenship at its core (Drache and Glasbeek, 2008).

In essence, the postwar compromise between organized labor and corporate giants like GM and US Steel with automatic wage increases to the base rate in the United States. Regularized collective bargaining in the mass production industries with automatic annual wage increases lifted blue collar America into middle class status. The newly minted affluent blue-collar male worker gave American families access to a home, mass consumer goods, education for their kids, and privately funded pensions on retirement (Piore and Sabel 1984).

What collective bargaining achieved for the first time in the history of late industrial capitalism was to link collective bargaining to mass consumption. Consumption and wages aligned through the collective bargaining cycle transformed the U.S. postwar order into a modern economy founded on the consumer appetite for mass consumption and financed by the expansion of credit provided by banks through credit cards and personal loans. Keynes and others would say that managing the demand side was an essential part of a larger macro strategy to stabilize the business cycle. For workers, the tangible benefit was dramatically evident: as Amstrong et al. (1984) have shown in their empirical work, in each decade between the 1950s and 1970s, blue-collar incomes in the United States and Western Europe doubled – an amazing redistribution of income unlike anything the world had seen up to that point. Class divides were bridged by a growing appetite for a middle-class life, but social exclusion and race discrimination were not eliminated. Blue-collar America was transformed and integrated into the mainstream. In terms of social opportunity, the playing field was leveled to a degree no one could have predicted, For Krugman and other empirical economists, the great uncoupling of wages from productivity growth since the end of the golden era of capitalism in the 1980s is a primary reason why the share of wealth going to the top 3 percent of all income earners is unparalleled. By 2011, the industrial standard across a majority of US industries is now the union-free workplace where workers are forced, once again as they were in the 1930s, to negotiate their wage and working conditions with their individual employer on an individual basis. It can be said without exaggeration that it is a wage relationship closely mirroring a market model of competitive capitalism of wage cuts in tough times and upward-sticky wages in good times. The critical difference is that particularly in contemporary American industrial relations norms, there is no productivity bonus added to base wage rates, and so without the upward pressure on wages, Krugman and other experts' fundamental point is right. The result is spiraling income inequality and very high debt levels for families faced with shrinking disposable incomes. It is this dwindling redistributive policy space that is now a hallmark of U.S. capitalism (Stiglitz, 2011).

It would be wrong to argue that convergence to the American industrial relations model is either automatic or has reached the same degree of magnitude in other jurisdictions. Still, the shrinking of the manual core of the old working class and the dismantling of collective bargaining system represent an easily observable deep structural change throughout the advanced capitalist world. Canada's bottom-up industrial relations policy space displays a certain resiliency because it is a strongly regionalized system with provincially based labor movements capable of striking deals with provincial premiers. These workers are also voters, and it is this kind of leverage that has forced provincial governments to calculate the costs of attacking their political vote banks. For example, compared to U.S. workers, Canadian workers are closer to Europe's social market than they are to U.S. laissez-faire capitalism. Seventeen percent of Canadian private-sector workers are unionized and the figure for public-sector workers is close to 80 percent. Wage settlements are about twice as high as those in the United States, averaging 1.8 percent in a period with inflation running below 3 percent (Jackson, 2011).

DIVERGENCE IN NORTH AMERICAN LABOR MARKETS DESPITE THE RHETORIC OF INTEGRATION

It is worth comparing briefly the U.S. system with its Canadian brethren. Superficially at least, Canada has a model of industrial relations practices similar to that of the United States. In fact, however, despite the enormous economic pressures for convergence, the Canadian system of collective bargaining practices has not buckled and remains stubbornly and distinctly divergent from its U.S. counterpart. Nonetheless, it is shrinking, and the hollowing out of Canadian industry is well advanced (see Figure 5.2). Theoretically it makes for a compelling case that globalization of markets is forced to adapt to local conditions with strong distinctive institutional practices and political values. Canada is a powerful case study of a system of collective bargaining that has evolved to the point where it now has both institutional features and practices sharply divergent from that of the United States. The policy space

FIGURE 5.2. Manufacturing Share of Jobs in Canada, 1976–2010 (%). *Source:* Daniel Drache (2012).

remains a hybrid of institutional guarantees and a union movement that has consolidated itself through mergers into larger bargaining units.

Most important is that collective bargaining remains embedded regionally in Quebec and British Columbia and in Canada's major urban areas. Organized labor has leverage with these governments and is able to mobilize its militant base at critical times. Neither governments nor employers have been able to dismantle Canada's system of workplace representation, despite a massive effort to import the U.S. union-free workplace into Canada. On paper Canada appears to have a fragmented structure, with not much possibility for solidaristic industry-wide collective bargaining. This perception hides much of the reality of the situation.

The fact that the Canadian system has so many decentralized features has worked to keep it strong regionally with a very small national footprint. Importantly, its strong survival instinct is owing to a younger generation of trade union leadership at the head of some of Canada's largest public and private unions. All these factors have allowed Canada's collective bargaining system to mature and evolve in a very hostile bargaining environment. On balance, Canada's labor movement has slowed its decline and defended its policy space from powerful domestic and continental interests bent on shrinking it further.[1]

Still, in critical ways, Canada's bottom-up space for industrial democracy is under tremendous pressure for a makeover.

CHINA'S INDUSTRIAL RELATIONS SYSTEM: BEGINNINGS OF A GREAT CONVERGENCE?

What can China learn from the North American system of workplace representation as it enters a period where its trade unions are neither representative nor autonomous according to commonly recognized international standards? With its highly legalistic features and the many restrictions regulating the right to strike and a factory-by-factory model, collective bargaining of the North American variety is not easily exportable. Western Europe's collective bargaining system premised on autonomous rights for citizens also faces large obstacles. As others in this volume demonstrate, China has its own three-legged system of collective bargaining, with state-run enterprise unions and a permanent presence of the Communist Party and local officials at the enterprise and industry-wide levels. The authoritarian command-and-control culture of Chinese institutions places visible structural limits on the possibility of emergence of a Canadian-style system of grievance-based workplace representation of industrial democracy.

Under the existing Chinese collective bargaining regime at the plant level, collective bargaining is organized to bypass the workers themselves. It gives them no right to independent representation (see Figure 3.3). Frequently collective bargaining is industry-wide, as seen in the new labor contract in Hubei province, which gives almost 500,000 catering services employees a 47 percent wage hike over the duration of the agreement. Even with Beijing pushing through "safe" process-driven reforms, there appears little chance for a bottom-up employer/employee-driven model of collective bargaining in the immediate future. Foxconn, maker of the iPad and other Apple products, unveiled a reform to permit workers to elect by secret ballot their union representatives, but the role of the Communist Party is much in evidence as it will have a major say in approving who gets on the ballot. The Party's pragmatism is evident. Faced with riots, factory occupations, and suicides, its reforms reflect its priority to ensure social stability.

Despite industrial relations being under tight centralized control, the collective bargaining's outlook for the future is not static. Wages are set to rise and take a larger share of the huge productivity growth of the past decade. In this volume, Chang-Hee Lee (Chapter 16) shows empirically that at the national level – a very broad measure including the poorest regions of the country – the

The Hollowing Out of the American Model	The "Glacier-Like" Filling in of China's Industrial Relations Practices
Factory-by-factory opt-in system; twenty-three states have right-to-work laws – almost union free but with silos of unionized workers in auto and other industries.	Industry-wide enterprise unions covering millions of production workers.
Social wages such as pensions and health care are shrinking.	Social wages such as food, accommodation, and clothing are provided by employer.
Ninety-five percent of contracts signed without a strike. Strike conditions for majority of workers are rare.	Unauthorized work stoppages with negotiations resulting in 43% rise in wages in affected industries. Right to strike tightly controlled by the state and not guaranteed.
Wages flat or negative uncoupled from productivity.	Annual increase below productivity growth.
Shrinking pension, medical, and other benefits.	A growing social wage still in an embryonic state.
Radical downsizing of production workers employed in mass production industries.	Insatiable demand for new hires, though highly sensitive to the business and export cycles.
Two-tier wage scale: new hires are paid 20–40% lower wages than the existing workforce's average.	Wage ladders and increased recognition of seniority and skill but also reliance on labor contractors.
Collective bargaining lacks critical mass – only 8% of private-sector workers are unionized.	Rudimentary kinds of workplace representation specific to regions and industries, but mass production workers are excluded from independent bargaining and belong to enterprise unions.
Only 30% of public-sector workers unionized, and numbers are expected to diminish after Wisconsin dismantled its public-sector benefits.	Public-sector workers remain covered by an extensive system of welfare benefits and rights, which are likely to increase.
Heavy reliance on contractual, part-time, third-party labor.	Unlimited labor supply but rising labor costs means that the country can no longer rely on a reservoir of cheap labor as its engine of growth.
Minimum training – reliance on more skilled immigrants.	As-needed on-the-job training with a minimum career ladder.
Weakening of minimum wage and discharge rights (without cause) in union-free workplaces.	Industry-wide workplace standards fixed by national/local government officials. Discharge rights and due process are rudimentary in practice.

FIGURE 5.3. China–US Industrial Relations Systems Contrasted: Beginnings of a Great Convergence?

share of national income going to labor has actually shrunk in the last decade, falling from 52 percent in 1999 to 40 percent in 2007.

ESCAPING THE LOW-WAGE STRATEGY: WILL CHINA ADOPT A MEDIUM-HIGH WAGE GOAL?

By contrast, what is also true is that wage negotiations for industrial workers inside the golden handcuffs have doubled the average worker's income in the past fifteen years or so. The idea that China will continue to be a low-wage mass producer of goods is a misconception. For China's elites, these rising wage costs challenge China's ability to use more technology, especially in electronics industries, to be cost effective. According to a study by Germany's Centre for Economics Studies (IFO) economics institute, between 2008 and 2010, the average year-on-year rise in labor costs in China's engineering sector was 11.6 percent, compared to a comparable rise of 1.9 percent in the EU and a decline over the same period of 8.5 percent a year in the United States and of 3 percent in Japan (Marsh, 2012). A decade ago, China's low-wage strategy gave it its competitive edge. The shift to a consumption-based, demand-driven economy has yet to occur, but China wants more industrial champions capable of producing sophisticated products for its booming domestic market. At first glance, this kind of mutation is confusing. After all, China is still a low-cost producer keen to fuel corporate profits by developing new technologies that will require better trained and skilled workers with pay and benefits to match. China is gearing up to re-engineer its industrial footprint and its investment in innovative technology and the record number of filing of new patent applications has surprised many seasoned China experts. (See Figure 5.4.) This is evidence that China is moving more rapidly toward higher-end goods, prodded by increased wage costs. If this is the case, experts predict that China will move away from "building up cheap production bases for exports" and prepare to move up the value-added chain by investing in innovative technologies (Marsh, 2012). As a possible harbinger of things to come, Foxconn, China's largest manufacturer of electronic products, has placed an order for 3 million labor saving production line industrial robots for 2015.

It is not surprising to learn that China's manufacturing capability, measured by the quality of local suppliers and design expertise, is about 75 percent of the level of Germany, whereas five years ago it was only 50 percent. (See Figure 5.5.) Chinese factory labor is still 80–90 percent cheaper than in many Western countries (Marsh, 2012). China has to acquire a factory system different from the one based on a crude model of mass production rooted in the nineteenth-century mind-set of hundreds of millions of workers laboring in the "satanic

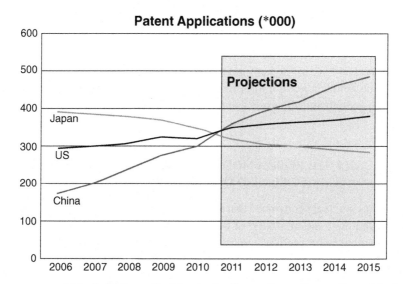

FIGURE 5.4. China's Sprint to Be First in the Patent Race. *Source:* Peter Marsh, *Financial Times* (2012).

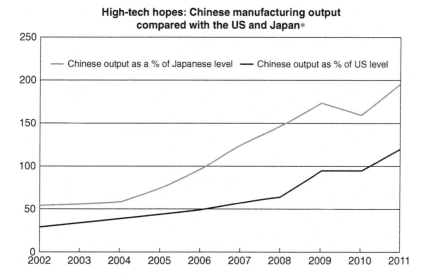

* Gross value measured in dollars

FIGURE 5.5. Tough Competition: China's Targeting the Productivity Gap. *Source:* Peter Marsh, *Financial Times* (2012).

mills" of capitalism. These are Blake's apt words, which he once employed to describe England's primitive industrial capitalism, but they are no less applicable to China's factory system. The question is what will happen to China's command-and-control system of industrial relations that stands in the way of China being "a normal industrial country with an autonomous industrial relations system and alongside it authentic workplace representation" (Marsh, 2012).

WILL THERE BE A MODERN DEMOCRATIC CHINESE MODEL OF INDUSTRIAL RELATIONS?

Chinese experts are convinced that as China's manufacturing capability grows, it will require a different kind of workforce. The need for stronger work and employment rights are likely to trend up rather than down. We can see that non-authorized work stoppages have a momentum of their own, and there is a propensity for workers to take initiatives in highly authoritarian settings. Similar kinds of strikes shook Egypt's cotton industry periodically in the 1950s, 1960s, 1970s, and 1990s, which had a profound impact on working-class collectivism even when crushed by Nasser and later by the army. The parallel is not exact, however; labor collectivism and work stoppages in authoritarian regimes follow a well-established pattern of episodic actions of worker defiance and insurgency movements directed against an authoritarian "law and order" regime run by state police and employing fierce repression. Inevitably there is a harsh crackdown and order often brutally restored.

One example among many spontaneous demonstrations occurred in July 2012. Chinese workers and middle-class activists took to the streets in Shifang, an ancient city in Sichuan, to protest the building of a factory project to make environmentally toxic copper and molybdenum products. Faced with bloodied protesters and police firing tear gas, the municipal authorities suspended construction (Bradsher, 2012). The construction may indeed recommence in the future. Pushback in this case is local and organized by the country's environmental movement. The Shifang protests are not an isolated event, but how and when something amounting to a reform of industrial relations system will occur is impossible to predict. Still, the proliferation of bottom-up collective spaces like this one is on the upswing despite police repression.

There is also a larger, macroeconomic point to this. Chinese workers are at the margins in terms of per capita income and a better standard of living with a modern set of human rights including speech, association, and personal freedom. From a macro perspective, China's economic ascendancy has left behind hundreds of millions of its own citizens. Wages are sticky downward, and the Chinese state's low-wage strategy has disenfranchised its laboring masses. Robert Boyer, one of the founders of the French Regulation School, in an influential and seminal study of wage movements for industrial workers in the nineteenth and twentieth centuries showed that productivity growth in Europe and the United States grew by leaps and bounds when new labor-saving technologies revolutionized production methods, but at the same time wages plummeted. Underconsumption and overproduction was the observable outcome (Boyer, 1990).

Boyer's explanation is that the introduction of scientific management in the workplace, combined with the Pareto efficiency gains of industrial technology to revolutionize production methods, pushed productivity growth to record heights. On the ground, something very different was happening. Wages in the mass production industries of steel, auto, and textiles were cut and working conditions worsened. Class warfare moved from the margins to the mainstream throughout the industrial world. The consequence was that a simple strike for wages and union recognition turned into a bloody encounter between the state and its citizens. For the first forty years of the twentieth century, there was no resolution of this fundamental problem for a bitter and angry workforce without the right of assembly and the right to choose a bona fide union. But the extension of industrial democracy into the workplace arrived in 1945, as discussed previously; wages in leading sectors became aligned with rapid productivity growth, which also led to the regularization of collective bargaining as industrial relations became institutionalized. We have already mentioned that this tumultuous and singular transformative change sustained a culture of mass consumption, home ownership, and access to a university education for the children of Marx's "industrial proletariat" on both sides of the Atlantic.

Is there a lesson to be learned for China, with its own industrial revolution in full ascendancy? China has its own trajectory but will have to learn the painful lesson that rising inequality is unsustainable. Shifting to a reliance on domestic demand is going to be an immense challenge for China that is short on democratic values and participation. It would be an error to underestimate the processes that will lead to more innovative kinds of breakthroughs and reforms. Its industrial relations system is far from broken but is in a turbulent period of transition, propelled by the sheer numbers of unauthorized stikes, work stoppages, and rural activism against land theft and corrupt party officials. The question is: Can the Chinese state implement reforms fast enough to ensure stability and build a democratic society? Will these new bottom-up spaces consolidate into change that is more formidable and long term, and transform China's industrial relations practices beyond where they are now?

A FINAL WORD: COLLECTIVE BARGAINING DYNAMICS
IN A WEB 2.0 AGE

With fewer workers bargaining collectively worldwide, industrial relations systems have to find new ways to operate in a Web 2.0 global age. The hollowing out of the U.S. industrial relations system marks the great reversal of the age for work and employment, and the ramifications are still being felt. The 2012 pattern-setting agreement between U.S. Caterpillar and its workers has pushed U.S. collective bargaining into a new, fragile, and more constricted policy space. Embedding collective bargaining rights in individual workers constitutes a fundamental change where the rights of the individual have been elevated above the effective workplace representation of the trade union. In this environment the deregulation of labor law has weakened and downgraded the role of unions (McCallum, 2011). The individual choice of workers becomes subordinated to the collective needs of the multinational.

We have argued that a very different phenomenon is observable in China, and it remains to be seen whether Chinese practices "kick away" the ladder of the state-run system. Canada occupies the unsteady middle ground, divergent from the U.S. model because of strong domestic institutions and values of equity and fairness. It remains to be seen if the culture of adaptation pushes Canada's industrial relations practices to the lower U.S. standard. Across the world, social rights have plateaued and bottom-up spaces for work and employment are under intense pressure to turn inward.

In a more fundamental sense, the interdependency of global markets offers an important lesson. The information age continues to surprise, disappoint, and challenge our ways of theoretically mapping and tracking its diverse social impacts on workplace representation and collective bargaining rights. Handheld cell phones provide hundreds of millions of workers a way to communicate cheaply and effectively in the emerging market economies where trade unions have not gained the legitimacy and muscle needed to be effective social actors. With more than 1.5 billion handheld phones in the hands of the poor and the powerless have tipped the scales in favor of the disenfranchised taking steps, both big and small, toward changes. To be informed means that hundreds of millions can become social actors. It is not only a theoretical possibility but an on-the-ground phenomenon from the factories in southern China to the favelas in Sao Paulo. Mobile communications afford those in every kind of workplace and agrarian setting to share information and mobilize for a better life. Self-organizing locally and transnationally has been a primary factor in the growth of new rank-and-file movements outside the formal institutions of industrial relations. So far their impact in the policy sense has been mixed, but pessimists would be wrong to write them off as complete failures.

Still, social income and industrial citizenship remain the essential components of building a modern, citizen identity. Up until now, rapid development of emergent market economies has not required them to answer what lessons are to be taken away from the financial crisis. The lack of engagement addressing long-term structural change is disquieting, and the obvious question is: What kinds of bottom-up spaces are required to tame globalization?

REFERENCES

Armstrong, Philip and Glyn, Andrew. (1984). *Capitalism since 1945*. Oxford, Blackwell.

Arthurs, Harry W. (1971). "Collective Bargaining by Public Employees in Canada: Five Models." Ann Arbor, Michigan, Institute of Labor and Industrial Relations at The University of Michigan, 166 pp.

Arthurs, Harry W. (2007). "Labour and the 'Real' Constitution," *Les Cahiers de droit* 48, 43–64.

Barber Lionel. (2011). "The End of U.S. Hegemony: Legacy of 9/11," *Financial Times*, September 5.

Blinder, Alan S. (2006). "Offshoring: The Next Industrial Revolution," *Foreign Affairs*, March/April.

Boyer, Robert. (1990). *The Regulation School: A Critical Introduction*. New York. Columbia University Press.

Boyer, Robert. (1996). "State and Market: A New Engagement for the Twenty-First Century?" In *States vs. Markets, The Limits of Globalization*, Eds. R. Boyer and D. Drache. London: Routledge.

Bradsher, Keith. (2012). "Chinese City Suspends Factory Construction Following Protests," *New York Times*, July 3.

Canada Watch. (2012). "India the Most Fragile of Democracies." Robarts Centre For Canadian Studies. Winter. http://www.yorku.ca/drache/Canada%20Watch/canada-watch/pdf/CW_Fall2011.pdf, September 10.

Chomsky, Noam. (2012). "Plutonomy and the Precariat," *The Huffington Post*, May 8.

Cohen, Norma. (2012). "World Economy Caught in a Vicious Cycle," *Financial Times*, June 24.

Drache, Daniel. (1999). "Globalization: Is There Anything to Fear?" Coventry, University of Warwick, Centre for the Study of Globalisation and Regionalisation. Available at: http://wrap.warwick.ac.uk/2102/1/WRAP_Drache_wp2399.pdf September 10.

Drache, Daniel. (2005). *Bon Anniversaire NAFTA: The Elusive and Asymmetrical Benefits of a Decade of North American Integration*. Toronto: York University Press.

Drache, Daniel. (2010). "The Structural Imbalances of the WTO Reconsidered: A critical Reading of the Sutherland and Warwick Commissions," available at http://papers.ssrn.com/sol3/papers.cfm?abstract_id=1858467, September 10 2013.

Drache, Daniel. (2011). "Reform at the Top: What's Next for the WTO? A Second Life? A Socio-Political Analysis," *Oñati International Institute for the Sociology of Law* vol. 1:4.

Drache, Daniel and Glasbeek, Harry. (1992). *The Changing Workplace: Reshaping Canada's Industrial Relations System*. Toronto: Lorimer.

Fudge, Judy. (2009). "The New Workplace: Surveying the Landscape," *The Manitoba Law Journal* 33, 139–141.

Greenhouse, Steven. (2012). "Caterpillar Workers Ratify Deal They Dislike," *New York Ttimes*, August 18.

Hille. Kathrin and Rahul Jacob. (2013). "Foxconn Workers in Landmark China Vote," *Financial Times*, February 4.

International Labor Organization (ILO) (2010). World of Work Report. Geneva:ILO. http://www.ilo.org/global/about-the-ilo/newsroom/news/WCMS_145182/lang-nl/index.htm, September 10.

International Institute for Labour Studies. (2011). "World of Work Report 2011: Making Markets Work for Jobs." Geneva: ILO.

International Monetary Fund. (2012). "Annual Report 2011: Pursuing Equitable and Balanced Growth." Washington, DC: IMF Publications.

Marsh, Peter. (2012). "Industry: In Search of Inspiration," *Financial Times*, June 11.

McCallum, Ron. (2011). "American and Australian Labor Law and Differing Approaches to Employee Choice," *ABA Journal of Labor & Employment Law* 26 (2), 181–200.

Murray, G. and Yates, C. (2010). *The Future of Collective Representation: Concepts for Union Renewal*. Oxford: Oxford University Press.

Organization for Economic Cooperation and Development. (2011). *Employment Outlook*. Paris: OECD Publications.

Piore, Michael and Sabel, Charles. (1984). *The Second Industrial Divide: Possibilities for Prosperity*. New York: Basic Books.

Reich, Robert. (2012). "A Diabolical Mix of Wages and European Austerity," *Financial Times*, May 30.

Rodrik, Dani. (1997). *Has Globalization Gone Too Far?* Washington, DC: Institute for International Economics.

Rodrik, Dani. (2003). *In Search of Prosperity: Analytic Narratives on Economic Growth*. Princeton: Princeton University Press.

Rodrik, Dani. (2011). *The Globalization Paradox*. New York: Norton & Company.

Standing, Guy. (2011). *The Precariat: The New and Dangerous Class*. London: Bloomsbury.

Stanford, Jim. (2010). "NAFTA's Chapter 11: The Latest Giveaway." *Real World Economics Review* Blog June 10, http://rwer.wordpress.com/author/jimdownunder/, September 10, 2013.

Stiglitz, Joseph. (2010). "Time for a Visible Hand: Lessons from the 2008 World Financial Crisis." Jones, S. G., Ocampo, J. A., and Stiglitz, J. E. (Eds.), *Time for a Visible Hand: Lessons from the 2008 World Financial Crisis (The Initiative for Policy Dialogue)*. Oxford: Oxford University Press, pp. 19–49.

Stiglitz, Joseph E. (2011). "Of the 1%, by the 1%, for the 1%," *Vanity Fair*. May.

Tucker, Eric and Fudge, Judy. (2010). "The Freedom to Strike in Canada: A Brief Legal History," *Canadian Labour and Employment Law Journal* 15(2), 333–353.

Wade, Robert (2009) "From global imbalances to global reorganizations", *Cambridge J. Economics* 33(4), 539–562.

Yalynizan, Armine. (2010). "The Rise of Canada's Richest 1 Percent." http://www.policyalternatives.ca/publications/reports/rise-canadas-richest-1.

6

Global Tobacco Control Law and Trade Liberalization: New Policy Spaces?

Lesley A. Jacobs

INTRODUCTION: POLICY SPACE AND THE DYNAMIC OF INTERNATIONAL LAW

Policy space as an arena where national governments have the freedom and capacity to design and implement public policies of their own choosing is ordinarily juxtaposed to the expanding circle of international trade and human rights law (Gallagher, 2005; Koivusalo et al., 2010). Over the past twenty years, the function of newly developed international law instruments has predominantly been understood to shrink national policy spaces or limit greatly the flexibility of governments to exercise their options within those spaces. This view has had particular currency in the field of international economic regulation. Indeed, this view ironically has been shared by both proponents and critics of greater international economic regulation through organizations like the World Trade Organization. The diverse policy responses by national governments to the 2008 global economic crisis show, however, that there has been a failure to appreciate that the dynamic relation between international law and national policy spaces is much more complex than a simple inverse one where the expansion of international law and regulations diminishes national policy spaces.

This chapter argues that in some instances new international law and regulations can enrich national policy space rather than diminish it. The policy arena for this argument is the integration of tobacco control into the global health and human rights agenda. The specific focus is on the Framework Convention on Tobacco Control (FCTC), an international law enacted by the World Health Organization (WHO), which came into effect in 2005. The purposes of the FCTC include the regulation of trade liberalization in tobacco products. The regulations are grounded on a right of all persons to the highest standard of health. I advance in this chapter two central observations. The first observation is that the FCTC has quickly and effectively placed tobacco control on the global health agenda by acting as a counterbalance to the international trend toward greater trade liberalization in the tobacco industry. The second observation is that although the FCTC sets global norms and standards for domestic tobacco control laws and policies, in practice it has had the effect of prioritizing tobacco control as a public health issue in developing countries while allowing individual countries immense flexibility in their policy decisions about how to implement tobacco control. Examples from China and India are used to illustrate this second observation.

ENHANCING POLICY SPACE: SOME GROUNDS FOR OPTIMISM

These two observations suggest that an international law like the FCTC can indeed function to enrich national policy spaces. Why has the FCTC had this enriching effect when other new international laws have had the effect of diminishing national policy space? I argue here that the explanation lies in the fact that the FCTC is grounded on an international human rights claim. The finding that international law in the context of health issues can allow immense flexibility for policy making by national governments is not unique to tobacco control. It has been noted, for example, that India has found great flexibility in its regulation of the pharmaceutical industry despite the alleged harmonizing implications of the Trade-Related Aspects of Intellectual Property (TRIPS) Agreement (Kapczynski, 2009). But there does not exist at present a persuasive theory that predicts when international law instruments will function to enrich national policy spaces.

The argument advanced here distinguishes between two ways – one substantive, the other procedural – in which the FCTC, because it is grounded in international human rights, enriches national policy spaces. One way it does so is substantive in nature. I illustrate this by showing how the FCTC has contributed effectively concerns about gender inequalities and tobacco control into domestic policy spaces. The other way in which the FCTC has enriched national policy space is by facilitating domestic efforts to ensure that tobacco control policy be taken seriously as a priority in the context of competing policy claims that all national governments face. This enrichment also flows from the FCTC's grounding on the human right to health. International law recognizes that international human rights such as the right to the highest attainable standard of health are designed in part to be progressively realized at the national level, and that this feature of the right to health requires flexible national policy space for governments to implement diverse and context-specific policies that enable the progressive realization of that right (Jacobs, 2012). China and India are taking different paths toward implementing tobacco control policy within the enriched national policy space created through the FCTC, but both paths involve obstacles that stem from competing policy claims from other areas of the government's agenda. The international human rights commitments that ground the FCTC have in both countries enabled unique efforts to overcome these obstacles.

TRADE LIBERALIZATION AND THE TOBACCO INDUSTRY

Tobacco use is globally the single biggest cause of chronic disease, in particular cancer, stroke, and heart diseases. Worldwide, tobacco use causes more than 5 million deaths annually and those numbers are expected to rise to 8 million in the next fifteen years (CDC, 2012). Although historically many countries had their own domestic cigarette companies, over the past three decades the tobacco industry has become increasingly concentrated in the hands of six transnational companies. Four of these companies – Philip Morris International, British American Tobacco, Imperial Tobacco, and Indian Tobacco Company – are privately owned and publicly traded. One company – Japan Tobacco – is 50 percent owned by the Japanese government. The remaining one – China National Tobacco – is owned entirely by the Chinese government. The concentration of the tobacco industry in these six companies makes clear why it now makes sense to characterize the market for cigarettes as a global one.

Tobacco usage is not, however, uniform across nations. In advanced industrial societies, cigarette use has been on a steady decline. In Canada, for example, tobacco use among adults has declined from 25 percent of the population in 1999 to 17 percent of the population in 2010 (Health Canada, 2010). Similarly, in the United States, smoking declined from 24.1 percent of the population in 1998 to 20.6 percent in 2008 (CDC, 2012). This contrasts the smoking trends in developing countries, which saw a dramatic increase in smokers from 1971 until 2001, followed by a levelling off. There are at present about 1.2 billion smokers globally, of which approximately 800 million live in developing countries. Table 6.1 represents the estimated number of smokers worldwide and their distribution.

Global cigarette production has continued to grow each year. Over the past decade, the increase has been 16.5 percent, which is on average 800 billion more cigarettes per year (The Tobacco Atlas, 2012). China and India not only are the most populated countries in the world; they are also now the two largest producers of tobacco products. India is the third-largest consumer of tobacco

Lesley A. Jacobs

TABLE 6.1. *Smoking prevalence in the developed and developing world*

| Countries | Smokers | | | Smoking Prevalence | |
	Males	Females	Total	Males	Females
Developed	275 million	150 million	425 million	35%	22%
Developing	700 million	100 million	800 million	50%	9%
World	975 million	250 million	1,125 million	47%	12%

Source: ASH (2007).

products after China and the United States (Reddy and Gupta, 2004). In other words, the expanding global market has been in developing countries and this is where the money is (http://www.articlesbase.com/addictions-articles/global-smoking-trends-where-tobacco-companies-make-money-these-days-354416.html). Access to these markets through trade liberalization is fundamental for transnational cigarette companies.

GLOBAL TOBACCO CONTROL THROUGH INTERNATIONAL TREATY LAW

In the mid-1990s, the WHO began to expand its traditional focus on infectious diseases to include chronic diseases. It is in this context that the WHO concentrated much of its efforts on tobacco control. In 1998, the new Director-General of the WHO Gro Harlem Brundtland explained both why tobacco control has urgency and why a transnational organization like the WHO should be in a leadership role:

> Tobacco-related diseases are spreading like an epidemic and are likely to be killing 10 million people a year around 2020. Into the next century, tobacco will climb the ladder to be the leading cause of disease and premature death worldwide.... We have the evidence. We know what works. Tightening legislation against advertising, increasing tobacco taxes and controlling the marketing of cigarettes will make a difference for the health of future generations worldwide.... This is not a challenge confined to independent states. It is a global challenge. (Brundtland, 1999)

Brundtland proposed that the WHO meet the global challenge of tobacco control in a new and innovative way. The World Health Assembly, the legislative assembly of the WHO, has had the power to create international treaty law since its inception in 1946, but had for fifty years never exercised that power. This changed when the WHO decided that an effective way to meet the global challenge of tobacco control is through the development of international law.

In 2004, the WHO enacted the FCTC and it entered force on February 27, 2005. The WHO FCTC creates an obligation for Parties to "reduce continually and substantially the prevalence of tobacco use and exposure to tobacco smoke" by adopting and implementing "effective legislative, executive, administrative and/or other measures" (WHO, 2003). There are now 176 countries that are parties to the convention, and 10 more such as the United States have signed the convention but not yet ratified it. This makes the FCTC one of the most successful international treaties in history. Several countries in the Asia-Pacific region, most notably Japan, China, and India, have been early strong supporters of the FCTC.

From a human rights perspective, the FCTC is significant because the preamble states clearly that the foundation for the legislation are the right to health, citing both the WHO Preamble and the ISEREC statement of the right to highest attainable standard of health provision. Tobacco control is presented, in other words, as a human rights issue (Crow, 2004; Dresler and Marks, 2006). As the Forward states, "The FCTC is an evidence-based treaty that reaffirms the right of all people to the highest standard of health" (WHO, 2003, p. iv).

What is the relevant evidence when it comes to global tobacco control? From the perspective of the WHO, cigarette companies have thrived in the neoliberal era of trade liberalization and the global movement of capital and goods. The treaty states:

> The FCTC was developed in response to the globalization of the tobacco epidemic. The spread of the tobacco epidemic is facilitated through a variety of complex factors with cross-border effects, including trade liberalization and direct foreign investment. Other factors such as global marketing, transnational tobacco advertising, promotion and sponsorship, and the international movement of contraband and counterfeit cigarettes have also contributed to the explosive increase in tobacco use. (WHO, 2003, p. v)

The significance of a rights-based approach to the global health epidemic created by the tobacco industry is that its available toolkit includes international treaty law, which is seen by the WHO as an instrument to regulate trade liberalization and foreign investment.

The FCTC is designed to reflect precisely the themes Director General Brundtland identified in 1998. It includes provisions on tobacco advertising, health warnings on cigarette packages, higher taxation, prohibitions against sales to minors, regulations on illicit trade, as well as some commitments to supporting smoke cessation. What these provisions reflect is the viewpoint that global tobacco control should include a focus on international trade liberalization and that the regulation of this trade is grounded in a human rights concern.

It is important from an international law perspective that the FCTC is only a framework convention, not a fully entrenched international convention – this means that it is a work in progress, with what are being called Protocols in particular aspects of the convention. Since 2005, the Secretariat of the FCTC has slowly been filling out the substantial content of the convention and the obligations of states that have ratified it. In practice, much of this work has been carried out with support from the Framework Convention Alliance on Tobacco Control (FCA), the major international nongovernmental organization working on the development and implementation of the WHO FCTC. Indeed, the head of Japan's leading tobacco control organization once commented to me that it is the FCA, not the FCTC per se, that has had a dramatic impact on the evolution of tobacco control in Japan and, he suspects, elsewhere in Asia since 2005.

GLOBAL TOBACCO CONTROL POLICY AND HUMAN RIGHTS

Why does it matter that the FCTC is grounded in the human right to the highest attainable standard of health? Global health policy has in recent years become increasingly shaped by human rights concerns (Farmer, 2005; Gruskin et al., 2005; Aginan, 2005). How are human rights concerns reflected in health policy? It is instructive to distinguish two ways that human rights can affect how global health policy is approached. This distinction enables me to identify two different ways in which the FCTC can be seen to enrich national policy space.

One way in which human rights impact health policy is through the substantive concerns of human rights, in particular, their distinctive emphasis on nondiscrimination and equality as regulative norms in the development and implementation of global health policy (Gruskin and Tarantola, 2005). The impact of this emphasis on nondiscrimination is most visible in the global response to HIV/AIDS, but its reach is also evident in, for example, the coordinated efforts by major charitable organizations such as the Bill and Melinda Gates Foundation to combat neglected infectious diseases. Human rights norms are applicable in these instances because of the overwhelming evidence that health policies and programs in many countries risk discriminating against, for example, persons with AIDS. China's response to the prevalence of AIDS among its rural population is often held up as a case in point (Jacobs and Potter, 2006).

The second way in which human rights approaches can affect global health policy stems from the widespread acknowledgment in the international human rights community that the fulfillment of social and economic rights including the right to health should be flexible and contingent on the particular socioeconomic and cultural circumstances that exist in the country where the right holder lives (Jacobs, 2012). The best-known statement of this idea is found in Article 2 of the ICESCR, which allows that social rights, including the right to the highest attainable standard of health, can be fulfilled through progressive realization. The right to the highest attainable standard of health differs from civil and political rights, such as the human right not to be tortured, in the sense that there is not a universal and uniform basis for determining what that right might require of others. There is, I believe, a clear implication that the fulfillment of the right to the highest attainable standard of health requires member states to have national policy space that allows them to develop health policy that reflects the diversity in cultural and socioeconomic conditions between countries.

GENDER-SPECIFIC TOBACCO CONTROL AND HUMAN RIGHTS

Substantive human rights concerns are reflected in the FCTC in a variety of ways. A concrete illustration can be provided by way of its emphasis on taking gender inequalities seriously in the design and implementation tobacco control policies. (For a much more detailed discussion, see Jacobs, 2012.) Gender discrimination has been one of the principal targets of the international human rights framework in the post–World War II period. This commitment runs through the entire series of the UN treatises that constitute the core of the framework, including the 1980 Convention on the Elimination of All Forms of Discrimination Against Women. The right to the highest attainable standard of health has been interpreted by the United Nations as involving two distinct components: freedoms and entitlements (UN ESOSOC, 2000). The essential freedoms at stake are the right to make one's own decisions about health and body, including consensual medical treatment and the right to be free from interference and discrimination. Entitlements are held against an individual's state or government. These entitlements do not include good health because that cannot be ensured by a state. Thus, observes the UN Economic and Social Committee, "the right to health must be understood as a right to the enjoyment of a variety of facilities, goods, services and conditions necessary for the realization of the highest attainable standard of health" (UN ECOSOC, 2000, para. 9). The right to health is seen, on this interpretation, as providing grounds to protect women from infringements on their basic freedom to make choices about medical treatment and care. But it is also interpreted as providing grounds for special provisions that give priority to women's health issues such as reproductive health care, given the unfair treatment and neglect of women's health issues in the past.

From a health risk perspective, smoking affects men and women in many ways that are similar, for example, in terms of heart disease, lung cancer, bronchial and digestive tract cancers, stroke, vascular diseases, bronchitis, and emphysema. Men who smoke also risk distinctive sexual and fertility problems. Women risk increases in cervical and breast cancer, cardiovascular disease, infertility, premature labor, low-weight births, early menopause, and bone fractures.

The most important gender differences have to do, not so much with the effects of smoking, but with the prevalence of smoking about men and women. As Table 6.1 indicates, in the developed world, 35 percent of men smoke, compared to 22 percent of women. The gap is steadily narrowing. Trends suggest that in advanced industrial countries such as the United States, United Kingdom, Germany, and France, socioeconomic class is emerging as the most important variable identifying who continues to smoke (Feldman and Bayer, 2011). The dramatic difference, however, is in the developing world where, on average, men smoke at more than five times the rate of women. China currently has more smokers than any other country in the world, and it is estimated that at least one million deaths a year are caused by smoking. There, the gap between men and women smoking is especially pronounced. In the Global Adult Tobacco China Survey for 2010, it was found that smoking rates for men in China were 52.9 percent but only 2.4 percent for women (WHO Representative Office in China, 2010a). The Global Adult Tobacco India Survey revealed that 35 percent of adults in India use some form of tobacco product (WHO India, 2010). Among them 21 percent of adults use only smokeless tobacco, 9 percent only smoke cigarettes, and 5 percent smoke as well as use smokeless tobacco. The prevalence of overall tobacco use among men in India is 48 percent; half of these men smoke. Twenty percent of women in India use tobacco products. Most women, however, use smokeless tobacco products; only 3 percent smoke. In other words, the GATS India findings show that six times more women chew tobacco than smoke cigarettes.

What follows from these differences in tobacco usage rates in developing countries like China and India? There are two important implications for tobacco control pertaining to women. The first is that it suggests that the overwhelming harm done to women in China regarding tobacco usage at present is a consequence of secondhand smoke. The second important implication is that from a marketing perspective, there is a huge potential for the tobacco industry to expand its customer base by encouraging the increase of smoking among women in China and India. The Government of India's 2004 *Report on Tobacco Control in India* observed:

> Gender-based psychosocial aspirations are blatantly exploited to promote tobacco. Almost all cigarette and chewing tobacco advertising imagery in India includes women, taking advantage of the changing position of women in society, and their increasing socioeconomic independence. As a result, many educated young women perceive smoking as a symbol of liberation and freedom from traditional gender roles. Peer and advertising pressure encourages even knowledgeable women to smoke. (Reddy and Gupta, 2004)

There are also important implications pertaining to men and tobacco control. The first is that smoke cessation efforts in China and India are predominately about ending tobacco addiction among men. Likewise, curtailing smoking behavior in China and India means in effect changing when and where men smoke.

Significantly, prior to the FCTC, tobacco control in the Asia-Pacific region was predominantly gender-neutral (Morrow and Barraclough, 2001). From a human rights perspective, however, it would be wrong to ignore the differences between men and women when developing tobacco control law and policy. Fair treatment of men and women demands sensitivity to differences in their situations regarding tobacco usage and exposure of its health risks. Gender-neutral tobacco control measures may not, in other words, always be consistent with the core values of nondiscrimination and equality.

The FCTC provides a clear expression of this sort of reasoning. It identifies women as especially vulnerable to the harmful effects of globalization and trade liberalization in the tobacco industry. Member states are said to be "*[a]larmed* by the increase in smoking and other forms of tobacco consumption by women and young girls worldwide" (WHO, 2003, p. 1; emphasis in the original). In response to this "alarm," the huge differences in smoking prevalence among men and women, and the gender differences between how tobacco usage causes harm, the WHO FCTC embraces as a matter of guiding principles "the need to take measures to address gender-specific risks when developing tobacco control strategies" (WHO, 2003, p. 6).

Substantive Enrichment of Policy Space in China

Tobacco control law and policy in China did not have gender-specific provisions prior to its ratification of the FCTC in 2005. In this respect, it was similar to other countries in the Asia-Pacific region. This absence of gender-specific tobacco control provisions in China existed, even though in China there has long been awareness of the differences in smoking rates between men and women and that foreign cigarette companies have an interest in targeting Chinese women as a huge potential market for their products.

The gender-specific tobacco control measures in the FCTC have enriched substantively Chinese tobacco control policy. Two examples illustrate the point. China has, since the early 1990s, experimented with bans on tobacco advertising and smoking in public places, with little success or impact. In May 2010, however, the WHO Representative Office in China released a special initiative titled Protect Women from Tobacco Marketing and Smoke, which is linked explicitly to the FCTC's provision for gender-specific tobacco control measures and has a twofold focus: a comprehensive ban on tobacco advertising and on smoking in public places. The rationale for the first ban is explained in the following way: "Advertisements falsely link tobacco use with female beauty, empowerment and health. In fact, addiction to tobacco enslaves and disfigures women" (WHO Representative Office in China, 2010b). The rationale for the ban on smoking in public places has a similar tone: "[T]he bigger threat to women is from exposure to the smoke of others, particularly men . . . in China more than 97% of smokers are men. Yet more than half of Chinese women of reproductive age are regularly exposed to second-hand smoke, which puts themselves and their unborn babies at risk" (WHO Representative Office in China, 2010b). This new way to rationalize advertising bans and prohibitions on smoking in public places has helped reinvigorate these kinds of tobacco control policies. Hundreds of Chinese cities have introduced bans on smoking in at least some public places including, for example, public transportation, and there is much more rigorous enforcement of the advertisement bans, especially on billboards.

From a different angle, China is also focusing on smoke cessation among men. The challenge, explains Douglas Bettcher, director of WHO's Tobacco Free Initiative, is that "among men [in China], there is enormous social pressure to smoke, and this is facilitated by the policy environment" (WHO Representative Office in China, 2010a). This pressure comes in the form of business practices as well as socializing with friends. Bettcher's point is that tobacco control requires at some level addressing the social pressure on men to smoke and changing the business and social culture for men in China. The WHO in China holds that this change can come with the sort of tobacco control measures mandated in the FCTC, but these should be implemented with a particular view to changing male norms around tobacco usage – in effect, gender-specific measures.

Changing social and cultural norms around smoking for men is a difficult one that until ratification of the FCTC was not an aspect of tobacco control policies in China. Since 2005, however, China has developed new and innovative ways to change cultural practices involving smoking by men. Most interesting are, I think, the "Bad Manners" campaigns. These campaigns are designed around the idea that many of the smoking habits of Chinese men in public constitute bad manners and for this reason should change. These campaigns received their highest visibility when Beijing hosted the 2008 Olympics and during the Shanghai World Exhibition in 2010. During the Olympics, bad manners were described as four pests – spitting, queue-jumping, smoking, and bad language – which, like the four pests – flies, mosquitoes, rats, and bed bugs – that tormented China in the 1950s would be extinguished. Shanghia developed a similar campaign in 2010 called the "Seven No's" – no spitting, no jaywalking, no cursing, no destruction of greenery, no vandalism, no littering, and no smoking – campaign. Both campaigns were judged to be very effective by Chinese public health officials and the use of these bad manners campaigns to curb men smoking in public places and at work are now widespread in China, perhaps most visibly on trains and other forms of public transportation.

HUMAN RIGHTS AND PROCEDURAL ENRICHMENT OF NATIONAL POLICY SPACES

Earlier I claimed that the commitment to progressive realization of the right to the highest attainable standard of health requires member states to have flexible national policy spaces that allow them to develop health policy that reflects the diversity in cultural and socioeconomic conditions between countries. China and India are taking different paths toward implementing tobacco control policy within the enriched national policy space created through the FCTC. India has followed a path of national legislation. In 2003, it enacted The Cigarettes and Other Tobacco Products (Prohibition of Advertisement and Regulation of Trade and Commerce, Production, Supply and Distribution) Act, in order to meet their obligations under the FCTC (Rao, 2004). This law was designed to protect public health by prohibiting smoking in public places, banning tobacco advertisements, forbidding the sale of tobacco products to minors and near schools, requiring health warnings on tobacco products, and regulating tar and nicotine contents. China's tobacco control policy has unfolded in a much more piecemeal fashion, reflected in new laws at all levels of government but also initiatives such as the Bad Manners campaigns described in the previous section.

In both countries, however, tobacco control policy has struggled with compliance issues, often arising from the fact that the tobacco industry is a powerful political actor in India and China. In India, the 2003 legislation is often ignored or simply not implemented. In China, making tobacco control a priority is often a problem because of the immense state revenues that are raised through the sale of cigarettes. How does the FCTC enrich the tobacco control policy toolkit for public health officials in these countries to overcome these obstacles to developing and implementing tobacco control policy? In other words, procedural enrichment is about improving national performance on tobacco control. China provides an example of one sort of procedural enrichment, India a different sort of procedural enrichment of the national policy space for tobacco control. Each fits with the particular political context in which it is used.

PRAISING AND SHAMING CHINA'S PERFORMANCE ON TOBACCO CONTROL

From an international human rights perspective, international nongovernmental human rights organizations such as Amnesty International and Human Rights Watch have a long history of pressuring countries, including China, to improve their human rights performance through naming, blaming, shaming, and praising exercises. The WHO in China appears in my view to have learned from these human rights organizations and is pursuing similar strategies to improve China's public health performance on global health issues. This is already clearly evident in the WHO's treatment of China in the context of emerging infectious diseases (Jacobs, 2011). Likewise, I think the WHO has effectively pursued the same strategy to help Chinese public health officials overcome political obstacles to implementing tobacco control in China. The fact that the FCTC is grounded on a human right makes this strategy an obvious one to pursue.

The best evidence that the WHO's naming, blaming, shaming, and praising strategy has been effective in supporting the tobacco control agenda of Chinese public health officials is the adoption of the new 2011 national law banning smoking in restaurants, most forms of public transportation, and some public places. China has also been very cooperative with the WHO in the information- and evidence-gathering requirements of the FCTC, as is clear in the case of the 2010 Global Adult Tobacco Survey (WHO Representative Office in China, 2010a).

Another clear example of the praise strategy came on July 18, 2012, when the WHO awarded Professor Chen Zhu, Minister of Health, People's Republic of China, with a Director-General's Special Recognition Certificate for his commitment to tobacco control (WHO China, 2012). There is a marked similarity here to the praise they gave Margaret Chan in her handling of the SARS crisis in Hong Kong in 2003.

But the human rights strategy is not always effective in overcoming obstacles to developing tobacco control policy in China. The recent increase in tobacco taxation shows this. Taxation is presented in the FCTC as likely the single most effective policy tool for reducing smoking. Article 6 of the FCTC states: "The Parties recognize that price and tax measures are an effective and important means of reducing tobacco consumption by various segments of the population, in particular young persons" (WHO, 2003, p. 7). The logic is that by increasing taxation on tobacco products and thereby increasing their retail price, individuals will choose not to buy the products. In 2009, the Chinese government increased the ad valorem tax on cigarettes with the explicit purpose of increasing government revenue in light of the economic slowdown. But the government also mandated that the new tax not be passed on to consumers but rather be absorbed by the cigarette manufacturer, the China National Tobacco Company (Feldman and Bayer, 2011). The point is that if China was genuinely interested in reducing tobacco consumption, it would have passed the tax on to consumers.

LITIGATING INDIA'S PERFORMANCE ON TOBACCO CONTROL

There is little evidence of the WHO using a naming, blaming, shaming, and praising strategy to enhance India's performance on FCTC tobacco control. The Cigarettes and Other Tobacco Products (Prohibition of Advertisement and Regulation of Trade and Commerce, Production, Supply and Distribution) Act made sense for the government of India to enact in 2003, given the compelling economic self-interest the government has in reducing the health costs of tobacco use. In practice, like many of India's public health laws, weak enforcement is a problem. India has, however, been very active in its tobacco usage surveillance, as is evident from its comprehensive GATS report in 2010. It is also important to note that India has not instituted taxation on tobacco products at the level required by the FCTC (Feldman and Bayer, 2011). This can be attributed in part to the lack of institutional capacity to collect such a tax.

Unlike China, India has a robust court system with a long history of judicial independence and engagement with policy development. Legal adversarialism is ordinarily understood as a form of policy development that revolves around the uses of the courts. In Canada and the United States, legal adversarialism is a well-known, albeit controversial, policy path. In one of the best-known American formulations, it is a "particular style of policymaking, policy implementation, and dispute resolution by means of lawyer-dominated litigation" (Kagan, 2002, p. 3). In India, legal adversarialism has evolved in a very different direction (Jacobs and Sen, 2012). Rather than being centered on lawyers, legal adversarialism is centered on judges, in particular Supreme Court judges. In India, legal adversarialism is a style of policy making, policy implementation, and dispute resolution by means of Supreme Court judge-dominated litigation. This sort of litigation is driven by a concern with the public interest and originated three decades ago. It has allowed the Supreme Court of India to take on a leadership role in the formulation of policy where other major government institutions – most notably the legislatures and the public service – have failed to act.

The principal architect of this form of legal adversarialism in India, often called public interest litigation or social action litigation, was Supreme Court Chief Justice P. N. Bhagwati. Bhagwati explains:

> The primary focus is on state repression, governmental lawlessness, administrative deviance, and exploitation of disadvantaged groups and denial to them of their rights and entitlements. The public interest litigation model that we have evolved in India is directed towards 'finding turn around situations' in the political economy for the disadvantaged and other vulnerable groups. It is concerned with the immediate as well as long term resolution of problems of the disadvantaged. It also seeks to ensure that the activities of the state fulfill the obligations of the law under which they exist and function. (Bhagwati, 1985, p. 569)

In broad objectives, there is little here that is exceptional about public interest litigation. The primary difference is that Supreme Court judges in India have a proactive role in public interest litigation that is exceptional for a common law legal system.

What differentiates legal adversarialism in India's Supreme Court from other jurisdictions? In India, the court has redefined the traditional "adversarial" judicial process as embodied in the Civil Procedure Code and the rules of evidence. It has allowed for the departure in public interest litigation from the traditional adversarial procedure, where each party produces its own evidence, tested by cross-examination by the other side, with the judge as a neutral umpire deciding the case on the basis of materials produced by both parties. Instead, the Supreme Court of India allows any party, including nongovernmental health organizations, to initiate court actions on behalf of the disadvantaged, appoints independent commissioners to gather information and evidence in support of these actions, and has monitoring mechanisms that allow it to follow up on its earlier decisions (Bhagwati, 1985).

Two recent examples of legal adversarialism in tobacco control by the Supreme Court of India illustrate how the FCTC has enriched policy space for tobacco control in India. In both examples, the Supreme Court has appealed to India's ratification of the FCTC to justify in part taking action on tobacco control. One example concerns the harmful health effects of smokeless tobacco. In December 2010, frustrated with the Department of Health and Family Welfare's lack of action to present findings on the health benefits of banning smokeless tobacco products, the Supreme Court ordered the department to gather evidence about oral cancer and other diseases caused by these sorts of tobacco products in the case *of Ankur Gutkha v. Indian Asthama Care Society & Ors* (http://www.tobaccocontrollaws.org/litigation/decisions/in-20101207-ankur-gutkha-v.-indian-asthama). The subsequent evidence presented to the Supreme Court in 2011 overwhelmingly showed to policy makers the health risks of these products (http://www.governancenow.com/news/regular-story/high-time-smokeless-tobacco-was-banned). In 2012, six states banned gutka and other tobacco foods, citing the Supreme Court of India's leadership on the issue (http://ibnlive.in.com/news/will-the-ban-on-gutka-curb-tobacco-use/274723-64.html).

Another example revolves around the government's lack of enforcement of a 2008 law requiring health warnings and pictures on tobacco products that meet the requirements of the FCTC provisions. In response to a petition from a nongovernment organization Health for Millions, the Supreme Court received from the government a commitment to not extend the implementation date of the law any further, "under any circumstances" (http://www.tobaccocontrollaws.org/litigation/decisions/in-20090506-health-for-millions-v.-union-o). The Supreme Court also directed that "no Court in the country shall pass any order, which is inconsistent with this order" (http://www.tobaccocontrollaws.org/litigation/decisions/in-20090506-health-for-millions-v.-union-o). Despite the ruling, however, the government was found to have continued to delay enforcement of the law in 2010 (http://articles.timesofindia.indiatimes.com/2010-12-16/chennai/28253618_1_tobacco-packs-pictorial-warning-current-warnings). Subsequently, in February 2011, the Supreme Court of India in another case, *Miraj Products Pvt. Ltd. v. Indian Asthama Care Society & Ors*, again requested and received from the government evidence of the harmful effects of tobacco products on the health of users and the necessity of labeling and packaging to reflect those dangers (http://www.tobaccocontrollaws.org/litigation/decisions/in-20110217-miraj-products-pvt.-ltd.-v.-in).

Conclusion: Augmenting Policy Space in a Dismal Economic Time

This chapter has been designed to provide insight into how new international law and regulations can enrich national policy space rather than diminish it. It shows how the FCTC enriches national policy space in two ways. One way is to enrich substantively how policy space is used by governments. I illustrate this by showing how the FCTC has influenced China to adopt gender-specific tobacco control measures since 2005. The other way in which the FCTC has enriched national policy space procedurally is by facilitating domestic efforts to ensure that tobacco control policy be taken seriously as a priority in the context of competing policy claims that all national governments face. China and India both provide concrete illustration of procedural enrichment. In China's case, the traditional international human rights strategy of naming, blaming, shaming, and praising has been effective in prioritizing tobacco control measures on the national policy agenda. In India, the Supreme Court has drawn on the FCTC to help influence the uses of policy space in area of tobacco control.

The broader point of this analysis of how the FCTC enriches national policy spaces has been to link the enrichment to the human rights foundation of that international law. That foundation is pivotal to appreciating both the substantive enrichment and the procedural enrichment of national policy spaces for tobacco control in China and India. When pondering in the future whether new international laws and conventions will diminish national policy spaces or enrich them, the extent to which those new laws or conventions are grounded on human rights provides an instructive guide.

REFERENCES

Action on Smoking and Health (ASH). (2007). Retrieved March 22, 2012, from http://www.ash.org.uk/files/documents/ASH_562.pdf.

Aginan, O. (2005). *Global Health Governance: International Law and Public Health in a Divided World*. Toronto: University of Toronto Press.

Bhagwati, P. (1985). "Judicial Activism and Public Interest Litigation." *Columbia Journal of Transnational Law*, 23, 561–577.

Brundtland, G. H. (1999). Why Investing in Global Health Is Good Politics. Retrieved July 28, 2012, from http://www.who.int/director-general/speeches/1999/english/19991206_new_york.html.

Centers for Disease Control and Prevention (CDC). (2009). Cigarette Smoking Among Adults and Trends in Smoking Cessation – United States, 2008. Morbidity and Mortality Weekly Report, 58(44), 1227–1232. Retrieved March 22, 2012, from http://www.cdc.gov/mmwr/preview/mmwrhtml/mm5844a2.htm.

Centers for Disease Control and Prevention (CDC). (2012). Smoking and Tobacco Use – Fast Facts. Retrieved February 18, 2012, from http://www.cdc.gov/tobacco/data_statistics/fact_sheets/fast_facts/.

Crow, M. (2004). "Smokescreens and State Responsibility: Using Human Rights Strategies to Promote Global Tobacco Control." *Yale Journal of International Law, 29,* 209–250.

Dresler, C., and Marks, S. (2006). "The Emerging Human Right to Tobacco Control." *Human Rights Quarterly, 28,* 599–651.

Farmer, P. (2005). *Pathologies of Power: Health, Human Rights, and the New War on the Poor.* Berkeley: University of California Press.

Feldman, E., and Bayer, R. (2011). "The Triumph and Tragedy of Tobacco Control: A Tale of Nine Nations." *Annual Review of Law and Social Science, 7,* 79–100.

Forman, L. (2008). "'Rights' and Wrongs: What Utility for the Right to Health in Reforming Trade Rules on Medicine." *Health and Human Rights, 10,* 37–52.

Gallagher, K. (Ed.). (2005). *Putting Development First: The Importance of Policy Space in the WTO and IFIs.* London: Zed Books.

Gruskin, S., Grodin, M., Annas, G., and Marks, S. (Eds.). (2005). *Perspectives on Health and Human Rights.* London: Routledge.

Gruskin, S., and Tarantola, D. (2005). Health and Human Rights. In S. Gruskin, M. Grodin, G. Annas and S. Marks (Eds.), *Perspectives on Health and Human Rights* (pp. 3–61). London: Routledge.

Health Canada. (2010). Canadian Tobacco Use Monitoring Survey (CTUMS) 2010. Retrieved March 22, 2012, from http://www.hc-sc.gc.ca/hc-ps/tobac-tabac/research-recherche/stat/ctums-esutc_2010-eng.php.

Jacobs, L. (2004). *Pursuing Equal Opportunities.* New York: Cambridge University Press.

Jacobs, L. (2011). China's Capacity to Respond to the H1N1 Pandemic Alert and Future Global Public Health Crises: A Policy Window For Canada. In P. Potter and T. Adams (Eds.), *Issues in Canada-China Relations* (pp. 333–343). Toronto: Canadian International Council.

Jacobs, L. (2012). Gender, Trade Liberalization, and Tobacco Control in China. In Pitman Potter and Heather Gibb (Eds.), *Gender Equality Rights and Trade Regimes: Coordinating Compliance* (pp. 141–158). Ottawa: North South Institute.

Jacobs, L. (2013). Adapting Locally to International Health and Human Rights Standards: An Alternative Theoretical Framework for Progressive Realization. In Mikael Rask Madsen and Gert Verschraegen (Eds.), *Making Human Rights Intelligible: New Theoretical and Empirical Contributions* (pp. 233–246). Oxford: Hart Publishing.

Jacobs, L., and Potter, P. (2006). "Selective Adaptation and Health and Human Rights in China." *Health and Human Rights, 9*(2), 142–166.

Jacobs, L., and Sen. S. (2012). "The Distinctive Character of Legal Adversarialism in India." *Canada Watch, Special Issue on India: The Most Fragile of Democracies* (Winter), 20–23.

Joey, S. (2008). Global Smoking Trends – Where Tobacco Companies Make Money These Days? Retrieved March 9, 2012, from http://www.articlesbase.com/addictions-articles/global-smoking-trends-where-tobacco-companies-make-money-these-days-354416.html.

Kagan, R. (2002). *Adversarial Legalism: The American Way of Law.* Cambridge, MA: Harvard University Press.

Kapczynski, A. (2009). "Harmonization and Its Discontents: A Case Study of TRIPS Implementation in India's Pharmaceutical Sector." *California Law Review,* 97, 1571–1649.

Koivusalo, M., Schrecker, T., and Labonté, R. (2010). *Globalisation and Policy Space for Health and Social Determinants of Health.* Ottawa: Globalization and Health Knowledge Network.

Merry, S. E. (2006). *Human Rights and Gender Violence: Translating International Law into Local Justice.* Chicago: University of Chicago Press.

Morrow, M., and Barraclough, S. (2001). "Tobacco Control and Gender: A Need for New Approaches for the Asia-Pacific Region." *Development Bulletin,* 54 (March), 23–26.

Rao, J. (2004). Forward to Reddy, K., & Gupta, P. *Report on Tobacco Control in India.* Delhi: Ministry of Health and Family Welfare, Government of India.

Reddy, K., and Gupta, P. (2004). *Report on Tobacco Control in India.* Delhi: Ministry of Health and Family Welfare, Government of India.

Reubi, D. (2011). "The Promise of Human Rights for Global Health: A Programmed Deception?" *Social Science and Medicine,* 73, 625–628.

The Tobacco Atlas. (2012). Tobacco Industry. Retrieved March 22, 2012, from http://www.tobaccoatlas.org/industry.

United Nations Economic and Social Council (UN ECOSOC). (2000). *General Comment No. 14: Substantive Issues Arising in the Implementation of the International Covenant on Economic, Social and Cultural Rights.* Geneva: UN Human Rights Council.

United Nations Economic and Social Council (UN ECOSOC). (2004). *The right of everyone to the enjoyment of the highest attainable standard of physical and mental health.* Report of the special Rapporteur, Paul Hunt. Addendum: Mission to the World Trade Organization. (E/CN.4/2004/49/Add.1). Geneva: UN Human Rights Council.

World Health Organization (WHO). (2003). *WHO Framework Convention on Tobacco Control.* Geneva, Switzerland: WHO.

World Health Organization (WHO). (2011). *WHO Report on the Global Tobacco Epidemic.* Retrieved August 1, 2012, from http://www.who.int/tobacco/surveillance/policy/country_profile/chn.pdf.

WHO Representative Office in China. (2010a). China's Global Adult Tobacco Survey and its Global Context, by Dr. Douglas Bettcher, Director, Tobacco Free Initiative, WHO. Speech in Shenzhen, China, August 17, 2010. Retrieved August 1, 2012, from http://www2.wpro.who.int/china/media_centre/speeches/sp_20100817.htm.

WHO Representative Office in China. (2010b). *Protect women from tobacco marketing and smoke.* Retrieved August 1, 2012, from http://www2.wpro.who.int/china/sites/tfi/wntd2010_flyer.htm.

WHO China. (2012). China Health Minister receives award for tobacco control from Director General of World Health Organization. Retrieved August 1, 2012, from http://www2.wpro.who.int/china/media_centre/press_releases/PR_20120718.htm.

WHO India. (2010). *Global Adult Tobacco Survey India Report 2009–2010*. Retrieved September 30, 2012, from http://whoindia.org/EN/Section20/Section25_1861.htm.

PART III

Paradigm Shifts and Structural Change

7

Business, Policy Spaces, and Governance in India*

Kuldeep Mathur

INDIA'S GOVERNANCE TRANSFORMATION

In the last few years India has been described as an emerging giant. Its economic transformations are seen as nothing short of revolutionary (Panagriya, 2008; Subramaniam, 2008; Ganguly and Mukherji, 2011). This view is quite in contrast to the sluggish economy unable to lift itself beyond a 3 percent rate of growth for several decades before 1980. Despite this slow growth, optimism was felt after 1991, when liberal economic reforms were introduced. The rate of growth accelerated and hovered around 8 percent for several years after 2002. Most commentators have given credit to the adoption of liberal economic policies for this buoyancy.[1]

India went through a governance transformation introduced in 1991–1992, which included far-reaching economic reforms. It is common knowledge that the deregulation of the Indian economy was the major purpose of these reforms. Deregulation was an effort to create a favorable environment for the private sector to grow and invest in India's growth. The strategy was to prioritize growth as a state goal, to support large business houses in achieving this goal, and to keep labor under control (Kohli, 2006). Quite significantly, business houses were no longer seen as hostile actors out to subvert the goals of the state but as partners in achieving them.

The focus of this essay is the relationship between the organized industrial sector and the government of India within the framework of governance. It explores the concept of networks such as the Private Public Partnerships (PPPs) and shows how the analysis of the relationship between the state and the corporate sector is based on a transformed role of the state, a role defined in the neoliberal economic policies introduced in India in 1991. This transformed role for the state in India has created new policy spaces where the government

* The revised version has benefited from the comments of Daniel Drache and Les Jacobs.

and business jointly develop public policy. This chapter questions the effectiveness this joint decision making between business and government in the
social economic context of India. Can a new system where the state has abdi-
cated many of its roles possess a built-in capacity to create equal partnership
and platforms of equal exchange?

LIBERALIZATION AND THE AGENDA OF GOOD GOVERNANCE

As country after country was incorporated in the fold of neoliberalization and
globalization, India was not left behind. The core features of the neoliberal
model are the acceptance of the preeminent role of the market as the strategy
for development and the contraction of the role of the state in providing
public goods and services. The wide appeal of this model was rooted in the
political ideals of individual liberty and freedom long regarded as sacrosanct
banners of rebellion against the oppression of the state. These were what
Harvey (2006, p. 146) called "central values of civilization" that continued to
resonate throughout the world in the various shades of democracy.

However, social and economic policies generated by these lofty ideals have
yielded mixed results. Increases in income inequalities and poverty have
become endemic features of the development performance of many countries. The emphasis on the market and the downsizing of state institutions
have failed to give the appropriate amount of stimulus for growth and investment that would provide adequate economic and social protection to the poor.
To face up to this challenge, "good governance" measures with the goal of
"eradicating poverty" (a goal defined by the neoliberals themselves) became
an additional item of the agenda. In truth, these measures did little more
than facilitate the implementation of neoliberal policies (Marquis and Utting,
2006, p. 4).

The inclusion of "good governance" in the neoliberal agenda carried two
very important implications. One was that the pursuit of good governance
would be essentially a pursuit of establishing such institutions and processes
that would facilitate the functioning of markets. The state began to be seen as
a facilitator to business and not as an institution to intervene in social policy
spaces. Consequently, providing support for the successful operation of business became the central theme of the state's role and activity in Indian society.
Business duly assumed greater power and influence over other segments of
society as large corporations began to be seen as partners of the state in development. Good governance had come to mean the development of governing
styles in which boundaries between (and within) the public and private sectors became blurred (Stoker, 1998, p. 155). The new formulation underlined

that political institutions no longer exercise a monopoly over the orchestration of governance (Pierre, 2000, p. 4). The concept of good governance indicated a shift away from well-established notions of the way government sought to resolve social issues through top-down approaches, and toward a view of national policy space as a realm for shared decision making with business.

GOVERNANCE AS NETWORKS

Governance originally emerged as a network of relationships between three actors: the state, the market, and civil society. It was an interactive process where the government may have liked to impose its will but its acceptance depended on the compliance and action of others. One institution depended on another – what Stoker (1998) refers to as "power dependence." In these relationships and networks, it was believed, no one institution could easily dominate. The monopoly of political institutions in providing services was diluted, the private sector and institutions of civil society filling in their previously occupied policy spaces. New forms of institutions emerged as the boundaries between the public and private sectors were being intentionally eroded. Consequently, a range of voluntary agencies arose to respond to mounting collective concerns.

The network metaphor was readily adopted to represent the multiple dimensions of participation that were created and networks became the core of new style of governance; these networks were seen as the basis of the transformation from "government to governance" (Rhodes, 1997). Their focus was the production of public policy and the contribution of public and private actors to it (Sorenson and Torfing, 2004, p. 5). The networks were also opportunities for public-private partnerships. It was even widely believed that society would benefit from these partnerships between the state and nonstate actors such as civil society and the market. The "good governance" agenda promoted these partnerships much as the neoliberal agenda worked to downsize the state.

PUBLIC-PRIVATE PARTNERSHIPS

The emphasis on PPPs changed the pattern of governance management practices and perceptions regarding the roles and responsibilities of different development actors in the context of globalization and liberalization. This transformation has also been termed as a pragmatic turn in official development practice; as Utting and Zammit (2006, p. 2) point out, "approaches to development interventions, and in particular the role of the private sector, are said to be driven by "what works" and less by ideology."

PPPs appeared to have pragmatic qualities even more so because the financial circumstances of both the government and the private sector were changing. Governments were suffering from a financial crisis and fiscal deficits rose in the 1980s, while the corporate sector was doing well, with healthy returns and technological advancement. Across the world, a partnership between the three actors – state, market, and civil society – began to be promoted as a strategy of good governance.

The partnerships promised to avoid duplication of efforts and were seen to draw on their complementary resources and capabilities to design more effective problem-solving mechanisms. They promised to increase the responsiveness of policies and create accountability by including other actors – market and civil society – into decision-making processes. They are also presumed to improve compliance with political decisions and their implementation. In addition, the partnerships provided opportunities to the partners to learn from each other (Streets, 2004).

It is widely believed that networks played a significant role in the processes promoting social and economic development. Pingle (2000) has argued that shared understandings are vital for better functioning of economic decision making. Shared understandings help overcome bureaucratic resistance and allow the state not to fall prey to social and political interests. Industrialists in turn increase their ability to get the necessary infrastructure and collective goods for future growth.

However, this optimism is not shared by many. Critics point out that these partnerships can be a strategy for the state to evade responsibility. There has been considerable belief in the proposition that

> [t]he hierarchical governance of the society by the state is based on substantive rationality. The political values and preferences of the government – supposed to incarnate the will of the people – are translated into more or less detailed laws and regulations that are implemented and enforced by publicly employed bureaucracies. (Sorenson and Torfing, 2004)

Networks carry the risk of weakening traditional accountability mechanisms by shifting policy decisions to the realm of partnerships that can circumvent parliamentary control (Streets, 2004).

STATE-BUSINESS PARTNERSHIPS

Another fear is expressed over the fact that partnerships can be used by the corporate sector to embellish their own power and resources. Galbraith expressed this fear when he suggested, in his influential book, *The Affluent Society*, that corporations exercising social and economic power had made the Western societies rich in private goods but poor in public goods such as mass transport, public health, low-cost housing, and good schools for ordinary people (Das, 2000, p. 86).

Rosenau (2000, p. 224; quoted in Datta, 2009, p. 74) expresses similar concerns. He questions the consensus in policy literature that partnerships combine the best of both public and private worlds, and argues that if partnerships emphasize cost reduction or profit maximization at the price of significant quality compromises, then vulnerable populations may not be able to respond appropriately and aggressively. There is always the risk that the poor and the marginalized groups in the population may be excluded as a result of pricing policies.

Despite these concerns, optimism about the partnerships is prevailing and a complex web of networks is emerging worldwide that has a far-reaching impact on the nature of the state and the functioning of democracy. The notion of governance is transforming the organization of the state along with its relationships with the private sector and civil society actors. A considerable amount of scholarly attention is now being devoted to analyzing and debating this transformation of state and democracy. Attention is being directed toward an improved understanding of the wider public policy spaces where the institutions of government – far from being autonomous in their decision making – now appear to be involved in processes of negotiation, bargaining, and compromise with a host of other actors.

It is important to explore how the private sector seeks to incorporate its profiteering ideology – the overriding goal of its existence – even when pretending to pursue the public interest. Private-sector orientation is that of achieving returns on invested funds, daring to take business risks, having to anticipate markets and competitive developments, and realizing a corporate goal. The public orientation reflects political opinion and influence, formulation of legislation, regulations, and authorities, democratic decision-making processes, the minimization of risk, and the realization of a social goal (Reijners, 1994, p. 224; quoted in Datta, 2009, pp. 73–74). Are there conflicts arising from the two orientations working together? If yes, how are they resolved and in which direction are the bargains struck?

Miraftab (2004) forcefully argues that there is a widespread impression that networks have been cases of "privatization by stealth" and the bargains have been in general more favorable to corporate interests. He has argued that the large corporate sector has easier access to technology and financial resources and thus has more influence than do both government partners and community organizations in decision making. Organized business interests have been powerful actors in most societies, and the capacity of state institutions to work on equal terms is not always assured. Corporate business interests have gained legitimate entry into formal institutions of governance and have become co-producers of public policy without giving up their raison d'être: working for profit. Countries of the developing world in particular suffer from a weak framework of public institutions, and to expect them to regulate partnership with corporate business is a challenge that needs to be explored (Kapur and Bhanu Mehta, 2005).

Lindblom (1977, pp. 170–188) argues that business almost by default has a privileged position in a market-based society. Its activities have a greater influence on public policies than those of any other groups in society. This is primarily because business has control over investment decisions, and when it chooses to withdraw from investment, the impact on society is that of recession and depression in the economy. It is for this reason that government officials are more than willing to cater to the interests of business and shape public policy in response to these concerns.

THE "PLAN PERIOD" AND THE INDIAN ECONOMY

A brief narration of the features of the state-business relationship before the period introduction of neoliberal economic reforms is necessary to understand later policy developments. In the early twentieth century, India chose a strategy of centralized planning where the state would occupy the commanding heights of the economy and the private sector would be controlled and regulated to achieve the goals set by the planners.

As early as 1938, the Congress Party had appointed a National Planning Committee under the chairmanship of Jawaharlal Nehru to evolve a strategy of development for postcolonial India. A consensus for state-driven develop-ment had evolved, with Nehru advocating economic independence. Emphasis was placed on the critical role of heavy industry and import substitution in attaining this objective. A system of industrial licensing was introduced during the early 1950s; this was around the time the first Five Year Plan was being implemented. This meant that companies had to seek permission from the government to establish business in specified areas. Production targets were fixed by government planners and any change in them needed their approval. To administer the industrial licensing system, the Central Advisory Coun-cil with strong representation from private business interests was established, supplemented by separate Development Councils for a range of important individual industries. Private business interests were also represented in many other regulating bodies that were established during this period.

Considerable space was provided to the private sector to invest in the production of goods and services. The licensing regime was relatively liberal during the Nehruvian years and private sector investment grew more rapidly than anticipated. The government's attitude towards the private sector was flexible and pragmatic rather than rigid (Panagariya, 2008, pp. 37–40). Introducing the second Five Year Plan in parliament, Nehru declared:

> May I say that while I am for [the] public sector growing, I do not understand or appreciate the condemnation of the private sector. The whole philosophy underlying this plan is to take advantage of every possibility for growth and not to do something which suits some doctrinaire theory or imagine we have grown because we have satisfied some text-book maxim of a hundred years ago.

This period was also marked by another characteristic: the belief in a rational, technocratic state and its primacy in steering development (Chatterjee, 1998). Technical advice made a perceptible rise through the influence of the technocrats who manned important positions within the Planning Commission (Khilnani, 1997). These decisions left the lasting impression on the mind of Indian policy makers that most problems – social or political – were to be resolved through a committee of experts.

In another relevant development, policy advice was restricted to closed groups associated with the government or the Planning Commission. Alternative sources or dissenting voices were not encouraged. The alternative centers of policy advice that were established during this period were sponsored by the government and were meant to provide support to its planning strategy (Mathur and Bjorkman, 2009).

The relations between business and the government soured during the period of Nehru's successor, Indira Gandhi. New controls over industry were introduced, making the process of procuring licenses to set up a new industry or to expand the existing capacities more cumbersome and difficult. The period was marked by the emergence of lobbies representing individual business houses trying to extract concessions from the government. The role of these lobby groups was to influence government to get concessions in their favor, not to change the law (Kochanek, 1996).

At this time, the Indian private sector was dominated by a relatively small number of large family-controlled businesses. According to the Monopolies Inquiry Commission Report of 1965, there were seventy-five business houses that controlled almost half of the nongovernmental, nonbanking assets in the country. It is widely believed that many of these business houses used political connections to take business advantages and therefore prosper, in spite of the laws framed to limit their power. While the policy makers saw the control and regulatory laws as provisions for rational allocation of resources and the fulfillment of social goals, private capitalists put their faith in their ability to influence their implementation (or lack thereof). Large industrial houses and influential private capitalists manipulated these very regulations and controls to their advantage. The key was in bending the implementation, not in changing the law.

A kind of clandestine partnership emerged between state and business interests in India. As Kochanek (1987, p. 1284) points out, the political leadership came to depend very heavily on the system as quid pro quo for securing campaign contributions, and the bureaucracy depended on it for payoffs, employment, power, prestige, and patronage. The business community depended on the system to secure and maintain monopoly, protection, and guaranteed profitability. Considering this relationship, it does not come as a surprise that among business houses the larger ones commanded more power and influence within the government.

THE GRADUAL INTRODUCTION OF LIBERAL POLICIES

During the Nehruvian period, business relations were far more cordial than during the period of Indira Gandhi. Controls and regulations during Prime Minister Gandhi's period became the dominant concerns of industrial policy making; the licensing system was tightened and business began to be looked on with suspicion. However, this began to change with the second Gandhi term (beginning in 1980) as restrictions began to be relaxed. A gradual process toward a liberalized economy began. During this period, the government of India produced a number of important reports that were critical of the industrial regulations and suggested the urgent need to promote exports instead of emphasizing import substitution (Ganguly and Mukherjee, 2011, pp. 71–72).

Rajiv Gandhi (1984–1989), Prime Minister Indira Gandhi's successor, began initiating some reformist policies that aimed at technological modernization through the opening up of trade and loosening of state regulation.[2] He was a strong supporter of the Indian private domestic sector and, when faced with opposition, he played a crucial role in transforming an association of industries into the "Confederation of Indian Industry" that supported liberalization and could speak for the entire industry (Sinha, 2005). But the radical change really occurred in 1991 when, as a result of the foreign exchange crisis, India went on to accept the structural adjustment program offered by the IMF and the World Bank. The program called for the licensing system to be dismantled, investment to be opened up for foreign private investors, and trade to be liberalized.[3]

While a gradual process of liberalization had begun in the 1980s, the introduction of liberal economic reforms in 1991 was of historic significance. It signaled far-reaching changes in the government's economic policies and a change in the role of the state and the government. Policy and governance reforms were seen as an effort to create a favorable environment for the private sector to grow and invest in India's growth. Unlike the period of planning, business houses were no longer seen as hostile actors out to subvert the goals of the state but as partners in achieving them. The Minister of Company Affairs, speaking at a seminar in 2006, emphasized the role of the private enterprise in taking the country to increasingly higher growth paths. The government's role was now to provide an atmosphere in which business could flourish. He then went on to stress the need for freedom of action and initiative by business, sharply contrasting the pre-reform mind-set of viewing business with suspicion. "We are in the era of PPP," he said.[4] This theme found sustenance in the idea of the PPP, and a search began for institutional arrangements to promote it.

The government sought an alliance with big business in order to pursue the goal of accelerated economic growth (Kohli, 2006). It began with initiating many policies that withdrew the controlling and regulating role of the state and went on to establish institutional structures that provided a formal forum where big business could participate in policy making. The government-business alliance became explicit when the government of India appointed a three-member Investment Commission in 2004 to enhance and facilitate investment in India. The Commission made recommendations to the government of India on policies and procedures to facilitate investment; it recommended that projects and investment proposals be fast-tracked and promoted India to the world as an investment destination.[5]

The Commission chaired by Ratan Tata, with Deepak Parikh (Housing Development Finance Corporation) and Ashok Ganguly (Industrial Credit and Investment Corporation of India), produced an important vision for policy spaces. The importance of this policy document was not only in that the members of the Investment Commission are major business leaders of the country but also in that the notification of the appointment of the Commission itself laid down the procedure to process the recommendations of the report. The Commission mentioned it would be located in the Finance Ministry while enjoying operational autonomy and government support, and its recommendations would be processed in the ministry and put up for approval to the Cabinet Committee of Economic Affairs.

The Commission set the goal of sustained economic growth at eight percent and proposed that the investment levels in the economy needed to rise from 30 percent of GDP to 34 percent over the next five years. Having set this target, the Commission suggested expansion in foreign direct investment (FDI) of US$15 billion by the end of 2007–2008 budget year. One of the major thrusts of raising the rate of economic growth has been based on the strategy to attract FDI.

To create a climate conducive for investment, the report of the Investment Commission centered on the role of government in setting a firm policy and on its debilitating decision-making procedures. The recommendation about changing the procedures is broadly subsumed in what we now call governance reforms that facilitate investment. This report also set the pace for forging the government-business partnership that has become the cornerstone of India's strategy of development.

INSTITUTIONAL ARRANGEMENTS FOR NETWORKS

New formal institutions that reflected this partnership and developmental perspective began to emerge and the government began to open itself to the advice and consultation of the corporate sector. The economic ministries formed boards that included leading thinkers of the corporate sector as members. Bodies like the Federation of Chambers of Commerce and Industry and the Confederation of Indian Industry were recognized as legitimate forums for political and bureaucratic leadership to interact with the captains of industry. At the highest level, with the prime minister as chair, the Council on Trade and Industry was created as an institutional framework for partnership between government and business. The prime minster emphasized that the partnership flowed from the overall strategy of economic reforms.

This Council was appointed with a notification in 1998, and this practice has continued through the change of governments in 2004 and 2009. The Council provided an opportunity for a policy dialogue on important economic issues relevant to trade and industry between the prime minister and members of the council; it ordinarily met once every three months on such dates as decided by its chairman. The membership of the Council nearly doubled – from ten to eighteen members – between the years the governments changed. In addition, special subgroups were also appointed to interact directly with the different ministries. Such subgroups specialized in areas such as food and agricultural industries management policy, infrastructure, capital markets and financial-sector initiatives, knowledge-based industries, service industries, and administrative and legal simplifications.

A significant aspect regarding the membership of these councils is that trade unions, labor federations, and NGOs go unrepresented. It is presumed that gains in the rate of economic growth or in relaxing of government norms is a technical problem and can be decided within an expert body and those who can invest. Part of the effort is also to insulate economic decision making from the political process.

The events in India coincided with similar events happening in the Western industrialized countries. In Britain, for example, where a three-way partnership had been institutionalized in the National Economic Development Council launched in 1962, labor unions had had a seat at the negotiating table. During the 1980s, however, the Council diminished in its significance and met infrequently. As prime minister, Margaret Thatcher, was of the opinion that trade unions had no legitimate role in policy making and should therefore be excluded. The Council was finally disbanded in 1992 (Dorey, 2005, p. 125).

CORPORATE INCLUSION IN POLICY SPACES

Members of the corporate world are now even being invited to participate in policy processes regarding many other areas than just industry and trade. For example, the Ministry of Human Resource Development convened a round table for discussing policy issues regarding education. In its first meeting it was decided that Analjit Singh of Max India[6] would prepare a concept note on education. Hari Bhartia of Jubilant Life Sciences[7] would prepare a policy outline on PPPs in research, and Rajendra Pawar of NIIT Enterprise Learning Solutions[8] would recommend measures to ensure that meritorious students get funds for education in private unaided institutions as well as on how private investment could be incentivized.[9] The government announced that during the course of the eleventh Five Year Plan, 2,500 of 6,000 secondary schools in the country will be established under public-private partnerships.

Another area that has seen an increase in the interaction between business and government has been in the management of foreign trade, where close relations with private industrial interests have been established. During the Uruguay Round of trade negotiations (1986–1994), there was only little interaction between negotiators and private business. In May 1989, however, a new advisory body, the Board of Trade, was established in order to strengthen the dialogue between the government and private business.

A much closer interaction was established after the foundation of the WTO and the beginning of regular negotiations on the large variety of issues was included in the WTO agenda. The Indian delegations to the WTO

negotiations in Seattle 1999 and Doha 2003 thus saw a significant participation from Indian business including both the Confederation of Indian
Industry (CII) and the Federation of Indian Chambers of Commerce and
Industry (FICCI). These two bodies assisted in the preparation of the Indian
negotiating position. The initiative to this much closer interaction with private business came from the Department of Commerce and was prompted by
the need for more specific knowledge of the situation within Indian industry
given the enlarged agenda in WTO negotiations. A similar need for more
expertise motivated the establishment of new links to academic research institutions and individual experts, leading to the establishment of a new kind of
government-industry-academia partnership (Pederson, 2007, pp. 23–24).

To create an improved relationship between the bureaucrats and the private
sector, some informal measures have also been attempted. Senior civil servants
are being permitted to go on deputation to work in multinational corporations
or large corporate houses in the public interest.[10] Making good use of Section
6(2) of the Indian Administrative service IAS (Cadre) Rules (1954), which allow
officers to take up assignments outside government, as many as 115 members of
the approximately 5,000-member IAS cadre are holding assignments outside
government. At last count, 64 IAS officers were working with private firms
or NGOs while 51 were on foreign assignments, including those with India
offices of international organizations. Meanwhile, to meet the "shortfall" in
the IAS, the government has decided to recruit "more and more" officers –
110, 120, and 130, respectively, in 2008, 2009, and 2010.[11]

In addition, individuals who have a long background in senior policy positions with the private sector are being inducted at policy-making levels in the
government. In 2009, the Planning Commission opened its doors to one such
well-known person, Arun Maira, who had worked with the business houses
Tata Motors and Arthur D. Little and was senior advisor with a Boston Consulting Group in India.[12] In another recent decision, Nandan Nilekani, Co-
Chairman of Infosys Technologies and leading spokesman for the information
technology industry, was appointed Chairman of the Unique Identification
Authority of India with the rank of cabinet minister. Thus, policy networks are
being created and strengthened in various ways.

This growing partnership between the executive and big business is also
reflected in the membership of parliament. According to a National Election Watch Report, there are around 300 MPs in the parliament who are
"crorepatis"[13] or the Indian equivalent of millionaire. Out of these 300, 138
belong to the Congress Party, and Bihar alone accounts for 52 of them.[14] Many
of these crorepati MPs have connections with big business. Many of them are
leading Indian industrialists with interests in specific sectors. They now sit on

many parliamentary committees that deal with these sectors. The Committee on Labour, the Consultative Committee of Finance in 2007, the Consultative Committee on Commerce, and the Ministry of Civil Aviation all have such members.

RESPONSE OF INDUSTRY ASSOCIATIONS TO GOVERNMENT OVERTURES

Associations of industries have also geared themselves to provide platforms for the leaders of government and business to interact and deliberate on public policy. The FICCI is the rallying point for free enterprise in India. According to its website,[15] it has "empowered Indian businesses, in the changing times, to shore up their competitiveness and enhance their global reach." Thirty-four specialized committees stemming from the FICCI grapple with a wide variety of sectorial issues on a day-to-day basis to provide solutions to business and suggest pragmatic policies to the government. The government in turn provides its support to the activities of Joint Business Councils formed by the FICCI with India's trading partners. This is what it calls track two diplomacy; its objective is to open new business opportunities for Indian businessmen with overseas investors, technology suppliers, and multilateral or bilateral funding agencies. The annual general meetings of FICCI have been important national economic events. Contemporary developmental issues facing the nation are discussed and debated by the political leadership, business, and academia. These events have helped the government of India take stock of the developmental initiatives and evolve policy corrections based on industry responses.

The Confederation of Indian Industry (CII) is another significant business association that catalyses change by working closely with the government on policy issues, enhancing efficiency and competitiveness, and expanding business opportunities for industry through a range of specialized services and global linkages. With 47 offices in India and 12 overseas and institutional partnerships with 239 counterpart organizations in 101 countries, the CII serves as a reference point for industry and the international business community. It has paid special attention to its linkages in the United States and in 1995 set up an office in Washington, DC, with close working relations to organizations such as the U.S. Chamber of Commerce, the U.S.-India Business Council, the Aspen Institute, and the Brookings Institution. The CII has developed strong programs to brief members of the U.S. Congress and has sponsored a number of delegations of Congressmen to visit India. As a corollary it also sponsors visits of Indian parliamentarians to the United States.

The prime ministers and their reform-oriented colleagues have played an important role in seeking support from these associations in initiating policies of liberalization. The finance minister came to address the National Council of the CII in August 2009. He elaborated on the measures taken in the last budget and called for support from industry to carry out many programs in the fields of health and education. He underlined the significance of PPPs that were being promoted to solve difficulties in various sectors like infrastructure, health, and education. Lauding the members of the CII as leading members of industry, he exhorted them to play a "stellar role in making the Indian growth story a continuing one."

The role of the CII in influencing public policy is now well recognized and documented (Kochanek, 1996; Sinha, 2005; Kohli, 2006). CII has argued for a more open and competitive economy and promoted greater integration. As quoted by Sinha (2005, p. 15) Tarun Das, its long-time secretary-general states: "[D]evelopment [is] a partnership process between the government and industry and we (the CII) are the junior partner of the government." The CII has sent delegations to the WTO and accompanied the prime minister on state visits abroad.[16] The CII increasingly came to represent India's more "modern" industries, especially engineering firms, which were interested in exports. The CII was also run professionally and developed such close ties with the Indian bureaucracy that the government's budget in 1993–1994 came to be called the Tarun Das budget (Kochanek, 1996, p. 167).

Over the next decade, these patterns gradually came to be institutionalized; for example, Montek Singh Ahluwalia (Deputy Chairman of the Planning Commission and leading face of liberal policies) in 2004 was openly discussing the need for "public-private partnership' and inviting the private sector "to be part of decision-making" (*Indian Express*, December 29, 2004).

There are also attempts by the industry associations to reach out to the parliamentarians. FICCI, for instance, has a unique mechanism known as the "Forum of Parliamentarians," where any MP interested in joining can do so on a voluntary basis. "At present, about 185 MPs, including those of regional parties, are part of the forum," says Mitra, Secretary-General of FICCI. It is chaired by a member of the ruling party, while the co-chair is an MP from the opposition, the idea being to balance views. Says Mitra: "We send briefings to these MPs on various issues. We also put forward our views to all parties involved in policymaking."

The FICCI, in collaboration with the Indo-U.S. Forum of Parliamentarians, launched an India-Yale Parliamentary Leadership Program in 2007. Young Indian MPs have been sponsored by the FICCI to participate in this program every year since then. Apart from attending the program at Yale University, the parliamentarians are also provided an opportunity to meet with U.S. business leaders.

The CII and FICCI are relating themselves to government not only in terms of demands for enabling a business environment; they have gradually taken steps to organize themselves to influence other sectors. The emerging networks span many areas that were exclusive to government before liberalization took hold.

GOVERNMENT AGENCIES PROMOTING PUBLIC-PRIVATE PARTNERSHIPS

The government set out to attract private investment in critical sectors of the economy, including health and education. The Investment Commission in 2006 calculated that in infrastructure alone, the demand for next five years was of around US$246 billion, not including the health and education sectors. Special governmental agencies have been set up to facilitate the partnerships. The Prime Minister's Office has taken responsibility for infrastructural development through PPPs by setting up a committee reporting to it. The ministry of finance has established a PPP cell to support a coherent policy. Nodal officers of senior rank have been appointed in critical ministries to expedite approvals.

A key initiative of the government to promote PPPs is the Viability Gap Funding Scheme. Its purpose is to provide financial support to those infrastructure projects that are economically justifiable but not viable commercially. The government has also set up a fund of Rs.100 crores (approximately US $21 million) for supporting credible and bankable PPP projects that can be offered to the private sector. The eleventh Five Year Plan, which ended in 2012, was emphatic in highlighting PPP mode in both crafting policy and in implementing it, and this thrust is being carried forward in the vision for the twelfth Plan. An investment of US$1 trillion is proposed in this Plan, out of which half will come through the PPP model.

POLICY NETWORKS AND POLICY SPACES: SOME CONCLUDING OBSERVATIONS

The transformation of the Indian economy was not a singular event. Contrary to popular belief, while the 1991 policy represented a landmark change, the economy was already moving gradually toward greater emphasis on the private sector since the 1980s. As Sinha (2004) points out, 80 percent of investment in the Indian economy was under public control in 1978; by 1998, the public-sector share had fallen to 40 percent.

The increase in the share of the private sector has also ushered a change in governance styles. Openness toward the private sector was growing. Calls for a greater public-private partnership were also gathering momentum, despite anti-market political rhetoric. During the 1980s, several high-powered committees were appointed to review aspects of the economy. Most of them were chaired by senior civil servants who became acquainted with the role of liberal economic policies and directly recommended opening up of the economy. At the same time alternative policy research and think tanks were being established, offering different kinds of technical advice. Several steps taken during the regime of Prime Minister Gandhi (1969–1975) were widely believed to be populist in nature and defying economic logic. The return of technical advice in the policy arena was perceived as a welcome development.

There appeared to be some continuity with the Planning Commission having played this role in the early years when Nehru was prime minister (1947–1964). In that period, efforts were made to insulate technical advice from the rumble-tumble of daily politics. Policies that were now being framed by experts associated with PPPs found wide acceptance. Neoliberals also tended to favor governance by technocrats and elites; this development also found ready favor with the middle classes (Harris, 2011, p. 127).

Raising rates of economic growth became the dominant theme in public discourse, and ways of attracting private investment became a public concern. The state set about searching for market solutions to societal problems. Issues of poverty and inequalities, which were defined as major problems earlier, yielded place to the argument that as the rate of economic growth rose, poverty levels would begin to go down. Inequalities of wealth and incomes were deemed necessary and conducive in providing incentives for wealth creation.[17] The emerging styles of governance underline an "enabling state" whose role is to create conditions in which private investment can take place. The traditional government patterns of decision making became a problem and administrative reforms were aimed at relaxing government decision-making processes so that business enterprises could be set up within minimum time.[18]

In the pursuit of an enabling rather than an interventionist state, confusion prevails around the role of bureaucracy. During the Plan period, bureaucracy sought to scrutinize private investment and assess whether it served the public purpose. It saw itself as part of the mission to see the public sector position itself at the commanding heights of the economy. Rules and regulations in many ways strangled private initiative but were seen as part of the regulatory economy in which private business was distrusted. However, bureaucrats are now being molded into becoming missionaries for the private sector. Public-sector reforms are accompanied by the belief that public goods and services cannot be delivered efficiently by the state.

THE PIVOTAL ROLE OF THE PROFESSIONAL BUREAUCRACY

However, this efficiency is to a great extent a function of a professional bureaucracy committed to public interest. These new institutional structures of governance are a major challenge to the established bureaucracy and their respective policy spaces. In general, the raison d'être of the private sector is profit whereas that of the government bureaucracy is the public interest. From what we saw from the preceding discussion, the networks tend to blur the boundaries between public and private interests. In participative decision making it is the large corporations that exercise vast social and economic power. They have greater opportunities to push their own agendas and take advantage of this fuzziness as a weak and demoralized bureaucracy is being constantly berated for not playing an enabling role adequately. In any case, the bureaucracy itself, through changed rules of deputation and service rules, is being encouraged to expose itself to corporate goals and practices so that more harmonious relations develop in these networks.[19]

It is important to note, however, that the new governance structures are making the collaboration between the government and business more open and transparent; the era of clandestine lobbying is receding into the past. However, network governance also obscures the process and accountability for public policy formulation, decision making, and execution. It opens the door to involvement by a wider range of actors in ways that are less constrained than those applying to institutions of political authority (Mathur and Skelcher, 2007, p. 235). This can lead to many consequences, particularly in a situation in which business by default is given a privileged position in a market-oriented economy that tends to dominate all patterns of social and economic transactions. This privileged position can lead to conflicts with a government that does not want to appear weak in negotiations. As Lindblom (1977, p. 179) points out, inevitably the groups will show hostility toward each other and try to outwit each other to gain an upper hand. But these conflicts lie within a range of dispute constrained by their understanding that they together constitute the necessary leadership for the system. This understanding, however, is leading to more and more socially exclusive policies that are not accountable to politically elected authorities. The final product is a system of networks that tends to democratise policy making toward business and that carries the risk of insulating itself from general democratic structures.

The policy impact of governance networks on socially and economically deprived groups leads to their exclusion and not to the prophesized benefits from the market. The private sector is hesitant to partner with the government's nonprofit schemes. Primary education and primary health care suffer at the cost of market-responsive technical education or highly sophisticated speciality hospitals. For example, when the government promotes a PPP to structure the urban water supply that excludes those who cannot pay for water, it is in a very real way abdicating its own basic responsibilities.[20]

Network governance is assumed to contribute to the production of the public purpose. This public purpose is an expression of a social vision and the direction the policies should take to achieve this vision. But network governance relies on certain political and social processes at work in society that may not necessarily be conducive to the production of public purpose on all occasions (Sorenson and Torfing, 2004).

There can be cases of governance network failure (Jessop, 1998). Human development indicators have not shown significant improvement as the economic transformation continues to take place. Social demands and economic performance are increasingly showing disconnect in India. The multiplying numbers of billionaires in the country is a testament to the growing economic inequality. Private-sector intervention in the social sector has not improved the access of the poor and the deprived to primary health care or primary education.[21]

Social dissatisfaction to this situation is being reflected in at least two ways. Democratically elected governments rarely last for more than one term, a situation that has come to be known as the incumbency factor. The reason for this is really the failure to fulfill the demands of the people who elected them. The classic example has been the defeat of the Bharatiya Janata Party (BJP) in 2004 when it ran the election campaign "India Shining," based on the achievements of economic growth. The Congress Party–led coalition got reelected in 2009 on the promise of providing greater employment and facilities to the rural poor. It must be realized that an increasing number of poor and marginalized citizens are now more mobilized and participative in the elective democracy. There will be a rising tide of demands that growth policies may not be able to satisfy. The government-business networks will need to respond to processes generated by such democratization.

ATTEMPTS TO COUNTER PPPs

Responding to the rising demands of the poor and the marginalized in the democratization process, the government has taken another step. It created the National Advisory Council led by Sonia Gandhi to involve civil society in policy deliberations. This council consists of a mix of retired civil servants, representatives of nongovernmental organizations, social activists, and an industrialist. Although excluded from forums where government and business sit together, this council has been seen to act as a check on the formulation of exclusive policies and to promote the human face of development. The prestige of Gandhi as president of the Congress Party has made the Council influential in formulating more people-friendly laws in many cases.

What is important to point out is that the government-business partnership in India is embedded in an economic situation of continuing mass poverty, in a politics where leadership is thickly enmeshed in maximizing benefits from liberalization, and in a public system that is widely seen to be corrupt and mostly unaccountable. The National Advisory Council has been an attempt to rescue the people from the negative impact of such partnerships as have been discussed throughout this essay.

It is in large part because of this council that concern is being increasingly expressed about the direction of economic reforms and the impact of policy partnership with big business on society and policy spaces. Kohli (2006) has persuasively argued that what may be a good strategy to accelerate economic growth may not necessarily have positive consequences for democracy and politics. It may give rise to social conflicts based on regional caste and even ethnicity rather than those based on class.

The prime minister apparently also seems to recognize this emerging contradiction. Speaking at a public forum, he said he is "puzzled by the persisting regional imbalance in industrial development. . . in India." He expressed serious concern that most Indian businessmen operate in "oligopolistic markets in sectors where the government [gives] them special privileges." He then went on to ask: "Are we encouraging crony capitalism? Is this a necessary but transient phase in the development of modern capitalism? Are we doing enough to protect consumers and small businesses from the consequences of crony capitalism?"[22] This is a significant reflection on the way the partnership is being given shape. In a political economy where corruption is rampant, risk of cronyism is a genuine concern.

Policy networks are embedded in the assumption that the state has the capacity to negotiate with business on equal terms within the policy spaces that have been created. But the alliance that is being generated is one that supports the power and influence of big business.[23] This poses a real challenge to the state in India, for the essence of democratic governance is accountability and transparency. In the new policy spaces where government and business work together, rather than appearing captured by the country's most powerful and

influential business houses, the state must pursue policies that are inclusive
and consistent with these fundamental requirements of democracy.

REFERENCES

Chatterjee, Partha. (1998) Development Planning and the Indian State. In Byres, T. J.
(Ed.), *The State Development Planning and Industrialization in India.* New Delhi:
Oxford University Press.

Das, Gurcharan. (2000) *India Unbound.* New Delhi: Penguin.

Datta, Amrita. (2009) Public-Private Partnerships in India. *Economic and Political
Weekly 44,* 33, 73–78.

Dorey, Peter. (2005) *Policy Making in Britain: An Introduction.* London: Sage Publications.

Ganguly, Sumit and Mukherji, Rahul. (2011) *India Since 1980.* Cambridge: Cambridge
University Press.

Harriss, John. (1987) The State in Retreat: Why Has India Experienced Such Half-
Hearted Liberalization in the 1980s. *IDS Bulletin 18,* 4, 29–36.

Harriss, John. (2011) How Far Have India's Economic Reforms Been "Guided by
Compassion and Justice:" Social Policy in the Neo-Liberal Era. In Sanjay Ruparelia
et al. (Eds.), *Understanding India's New Political Economy.* London and New York:
Routledge.

Harvey, David. (2006) Neo-Liberalism as Creative Destruction. *Geography Annals 88
B,* 2, 145–158.

Jessop, B. (1998) The Rise of Governance and the Risks of Failure: The Case of
Economic Development. *International Social Science Journal 50,* 155, 29–45.

Kapur, Devesh and Bhanu Mehta, Pratap (Eds.). (2005) *Public Institutions in India
Performance and Design.* Oxford: Oxford University Press.

Khilnani, Sunil. (1997) *The Idea of India.* London: Hamish Hamilton.

Kochanek, Stanley. (1996) Liberalization and Business Lobbying in India. *Pacific
Affairs 34,* 3, 155–173.

Kochanek, Stanley A. (1987) Briefcase Politics in India: The Congress Party and the
Business Elite. *Asian Survey 12,* December, 27, 1278–1301.

Kohli, Atul. (1989) The Politics of Economic Liberalization in India. *World Development 17,* 3, 305–328.

Kohli, Atul. (2006) Politics of Economic Growth in India 1980–2005. *Economic and
Political Weekly,* April 1 (Part I) and April 8 (Part II), 1361–1370.

Lindblom, Charles E. (1977) *Politics and Markets: The World's Political-Economic
Systems.* New Delhi: Ambika Publications.

Marquis, Jose Carlos and Utting, Peter (Eds.). (2006) *Business, Politics and Public Policy
Implications for Inclusive Development UNRISD.* London: Palgrave MacMillan.

Marquis, Jose Carlos and Utting, Peter. (2006) Introduction: Understanding Business
Power and Public Policy in a Development Context. In Mathur Kuldeep and James
W. Bjorkman (Eds.), *Policy Making in India Who Speaks? Who Listens?* New Delhi:
Har-Anand Publishers.

Mathur Navdeep and Skelcher, Chris. (2007) Evaluating Democratic Performance:
Methodologies for Assessing the Relationships between Network Governance and
Citizens. *Public Administration Review 2,* 67, 228–237.

Mathur, Kuldeep and Bjorkman, James W. (Eds.). (2009) *Policy Making in India: Who Speaks? Who Listens?* New Delhi: Har-Anand Publishers.

Miraftab, Faranak. (2004) Public–Private Partnerships: The Trojan Horse of Neo-liberal Development. *Journal of Planning Education and Research*, 24, 89–101.

Mural, Kanta. (2006) Liberalization, Business-State Relations and Labour Policy in India. In Jose Carlos Marquis and Peter Utting (Eds.), *Business, Politics and Public Policy Implications for Inclusive Development UNRISD*. London: Palgrave MacMillan.

Panagriya A. (2008) *India: The Emerging Giant*. Oxford: Oxford University Press.

Pedersen, Jorgen Dige. (2007) The Transformation of Indian Business: From Passive resisters to Active Promoters of Globalization. *Pan European Conference on International relations, University of Turin, Italy, 12–15 September*.

Pierre, Jon (Ed.). (2000) *Debating Governance*. Oxford: University Press.

Pingle, Vibha. (2000) *Rethinking the Developmental State: India's Industry in Comparative Perspective*. New Delhi: Oxford University Press.

Ravillion, Martin. (2009) A Comparative Perspective on Poverty Reduction in Brazil, China and India. *World Bank Policy Research Paper no.5080*.

Reijners, J. (1994) Organization of Public-Private Partnerships Projects; The Timely Prevention of Pitfalls, *International Journal of Project Management*, 12(3), 137–142.

Rhodes, R. A. W. (1997) *Understanding Governance Policy Networks, Governance, Reflexivity and Accountability*. Buckingham: Open University Press.

Rhodes, R. A. W. (2006) Policy Network Analysis. In M. Moran, M. Rein, and R. Goodin (Eds.), *The Oxford Handbook of Public Policy*. Oxford: Oxford University Press.

Rosenau, P. V. (2000) *Public-Private Partnerships*. Cambridge, MA: MIT Press.

Sinha, Aseema. (2004) Changing Political Economy of Federalism A Historical Institutional Approach. *Indian Review*, 3, 25–63.

Sinha, Aseema. (2005) Understanding the Rise and Transformation of Business Collective Action. *India Business and Politics*, 7, 2, 1–37.

Sorenson, Eva and Torfing, Jacob. (2004) Making Governance Networks. *Democratic Working Paper 1, Roskilde, Centre for Democratic Governance*.

Stoker, Gerry. (1998) Governance as Theory: Five Propositions. *International Social Science Journal*, 50, 155, 17–28.

Streets, Julia. (2004) *Developing a Framework: Concepts and Research Priorities for Partnership Accountability*. Berlin: Global Public Policy Institute.

Subramaniam A. (2008) *India's Turn: Understanding the Economic Transformation*. New York: Oxford University Press.

Utting, Peter and Zammit, Anne. (2006) Beyond Pragmatism: Appraising UN Business Partnerships. *Markets, Business and Regulation Programme, Paper no.1*. Geneva: United Nations Research Institute for Social Development.

World Bank. (2009) *Doing Business Report*. Washington, DC: World Bank.

8

India's Pharmaceutical Industry: Policy Space That Fosters Technological Capability

Amit Shovon Ray and Saradindu Bhaduri

INTRODUCTION: THE LEARNING CURVE

India's pharmaceutical industry occupies an important position nationally and internationally. In the Economic Survey of 2009–2010 it was reported that India now ranks third among the drug-producing countries of the world in terms of volume of production, accounting for 10 percent of global production (Government of India, 2010). In value terms, India ranks fourteenth in the world. The size of the Indian pharmaceutical industry has expanded phenomenally from a mere 100 million rupees (US$1.5 million) (value of production) in 1947 to more than 1 trillion rupees (US$15 billion) in 2009–2010.

The evolution of the Indian pharmaceutical industry reveals an interesting story of emergence through technological learning and capability, nurtured by a well-focused policy framework. In this chapter, we relay this story to understand how the Indian pharmaceutical industry has emerged as a major global generics producer and how it is poised to take on the challenges posed by a changing landscape of the international political economy. In the first section we trace the historical origin and policy framework for the Indian pharmaceutical industry. The second section describes the trajectory of its technological learning and the evolution of its technological capability within this policy space. The third section outlines the challenges and adjustments for the Indian pharmaceutical industry in the changing global landscape, especially since the financial crisis of 2008. The last section synthesizes the major conclusions.

THE HISTORICAL ORIGIN AND POLICY FRAMEWORK

The origins of the pharmaceutical industry in India can be traced back to the colonial (pre-independence) era. Most of the pre-independence pharmaceutical companies were owned by the British. Perhaps the only exception was Bengal Chemical and Pharmaceutical Works established in 1901 by eminent chemist Prafulla Chandra Ray. However, during the British Raj, India remained import dependent. World War II boosted the pharmaceutical industry's size as well as product range. Besides vaccines for infective diseases, the industry started producing various other drugs including alkaloids, chemotherapeutic drugs, and calcium preparations.

SELF-RELIANCE IN MANUFACTURING: TWO DECADES POST INDEPENDENCE

In the first two decades after independence, India's overall development strategy of import-substituting industrialization acted as the key driving force behind the growth and expansion of the pharmaceutical industry. The first public-sector drug-manufacturing firm, Hindustan Antibiotics Limited, was established in 1954. Another public-sector company, Hindustan Organic Chemicals, also started operations around the same time. In 1958, the government of India entered into an agreement with the Soviet Union to manufacture antibiotics, synthetic drugs, and surgical equipment with a 80 million ruble loan. This led to the establishment of the Indian Drugs and Pharmaceuticals Limited in 1962 with Soviet technical know-how.

These steps, however, could not reduce foreign dominance of the industry, and many Indian-owned private firms found it increasingly difficult to survive and consequently closed down. The industry became largely dominated by multinational corporations (wholly or partly owned subsidiaries), British as well as others. In fact, according to a Reserve Bank of India survey for the 1964–1970 period, the overall domination of foreign firms was the highest in the pharmaceutical sector. Furthermore, these multinationals as well as the few Indian private firms that could survive the competition confined their production activities to packaging and, at best, preparing formulations, relying heavily on imports of bulk drugs and intermediaries. The establishment of the aforementioned three public-sector units was an attempt to reduce this dependence. But through the 1950s and 1960s, the industry remained largely dominated by foreign firms, and drug prices were among the highest in the world.

This makes it evident that trade policy alone is inadequate to foster self-reliance, especially in a process-driven sector where learning and technological capability building has to be actively nurtured through complementary policy instruments, intellectual property rights (IPR) in particular. This policy toward technological self-reliance started in 1970, which marked the beginning of a new era for the pharmaceutical industry in India.

TECHNOLOGICAL SELF-RELIANCE: 1970–1990

With the introduction of the Patent Act of 1970, there was a concerted effort at generating indigenous technological capability in the pharmaceutical sector with the goal of increasing access to drugs at affordable prices. In fact, the 1970s witnessed the passage of several government directives directly shaping the growth path of this sector, including the Drug Price Control Orders (DPCO) 1970 and 1979, Foreign Exchange Regulation Act (FERA) of 1973, and the New Drug Policy 1978. In this section we briefly discuss these policies.

Independent India inherited its Patent Law from the colonial past. The Patents and Designs Act of 1911 adopted by the British in India followed a strict regime of product as well as process patent protection for up to ten years (extendable by another six years) and acted as a major deterrent to the creation of indigenous technological capability, especially through reverse engineering.[1,2] The Patent Act of 1970 was a radical departure and granted only process patent for chemical substances including pharmaceuticals, reduced the duration of patents to seven years from the date of filing or five years from the date of sealing, whichever came first, excluded all imported substances from the domain of patent protection (i.e., only new substances manufactured in India were entitled to patent protection), and placed the burden of proof on the plaintiff in case of infringement. It is worth noting that the scope of the 1970 Patent Act remained confined only to chemicals and pharmaceuticals. One cannot view it as a general policy attempt to create technological self-reliance across the board.

The Drug Price Control Orders of 1970 was the first concerted effort to check rising drug prices in India. DPCO 1979 expanded the coverage of drug price control, bringing about 80 percent of the Indian pharmaceutical industry (in value terms) under price regulation. The price-fixing rules were made more rigid and stringent.

FERA 1973 was introduced to restrict and regulate the operations of foreign multinationals in India to protect and develop indigenous industrial and technological capability. A 40 percent ceiling was imposed on foreign equity share, with the exception of "Core" sectors (including pharmaceuticals), where up to 74 percent foreign equity was allowed to high-technology bulk and formulation producers provided 50 percent of the bulk is supplied to non-associated formulators and the share of own bulk in their formulation should not exceed one-fifth.

BUILDING A FAVORABLE POLICY ENVIRONMENT

The spirit of this policy regime was reinforced by Drug Policy 1978 with its threefold objective of achieving self-reliance in pharmaceutical technology, self-sufficiency in drug production, and easy and cheap availability of drugs. In a sense, this summarizes the policy framework adopted in the 1970s with its clear emphasis on import substitution and self-reliance in the production of bulk and formulations, as well as on creating indigenous technological capability of process development.

Within this favorable policy environment, the pharmaceutical industry in India embarked on a new trajectory of technological learning and acquired substantial technological capability for process development through reverse engineering, both infringing processes for off-patented molecules and non-infringing processes for patented molecules. This phenomenon has been often referred to as the "process revolution" in the Indian pharmaceutical sector. As a result, the bulk drug industry grew at a phenomenally high annual rate of 21 percent and 11 percent during the 1970s and 1980s, respectively. Along with process revolution, simple product development in conventional dosage forms, which had already started in the post-independence era, continued in post 1970s. As a result, the formulation industry also registered impressive annual growth rates of 13 percent and 10 percent, respectively, during the same periods. The impetus largely came from the massive expansion of bulk drugs, stemming from the process revolution and policies to deter captive consumption of bulk. Indeed, there was a marked increase in research and development spending during this period: it stood at Rs 50 Crores in 1986, accounting for nearly 2 percent of the industry's sales turnover, compared to less than 1 percent prior to 1970.

The policy environment also facilitated free entry of a large number of producers of both bulk and formulation, most of them in the small-scale and unorganized sector. The resultant market structure was characterized by a limited number of large organized-sector units enjoying the lion's share of the market and thousands of small producers each producing a microscopic fraction of the total industry sales. This implied a wide variation in the quality and price of drugs in the market and multiplicity of formulation resulting in spurious drugs and irrational combinations. Lack of adequate quality regulations and control mechanisms (often arising out of acute shortage of quality-monitoring infrastructure) resulted in the supply of suboptimal and ineffective drugs. In fact, not only were there major deviations from quality norms; norms were kept at a low level by the regulatory authority to encourage small producers who may not be able to afford sophisticated equipment for various tests and assays. Indeed, there has been a noticeable difference in the parameters of acceptable drug quality in India compared to that in the developed world. But most drugs were by then available in India at affordable prices, quality variations notwithstanding.

As an outcome of this policy framework, multinational corporations became reluctant to launch their new drugs in India. But that did not deprive Indian patients from the latest drug discoveries. Indian firms introduced these new drugs in the market using non-infringing processes, perhaps with a time lag marginally exceeding the demand lag. Examples are numerous.[3]

THE NEW WORLD ORDER AND A SHIFT IN POLICY PARADIGM: POST-1990

The success story of the pharmaceuticals, however, could not be replicated in many other sectors. As a result, India's overall quest for self-reliance remained a largely elusive goal. For one thing, within the protectionist policy framework, there was no incentive to keep pace with the fast-changing global technology frontier in many of the manufacturing sectors. This resulted in the Indian industry becoming technologically backward and inefficient with respect to global standards of cost and quality. This could be attributable to the failure of the Indian entrepreneurial class to reinvest its surpluses, which meant that many Indian industries remained apathetic to focusing on research, development, and technological learning (Gorter, 1996).

From the mid-1980s, we observe a changing norm of development in India's policy-making circles. With Rajiv Gandhi taking over as a prime minister characterized by youth and dynamism, along with his team of technocrat advisers, a technological view of development gained momentum in India's development policy. A shift began away from self-reliance as the sole focus. It was apparent that being able to produce everything could not be the end-all objective. It is very important to be able to do things efficiently as well. This period also witnessed a departure in the scholarship on economic development, with greater emphasis being placed on free trade and moving away from protectionism as a viable means of achieving economic development. India started opening its doors to the latest global technological developments, quite a departure from its earlier inward-looking policy regime. This, in a sense, marked the beginning of India's policy of liberalization. These attempts at liberalization, however, remained arguably piecemeal and somewhat ad hoc (Ray, 2006).

The year 1991 marked a radical departure from the past when, faced with an exceptionally severe balance-of-payments (BoP) crisis, India launched a massive package of economic reforms consisting of short-term stabilization measures along with a longer-term program of structural reforms. In contrast to the feeble attempts that characterized policy making during the 1980s, liberalization post-1991 was better orchestrated, wider in scope, and deeper in coverage. A larger role was granted to the private sector as the engine of growth, market and competitive forces were freed up to boost efficiency, and greater integration with the world economy was encouraged. Incidentally, the BoP crisis of 1991 that precipitated India's economic reforms package coincided with the Uruguay Round of negotiations culminating in the establishment of the WTO in 1994. Hence, one gains a better perspective on the Indian reforms process by viewing it against the evolution of the WTO-driven new world order, instead of regarding it as merely an isolated occurrence.

India's reform process began with trade reforms that sought to reduce, rationalize, and eventually eliminate all forms of trade restrictions, including tariffs, quantitative restrictions, and other nontariff barriers. Reduction and removal of subsidies have accompanied trade reforms. Policies toward foreign investment and foreign technologies have been relaxed. FERA 1973 was modified to the less stringent Foreign Exchange Management Act in 1999. The monitoring of payments for imported raw material and technical know-how was deregulated, but the Reserve Bank of India (RBI) retained the monitoring authority of the dividend payment. The Foreign Exchange Management Act allowed the pharmaceutical multinational corporations to hike their stakes in India up to 74 percent. Automatic approval can be granted for foreign technology agreements in high-priority industries up to a lump sum payment of Rs.10 million, or if the royalty is less than 5 percent of domestic sales or 8 percent of exports, subject to a maximum ceiling. For other non-priority industries, automatic permission is given according to the same guidelines if no free foreign exchange is required for any payments.[4]

The Patent Act of 2005 was a direct fallout of the WTO agreements. This act allowed product patents in all fields of technology with a uniform duration of twenty years in pharmaceuticals, food products, and agrochemical from the date of application. The burden of proof was reversed to rest with the party that infringes. However, India, in designing its Patent Act, has made use of some of the flexibilities of the TRIPS provision, for example, in defining patentability criteria (article 3(d)) and in the use of compulsory licenses. The former (patentability criteria) disallows patenting of a new form (with no increase in efficacy), a new property, or a new use of known substances or known processes, and the latter (compulsory licensing) allows granting licenses to produce a patented drug in case of national emergency.

The enactment of this law signaled the end of the era of process-development-oriented research and development in the pharmaceutical industry. But the strong product patent regime was supposed to encourage basic and frontier research in the industry by correcting the incentive structure. Moreover, the new IPR regime was also supposed to expedite launches of new drugs further.

The overall philosophy of the new policy regime was echoed in the Drug Policy Statements of 1986, 1994, and 2003. Licensing requirements for all bulk drugs and formulations were mostly abolished and restrictions on import substantially relaxed. The new policy framework also allowed captive consumption of bulk drugs. Importantly, drug quality received a renewed emphasis. The need to monitor and regulate quality was recognized, along with placing increased stress on overall manufacturing quality, deviating from the earlier focus on the quality of only the final products. Implementation of a suitable form of good manufacturing practices became compulsory for firms across the board.

The regime of drug price control also gave way to this new policy direction of liberalization. DPCO 1987 followed by DPCO 1995 appeared as major landmarks aimed at progressive decontrol of drug prices. It is interesting to note the clear policy shift in the stated principle for controlling drug prices during this period. As opposed to the earlier objective of making drugs available at affordable prices, the DPCO 1995 clearly stated that the objective is to prevent a monopoly in any market segment. Only 40 percent of the total finished dosage forms remain under price control in 2001, compared to 85–90 percent in 1979.

We now analyze the trajectory of technological learning by the Indian pharmaceutical industry during the so-called protectionist policy framework to help assess the preparedness of the industry to cope with the challenges of a liberalized policy regime in the long run.

TECHNOLOGICAL LEARNING AND THE EVOLUTION OF TECHNOLOGICAL CAPABILITY

The technological capability acquired by the Indian pharmaceutical industry since its inception may be grouped under three broad categories: (1) process development capabilities for bulk drug; (2) product development capabilities for formulations; and (3) new drug discovery research. We discuss each of these separately before presenting a summary of the evolutionary process.

PROCESS DEVELOPMENT BULK DRUG CAPABILITIES

Popularly, process development capability refers to reverse engineering. In the context of the pharmaceutical industry it essentially implies decoding an original process for producing an active pharmaceutical ingredient or bulk drug. One can distinguish between two types of capabilities in this context: capability to develop infringing and non-infringing processes. In case of the former, a reverse engineered process exactly matches the chemical specifications of the original process. Needless to say, such processes infringe on the intellectual property rights of the innovator of the original process. The second category of reverse engineering activities is somewhat more complex as it results in the development of non-infringing processes whereby the same bulk drug may be produced through a different combinations of chemical specifications (e.g., temperature, air pressure, solvents, excipients used), not patented so far.

There has been widespread reverse engineering for non-infringing processes since the 1970s. This is not to suggest that infringing process development (simple imitation) has never taken place. In fact, many firms reportedly began with such simple technological activities (perhaps on off-patent drugs) to acquire more complex capabilities at a later stage.

PRODUCT DEVELOPMENT FORMULATION

Formulation is the end-product of the pharmaceutical industry. Conventionally it takes the forms of tablets, capsules, syrups, and injectables. In the production of formulation, bulk drug (i.e., the active pharmaceutical ingredient) is used as raw material. Unlike process development, where cost reduction and import substitution were the key objectives, product development is driven to diversify product range, improve product quality, and create niche markets (to remain competitive) and retain market share. Indeed, these activities are not necessarily cost-reducing in nature.

In terms of complex research and development and level of technological capability, one can categorize pharmaceutical product development (formulations) into two broad groups: *conventional dosages forms* and *non-conventional drug delivery system*. Within the second group there can be further subdivision. In the absence of any standard nomenclature for these subgroups, we name them as *first-generation* and *second-generation* non-conventional delivery systems. Conventional dosage forms include traditional tablets, capsules, and syrups, whereas non-conventional delivery systems may take the form of sustained release, controlled release dosage forms, and targeted release formulations.

First-generation non-conventional delivery systems constitute a technological advancement over conventional formulations because the former has the capacity to manipulate the release of medicine in the body over a specified period of time and thus requires a better understanding of the chemical reactions between medicine and the acids and fluids within the human system. Second-generation non-conventional delivery drugs hit the target (the diseased part of the body) directly and exclusively without reacting with any other organs, therefore manufacturing them requires knowledge of biology and anatomy as well.

The evolutionary trajectory of firms in India suggest that only a handful of firms ventured into second-generation non-conventional formulations, compared to a number of firms actively producing conventional dosage forms and first-generation non-conventional formulations. The research and development on second-generation non-conventional delivery formulation in India is constrained by both demand and supply side factors. On the demand side, a majority of consumers are not quality sensitive or bothered by the hazards associated with over-intake of drugs, as is the case with conventional dosage formulation. As a result, second-generation non-conventional delivery formulation caters only to a small group of quality-conscious consumers.[5] On the supply side, India lacks sufficiently skilled personnel in biology, which contributes to successful research on second-generation non-conventional delivery systems.[6]

BASIC RESEARCH FOR NEW DRUG DISCOVERY

In the context of the pharmaceutical industry, basic research essentially means research and development undertaken with the objective of new drug development. A new, hitherto unavailable drug is a patentable new chemical (molecular) entity able to cure or control a disease (or any particular aspect of it). New drug discovery research involves a series of steps, beginning with target identification and ending with clinical trials.

The cost of new drug discovery has been sharply rising and is currently estimated at more than US$3.5 billion. More than 60 percent of this cost is incurred for various safety studies, especially at the clinical trial phase (Cockburn, 2004; DiMasi et al., 2003). This is more than the critical mass (sales turnover) enjoyed by even the largest Indian pharmaceutical firms. Thus, carrying out new drug discovery research in its entirety (from target identification to clinical trials) is beyond their financial capability.[7] Also, there is a dearth of skills and expertise in biology, limiting India's technological capability to efficiently conduct all steps new drugs development. Accordingly, the financial and technological capability of the Indian drug industry has shaped the trajectory of new drug discovery research.

The attempts toward new drug discovery research in India have largely been confined to developing the *me-too* type of new chemical entities. This implies that Indian firms do not go for target identification as well as extensive use of advanced technologies to screen for new lead molecules. Their small size and lack of critical research and development deters them from exploiting the possible scale economies in such research and development practices as per the Schumpeterian doctrine. In India, conventional analytic chemistry tools are used to develop analogs of existing molecules to arrive at a *me-too* type new molecular entity. Such methods are highly human skill oriented, without much economies of scale. However, one should note in this context that some of the Indian firms use various tailor-made versions of medium throughput machines.

Even after getting the lead molecule, Indian firms do not have adequate financial resources to carry out most of the activities in the development phase of new drug discovery research. As a result, they either aim to partner up with or sell their patented lead to foreign firms that, in turn, undertake the developmental part of new drug discovery research. Such arrangements have clear implications for the choice of therapeutic area for research in India. Although infectious diseases are prevalent in India, implying a high demand for new antibiotic and anti-infective drugs, foreign firms aiming at global markets do not find such therapeutic areas lucrative enough for new drug discovery research. As a result most of Indian firms have chosen systemic, non-communicable diseases for their research-and-development activities. Such a focus, however distorted from a welfare perspective, enhances the probability of getting a foreign collaborator for developmental activities and, if successful, marketing new molecules.

At another extreme, new drug discovery research in India is also taking the form of contract research and development, where a foreign firm identifies a research area to a domestic firm, which then develops a new patentable lead molecule under contract. This route enables firms with some technological capabilities for new drug discovery research to overcome their financial constraints and reduce the search costs of identifying projects. Through contract research, such firms can also augment their technological capabilities.

SYNTHESIS: EVOLUTION OF TECHNOLOGICAL CAPABILITY

Figure 8.1 depicts the evolution of technological capability in the Indian pharmaceutical industry in a simple schematic framework. The solid arrows represent the path of evolution for domestic firms and the dotted arrows represent the research and development activities of multinational corporations. It is worth mentioning at the very outset that the trajectories of multinational corporation subsidiaries do not represent any efforts toward building up technological capabilities. They have largely relied on the technology shelf of

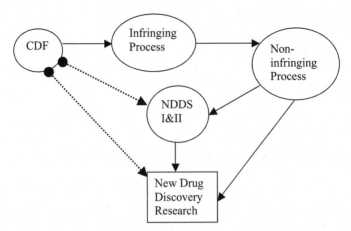

FIGURE 8.1. Evolution of Technological Capability in Indian Pharmaceutical Industry

their parent firms. However, during the 1970s, some multinationals reportedly made limited effort to develop cheaper processes to remain competitive in the Indian market.

The evolution of the technological capability of domestic firms begins with simple product development capability of conventional dosage forms. Eventually, within the framework of an inward-looking policy regime of industrialization, self-reliance, and weak IPR, they acquired process reverse engineering capabilities. Initially these capabilities were purely imitative in nature, and thus infringing processes. Over time, they acquired capabilities to invent around patentable processes through non-infringing routes. The technological capability to develop non-infringing processes requires not only scientific knowledge but also learning through experience and spillover. Until this stage, the evolution of technological capability in the Indian pharmaceutical industry resembles the technological trajectory followed by the manufacturing industry in Latin America as analyzed by Katz (1984, 1987).

However, we find a reversal from process development capability to further (advanced) product development capabilities known as *novel drug delivery systems*. These capabilities, however, could only be acquired by larger firms in the industry, which successfully combined the multidisciplinary skills required for such research and development. Moreover, controlled and targeted-release drugs usually cater to wealthier consumers, who are able and willing to pay a premium for reduced hassles of drug intake. However, these consumers are also more conscious about finer dimensions of quality. Large firms, either because of their brand reputations or because of their better in-house quality control facilities, are in a stronger position to venture into these quality-conscious market segments.

Acquisition of advanced product development capabilities embodied in novel drug delivery systems facilitated acquisition of new drug discovery research capabilities by the Indian firms. The existing skills in chemistry, along with strengthening biology expertise (molecular and structural biology, in particular) required for novel drug delivery system research, as well as experience in handling new sophisticated quality-testing equipment, have helped them venture into more risky projects of new drug discovery research. However, the nature, process, and steps of new drug discovery research in India typically reflects the evolution of technological capability of a less developed country with limited risk-taking, financial, and research capabilities. The *me-too* type new drug discovery research, predominantly focusing on inventing around an existing inhibitor for a given target, are far less risky and less expensive than finding a new target itself. The same factors explain the move toward contract new drug discovery research.

To overcome their financial constraints, some firms have engaged in contract research to augment their technological capabilities. We thus see a diverse pattern of path-dependent learning trajectories of domestic firms, shaped by a complex interaction of skill availability, division of labor in research and development, a risk-taking attitude, finance, firm size, policy regimes, and the institutional parameters of drug research. All this suggests that technological capability in this industry has been a path-dependent and incremental process rather than one consisting of discrete jumps.

CHALLENGES AND ADJUSTMENTS POST-1990: INDIAN PHARMACEUTICAL INDUSTRY AT A CROSSROADS

Although the Indian pharmaceutical industry has continued to expand both in terms of production and trade post-1990, the new global policy environment poses major challenges to the sector. As a result, the Indian pharmaceutical industry is going through a turbulent phase of adjustments. In this section we attempt to trace this adjustment process for the organized segment of the industry.[8]

The new patent regime makes the non-infringing process-led growth unviable. Reverse engineering on patented drugs will come to complete halt, raising a big question as to how far the Indian pharmaceutical industry can exploit its process development, acquired through conscious research-and-development effort during the last quarter of the twentieth century prior to the existence of the new IPR.

Reverse engineering off-patent drugs can, of course, continue to give them an edge in the generic market. In fact, a market of about US$50 billion of currently proprietary drugs will come off patent in the next few years. We must note, however, that the global pharmaceutical market is becoming increasingly competitive with respect to both price and quality. In the post-TRIPS environment, new drugs become the exclusive monopoly of the innovating firm, and all non-innovating firms will now rely on the generic market, making it extremely crowded. Moreover, the scope of business development based on the generic market may be further limited by the high rate of new drug discovery. This could work via two routes. First, with a faster pace of new drug discovery research, the new drugs rarely have a pioneering therapeutic use. Rather, they usually offer better therapeutic efficacy or lower side effects and hence replace an earlier drug. New drug discovery might therefore reduce the life span of existing drugs, which, in turn, implies a high rate of obsolescence in the generic pharmaceutical market. Secondly, we could alternatively argue that in the era of faster new drug discovery research, most new drugs are not "new" in the sense of offering a major therapeutic advancement. They are usually outcomes of inventing around an existing drug and making marginal changes. This often leads to an ever-greening of patents, provided the regime allows for such narrow patentability criteria. This naturally delays the entry of generics into the market.

Under these circumstances, the India pharmaceutical industry remains at a watershed. It could emerge as a major and successful global generic producer. It may also aspire to enter the top league of global innovating firms and get into new drug discovery research. We examine these possibilities in the next section.

INDIA AS A GLOBAL GENERIC PRODUCER

One could argue that Indian firms with their process capabilities are eminently poised to emerge as global suppliers of generic drugs. Indeed, we do see this trend emerging in the last decade or two. However, there are serious roadblocks in the form of protectionist moves through various channels by the advanced nations to protect their pharmaceutical industries.

The WTO allows for imposition of product regulations and standards to create barriers to the free flow of trade. This is being fully exploited by developed countries to protect their large pharmaceutical markets from low-cost imports from the developing world. Therefore, new norms of drug quality are being introduced worldwide, which will further limit the scope of access to the world generic market. With a move toward quality harmonization, drug quality will act as the principal parameter of success even for Indian firms in years to come.

Drug quality is a complex and multidimensional concept. First and foremost, quality implies therapeutic efficacy and safety. A high-quality drug must be effective and should not produce any toxicity or side effects. In this regard, bioavailability acts as an important parameter of drug quality. A second and more commonly stated parameter of quality pertains to the impurity profile and stability of chemical ingredients. A related quality parameter affecting product purity is contamination during the production process. Not only is maintaining minimum impurity important, but consistency in the specified impurity profile over all batches of production must be adhered to. Detailed documentation of all the production stages along with the quality control operations constitutes an added dimension of quality specification as it creates institutional memory and makes the entire production process transparent to all concerned parties. The third set of quality parameters stipulates that the production process should be environmentally friendly and should not create any health hazards within and/or outside the production unit. The intermediates and excipients of the production process must also be nonhazardous and environmentally friendly (Ray and Bhaduri, 2003).

The relative importance of each of these diverse parameters in the final quality specification would vary from country to country depending on the composition of their pharmaceutical industry and the socioeconomic priorities of the government. This has resulted in the divergence of technical requirements for quality specification and control in different countries, compelling the globalized industry to replicate many test procedures, including clinical trials, in order to market new products in different countries. To overcome this problem, the governments of the three largest pharmaceutical markets (the United States, EU, and Japan) have jointly initiated a move toward harmonization of drug quality through the International Conference on Harmonisation from the late 1980s. The U.S. pharmaceutical industry has dominated this harmonization movement with a built-in bias toward increasingly stringent norms for impurity profiling through sophisticated instrumentation and analytical methods.

Prior to the 1990s, drug quality in India was loosely defined and remained far below international standards. This is not to suggest that there were no high-quality producers even during this period. But quality parameters did not receive much attention by the industry and the regulatory authorities in general. In the new era of globalization, however, characterized by a strict IPR regime, a fast-moving technology frontier, and moves toward international harmonization of quality standards, firms will have to explore the growing international market for generic drugs, the U.S. market in particular. Entry into this highly competitive market calls for stringent quality requirements. Indeed with the threats of the International Conference on Harmonisation, not only the U.S. but the entire global market will be subjected to stricter quality norms that entail increased automation of the production process. In many cases this would require completely overhauling of the plant setup to install sophisticated (often imported) machinery and equipment for production and quality control. Thus quality norms act as an effective entry barrier for Indian generic exporters. Still, many of the Indian pharmaceutical players have made necessary adjustments to meet the challenges of global quality.

Apart from quality restrictions, yet another form of regulation that appears to be creeping in as a major nontariff barrier for generic exporters takes the form of Anti-Counterfeit trade agreements. While spurious drugs are a source of major health concern and require strict policy attention, one observes in recent years an attempt to expand the net of counterfeit drugs to include not only the spurious drugs but also drugs having disputed boundaries of intellectual property rights and quality norms. Both these extensions are problematic, given that quality and intellectual property are rarely uniform across countries, cutting across the wide spectrum of the levels of economic development and technological capability. Moreover, we have already noted that under the provisions of compulsory licensing, intellectual property rights can also be revoked by a country in the interest of public health during "national emergencies."

There is now a concerted attempt by innovating pharmaceutical firms, backed by their respective states, to thwart the challenges of the generic industries by labeling generic drugs as "counterfeit" and delegitimizing their therapeutic content. Recent incidents of seizing legally produced Indian generics en route to Latin American markets at EU ports on grounds of counterfeiting are clear indicators of how anticounterfeiting could pose a killer threat to legitimate Indian generics.

Interestingly, the first attempt to bring in anticounterfeit measures at the global level was initiated at the WHO under the International Medical Product Anti-Counterfeit Taskforce. It was strongly opposed by India and other emerging and developing nations. Now there are fresh attempts to activate a new forum, the Anti-Counterfeit Trade Agreement (ACTA), as a new plurilateral agreement. The Agreement has already been signed by thirty-one states including twenty-two members of the EU. So far India has resisted yielding to such moves. However, with an increasing number of nations signing up for such agreements, access to global markets for legitimate Indian generics becomes increasingly difficult. Such attempts go completely against the spirit of the Doha Declaration and its mandate to give priorities to public health concerns over trade interests.

DATA EXCLUSIVITY – TRIPS PLUS AGENDA IN FREE TRADE AGREEMENTS

A pharmaceutical product, whether patented or otherwise, requires marketing approval by a regulatory agency to certify its safety, efficacy, and quality. The producer, as a precondition for this approval, has to submit data relating to the safety, effectiveness, and quality of the drug to the marketing approval authority. This data is generated during the clinical trials and testing stage of the drug, carried out by the producer. Based on this data, the regulatory agency grants marketing approval for a new drug application only if it is satisfies all the conditions of testing. Because this data is submitted to the public authorities for approval, it allows the possibility of its use by a third party. The use of this data by a third party confers an unfair commercial advantage, and thus this data should be protected from disclosure. TRIPS includes provisions for data protection, contained in the Article 39.3 under Protection of Undisclosed Information.

However, data protection does not preclude public authorities from granting marketing approval to third-party (generic) producers relying on the data submitted by the original producer. This enables them to launch the generic product as soon as the patent period is over, facilitating early entry of generics. Data exclusivity goes one step further. It disallows the use of test data by public authorities for granting marketing approvals for generics. This effectively extends the monopoly protection enjoyed by the original producer over and above its period of patent protection. The global pharmaceutical giants argue that without data exclusivity, pioneer drug manufacturers are placed at a serious commercial disadvantage, and hence the incentives to innovate are weakened. It is in this context that developed country governments are demanding data exclusivity in international trade negotiations. This would be a form of marketing exclusivity for a fixed period of time prohibiting even the regulatory authorities to use the clinical trial data submitted by the original innovator for marketing approval of generics, providing a serious blow to the generics manufacturers. India being an emerging player in the global generics market, data exclusivity is clearly not in its interest.

Despite several attempts to prove that data exclusivity is an integral part of the TRIPS obligation, the verdict remains loud and clear – TRIPS mandates only data protection but not data exclusivity. With the WTO presently as a standstill, there has been a sudden explosion of free trade agreements among trading nations, and the developed countries are now trying hard to put in a TRIPS Plus agenda in these bilateral free trade agreements. The recent attempt to include data exclusivity as part of the India-EU free trade agreement under negotiation is a glaring example. Acceding to these pressures could prove fatal to the Indian generic industry.

NEW DRUG DISCOVERY RESEARCH IN INDIA: AN ELUSIVE GOAL?

At one time there was a wide optimism that with the enactment of the TRIPS compatible patent regime in India, the Indian pharmaceutical industry would ease into the process of new drug discovery research and make major therapeutic advances. This has not happened so far.

The previous sections clearly demonstrate that technological capability is an incremental, path-dependent process. Incentive alone cannot ensure success in drug discovery research. In India, advanced product development capabilities have slowly paved the way for new drug discovery research. However, the me-too new drug research effort in India focuses predominantly on inventing around an existing inhibitor for a given target. It has been primarily driven by existing skills and capabilities rather than venturing into new areas of capability building and research-and-development investments. India still lacks adequate skills in some of the specific areas (like biology, toxicology, and computer-aided drug design) and state-of-the-art infrastructure (for instance, high-throughput screening machines) that are critically important for new drug discovery research. In fact, almost ten years after the first batch of lead molecules were developed and sold for further development by an Indian firm, we have yet to see any Indian new molecular entities on the market.

In an earlier work (Ray, 2009), we argued that while technology has, in general, been a key driving force behind India's economic emergence, India's technological advantages have still, by and large, remained confined to the domain of minor as opposed to major innovative capabilities. India has demonstrated significant competitive strength in routine tasks like process development in pharmaceuticals, and perhaps less so in creativity and innovativeness. The myopic vision of the Indian industry, in general, has stood in the way of nurturing the creativity that can be achieved through large-scale investments in fundamental and long-term research-and-development projects. Indian entrepreneurs, by and large, remain interested only in immediate returns on their investments.

One way of stimulating creativity and innovation in India's technological trajectory is through nurturing India's large pool of research potential in the publicly funded institution (universities and laboratories) and harnessing it for effective commercial application and industrial development. Indeed, many of the pioneering drug discoveries in the world (e.g., penicillin, insulin, streptomycin, polio vaccine, hepatitis B vaccine) have been made in university laboratories. However, in India, the research partnerships between industry and public research institutes have been at best suboptimal and at worst stressful. Successful university-industry collaboration may hold some promise for meaningful drug discovery research in India, but energizing this "successful" collaboration could prove a tall order. There have been policy discussions to this effect. However, the approach of the Indian policy makers to solving this problem, primarily through intellectual property rights reforms in publicly funded institutions, suffers from short-sightedness and an inability to appreciate the complexity and multidimensionality of industry-university collaboration in basic research. Willy-nilly, new drug discovery research for major therapeutic advances may remain an elusive goal for the Indian pharmaceutical industry, at least in the near and medium future.

CONCLUSION: INDIA'S UNIQUE POLICY SPACE

In this chapter, we have attempted to portray the unique policy space India has created for itself to foster the technological capability of the domestic pharmaceutical industry. We have shown how endogenously determined homegrown policy models have helped this industry become self-reliant, not only in manufacturing but also in technology, and eventually compete successfully in global markets through technological capability. A few important questions arise from this discourse.

First, why can the success of Indian pharmaceuticals not be replicated in other sectors in India? As already mentioned, India made a concerted effort in the 1970s to create a new policy paradigm for its pharmaceutical sector only, leaving the rest of the manufacturing industries to operate within the earlier IPR framework. Hence, it is little surprise that we fail to see replication of India's pharmaceutical success in other sectors. The policy attention on pharmaceuticals can be understood in the light of India's public health concerns and rising drug prices, but there is very little by way of research to explain India's policy priority for pharmaceuticals over other manufacturing industries.

Second, is it possible to replicate this pharmaceutical policy framework elsewhere? It has been adequately highlighted by the innovation systems literature that policies need to develop various systemic linkages to be effective. Synchronization of policies with other institutional and organizational factors determines, to a large extent, the fate of policy outcomes, and one cannot deny the importance of historicity and path dependence in technological learning. India's historical roots in pharmaceutical production, coupled with its long-standing tradition of science education, especially in analytical chemistry, perhaps contributed to the policy success in building pharmaceutical technological capability. Therefore, one must contextualize the policy lessons to be able to replicate this success in other countries.

In addition, the creation of a policy space is influenced by national and international political economic interests. For instance, the pressure lobby from global pharmaceutical giants have often influenced policy making in developing countries to the detriment of indigenous capability building. In the 1970s, many believed India could succeed in resisting such pressures to pursue its primary goal of technological self-reliance. Similar attempts by other developing countries to create this policy space have often been foiled by political economy pressures created by pharmaceutical multinational corporations and their home governments.[9]

We would like to note that the space for endogenous policy making by national governments has been shrinking over the past two decades with the emergence of a new world order driven by neoliberal institutions like the WTO. Accordingly, the present global landscape poses a challenge for the Indian pharmaceutical industry to continue to compete and emerge through its technological capability. We have seen how it is becoming increasingly difficult to create a favorable policy environment for the pharmaceutical industry to flourish. For one thing, its transition to a new paradigm of technological trajectory through successful drug discovery research does not appear imminent. At the same time, the niche it has created for itself as global generic producer is also under major threats. Our contention is that at this juncture any policy move that may hurt the generic industry in India should be resisted. A vibrant generic industry in India will go a long way in serving the cause of global access to affordable medicines and upholding the spirit of the Doha Declaration, with its mandate to give priority to public health concerns over trade interests.

REFERENCES

Bhaduri, S. and Ray, A. S. (2006), "A Game Theoretic Model of Drug Launch in India", *Health Economics, Policy and Law*, 1(1), pp. 23–39.
Cockburn, I. M. (2004), "The Changing Structure of the Pharmaceutical Industry", *Health Affairs*, 23(1), pp. 10–22.
DiMasi, J., Hansen R. W., and Grabowski, H. G. (2003), "The Price of Innovation: New Estimates of Drug Development Costs", *Journal of Health Economics*, 22(2), pp. 151–185.

Gorter, P. (1996), *The Rise of a New Class of Industrialists: Economic and Political Networks on an Industrial Estate in West India*, Oxford University Press: Delhi.

Government of India (2010), *Economic Survey*, Department of Economic Affairs, Ministry of Finance: New Delhi.

Katz, J. M. (1984), "Domestic Technological Innovations and Dynamic Comparative Advantage", *Journal of Development Economics*, 16, pp. 13–37.

Katz, J. M. (1987), "Domestic Technology Generation in LDCs: A Review of Research Findings" in J. M. Katz (ed.) *Technology Generation in Latin American Manufacturing Industries*, Macmillan: London.

Ray, A. S. (2005), "The Indian Pharmaceutical Industry at Crossroads: Implications for India's Health Care" in Amiya Bagchi and Krishna Soman (eds.) *Maladies, Preventives and Curatives: Debates in Public Health in India*, Tulika Books: New Delhi.

Ray, A. S. (2006), "Going Global: India's Economic Aspirations and Apprehensions in the New Millennium" in F. Villares (ed.) *India, Brazil and South Africa: Perspectives and Alliances*, Editora UNESP: Sao Paulo.

Ray, A. S. (2009), "Emerging through Technological Capability: An Overview of India's Technological Trajectory" in Manmohan Agarwal (ed.) *India's Economic Future: Education, Technology, Energy and Environment*, Social Science Press: New Delhi.

Ray, A. S. and Bhaduri, S. (2003), "The Political Economy of Drug Quality: Changing Perceptions and Implications for the Indian Pharmaceutical Industry", *Economic and Political Weekly*, 38(23).

Reich, M. R. (1994), "Bangladesh Pharmaceutical Policy and Politics", *Health Policy and Planning*, 9(2), pp. 130–143.

PART IV

Contested Policy Space in Social Welfare

9

Reducing Poverty in Brazil: Finding Policy Space for Meeting Development Needs

Kathryn Hochstetler

INTRODUCTION: BRAZIL'S GOOD NEWS

The first decade of the twenty-first century brought an unprecedented mix of good economic news to Brazil. Strong aggregate macroeconomic outcomes made their effects felt deep in the Brazilian population, lifting millions out of economic misery and millions more into the middle class. Even Brazil's infamously high income inequality was reduced. A cover of the *Economist* magazine showed Rio de Janeiro's statue of Christ lifting off into the stratosphere, with a special section inside to tell "Latin America's Big Success Story."[1] This chapter examines that success story more closely, identifying the major components of Brazil's emerging economic model and its strengths and weaknesses. Overall, the lesson is that more inclusive growth contributed to sustained domestic demand, which in turn generated the employment and government revenues that could further support an ongoing positive cycle of investment and growth.

The economic approach that produced these Brazilian results is a heterodox mix. Increasing levels of state spending and planning were placed on a foundation of policies designed for macroeconomic stability and market opening. As such, the Brazilian model involves a larger state role than the neoliberal Washington Consensus would condone, but does not step away from market forces altogether. The chapter begins with a discussion of how Brazil found the "policy space" to make these development choices. From there I turn to the model itself. I focus on the two administrations led by former president Luiz Inácio "Lula" da Silva (2003–2010), pointing out elements of continuity and discontinuity with his successor, Fernando Henrique Cardoso (1995–2002). Lula's first term generally extended Cardoso's policy choices, while the second was marked by more significant departures. Thus Lula's Workers' Party (PT, *Partido dos Trabalhadores*) and Cardoso's Brazilian Social Democratic

Party (PSDB, *Partido Socio Democrático Brasileiro*) both claim – and deserve – credit for the recent successes.

FINDING POLICY SPACE IN A GLOBALIZED ECONOMY

For the last several decades, developing countries have seen their ability to choose their preferred economic policies circumscribed. The concept of policy space captures this problem of the frequently missing "flexibility under trade [and other international] rules that provides nation-states with adequate room to deploy effective policies to spur economic development" (Gallagher, 2008, p. 63). The rise of the World Trade Organization (WTO) and its enforceable trade rules notably restricted this space. For Latin American countries, even more dramatic constriction has come in moments of debt and/or currency crises, when international financial institutions have extracted numerous policy concessions in exchange for inflows of dollars (Akyüz, 2010; Kaufman and Segura-Ubiergo, 2001; Nooruddin and Simmons, 2006; Wibbels, 2006). During the years of the Washington Consensus, such institutions worked together to insist on less state spending of all kinds. This included both social and investment spending, obedience to open market rules in trade and investment, and limited regulation, among other tenets.

As we will see, the new Brazilian model violates many of these tenets, raising the question of how Brazil was able and willing to develop such a large policy space. The first set of answers comes from changes in the developed world: mired in economic crisis, reaching out for their own heterodox solutions, industrialized countries were in little condition to discipline a large developing country like Brazil in the 2000s. In fact, the comparatively good performance of the emerging powers like Brazil even gave them new influence among international financial institutions and their global rule-making in response to the crisis. The second set of answers comes from Brazilian policy choices after their last currency crisis and International Monetary Fund (IMF) loan in 1999. Presidents Cardoso and then Lula were determined to reduce their international financial vulnerability, and both took comparable steps to change the nature of their public debt and to build reserves. The boom in global commodity prices in the 2000s helped make this effort successful. The different political bases and ideologies of their political parties also eventually propelled Lula to employ more of his growing policy space.

NEW POLICY SPACE FROM THE GLOBAL FINANCIAL CRISIS

Beginning on the largest scale, the global financial crisis of 2007–2009 found countries around the world scrambling to respond, and doing so by violating many of the rules they had recently upheld. While trade protectionism largely did not recur as feared (Ocampo, 2011, p. 14), most states increased spending and their involvement in the economy considerably if they were able to do so. They put together stimulus packages, extended social safety nets for the unemployed and economically displaced, and supported national enterprises and banks with bailouts, inexpensive credit, and other initiatives (International Monetary Fund, 2009; Schelkle, 2010; Weber and Schmitz, 2011). A decade earlier, similar policies of public support for the aerospace conglomerate Embraer had led Canada to challenge Brazil at the WTO (Schrank and Kurtz, 2005), but there were few such cases this time, perhaps because so many countries would be vulnerable to counter-challenges for their own crisis responses.

This global crisis was also different in a more profound way for developing countries, and especially the set of emerging powers that included Brazil. They had been at the center of recent crises, but now were doing comparatively well (Hochstetler, 2011). The crisis accelerated their inclusion in global economic policy framing, as well as in policy implementation. The G-7 had already expanded to a G-20 of finance ministers in 1999, but beginning in 2008, the heads of state of a newly active G-20 began to meet regularly. The World Bank and the IMF shifted a small quota of voting shares to the global South and promised more. In short order, Brazil was invited to join the Financial Stability Board, the Basel Committee on Banking Supervision, the Technical Committee of the International Organization of Securities Commissions (IOSCO), and the Committee on Payment and Settlement Systems (Helleiner, 2010, p. 284; Woods, 2010). These invitations were part of a longer-term shift in economic power from Northern to Southern countries, which had begun a decade before. Their accumulation over time meant that Brazil and other emerging powers actually sat at the table and participated as global policy expectations were set for this new context. It seems likely that this contributed to new policy flexibility on the part of organizations like the IMF, which somewhat reluctantly went along with the use of foreign capital controls by countries like Brazil (International Monetary Fund, 2010, p. 35).[2]

REDUCING INTERNATIONAL ECONOMIC VULNERABILITY: STRATEGIES AT HOME

Beyond the broader policy space claimed by most countries in the wake of the crisis, Brazil had taken a number of additional steps to reduce its vulnerability to global economic controls well before the crisis. Its 1999 currency crisis – when investors pushed down the value of the Brazilian real by 42 percent in two weeks and another 8.5 percent in one day, causing Brazil's dollar-denominated foreign debt to balloon – issued an indelible warning about the dangers of exposure to foreign markets (Flynn, 1999, p. 287; Burges, 2009; Chin, 2010). Brazil had already begun to accumulate foreign reserves to help shore up the credibility of its new currency in 1994. Those were decimated in 1999, but by the start of the next crisis in 2008, Cardoso and Lula together had determinedly raised Brazil's currency reserves to a historic high of US$210 billion and gathered $80 billion more by 2010 (Barbosa 2010, p. 5; *Estado de São Paulo*, October 26, 2010). The broader backdrop for such historic reserves was a boom in global prices for Brazil's commodity exports throughout much of the 2000s (Gallagher and Porzecanski, 2010, p. 27).

Other policy choices and features of the Brazilian economy joined with the new reserves to expand Brazil's policy space. Both Cardoso and Lula used the commodity price windfall to pay down the national debt rather than spending it profligately. While Brazil still has heavy debts, it came into the crisis with net public debt at 41.8 percent of GDP in August 2008, quite a bit lower than recent levels. Even the stimulus and crisis response spending brought the total debt to just 44 percent of GDP a year later (Barbosa, 2010, p. 8). A second step was a deliberate choice to pay off all public-sector foreign-denominated debt by 2008, including early repayment of the IMF loan (Kingstone, 2009, p. 120). Most government debt through the crisis continued to be issued in local markets. This choice further strengthened the domestic orientation of the Brazilian economy, which already had very low trade dependency at just 25 percent of GDP in 2007 (Kingstone, 2009, p. 106). This profile gave external actors comparatively few direct levers of influence over Brazil's crisis response, creating a policy space that allowed for a good deal of national determination of the appropriate domestic response.

To this point, I have discussed developments that would have enlarged the policy space for anyone who might have governed Brazil during the first decade of the twenty-first century. By definition, a large policy space does not itself determine the policies chosen; it just establishes that domestic actors exercise a larger amount of control than they might otherwise. The remaining task is to examine the economic model(s) Brazil put into place under Lula, and to trace how and why Lula's administrations took steadily greater advantage of the opened policy space.

REDUCING POWER AND INEQUALITY IN BRAZIL

Brazil has always been a large country of impressive resources and potential. However, for much of its history, it has struggled with turning that potential into actual political and economic achievements. Even prosperous moments for the country as a whole usually failed to trickle down to large parts of the

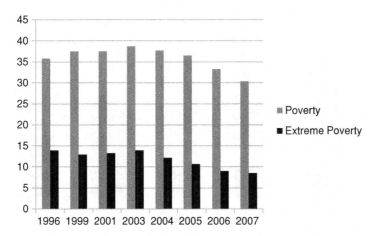

FIGURE 9.1. Poverty and Extreme Poverty in Brazil, 1996–2007. *Source:* Constructed with data from Kingstone and Ponce (2010, p. 114).

population. As one of Brazil's last military presidents said about the country's economic miracle at the beginning of the 1970s, "Brazil is doing well, Brazilians are not." As the country became one of the world's largest economies in the 1990s, it continued to have problematically large numbers of poor and illiterate citizens, and has been among the most economically unequal of all countries in the world for decades.

OUTCOMES SHOW ECONOMIC PROGRESS

The last decade, then, represents real progress for Brazil. Figure 9.1 shows that poverty and extreme poverty both rose during the Cardoso administrations (1994–2002) as economic decision makers focused on fighting inflation and achieving economic stability, but have dropped steadily since their peaks in the year of Lula's inauguration. Twenty million people moved into the middle class between 2003 and 2007 (Kingstone and Ponce, 2010, p. 105). Figure 9.2 tracks the steady fall in income inequality since 1989, with steeper drops under Lula. These significant national achievements benefit from being put into a comparative perspective: by national definitions of poverty, the Brazilian rate between 2004 and 2008 was second-lowest among Latin American countries with available data, although Brazil is in the regional midrange by the standard of the percentage of the population who live on US$2 per day or less, at 12.7 percent (IILS, 2011, pp. 109–110). Finally, Brazil was still among the most unequal of its Latin American and emerging powers peer groups even

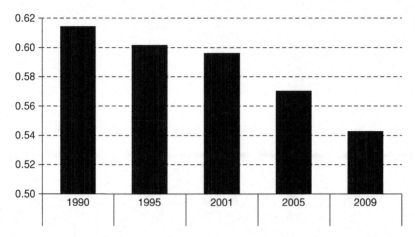

FIGURE 9.2. Inequality in Brazil, 1990–2009 (measured in Gini coefficient). *Source*: Figure 1.10 (IILS 2011: 16), with data from Instituto de Pesquisa Econômica Aplicada (IPEA).

after the two decades of declining inequality (IILS, 2011, p. 110) – although it is steadily improving while many are not.

DEBATING THE CAUSES OF ECONOMIC PROGRESS

The reasons behind Brazil's improvements in poverty and inequality have been much debated. Some causes were clearly outside Brazil's control. Beginning in 2002, both the prices and terms of trade for Latin America's (and Brazil's) commodity exports took a leap upward (Gallagher and Porzecanski, 2010, p. 27), as already noted. That was reflected by a similar burst in the value of Brazilian exports and spilled over into domestic growth, and obviously helped create the results of interest here. That surge was quickly ended by the equally abrupt collapse in the global economy, which removed external drivers of Brazilian success. Yet most of the outcomes of interest continued to improve. In addition, Brazil often had aggregate economic growth that has not improved conditions for its poorest citizens. Thus the commodities boom and global expansion are not the answer on their own.

The critical part of the explanation lies in government policies, and the remainder of this chapter focuses on Brazilian policy strategies, keeping the global dynamics in the background. Lula's first term in office was dominated by policies that Cardoso began and that are now largely consensual across the two major parties and their associated coalition partners. These were policies of economic stabilization with the aim to increase the trickle-down effects to the poorer parts of the population, including the well-known *Bolsa Familia* (Family Grant) program. While the policies proved successful in curbing poverty, historic supporters of Lula's Workers' Party and many observers thought the "compensatory" policies of the first term fell far short of what might have been expected from a leftist, union-oriented government (Hochstetler, 2008; Kingstone and Ponce, 2010; Silva, Braga, and Costa, 2010). In Lula's second term, his economic policies came closer to the historic agenda, as he used the state's economic resources to augment private and international economic forces, especially after they began to falter with the global recession. These were more explicitly growth-oriented policies directed toward promoting formal employment and public investment.

CARDOSO'S POLICY BASELINE: STABILIZATION AND SMALL-SCALE SOCIAL POLICIES

Cardoso earned a presidential election victory in 1994 for having tamed Brazil's hyperinflation while finance minister. As president, he introduced policies that kept stringent controls on government spending, maintaining a primary account surplus and paying down public debt as a first priority for new revenues. Cardoso's government also privatized some state-owned corporations and functions and reduced public controls on flows of capital, currency, and goods. While these policies obviously have many of the hallmarks of the Washington Consensus, economic policy making in Brazil has never displayed tight ideological or international constraints. The fact that Brazil's neoliberal transition came under a president who was an important formulator of dependency theory in his sociologist days may have contributed to this (Cardoso and Faletto, 1979), but the state-led development model was also comparatively successful in Brazil. In any event, market reforms came late to Brazil compared to the rest of Latin America. They also took shape in uncoordinated, small reform efforts across a number of different administrations. The reforms in Brazil reflected a pragmatic, problem-solving logic rather than the ideological neoliberalism that appeared elsewhere (Castelar Pinheiro, Bonelli, and Schneider, 2007).

Under Cardoso, social policies were small-scale and targeted, but they did begin the positive developments of the 2000s. In a series of econometric studies, Brazilian economists concluded that one significant cause of the recent decline in inequality (31–46% of the drop) came from a more equitable distribution of labor income. The studies credit the 1990s policy period when Cardoso's government broadened access to education for creating first a drop in the inequality of education access, then a fall in wage differentials by education level, and ultimately the visible drop in income inequality. Reduced geographical wage differentials also played a part.[3] Cardoso's administration also drew on experiments by PT and PSDB governments at subnational levels to develop a School Grant program (*Bolsa Escola*) that gave families small cash payments for keeping their children in school (Power, 2010, p. 229). The latter program was eventually built into the much bigger Family Grant (*Bolsa Familia*) under Lula. Brazilians appreciated the stabilization of the Cardoso years, but the accompanying economic stagnation, declining real wages, and chronically high levels of unemployment helped sweep Lula into office in 2003 (Kingstone and Ponce, 2010, pp. 103–104).

LULA'S FIRST TERM: REDUCED POLICY SPACE AND POLICY CONTINUITY

Voters did not necessarily get the policy changes they expected from the turnover in presidents. While Brazil eventually gained significant policy space, it was less clearly present at the beginning of Lula's presidency. As Lula's win began to look likely, nervous foreign investors drove down the value of Brazilian currency and stocks, warning there would be "economic crisis unless Lula strongly signaled neoliberal" – which he did (Amaral, Kingstone, and Krieckhaus, 2008, pp. 146, 148; Jensen and Schmith, 2005). Monetary stability has been a consistent aim of recent administrations from both parties, with pragmatism on other aspects of market reform (Kingstone and Ponce, 2010, p. 99). Not only did Lula publicly promise to follow Cardoso's stabilization and austerity policies in this reduced policy space; he actually raised the primary surplus target to 4.5 percent of GDP in his first term (Kingstone, 2009, p. 117).

A social security reform put that policy area on a firmer fiscal footing by increasing the number of years workers had to work and putting a cap on pension benefits (Kingstone and Ponce, 2010, p. 115). It was so strongly resisted by unions that Lula – who rose to national prominence as a union leader – had to drive the one block from the executive building to the congress to take the legislative project there (Hochstetler, 2008). Such policies were deeply disappointing to the PT's historic constituencies, although they were clearly signaled before the election and were part of an ongoing movement away from socialism by the party (Samuels, 2004). After the social security reforms, some of the party's legislators and union supporters broke off to form the PSOL party and its associated Conlutas trade union central (Hochstetler, 2008; Silva, Braga, and Costa, 2010).

THE *BOLSA FAMILIA* PROGRAM: CHEAP AND EFFECTIVE

Yet equity-enhancing changes were coming from the PT, if not those originally expected. A recent quantitative study of the decline in income inequality in Brazil concluded that 40–50 percent of the drop (and its concomitant decrease in poverty) could be attributed to non-labor income. Most of this, in turn, was a series of public transfers including pensions, an income program for the poor elderly and disabled, called the Continuous Welfare Benefit (BPC, *Benefício de Prestação Continuada*), and the *Bolsa Familia* program.[4] The final program is the largest and best known, reaching almost one-quarter of the total Brazilian population and more than 90 percent of its poor population by the end of Lula's time in office (Lopez-Calva and Lustig, 2009, pp. 13–15). Lula's administration took Cardoso's smaller School Grant program and joined it with several other existing stipend projects to create this new program. All of them work as conditional cash transfer programs, offering small amounts of cash to poor families that meet basic requirements such as keeping their children in school and having them vaccinated. Lula raised spending on the joint set of programs by 24 percent from 2002 to 2005 (Kingstone and Ponce, 2010, p. 116), and then steadily increased it after that to its current near-universal coverage of Brazil's poor (IILS, 2011, p. 80). The *Bolsa Familia* program is now one of the most consensual policies in Brazil (Power, 2010, p. 229).

The poverty and inequality impacts of these programs are all the more remarkable given the very small sums of money involved. *Bolsa Familia* recipients receive just tens of dollars per month, and its program expenditures totaled just 0.4 percent of GDP in 2009 (IILS, 2010, p. 80). In another calculation, Peter Kingstone and Aldo Ponce put the entire package of non-pension transfer programs at 2.58 percent of GDP (plus administrative costs) (Kingstone and Ponce, 2010, p. 116). The combination of immediate benefits for Brazil's neediest families and the small price tag should place this kind of policy in the toolkit of every government looking to raise the fortunes of the bottom of the economic distribution. Indeed, *Bolsa Familia* and a related program in Mexico have been widely copied throughout the Latin American region (Handa and Davis, 2006).

LONGER-TERM EFFECTS OF THE *BOLSA FAMILIA*

As is well known, however, such programs alleviate poverty in the short term without necessarily contributing to sustainable income independent of ongoing government transfers (Hall 2006; Handa and Davis 2006; Silva, Braga, and Costa 2010; Teichman 2008). Well-monitored conditions could arguably contribute to more structural improvements, including in priorities like "primary and professional education, health care, basic sanitation, and job and income generation" (Silva, Braga, and Costa, 2010, p. 130). The Brazilian government has been lax on monitoring its comparatively few conditions, and government spending in those areas continues to lag, so these are clear areas for potential improvements.

Beyond these caveats, the true long-term impact will take some time to assess, especially given that the ultimate goals are couched in terms of human capital development that cannot yet be evaluated in child-focused programs that began nine years ago. It is possible too that some of the more important effects may prove to be serendipitous ones. For example, the promise of access to cash transfers has led to a bulge in the number of Brazilians seeking birth certificates and other documents of identity in a country where the parents of about 30 percent of children born in the 1990s did not officially register their births (Hunter and Sugiyama, 2011, p. 3). The birth certificate is also required for access to the formal labor market and other government benefits in turn, and so recipients of *Bolsa Familia* may find themselves better able to take advantage of real economic opportunities later on – an unanticipated effect of a temporary cash transfer program.

FORMAL EMPLOYMENT GAINS

Taking up another critique, some have worried that the drop in inequality is an artifact of a presumed drop in formal employment, with the poorest no longer measured (Silva, Braga, and Costa 2010, pp. 129–130). Instead, the drop in poverty and inequality is in part attributable to a surprising gain in formal employment, which rose steadily after 2002 and especially steeply after 2005 (see Figure 9.3). The formal sector now includes about half of the employed labor force, after rising from a low of 43.9 percent in 1999 (Berg, 2011, p. 128), immediately after the privatization push of the first Cardoso administration. Average annual growth in the formal labor force between 1999 and 2008 was 5.3 percent, with gains in salaried private-sector workers with a signed labor card (6.6 percent) almost doubling the rates of the increase in government workers (3.6 percent) and domestic workers (3.4 percent) (Berg, 2011, p. 129). Even the global economic crisis only temporarily slowed the growth (IILS, 2011, p. 15). Janine Berg traces the rise in formalization to growth-generated demand for formal workers, demographic and educational changes that reduced the availability of young workers, and a series of "micro-level policy interventions that have altered the behavior of firms and employers"

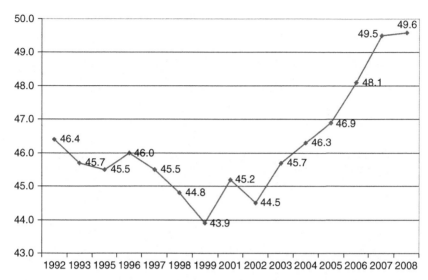

FIGURE 9.3. Share of Formal Employment in Brazil, ILO Definition, 1992–2008 (percent). *Source*: Figure 2 in Berg (2011: 128), based on data from IBGE/PNAD.

(Berg, 2011, p. 130). These policies included labor inspections and tax breaks, but also the formalization of domestic work, which brought many women into the formal labor force for the first time. The rise in formal employment is clearly part of the story on the drop in poverty and inequality, especially since it was paired with regular increases in the official minimum wage. This is discussed in more detail later in the chapter.

LULA'S POLICY TRANSITION

To this point, the policies described have been among those that could be considered broadly part of a consensual Brazilian economic model. Economic stabilization and modest income transfer programs for the poor, like *Bolsa Familia*, were defended by essentially all of Brazil's major political parties in the 2010 presidential election, and certainly by the dominant PT and PSDB. They continued in Lula's second term and that of current PT president, Dilma Rousseff. Beginning in 2006, however, Lula's administration began to add some policies that are less Brazilian than they are of the Worker's Party itself in their focus on labor and public investment.

The policy transition has several apparent origins. Politically, 2006 found Lula running for a second term in office and needing to rebuild bridges with

the disappointed labor activists and voters who were part of the PT's historical base (Hochstetler, 2008). Economically, the spurt in exports and reserve
accumulation had begun, and the general economic expansion increased
government revenues so that more spending could accompany ongoing debt
paydowns. Insiders also speak of an administration whose economic team
always had a variety of orientations, with those who favored a larger state
role rising in influence after Lula's first finance minister, Antonio Palocci,
was forced to resign over corruption charges.[5] In Lula's second term, coupled with the global recession, their arguments had more weight. The pre-
crisis timing suggests that the shift in focus was grounded in the domestic
changes.

SITTING DOWN WITH ORGANIZED LABOR

In 2006, the final year of Lula's first term, the government sat down with labor
activists to establish dates and a formula for increasing the minimum wage from
April 2007 to 2011. The schedule was maintained after the global crisis set in and
even helped Brazil weather the crisis (IILS, 2011, p. 17). With many government
benefits, including retirement benefits, indexed to the minimum wage, these
increases supported strong continuous household buying power after 2007.
The domestic consumer demand in turn sustained national firms, creating
a positive cycle between employment, consumer demand, production, and
more employment in this domestically oriented economy. The coexistence of
a rising minimum wage and stronger formal labor force participation – often
presumed to represent a trade-off of policy goals – is further evidence that the
first decade of the 2000s was a time when many economic stars aligned for
Brazil.

The rise in the minimum wage was attributable to an explicit government policy, notable for its process as well as its content. The government
negotiated with labor, business, and retirees' representatives, in the spirit of
corporatist social consultation (IILS, 2011, p. 83). The normally oppositional
Força Sindical union central joined the PT's associated CUT union in praising the government at the May Day celebrations in 2007. The Força Sindical
leader explained: "When you have space for negotiation, you don't have to
criticize anyone" (*Estado de São Paulo*, May 2, 2007). Similar consultations
set the tone for the response to the global economic crisis, when the near-
moribund Economic and Social Development Council (Hochstetler, 2008)
helped develop proposals for what became a job-rich recovery in Brazil. The
government extended credit to support businesses when the crisis stopped
access to international sources of credit, setting aside designated funds for the

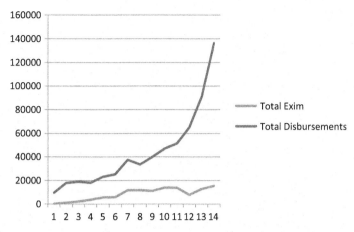

FIGURE 9.4. BNDES total and Exim disbursements, 1996–2009. *Source*: BNDES, in millions of reals, not corrected for inflation, based on data from BNDES.gov.br.

small and medium enterprises that create many jobs (IILS, 2011, pp. 50–53). It also chose sectors for special support if critical employment was at stake, notably providing tax cuts for the purchase of motor vehicles (IILS, 2011, pp. 53–54).

A NEW PROGRAM OF PUBLIC INVESTMENT

Finally, formal employment, wages, and economic growth all received additional impetus from new programs of public investment that began to be spent in Lula's second term. Anemic investment rates, whether public or private, foreign or domestic, have long been a barrier to Brazilian development (Stallings and Studart, 2006). The Brazilian National Development Bank was created in the 1950s to support Brazil's ambitions for development, stepping in at a time when there was literally no long-term source of investment finance in the country. Cardoso had used the Bank primarily to carry out his privatization programs (Montero, 1998), and many of Lula's supporters had expected a national PT administration to restore it to its central role in public development finance. Yet public investment grew only slowly in his first term, as shown in Figure 9.4. The same figure also illustrates the very rapid rise in the Bank's disbursements in Lula's second term, the development of interest here. By 2010, the Bank had disbursed three times as much in new loans annually as the World Bank had (*Estado de São Paulo*, March 10, 2011).

Much of the spending was packaged in a new Program for Growth Accel-
eration (PAC, *Programa de Aceleração do Crescimento*), launched in 2007. Its
transport, energy, and urban and social infrastructure projects brought federal
public investment from 0.6 percent of GDP in 2006 to an estimated 1.0 percent
in 2009. State enterprises nearly doubled their investment, from 1.0 percent
to 1.9 percent of GDP (Government of Brazil, 2010, p. 10). Tax breaks, credit
lines, and measures that improved the investment climate were central mechanisms of the PAC. Similar measures were used in the new industrial plan
policy (PDP, *Política de Desenvolvimento Produtivo*) of 2008, but that policy
was designed to "conduct planned and coordinated initiatives for the broad-
ening of the competitiveness of the Brazilian productive structure" (Oliva and
Zendron, 2011, p. 81). In other words, it targets economic activities that will
generate innovation, greater global competitiveness, and the future infrastructure of continued growth. Substantial parts of both programs remain to be
implemented, but Lula's successor Dilma Rousseff has continued them and
even deepened their industrial policy orientation.

THE "BOLSA BRAZILIAN NATIONAL DEVELOPMENT BANK"

The details of the programs are beyond the scope of this chapter, but several
features should be noted. First, even parts of the PAC that had Brazil's poor as
their ultimate beneficiaries, like the Lights for All (*Luz para Todos*) program,
were first construction, engineering, and industrial projects that brought large
numbers of new government contracts to a familiar assortment of Brazil's large
private companies. One newspaper calculated that 57 percent of the Brazilian
National Development Bank's disbursements from 2008 to June 2010 went
to just twelve firms – Parastatals Petrobras, Eletrobras, and ten private firms,
including three construction firms, a mining company, and a cement and
pulp manufacturer. A blogger for the *Veja* newsmagazine had called this the
"Bolsa Brazilian National Development Bank" already in 2007. Needless to
say, the resources dwarfed those spent on the *Bolsa Família*.

At the same time, these contracts and their economic spillovers to upstream
and downstream firms were central components of the surge in formal employment. Although the projects are not technically stimulus programs because
they were underway before the recession began and have long-term aims, they
clearly stimulated the Brazilian economy and helped maintain growth when
foreign demand was low after 2008. Projects for the PAC in particular were
designed to be job rich by a working subgroup of the Economic and Social
Development Council, which contained representatives of government, business, labor, and civil society (IILS, 2011, pp. 67–68).

AREAS OF VULNERABILITY IN THE BRAZILIAN MODEL

As the preceding section has shown, the package of policies of the Lula years, some building on those of the Cardoso years, have gradually come together to create an unusually good run by many economic indicators. In conclusion, I briefly mention several areas of vulnerability, where policies should be added and/or outcomes closely monitored. The first is education, as good-quality education continues to elude many Brazilians. Small steps in the 1990s helped erase some of the income inequality, but educational inequality persists (Lopez-Calva and Lustig, 2009) and needs to be addressed for its own sake and for the long-term economic innovation Brazil craves. A second area of vulnerability is environmental. The infrastructure projects of the PAC have heavy environmental impacts, and the government's inclination has too often been to try to downplay them (Hochstetler, 2011). The Brazilian National Development Bank is often the target of environmentalists, with a transnational social movement coalition challenging many of its projects,[6] although it has an increasingly sophisticated internal discourse that links environmental protection and a low-carbon economy to economic innovation and global competitiveness.[7] Finally, large government spending programs inevitably raise the possibility of corrupt contractual and spending practices, long endemic in Brazilian public finance (Power and Taylor, 2011). While the *Bolsa Familia* program has had comparatively few of these kinds of problems, the PAC and other infrastructure projects have more. In current president Rousseff's first year in office, she removed six of her ministers after evidence of systematic improbity, and all had occupied their positions under Lula as well. Such problems have both economic and political legitimacy costs for a state that takes a larger economic role.

CONCLUSION: THE CLIMB OUT OF POVERTY AND
NEW POLICY SPACES

Brazil has had a strong run in the 2000s. Long a country with a great deal of potential, it began to live up to that potential with strong economic growth that improved the lives of ordinary Brazilians. It did so by following a heterodox economic model that was shaped over a series of presidencies starting in the 1990s. On the one hand, the model prioritizes macroeconomic stabilization and steady debt repayment, hallmarks of the Washington Consensus. On the other hand, comparatively inexpensive educational and income transfer programs gave many of Brazil's poor the hand up that they needed to begin the climb out of poverty. The final pieces of the model came into place during President Lula's second term, as job-rich policies and expanded public investment gave Brazil enviable economic outcomes while much of the rest of the world sunk into crisis.

The heterodox model was made possible by a number of developments, both inside and outside Brazil. Outside Brazil, the economic crisis and Brazil's comparative success within it made the country one of the global economic rule-makers as countries widely sought a mix of strategies in response. Brazilian presidents Cardoso and Lula had also taken important steps to reduce Brazil's dependence on the international financial system, paying off debt and especially foreign-denominated debt. A rise in the prices of Brazil's commodity exports in the middle of the 2000s brought new resources and revenues that were generally well spent. These were significant cross-partisan continuities in Brazilian economic policy. During Lula's final term, he went further to develop the state's role in the economy, filling the expanded policy space with a wide-ranging agenda that reflected his party's historical constituencies and priorities. These policies facilitated a rise in formal employment, real wages, and public investment. While the Brazilian model is not without its flaws, it does suggest the possibility of alternative development strategies and shows some of the conditions of their success.

What created this policy space, and can those strategies be duplicated elsewhere? Will the mix of policies Brazil chose within that policy space work as well in other countries? As just noted, Brazil gained policy space from conditions both within and outside its control. Within its control, it made prudent economic choices. Brazil paid down its foreign debt and reduced the external leverage of international financial institutions. It had plenty of reserves and did not require any emergency assistance in the crisis. Outside its control, the global economy and the prices of its exports boomed for several critical years in the mid-2000s. Other countries cannot count on such a felicitous context, of course, but they can learn from the strategy of putting aside resources for the bust that inevitably comes.

At the same time, the lesson of the Brazilian model is not a simple one of austerity and saving for the future. There is also a considerable amount of state spending in it, with both the comparatively cheap policies like the *Bolsa Familia* and the comparatively expensive policies of investment funded by the Brazilian National Development Banks responsible for the recent results. *Bolsa Familia* appears to have enough concrete positive effects that it is worth making part of the policy framework in many countries, and it is indeed being copied widely. Not all of these copies are as successful as the original, and the details should be examined closely, especially the controls that reduce the levels of politicization and fraud. Countries where the numbers of very poor constitute a much higher percentage of the population than Brazil's one-quarter will probably not be able to fund even these very modest programs without external assistance, but they are within the reach of many states.

The applicability of the Brazilian National Development Bank's style of investment spending is less wide. On the one hand, this kind of public investment is very expensive and has been unaffordable for many years in Brazil itself. It also has its most expansive effects when it is partnered with private investments and is spent on firms that are at or near global competitiveness levels. Those features are more likely in an economy as big as Brazil's, where firms can grow to competitive size in a large domestic economy and where investors see good prospects. The positive cycle where more inclusive growth contributed to sustained domestic demand, which in turn generated the employment and government revenues that supported an ongoing positive cycle of investment and growth, is also easier in a large domestic economy.

REFERENCES

Akyüz, Yilmaz. 2010. Global Rules and Markets: Constraints on Policy Autonomy in Developing Countries. In *Commodities, Governance and Economic Development Under Globalization*, eds. M. Nissanke and G. Mavrotas. Houndmills: Palgrave Macmillan.

Amaral, Aline Diniz, Peter R. Kingstone, and Jonathan Krieckhaus. 2008. The Limits of Economic Reform in Brazil. In *Democratic Brazil Revisited*, eds. Peter R. Kingstone and Timothy J. Power. Pittsburgh: University of Pittsburgh Press.

Barbosa, Nelson. 2010. Latin America: Counter-Cyclical Policy in Brazil: 2008–09. *Journal of Globalization and Development* 1(1): 1–12.

Berg, Janine. 2011. Laws or Luck? Understanding Rising Formality in Brazil in the 2000s. In *Regulating for Decent Work: New Directions in Labour Market Regulations*, eds. S. Lee and D. McCann. Geneva and Basingstoke: ILO and Palgrave Macmillan.

Burges, Sean W. 2009. *Brazilian Foreign Policy after the Cold War*. Gainesville: University Press of Florida.

Cardoso, Fernando Henrique and Enzo Faletto. 1979. *Dependency and Development in Latin America*, trans. Marjory Mattingly Urquidi. Berkeley and Los Angeles: University of California Press.

Castelar Pinheiro, Armando, Regis Bonelli, and Ben Ross Schneider. 2007. Pragmatism and Market Reforms in Brazil. In *Understanding Market Reforms in Latin America*, ed. J. M. Fanelli. London: Palgrave Macmillan.

Chin, Gregory. 2010. Remaking the Architecture: The Emerging Powers, Self-Insuring and Regional Insulation. *International Affairs* 86(3): 693–715.

Flynn, Peter. 1999. Brazil: The Politics of Crisis. *Third World Quarterly* 20(2): 287–317.

Gallagher, Kevin P. 2008. Understanding Developing Country Resistance to the Doha Round. *Review of International Political Economy* 15(1): 62–85.

Gallagher, Kevin P. and Roberto Porzecanski. 2010. *The Dragon in the Room: China and the Future of Latin American Industrialization*. Stanford: Stanford University Press.

Government of Brazil. 2010. *Balanço 3 Anos [Programa de Aceleração do Crecimento]*.

Hall, Anthony. 2006. From *Fome Zero* to *Bolsa Família*: Social Policies and Policy Alleviation under Lula. *Journal of Latin American Studies* 38: 689–709.

Handa, Sudhanshu and Benjamin Davis. 2006. The Experience of Conditional Cash Transfers in Latin America and the Caribbean. *Development Policy Review* 24(5): 513–536.

Helleiner, Eric. 2010. What Role for the New Financial Stability Board? The Politics of International Standards after the Crisis. *Global Policy* 1(3): 282–290.

Hochstetler, Kathryn. 2008. Organized Civil Society in Lula's Brazil. In *Democratic Brazil Revisited*, eds. P. R. Kingstone and T. J. Power. Pittsburgh: University of Pittsburgh Press.

Hochstetler, Kathryn. 2011a. The Politics of Comparatively Good Times: Brazil in the Global Financial Crisis. Paper presented at the 2011 Annual Meeting of the International Studies Association, Montreal.

Hochstetler, Kathryn. 2011b. The Politics of Environmental Licensing: Energy Projects of the Past and Future in Brazil. *Studies in Comparative International Development* 46(4): 349–371.

Hunter, Wendy and Natasha Borges Sugiyama. 2011. Documenting Citizenship: Contemporary Efforts toward Social Inclusion in Brazil. Paper prepared for presentation at the 2011 APSA Annual Meeting, September 1–4, 2011, Seattle, Washington.

Hunter, Wendy and Timothy J. Power. 2008. Rewarding Lula: Executive Power, Social Policy, and the Brazilian Elections of 2006. *Latin American Politics and Society* 49(1): 1–30.

IILS (International Institute for Labour Studies). 2011. *Policy Matters Brazil: An Innovative Growth-with-Equity Strategy*. Geneva: International Labour Organization, International Institute for Labour Studies.

International Monetary Fund. 2009. Note by the Staff of the International Monetary Fund to the Group of Twenty, January 31–February 1. Washington, DC: International Monetary Fund. Online at http://www.imf.org/external/np/g20/pdf/020509.pdf.

International Monetary Fund. 2010. *Global Financial Stability Report: Sovereigns, Funding, and Systemic Liquidity*. Washington, DC: International Monetary Fund, World Economic and Financial Survey, October.

Jensen, Nathan M. and Scott Schmith. 2005. Market Responses to Politics: The Rise of Lula and the Decline of the Brazilian Stock Market. *Comparative Political Studies* 38(10): 1245–1270.

Kaufman, Robert and Alex Segura-Ubiergo. 2001. Globalization, Domestic Politics, and Social Spending in Latin America. *World Politics* 53(4): 553–587.

Kingstone, Peter. 2009. Sobering Up and Going Global: Brazil's Progress from Populism and Protectionism. *Law and Business Review of the Americas* 15: 105–126.

Kingstone, Peter and Aldo Ponce. 2010. From Cardoso to Lula: The Triumph of Pragmatism in Brazil. In *Leftist Governments in Latin America: Successes and Shortcomings*, eds. K. Weyland, R. L. Madrid, and W. Hunter. Cambridge: Cambridge University Press.

Lopez-Calva, Luiz F. and Nora Lustig. 2009. The Recent Decline of Inequality in Latin America: Argentina, Brazil, Mexico, and Peru. Working Paper, Society for the Study of Economic Inequality, ECINEQ WP 2009-140.

Montero, Alfred P. 1998. State Interests and the New Industrial Policy in Brazil: The Privatization of Steel, 1990–1994. *Journal of Inter-American Studies and World Affairs* 40(3): 27–62.

Nooruddin, Irfan and Joel Simmons. 2006. The Politics of Hard Choices: IMF Programs and Government Spending. *International Organization* 60(4): 1001–1033.

Ocampo, José Antonio. 2011. Global Economic Prospects and the Developing World. *Global Policy* 2(1): 10–19.

Oliva, Rafael and Patricia Zendron. 2010. Politicas Governamentais Pró-Investimento e o Papel do BNDES. In *O BNDES em um Brasil em Transição*, eds. A. C. Além and F. Giambiagi. Rio de Janeiro: BNDES.

Power, Timothy J. 2010. Brazilian Democracy as a Late Bloomer: Reevaluating the Regime in the Cardoso-Lula Era. *Latin American Research Review* (Special Issue): 218–247.

Power, Timothy J. and Matthew M. Taylor, eds. 2011. *Corruption and Democracy in Brazil: The Struggle for Accountability*. South Bend: University of Notre Dame Press.

Samuels, David. 2004. From Socialism to Social Democracy: Party Organization and the Transformation of the Workers' Party in Brazil. *Comparative Political Studies* 37(9): 999–1024.

Schelkle, Waltraud. 2010. Good Governance in Crisis or a Good Crisis for Governance? A Comparison of the EU and the US. *Review of International Political Economy* iFirst: 1–25.

Schrank, Andrew and Marcus Kurtz. 2005. Credit where Credit Is Due: Open Economy Industrial Policy and Export Diversity in Latin America and the Caribbean. *Politics and Society* 33(4): 671–702.

Silva, Pedro Luiz Barros, José Carlos de Souza Braga, and Vera Lúcia Cabral Costa. 2010. Lula's Administration at a Crossroads: The Difficult Combination of Stability and Development in Brazil. In *Leftist Governments in Latin America: Successes and Shortcomings*, eds. K. Weyland, R. L. Madrid, and W. Hunter. Cambridge: Cambridge University Press.

Stallings, Barbara with Rogerio Studart. 2006. *Finance for Development: Latin America in Comparative Perspective*. Washington, DC: Brookings and ECLAC.

Teichman, Judith. 2008. Redistributive Conflict and Social Policy in Latin America. *World Development* 36(3): 446–460.

Weber, Beat and Stefan W. Schmitz. 2011. Varieties of Helping Capitalism: Political Determinants of Bank Rescue Packages during the Recent Crisis. *Socio-Economic Review* 9(4): 639–669.

Wibbels, Erik. 2006. Dependency Revisited: International Markets, Business Cycles, and Social Spending in the Developing World. *International Organization* 60(2): 433–468.

Woods, Ngaire. 2010. Global Governance after the Financial Crisis: A New Multilateralism or the Last Gasp of the Great Powers? *Global Policy* 1(1): 51–63.

The Global Health Agenda and Shrinking Policy Spaces in the Post-Crisis Landscape

Ronald Labonté

INTRODUCTION: POLICY SPACE, TRADE, AND GLOBAL HEALTH STANDARDS

A policy space describes "the freedom, scope, and mechanisms that governments have to choose, design and implement public policies to fulfill their aims" (Koivusalo, Labonté, and Schrecker, 2008, p. 7). Policy capacity refers to the fiscal ability of states to enact those policies or regulations, which depends on their ability to capture sufficient revenue through taxation for this purpose.

Most of the attention on health-related issues in trade focuses on two areas. One is intellectual property rights (IPRs) and access to essential medicines and the other is the potential of commitments to liberalized services resulting from an expansion of private financing and provision of services essential to health, such as health care, water, and sanitation. While these concerns merit continued attention, three themes are of arguably greater importance to health. This chapter explores these three themes, before concluding with an idealized snapshot of potential reform measures.

The first theme is the impact of liberalized investment flows and their consequent financial crises. It used to be an axiomatic belief that liberalization led to both economic growth and new state capacity, which in turn generated new wealth that would lift increasing numbers out of poverty, with health improving as poverty declined. Increases in wealth can be taxed and used to invest in human capital, namely health, education, and gender empowerment, creating more productive and skilled workers that spur the economy to greater growth and more trickle-down health. Each of these links, however, is empirically moot.

The second theme is the "behind-the-border" effects of trade treaties on governments' policy spaces. Most econometric studies find that trade liberalization is associated with better growth, but a recent review of these studies concluded that this positive relationship "is neither automatically guaranteed nor universally observable" (Thorbecke and Nissanke, 2006, p. 1334), and there remains doubt about the causal flow: Does openness lead to growth, or does growth give rise to openness? While extreme poverty (US$1.25/day) has decreased globally since the era of liberalized trade, the "rising tide" of economic growth has not lifted people very far, with poverty at the US$2.50/day level increasing by almost the same number (Chen and Ravallion, 2008), with the majority of those in developing countries whose incomes have improved residing in the vulnerable "precariat" of informal labor markets, sandwiched between the desperately poor and the marginal middle class (De Barros et al., 2009; Standing, 2011; Chen and Ravallion, 2012).

The third theme and a major subject of this paper is the capacities and roles trade plays in the global diffusion of unhealthy "lifestyles." Of greater health concern is the increasing scale of income and wealth polarization within countries. China and India, two fast-growing and increasingly unequal societies, are far from alone in this trend, with income polarization affecting many high-income countries on scales not seen since before the 1929 market crash. While global trade is not the sole perpetrator of this growing gap, the underpinning economic orthodoxy for global trade supports the domestic neoliberal policies that lead to such inequalities. The excessive CEO salaries and lower tax margins at the top have coincided with the labor market "flexibilities" and insecurities worldwide that have seen labor's share of global wealth decline relative to capital's (World Bank, 2007).

DEREGULATED GLOBAL FINANCE AND THE 2008 CRISIS

Growing income and wealth polarization, troubling in its association with health inequalities and the loss of social cohesion, owes at least as much to the liberalization of capital markets as it does to liberalized trade in goods and services, and probably much more. The focus of critical analysis and civil society's opposition to globalization's negative consequences has shifted in recent years from the WTO and trade in goods and services to the financial institutions and the lack of effective regulation over "footloose" global capital. Although the two types of liberalization differ, they cohabit many regional and bilateral trade treaties.

Investment liberalization remains somewhat marginalized within the WTO (GATS mode 3: commercial presence, and the TRIMS agreement on trade-related investment measures) and is supposed to be off the table in the Doha Round, despite continued efforts by high-income countries to introduce investment liberalization during Ministerial meetings. The health risks of investment liberalization lie instead in the proliferation of bilateral and regional trade treaties that have emerged in the wake of stalled WTO negotiations and which for some time have constituted the major negotiating arenas for new trade deals; indeed, thousands of bilateral investment treaties have been ratified over the past two decades.

The health risks associated with investment liberalization were first realized in the recurrent developing-country financial crises over the past two decades; these crises were extreme consequences of the hypermobility of portfolio investment that followed the liberalization of capital markets. Portfolio investment (essentially trade in currencies) and the huge explosion in over-the-counter trade in financial derivatives dwarf all other forms of capital flows. Such growth in portfolio capital led to a greater likelihood for panics, manias, and crashes (Bhagwati, 2000), with generally devastating effects on human health through the depreciation of national currencies and purchasing power (Carranza, 2005; World Bank, 2000). Subsequent austerity measures reduced public revenues and expenditures on health and social program transfers (Lee and Crotty, 2005; Kaminsky, 2005; Pirie, 2006). Most alarming is the fact that the impact of these crises and the subsequent austerity responses are felt first and most severely by women, children, and the rural poor (Floro and Dymski, 2000; Parrado and Zenteno, 2001).

The global financial crisis of 2008 is the most recent case in point, albeit differing from other recent crises in its origin (high-income countries) and reach.

HYPER-GLOBALIZATION, THE NEOLIBERAL AGENDA, AND THE 2008 CRISIS

The 2008 crisis is an example of the hyper-globalization of financial markets and its social cost in human terms. These dynamics between global reach and local impacts need to be untangled, particularly when examining the sustainability of the deregulatory imperative. A good place to begin is with the role of the corporation.

As corporations outsourced their manufacturing to lower-waged and usually lower-regulated and taxed countries in the 1990s (notably Asia, and especially China), these countries experienced a surge in foreign currency investments. To protect themselves from future attacks against their own currencies, they purchased enormous sums of low-interest long-term U.S. Treasury Bills, because the U.S. dollar was still functioning as the currency of last reserve. The difference between their borrowing costs on the international market and their investments in low-interest treasury bills was effectively a transfer of between US$750 billion and US$1 trillion in capital each year to high-income countries. This capital transfer went into U.S. banks that pushed loans to high-risk consumers, who in turn used the real estate bubble to finance their continued consumption of goods imported from countries like China. This external debt-financed consumption was essential to the high growth trajectory of these outsourced developing countries, and to maintaining the consumption lifestyles of workers in high-income countries who had seen their jobs or earnings dissipate with technological innovation and outsourcing.

Although concern was expressed in some quarters about the economic unsustainability of this arrangement, the real threat came when underregulated financial institutions began bundling their mortgage (and other) debts and marketing them as investments. These mortgage-backed securities were sold to individuals, other banks, mutual funds, and government pensions around the world, effectively reducing the original lender's risk of loan defaults by spreading said risk across the entire global financial system. The extent of this "debtonation" did not become clear (at least to regulators and the media) until the U.S. real estate bubble began to burst in 2007. The diffusion of toxic debt throughout the liberalized global financial economy led to a worldwide credit crunch (banks hoarded cash and stopped lending to each other) and the collapse of several banks and investment firms. The steep recession triggered by the credit crunch among the high-income countries most at risk became global in 2008, as all forms of financial transfers to developing countries began to shrink along with markets for their exports.

HEALTH IMPACTS AND THE DEVELOPMENT CONSEQUENCES OF THE CRISIS

The depth of global production chains (whose growth was an outcome of liberalization in both trade and financial markets) meant that the credit crunch – "sudden, severe, and synchronized" (Yi, 2009, p. 45) – rippled rapidly across supply chains. Negative health implications via increased unemployment and poverty as well as decreased public revenues for social investment were both consequences of the crisis in low- and middle-income countries. Multilateral agency estimates suggest a rise in extreme poverty of between 50 million and 200 million, leading to an excess of 200,000 to 400,000 childhood deaths and an increase in child labor and domestic violence. Estimates also show a decline in remittances and health/social protection policies, a decline in net development assistance flows, and a decline in overall financial flows to developing countries (World Bank, 2009; Marmot and Bell, 2009; International Labour Organization, 2009).

In effect, the poorer groups in the poorer countries are bearing the brunt of unregulated financial speculation carried out by investment bankers in the high-income countries. The "rescue" of these banks and the massive countercyclical infusion of public monies by governments in many high-income countries, in turn, created a massive moral hazard and a huge public debt. This debt is already reducing health expenditures in several of the most affected nations, notably the United Kingdom and other Eurozone nations, as well as in the United States, which, by one estimate, has effectively transferred US$2 trillion in bank losses into sovereign debt (Olive, 2011). Other estimates place the total value of public bank bailouts in the G20 at more than US$9 trillion. While some of this amount has already been repaid or recovered through sale of government shares in quasi-nationalized failed banks, the interest rate spreads on what governments and their central banks provide to banks, and what they then borrow back to cover this lending, has been a massive transfer of public wealth to the very corporations and individuals who first created the crisis (Altvater and Mahnkopf, 2012; Ortiz and Cummins, 2012).

The financial crisis is expected to have mixed health impacts on populations in the rich countries. On the one hand, it will potentially reduce discretionary expenditures on tobacco or excess alcohol consumption, but on the other hand, it will increase poverty rates for those in less secure employment settings (Bezruchka, 2009; Dávila Quintana and Gonzalez Lopez-Valcarcel 2009), which in turn will lead to homelessness (particularly in the United States) and increased reliance on low-cost, highly processed obesogenic foods. Unemployment along with poverty- and insecurity-related stress levels are also predicted to rise, and suicide rates since the crisis have indeed increased by 12–15 percent in the worst affected European countries. At the same time, health and social protection financing has been dramatically cut and user charges are being imposed on many services (Stuckler, Basu, Suhrcke, Coutts, and McKee, 2011; Stuckler, Basu, and McKee, 2011; Kentikelenis, Karanikolos, Papanicolas, Basu, McKee, and Stuckler, 2011).

The draconian extent of the austerity measures being imposed in the EU at the behest of bankers' interests almost defies reason. As the Secretary-General of UNCTAD commented rather pointedly in that agency's 2011 report:

> Those who support fiscal tightening argue that it is indispensable for restoring the confidence of financial markets, which is perceived as key to economic recovery. This is despite the almost universal recognition that the crisis was the result of financial market failure in the first place. (UNCTAD 2011a, V)

Conventional economics logically contradicts these official motives and sees such austerity plunging the EU into a double-dip recession (Wade, 2009;

Spratt, 2011). China is complaining loudly (alongside UNCTAD) that the rich world's retreat into fiscal compression is beggaring the economic prospects of developing countries. It is also worth bearing in mind that, unlike the last great global crash of 1929, this time the global rich have emerged relatively unscathed and comparatively richer. Belt-tightening has not been an equally shared exercise, and some analysts contend that much of the austerity being imposed has more to do with completing the neoliberal project of state retrenchment begun in the 1970s than with managing structural deficits.

AUSTERITY AT HOME AND TRADE LIBERALIZATION ABROAD

The post-crisis period has also been accompanied by a series of "murky protectionist" measures worldwide, most enacted by middle- and high-income countries engaged in countercyclical spending. Their "murky" quality resides in their being permissible under existing trade treaties but liable to spark equally permissible retaliatory measures, leading to declines in international trade. International trade rates did decline in 2008, bounced back briefly in 2009, but in 2010 began another downward slide that, at time of this writing (early 2013), is continuing. To minimize this slowdown, first the G20 in 2009 and then the 2011 WTO Ministerial issued an "anti-protectionist pledge" (Foreign Affairs and International Trade Canada, 2011). Not all developing countries were pleased with its insertion into the WTO Ministerial, however, noting that the recipe of austerity at home and liberalization abroad for resolving the post-crisis recession was not meeting the needs of most emerging economies. Of particular concern was the pledge's reference to roll back protectionist measures introduced since 2008 and to avoid any new ones that could impede global trade, even if these measures are WTO compliant.[1]

Even if we accept that global growth should be the most important international policy goal at the moment,[2] there is little evidence that financial reforms so far announced or currently under discussion would help much. The government-initiated recapitalization of banks, such as the two doses of quantitative easing undertaken in the United States, did not lead to increased commercial and personal lending to reboost production, consumption, and trade, as intended. Instead it was used by the banks in investments, including speculation in food futures (Hudson, 2010), earning profits for the banks by driving up food prices globally. A similarly large infusion of capital from the European Central Bank to private banks in the Eurozone, intended to encourage the purchase of new government bond issues and thus reduce the risk of sovereign defaults, led instead to banks hoarding large amounts of cash

(Eavis, 2012). The UK's Independent Commission on Banking in its September 2011 report failed to call for a complete separation of commercial from investment banking (as had been urged by economists concerned about a replication of the 2008 collapse), although it did recommend a "ring-fence" strategy in which banks would be required to sequester one-sixth to one-third of their total capital in their commercial operations. This still leaves enormous leveraging for casino capitalism, and the reforms are not even expected to be in place until 2019 (Treanor, 2011). The "Volker Rule" presently under debate in the United States would substantially restrict proprietary trading by banks in that country, but is under sustained criticism from governments in Europe, Canada, and Japan, as well as from American financial institutions (Braithwaite, Mackenzie, McLannahan, and Nasirpour, 2012). Whether it succeeds in becoming law, and what its effects would be, remains unknown.

POLICY SPACE AT RISK: ERODING POLICY FLEXIBILITY

Another aspect of market liberalization with an indirect health outcome is the loss of governments' policy space and policy capacity. The increasing "behind the border" reach of trade treaties is shrinking policy space by prohibiting a range of domestic regulatory options that could be used to promote more equitable population health outcomes. Although governments retain substantial policy flexibilities within existing trade treaties, these flexibilities continue to be eroded through ongoing negotiations, notably the shift to bilateral and regional treaty negotiations which are often categorized as WTO Plus, limiting policy space to a much greater extent than current WTO rules do. Of particular concern is the proliferation of investor state dispute settlement (ISDS) provisions in bilateral and regional treaties, which allow corporations to sue governments for regulations that result in expropriation of their investments, with expropriation generally defined in very broad terms. Such provisions could be used to challenge compulsory licensing of patent drugs, even if such licensing was in compliance with the TRIPS agreement (Hsu, 2012).

The protection of environmental, animal, and human health can be enough grounds for abrogating a trade treaty commitment. Both the GATT and the GATS agreements allow exceptions for measures 'necessary to protect human, animal or plant life and health' (GATT article XX(b), GATS XIV(b)).

However, WTO dispute panels until recently have applied a very stringent necessity test to these exceptions. An example of this is the 2007 decision involving Brazil's attempted ban on imports of European used and retreaded tires. Since regional trade treaty obligations with other MERCOSUR countries allowed some tire imports similar to those from the EU, until Brazil could ban these (numerically much smaller) imports, its ban on EU imports was ruled discriminatory. Similarly, the United States in 2010 lost a WTO dispute involving a ban on imported flavored cigarettes, which it claimed would be particularly popular with adolescents because it did not similarly ban domestic menthol-flavored cigarettes, also known to be particularly popular with adolescents. Such dispute rulings can create momentum for stronger domestic public health regulations (ban all used tire imports, ban menthol cigarettes) or, in the absence of such a move, could worsen public health outcomes. As was noted with the Brazil case, a public health risk associated with large-scale used tire imports (which stack up and become breeding grounds for disease-carrying mosquitoes) is still allowed to persist in pursuit of protecting a free trade law (Lavranos, 2009).

Another limitation on the health defense (under WTO rules) is that domestic regulations that could affect foreign imports, even if these are treated no differently than national goods, must be based on international standards or scientific risk assessments (Labonté, 2010). This loss of policy space was most famously encountered with the EU's refusal to accept hormone-treated beef imports, a dispute it lost and for which it subsequently paid in retaliatory trade penalties.[3]

DECLINING PUBLIC REVENUES AND THE SCARCITY OF PUBLIC GOODS

Policy capacity can be affected by liberalization's requirements for progressive reductions in tariffs. Many developing countries still rely much more heavily on tariffs for their tax revenue than do developed nations. These tariff rates have come under intense trade negotiation pressures from developed countries, which want to see them "locked in" and rapidly reduced, especially in those developing countries with a growing middle class that could represent new consumer markets. In theory, developing country governments should be able to shift their tax base from tariffs to sales or income taxes, assuming their economies grow with increased liberalization.

In reality, many developing, and most low-income, countries subject to tariff reductions as conditions for loans from the international financial institutions (the World Bank and IMF) were unable make the shift described above (Glenday, 2006; Baunsgaard and Keen, 2010), partly as a result of inadequate institutions to implement alternate tax regimes (Aizenman and Jinjarak, 2009). For a majority of these countries there was a net decline in overall public revenues (Labonté et al., 2008) and a loss in policy capacity with implications for spending in health, education, and public regulations, which in turn affect primary and secondary prevention of disease.

There are, however, instances where liberalization can increase policy capacity. This can occur if improved market access for developing country exports increases growth and decreases the portion of government revenues that go toward servicing public debt, as was the case in Thailand in the late 1980s and early 1990s; although notably this was a period that preceded a loosening in import restrictions now required of many developing countries under WTO rules.

Estimates of winners and losers in global trade implicate liberalization's tendency to reward disproportionately those countries with already deep resource pockets (Birdsall, 2006). Notwithstanding the economic growth of certain Asian and Latin American developing countries over the past decade, estimates of aggregate gains from a completed WTO Doha Development Round under the "most realistic scenario" found that developed countries by 2015 could expect to gain US$80 billion while developing countries would gain only US$16 billion (World Bank, 2008). Global annual gains of a completed Doha Round range between US$60 billion and $160 billion (Prowse, 2009) – less than 0.23 percent of gross global economic product at the high estimate (CIA, 2011) and a fraction of the trillion-dollar-plus in annual illicit capital flows from developing countries via trade mispricing (transfer pricing), tax havens, and bribery (Kar and Curcio, 2011). An earlier (2006) analysis of aggregate economic gains and losses using four different scenarios of a Doha Round completion estimated annual real income gains for developed countries of between US$6 billion and $8 billion each for Japan, the United States, and the EU 15 group of nations;[4] but annual real income losses of almost US$250 million for Sub-Saharan Africa (Polaski, 2006).

GLOBAL GOVERNANCE AND THE NEOLIBERAL AUSTERITY AGENDA

The 2008 financial crisis has also contributed to eroding policy capacity in two ways. First, despite a near-universal call among UN agencies for increased social protection spending to buffer the negative externalities of the crisis-induced recession, 70 of 128 developing countries surveyed by UNICEF reported spending cuts of at least 3 percent of GDP in 2010, with 91 planning deep cuts in 2012 (Ortiz, Chai, and Cummins, 2011). Such actions may be prudent for countries facing losses in remittances, export markets, and foreign investment, but UNICEF cautions that the "austerity agenda" emanating from the high-income countries is causing irreversible harm to children's health. Second, such cuts are actually being demanded under new regimes of conditionality required by the IMF in its post-crisis bailout packages. Despite the

IMF arguing the importance of governments sustaining their social protection programs, a 2009 EURODAD[5] survey of IMF conditions attached to post-crisis loans to ten low-income countries found that all recipient governments were expected to cut spending; none were given flexibility to defer debt payments, and half were instructed to reduce deficits and introduce wage freezes. Recipient governments were also advised to increase VAT (regressive) taxes, privatize the financial and energy sectors, and deepen liberalization, though these were highly contentious policy directions and none were advised to increase progressive forms of taxation (Molina-Gallart, 2009).

Similar austerity measures are being imposed on many of the affected Euro-zone countries by the IMF and the European Central Bank, with requirements for further financial liberalization despite the record of how such underregulated liberalization led to the private market and subsequent sovereign debt crises in the first place. Interestingly, developing countries at the 2011 WTO Ministerial organized a well-attended session arguing the importance of countries retaining flexibilities in regulating financial services rather than pursuing more rapid liberalization, with the IMF in late 2012 suggesting that austerity in Europe was now doing more harm than good, and that (perhaps) capital controls may not be the bad idea it had been denouncing for decades.

GLOBAL PUBLIC HEALTH COSTS BACK ON THE AGENDA

There also exist more quotidian public health concerns with global trade: the "communicable" vectors of noncommunicable diseases (NCDs). NCDs were ignored in global health and developing country policy during the 1990s; the Millennium Development Goals focus entirely on infectious disease and conditions associated with acute infant and maternal mortality. This complacency is changing, but there is as yet little appreciation for (or even much acknowledgement of) the role trade and investment liberalization has played in globalizing exposure to the major individual risk factors for these NCDs: tobacco use, poor diets, excess alcohol use, and lower rates of physical activity.[6]

TRANSNATIONAL TOBACCO CORPORATIONS (TTCs) AND THEIR IMPACT ON THE GLOBAL HEALTH AGENDA

As smoking rates decline in developed countries (the result of decades of public health activism and regulation), transnational tobacco corporations (TTCs) have come to target developing nations. Trade treaties have been used successfully to block developing countries' efforts to limit the introduction of new foreign brands through tariffs or other measures, with WTO dispute panel rulings finding such policies (even if invoked under the health defense) discriminatory. Instead, countries are obliged to use often inadequate domestic regulations to curb tobacco use. This "least trade restrictive" argument ignores that as tobacco product exposure increases in any given market, price competition, advertising, and other corporate practices invariably lead to increased consumption. Liberalized investment is the more important means by which tobacco consumption rises, with TTCs buying out domestic tobacco manufacturers or creating manufacturing facilities within developing countries. As foreign direct investment (FDI) in tobacco rises, with the two largest TTC investors being British American Tobacco and Philip Morris International, consumption rises, sometimes quite dramatically.

The 2003 Framework Convention on Tobacco Control (FCTC), negotiated under the WHO system and in force since 2005, encourages stronger national tobacco controls by all WHO member states through a number of nonbinding protocols. The FCTC is grounded on an international human right to health and includes specific provisions against for example gender discrimination (Jacobs, 2012). The FCTC also states that, assuming foreign tobacco products are treated the same as domestic ones (the nondiscrimination standard of the WTO), a country's tobacco control measures should not be subject to a trade dispute. The FCTC is silent on the role of FDI, which allows the TTCs – giant corporate entities – to avoid any possible tariff barriers on finished goods while still increasing their presence in domestic markets. Moreover, "nearly every investment and trade agreement negotiated by the United States eliminates or reduces trading partners' tobacco tariffs and protects US tobacco companies' overseas manufacturing and investment" (Bollyky and Gostin, 2010, p. 2637).

Indeed, trade treaties have become the weapon of choice for TTCs to challenge the (nonbinding) protocols for tobacco control advanced by the FCTC. Eleven trade disputes have been or presently are being brought against tobacco control policies. Three disputes involved tariff policies that discriminated against foreign products and all were judged to be trade discriminatory. Five involved promotion strategies while three involved product policies. Many of these challenges are only expressed "concerns" or have just entered a dispute resolution stage. Philip Morris through its regional companies has been particularly aggressive in challenging control measures using obscure bilateral investment treaties (specifically packaging measures in Uruguay and Australia), as well as initiating disputes at the WTO with the help of proxy states (Ukraine, Honduras, and the Dominican Republic). What is ironic is that countries enacting a control policy within their own borders have often lodged concerns with other countries attempting to do the exact same within their borders – a sign of a lack of coherence between domestic health and global economic policies.

FAST FOOD, OBESITY: WHAT IS THEIR LINK TO GLOBAL TRADE?

By one account, the most universally recognized symbol in the world is the Golden Arches of McDonald's – an icon of a global shift toward energy-dense foods high in fat, salt, and sugar but often low in nutrient value. Trade liberalization, either through trade treaties or structural adjustment loan requirements, facilitated this spread and the consolidation of global food production, distribution, and retailing into a small number of transnational food corporations (TFCs). Food products now account for at least 11 percent of all global trade, with the rise of processed food occurring more quickly than that of primary agricultural products. There is some evidence, notably from India and the Pacific islands, that the increase in international food trade has shifted dietary patterns from local "healthy" diets to the consumption of fattier diets. This has also been eased by liberalization of foreign direct investment, which has targeted highly processed foods. Food retailers, in turn, have undergone an intense and rapid transformation, with TFC-dominated supermarkets replacing local retailers and traditional markets in the urbanizing centers of most developing countries. Supermarkets in developing countries have focused on highly processed foods because of their long shelf lives and their potential economies of scale.

Weight and obesity problems are no longer plagues exclusively of the wealthier nations. The United States continues to have the highest rate of obese citizens, but it is followed by Mexico and South Africa, with rates of overweight children growing more rapidly in middle-income countries such as Brazil and Chile than in the United States. Advertising and product marketing have played their role through the "systematic molding of taste by giant corporations" (Chopra and Darnton-Hill, 2004, p. 1559). Marketing has been especially directed at the youth. During the late 1990s, soft-drink companies targeted school children by selling products in attractive combination packages in schools in Mexico and Colombia, which led to a 50 percent increase in soft-drink sales among children. There is also a direct relationship between global food trade and the growth in snack/fast food outlets and consumption in most developing nations.

In theory, trade treaties could be used to restrict unhealthy foods. One effort to do so, however – a Mexican tax on high-fructose corn syrup sweetened soft drinks from the United States – failed under a NAFTA and WTO challenge.

The tax Mexico charged on syrup-sweetened beverages was higher than the tax on soft drinks sweetened with domestic cane sugar. Corn syrup production, however, is heavily subsidized in the United States and is cheaper than sugar, leading to lower final beverage cost, price competition, and increased consumption (Labonté, 2010).

THE UN SUMMIT ON NONCOMMUNICABLE DISEASES

NCDs have become an important issue for global health experts. The Final Declaration of the September 2012 UN Summit on this theme is important to examine. The summit was only the second UN high-level meeting convened on a health issue and the first concerning the security risks posed by an unchecked HIV pandemic. Its outcome, however, was more a commitment to individual behavior change than a regulation of the market practices that create obesogenic environments. When a U.S. representative to the run-up meeting for the September Summit was asked why the American program aimed to reduce childhood obesity was not being highlighted for adoption by developing countries, the representative was straightforward: "It may damage US trade export interests."

FUTURE SCENARIOS TO PROTECT AND EXPAND POLICY SPACE: FUNDAMENTALS OF REFORM

If we accept that some system of trade between peoples and nations is needed and will (or should) continue, it is better it be based on rules. How might present trade rules be altered to be more globally equitable, providing countries and their governments the capacities to respond to the health and development needs of their citizens? Some of these reforms have been implied throughout this chapter, but a consolidated short list would look something like this:

1. Development, not trade, at the center of the treaties.
    Piecemeal approaches to this issue include strengthening special and differential treatment provisions for developing countries; ending demands for tariff reductions from developing (and especially smaller or lower-income developing) countries until viable alternative tax systems and competitive industries are in place, thus addressing the long-standing implementation issues faced by developing countries; and ending new treaty negotiations until these issues are resolved.
    A more dramatic approach would be to require developed countries to negotiate nonreciprocal market access and subsidies for developing

countries outside of any other trade treaty negotiations (Y.-S. Lee, 2006). Only when these are complete would multilateral negotiations on other trade treaties be allowed to proceed. These initiatives may now be beyond implementation, however, given the implosion of consumer markets in high-income countries.

The 2011 UNCTAD Report on Least Developed Countries (many of which are in Africa) urges much greater exchange between developing nations and an emphasis on poor countries developing their domestic industrial capacity and internal markets, rather than relying on the model of export-led growth through cut-price consumer goods. This would almost be a return to the import substitution model that disappeared with the oil price shocks, developing world debt, and subsequent structural adjustment policies of the 1980s and 1990s (UNCTAD, 2011b).

2. Incorporate provisions for derogation from trade rules for purposes of meeting obligations under human rights treaties.

The role of the WTO as perhaps the most effective existing institution for supranational economic regulation raises questions about how the trade policy regime interacts with the international human rights framework. The UN Special Rapporteurs on globalization and human rights concluded several years ago that "it is necessary to move away from approaches that are ad hoc and contingent" in ensuring that human rights are not compromised by trade liberalization (Oloka-Onyango and Udagama, 2003, p. 10). Assessing trade policy against other metrics than liberalization or growth is consistent with the argument for establishing other measures of social progress besides the GNP/GNI.

3. Cease incorporation of investor-state provisions in bilateral or regional trade treaties, and remove provisions from existing treaties.

If such provisions remain, there should be clearer guidelines on what constitutes an expropriation and language that would prevent corporations from forum-shopping. The manner in which such treaties are structured tends to favor the already wealthier and more powerful side of the negotiating table; a broader reform area would cover the "spaghetti bowl" of bilateral and trade treaties more generally. While the United States is often singled out negatively for its bilateral and regional efforts, especially its recent Dominican Republic and Central American Free Trade Agreement (CAFTA), the EU is little better, having imposed highly skewed terms on its former African, Caribbean, and Pacific (ACP) colonies in its (still being finalized) Economic Partnership Agreements (Stevens et al., 2008; Lee, Sridhar, and Patel, 2009).

FINANCIAL REREGULATION AND NEEDED REFORMS

For many observers of the global economy, however, its financialization over recent decades is a more pressing concern than trade per se. Some of the key reforms that have been mooted include:

1. An effective closure of offshore financial centers (OFCs, or tax havens) and an end to the transfer pricing practices of transnational corporations.
   - The need to clot the hemorrhaging of wealth away from taxable territories has been argued for years, even gaining the attention of the OECD and the IMF. Between US$21 trillion to $32 trillion in personal capital sits in sheltered accounts, with estimates of foregone annual tax revenues exceeding on growth alone of US$180 billion to $250 billion (Henry, 2012; Oxfam, 2013), to say nothing of tax on what (unknown) amount of the principal leaked offshore before any significant tax bite was made. In the immediate aftermath of 2008 many of the G20 countries again began to talk tough on tax havens, with some successes in prying open private Swiss accounts, but the requirements were so lax that the one study subsequent to G20 reforms found that nothing had changed, and that the top ten investment banks (all operating in tax haven countries) saw their "wealth management" jump from US$2.3 trillion to US$6 trillion since the financial crisis (Johannesen and Zucman, 2012; *Guardian Weekly*, July 27, 2012, p. 18).

2. Introduce a financial transaction tax.
   - As with tax havens, there have been episodic calls for, and the occasional unilateral adoption of, such a "Tobin tax" (named for the economist who first proposed it). The theory was that such a tax would dampen destabilizing speculative capital flows, although evidence to date indicates that this may not be the case as the rate (0.05 or 0.005 percent) may be too low to affect speculators. Some have called for an additional "Spahn tax," with rapidly escalating rates in the case of panic outflows or evidence of significant capital flight. Post-2008, interest in a financial transaction tax has gained new adherents, no longer as a means to dampen speculation or to finance global development (the intent around which many of the NGOs and some country proponents for such a tax had long gathered around) but to recapitalize central banks weakened by private bank bailouts or emergency relief for countries at risk of sovereign default. The potential revenues could be large: a low rate of 0.05 percent applied to bond and share sales globally could raise US$410 billion. Indeed, a much lower tax of 0.005 percent (or 5 cents for every 1,000 dollars), if applied to all

foreign exchanges, derivatives, shares, and over-the-counter trading globally, would raise US$863 billion annually, which means that at the 0.05 percent rate, it would total US$8.63 trillion (McCulloch and Pacillo, 2011). Eleven of seventeen EU countries (as of January 30, 2013) have now agreed to implement such a tax, albeit at a low level that would raise about €35 billion annually (Inman, 2013).

3. Separate savings/consumer banking from investment banking, limit the leverage of all banking to avoid speculative bubbles, and break up global banks too big to fail.
   - These reforms have already been discussed, along with the apparent reluctance by governments to act decisively in any of these areas.

4. Reinstitute restrictions on capital flows and develop multilateral rules for their use, and reduce the flexibility in exchange rates by developing a global currency unit and an international clearing agency to stabilize global imbalances.
   - These policies were urged (unsuccessfully) by Keynes in the Bretton Woods meetings. But as Wade (2009, p. 551) argues, "The post–Bretton Woods combination of flexible exchange rates and free capital movements has failed spectacularly in keeping the world economy stable."

FINAL THOUGHTS

Has the WTO lost its relevancy in global economic governance? The proliferation of bilateral and regional treaties would suggest that multilateralism is being replaced by regionalism, and the lack of movement in the dead, dying, or simply narcoleptic Doha Round renders the WTO more an arbiter of past treaties than a venue for the creation of new ones. What is clear is that the balance of power in multilateral negotiations has shifted enormously, with the so-called BRIC[7] countries (but perhaps most importantly China and Brazil) flexing much more trade and economic muscle. However, there is as much antinomy as there is solidarity between the waking giants: China grows its economy through government financing and subsidies, whereas Brazil uses tariffs to protect its private sector. The two clash over this, with both aspiring to be seen as the spokespersons for the interests of the developing world. What is also clear is that developing countries are loathe to give up on multilateral trade negotiations, recognizing that such a venue offers more potential for a global development rather than the mercantilist outcome. How well health or health equity fares as a result of multilateral trade remains very much a matter of how powerful health diplomats can exert their influence over the pace and content of trade negotiations; their power is strengthening, but it is still a minor voice amid the liberalizing chorus that dominates the economic policy making of most states.

REFERENCES

Aizenman, J. and Jinjarak, Y. (2009). Globalisation and developing countries – a shrinking tax base? *The Journal of Development Studies*, 45(5), 653–671.

Altvater, E. and Mahnkopf, B. (2012). European integration and the crossroads: Deepening or disintegration? In Pons-Vignon, N. and Ncube, P. (eds) *Confronting Finance*. Geneva: International Labour Organization Global Labour University.

Baunsgaard, T. and Keen, M. (2010). Tax revenue and (or?) trade liberalization. *Journal of Public Economics*, 94(9–10), 563–577.

Bezruchka, S. (2009). The effect of economic recession on population health. *Canadian Medical Association Journal*, 181(5), 281–285.

Bhagwati, J. (2000). *The wind of the hundred days: How Washington mismanaged globalization*. Cambridge, MA: The MIT Press.

Birdsall, N. (2006). *The world is not flat: Inequality and injustice in our global economy*. Helsinki: World Institute for Development Economics.

Bollyky, T. J. and Gostin, L. O. (2010). The United States engagement in global tobacco control. *The Journal of the American Medical Association*, 304(23), 2637–2638.

Braithwaite, T., Mackenzie, M., McLannahan, B., and Nasiripour, S. (2012, January 11). Japan and Canada warn on Volcker rule impact. *FT.com*.

Carranza, M. E. (2005). Poster child or victim of imperialist globalization? Explaining Argentina's December 2001 political crisis and economic collapse. *Latin American Perspectives*, 32(145), 65–89.

Central Intelligence Agency (CIA) (2011, December 1). *The World Factbook – Economy – overview*.

Chen, S. and Ravallion, M. (2008). *The developing world is poorer than we thought, but no less successful in the fight against poverty*. World Bank Policy Research Working Paper 4703.

Chen, S. and Ravallion, M. (2012). *An update to the World Bank's estimates of consumption poverty in the developing world*. World Bank Briefing Note 03-01-12. Retrieved February 18, 2013 from: http://siteresources.worldbank.org/INTPOVCALNET/Resources/Global_Poverty_Update_2012_02-29-12.pdf.

Chopra, M. and Darnton-Hill, I. (2004). Tobacco and obesity epidemics: Not so different after all? *British Medical Journal*, 328(7455), 1558–1560.

Dávila Quintana, C. D. and González López-Valcárcel, B. (2009). The economic crisis and health. *Gaceta Sanitaria*, 23(4), 261–265.

De Barros, R. P., Ferreira, F. G. P., Vega, J. R. M., and Chanduvi, J. S. (2009). *Measuring inequalities of opportunities in Latin America and the Caribbean*. Washington, DC: The World Bank.

Eavis, P. (2012). For Europe, few options in a vicious cycle of debt. *DealBook – The New York Times*.

Floro, M. and Dymski, G. (2000). Financial crisis, gender and power: An analytical framework. *World Development*, 28(7), 1269–1283.

Foreign Affairs and International Trade Canada (2011). *Pledge against protectionism.* Joint Ministerial Press Statement.

Henry, J. (2012). *The Price of Offshore Revisited.* Tax Justice Network. Retrieved February 18, 2013 from: http://www.taxjustice.net/cms/upload/pdf/Price_of_Offshore_Revisited_120722.pdf.

Hsu, L. (2012). Public health regulation: The impact of intersections between trade & investment treaties in Asia. Society of International Economic Law Online Proceedings, Working Paper 2012/32. Retrieved February 18, 2013 from: http://www/ssrn/com.link/sIEL-2012-Singapore-Conference.html.

Glenday, G. (2006). *Toward fiscally feasible and efficient trade liberalization.* Durham, NC: Duke Center for Internal Development.

Hudson, M. (2010). *US "quantitative easing" is fracturing the global economy.*[Working Paper No. 639. New York: Levy Institute of Bard College.

Inman, P. (2013, January 22). EU approves financial transaction tax for 11 eurozone countries. *The Guardian.* Retrieved February 18, 2013 from: http://www.guardian.co.uk/business/2013/jan/22/eu-approves-financial-transaction-tax-eurozone.

International Labour Organization (ILO) (2009). *Global employment trends: January 2009.* Geneva: International Labour Office.

Jacobs, L. (2012). Gender, Trade Liberalization, and Tobacco Control in China. In Pitman Potter and Heather Gibb (Eds.), *Gender Equality Rights and Trade Regimes: Coordinating Compliance* (pp. 141–158). Ottawa: North South Institute.

Johanessen, N. and Zucman, G. (2012). *The end of bank secrecy? An evaluation of the G20 tax haven crackdown.* Retrieved February 18, 2013 from: http://www.parisschoolofeconomics.eu/docs/zucman-gabriel/sub_jan31.pdf.

Kaminsky, G. L. (2005). *International capital flows, financial stability and growth.* ST/ESA/2005/DWP/10. New York: United Nations Department of Economic and Social Affairs.

Kar, D. and Curcio, K. (2011). *Illicit financial flows from developing countries: 2000–2009 (Update with a focus on Asia).* Washington, DC: Global Financial Integrity.

Kentikelenis, A., Karanikolos, M., Papanicolas, I., Basu, S., McKee, M., and Stuckler, D. (2011). Health effects of financial crisis: Omens of a Greek tragedy. *The Lancet* 378 (9801), 1457–1458.

Koivusalo, M., Schrecker, T., and Labonté, R. (2008). *Globalization and policy space for health and social determinants of health.* Globalization Knowledge Network, World Health Organization Commission on Social Determinants of Health.

Labonté, R. (2010). Liberalized trade and the public's health: What are the linkages? What is the evidence? What are the healthy options? In A. den Exter (Ed.) *International trade law and health care: In search of good sense* (9–36). Rotterdam: Erasmus University Press. WHO: Geneva. Accessed at www.WHO.int/social_determinants/resources/gnk_final_report_042008.pdf.

Labonté, R., Blouin, C., Chopra, M., Lee, K., Packer, C., Rowson, M. et al. (2008). Towards health-equitable globalisation: Rights, regulation and redistribution. *Globalization Knowledge Network, Final Report to the Commission on Social Determinants of Health.*

Labonté, R., Mohindra, K., and Lencucha, R. (2011). Framing international trade and chronic disease. *Globalization and Health,* 7(21), 1–15.

Lavranos, N. (2009). The Brazilian tires case: Trade supersedes health. *Trade, Law & Development*, 1(2), 230–258.

Lee, K., Sridhar, D., and Patel, M. (2009). Bridging the divide: Global governance of trade and health. *The Lancet*, 373(9661), 416–422.

Lee, K.-K. and Crotty, J. (2005). The effects of neoliberal "reforms" on the post-crisis Korean economy. Working papers, wp134. Amherst, Political Economy Research Institute, University of Massachusetts.

Lee, Y.-S. (2006). *Reclaiming development in the world trading system*. New York: Cambridge University Press.

Marmot, M. and Bell, R. (2009). How will the financial crisis affect health? *British Medical Journal*, 338(b1314), 858–860.

McCulloch, N. and Pacillo, G. (2011, May). The Tobin tax: A review of the evidence. Brighton, UK: Institute of Development Studies. IDS Research Report 68.

Molina-Gallart, N. (2009). *Bail-out or blow-out? IMF policy advice and conditions for low-income countries at a time of crisis*. Brussels: European Network on Debt and Development.

Olive, D. (2011, September 9). Should we raise taxes on the rich? *The Toronto Star*, p. B1.

Oloka-Onyango, J. and Udagama, D. (2003). Fifty-fifth session Item 4 of the provisional agenda. *Economic, social and cultural rights: Globalization and its impact on the full enjoyment of human rights – Final Report*. Geneva: United Nations Economic and Social Council.

Ortiz, I., Chai, J., and Cummins M. (2011). *Austerity measures threaten children and poor households: Recent evidence in public expenditures from 128 developing countries*. New York: UNICEF.

Ortiz, I. and Cummins, M. (eds.) (2012). *A recovery for all: Rethinking socioeconomic policies for children and poor households*. New York: UNICEF.

Oxfam (2013). *The cost of inequality: How wealth and income extremes hurt us all.* Retrieved February 18, 2013 from: http://www.oxfam.org/sites/www.oxfam.org/files/cost-of-inequality-oxfam-mb180113.pdf.

Parrado, E. A. and Zenteno, R. M. (2001). Economic restructuring, financial crises and women's work in Mexico. *Social Problems*, 48(4), 456–477.

Pirie, I. (2006). Social injustice and economic dynamism in contemporary Korea. *Critical Asian Studies*, 38(3), 211–243.

Polaski, S. (2006, March). *Winners and losers: Impact of the Doha round on developing countries*. Washington, DC: Carnegie Endowment for International Peace.

Prowse, S. (2009). *Doha and the global crisis: The preservation of the multilateral trading system is vital in the current international climate.* Briefing Paper 57. London: Overseas Development Institute.

Spratt, S. (2011). *Global financial turmoil part II: Five lessons from developing countries.* Retrieved September 8, 2013 from: http://www.ids.ac.uk/news/global-financial-turmoil-five-lessons-from-developing-country-crises.

Standing, G. (2011). *The precariat: The new dangerous class.* Cornwall, UK: Bloomsbury.

Stevens, C., Meyn, M., Kennan, J., Bilal, S., Braun-Munzinger, C., Jerosch, F. et al. (2008, March 31). *The new EPAs: Comparative analysis of their content and tasks for 2008*. (Policy Management Report 14). Maastricht: European Centre for Development Policy Management.

Stuckler, D. Basu, S., and McKee, M. (2011). Budget crises, health, and social welfare programmes. *British Medical Journal*, 341, 77–79.

Stuckler, D., Basu, S., Suhrcke, M., Coutts, A., and McKee, M. (2011). Effects of the 2008 financial crisis on health: A first look at European data. *The Lancet*, 378(9876), 124–125.

Sustainable Development Commission (2009). *Prosperity without growth: The transition to a sustainable economy?* London: UK Sustainable Development Commission.

Thorbecke, E. and Nissanke, M. (2006). Introduction: The impact of globalization on the world's poor. *World Development*, 34(8), 1333–1337.

Treanor, J. (2011, September 13). Banks face 'far-reaching' reform as 358-page report is released. *The Guardian*, p. 1.

United Nations Conference on Trade and Development (UNCTAD) (2011a). *Trade and development report 2011: Post-crisis policy challenges in the world economy.* Geneva: United Nations Publications.

United Nations Conference on Trade and Development (UNCTAD) (2011b). *The least developed countries report 2011: The potential role of south-south cooperation for inclusive and sustainable development.* Geneva: United Nations Publications.

Wade, R. (2009). From global imbalances to global reorganisations. *Cambridge Journal of Economics*, 33(4), 539–562.

World Bank (2000). *Global economic prospects and the developing countries 2000.* Washington, DC: World Bank.

World Bank (2007). *Global economic prospects 2007: Managing the next wave of globalization.* Washington, DC: World Bank.

World Bank (2008). *Global monitoring report 2008: MDGs and the environment.* Washington, DC: World Bank.

World Bank (2009). *The global economic crisis: Assessing vulnerability with a poverty lens.* Washington, DC: World Bank.

Yi, K.-M. (2009). The collapse of global trade: The role of vertical specialization. In R. Baldwin and S. Evenett (Eds.), *The collapse of global trade, murky protectionism and the crisis: Recommendations for the G20.* London: Centre for Economic Policy Research. Retrieved September 9, 2013 from: http://www.voxeu.org.

The World Trade Organization and Food Security after the Global Food Crises

Matias E. Margulis

INTRODUCTION: FOOD POLICY AND INTERNATIONAL TRADE

Following the 2008 and 2011 global food crises, the relationship between world food security and the international trade system has emerged as a significant issue in global policy.[1] The global food crises, most closely associated with the end of low food prices and a massive increase in the number of hungry people worldwide to more than 1 billion, have put the relationship between food security and international trade, and its implications for global food policy, under much greater scrutiny. Although states and international actors have not called for a return to national self-sufficiency or an end to free trade in agriculture, the new global food policy consensus indicates a significant erosion of international confidence in the status quo of trade in foodstuffs. The primacy of international trade in agriculture as an element of food policy has become more deeply contested since the establishment of the World Trade Organization (WTO).

Behind the new consensus lies an ongoing contest about the relationship between food security and international trade and its impact on the future of global food policy. The debate on food security remains at the top of the international agenda. It is extensively debated in key forums such as the United Nations, the World Bank, the WTO, and the G8/G20. The consensus is reshaping the purpose and destination of official development assistance and private philanthropy for food security. The consensus is also rescaling the politics of food security advocacy across traditional international NGOs and the rising food sovereignty movement.

This chapter analyzes the emergent transnational policy space for food security and its implications for understanding the WTO in a changing global landscape. Despite the collapse of Doha Round negotiations in July 2008, the debate over food security and international trade has intensified at the WTO since that time. There are observable changes in the WTO's role as an international institution, including its participation in new forms of global food security governance. We can also observe a substantial change in the content of interstate deliberations at the WTO on food security. Also examined is the purported right to food, which has been firmly established in the new global food security policy consensus. The legitimacy of the right to food provides a novel intervention into the food security/international trade debate. Repeated interactions between the UN Special Rapporteur on the right to food and the WTO illustrate conflicting visions about the role of international trade rules in addressing world hunger, which are emblematic of the political contests shaping the transnational policy space for food security.

THE GLOBAL FOOD CRISES AND INTERNATIONAL TRADE

The causes and consequences of the 2008 and 2011 global food crises have been exhaustively debated elsewhere in the scholarly and policy literature.[2] Rather than review these debates here, this section briefly discusses the drivers of the food crises, trade-related aspects of responses to the crises, the emerging transnational policy space, and the WTO's role in this new space.

DRIVERS OF THE CRISES AND THE END OF CHEAP FOOD

There is no single smoking gun behind the recent global food crises. Instead, they were precipitated by a confluence of factors. The most commonly cited drivers are: biofuel policies in the global North that diverted large volumes of agricultural production and supply such as corn and oilseeds away from food and feed markets into energy production; domestic policies of key agricultural producers encouraging the drawdown of buffer stocks; rising demand for agricultural goods from the emerging economies; increased financial activity and speculation in commodity and futures markets; and, unilateral agricultural export restrictions.

Reference is made to the global food *crises* instead of a *crisis* in this chapter. This is to recognize that global food prices have demonstrated continued volatility since 2008. Figure 11.1 clearly shows the "twin peaks" of world food prices that occurred in 2008 and 2011 and the significant volatility of prices, especially in the period between the 2008 and 2011 peaks. The same figure also shows that global food prices remain well above their pre-2008 levels. There has been no decline to pre-crisis levels. This is why the global food crises are commonly referred to as the end of cheap food. One must recognize

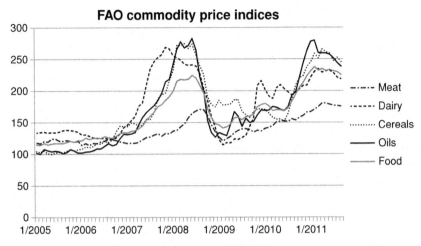

FIGURE 11.1. FAO Global Food Price Index, 2005–2011. *Source*: FAO.

that the long-standing trend of declining international food prices associated
with the post–World War II era appears to have come to an abrupt end. Most
international institutions and academic economists suggest there has been a
structural shift in the global food system. Food prices are expected to stay high
and continue to increase over the medium term, especially as the effects of
climate change on world food production become more pronounced. High
and rising global food prices are the "new normal" in the world economy.

The end of cheap of food is experienced unequally by people across the
globe. Price increases were less intensely felt in developed countries, where
food does not make up a major proportion of household consumption. In sharp
contrast, rising food prices have had profound income and nutritional impacts
in the global South. At the global level, the Food and Agricultural Organization
(FAO) has estimated that the global food crises pushed an additional 150–
200 million people into a state of undernourishment. The World Bank most
recently reported that more than 44 million people were driven into poverty as
a result of the food price spike of 2011. It is difficult to translate these statistics
into individual-level effects given that undernourishment and poverty interact
with a wider set of socioeconomic factors. Recent studies have confirmed
higher levels of food insecurity, leading to an increased global incidence of
malnutrition and child stunting (Ruel et al., 2010).

NATIONAL RESPONSES TO THE GLOBAL FOOD CRISES

States employed various policies and tools to cope with rising food prices. At the
national level these policies varied widely across developed and developing

countries and between net-food-importing countries and net-food-exporting countries. In addition, policy making was also influenced by public pressure on governments to respond to food price inflation.

Most relevant is the fact that trade measures were the principal form of national response to rising food prices. Other typical responses included lowering import tariffs and taxes on staple foods in net food importers and least-developed countries. Several countries imposed unilateral export restrictions to increase the supply of food available in domestic market and to check food price inflation. Export restrictions have been the most controversial of national responses, especially the restrictions placed on grain exports by major agricultural exporting countries such as Argentina, Ukraine, and Russia. These countries were singled out and blamed by several international institutions and Northern governments for exacerbating the crises. Indeed, export restrictions were often followed by pronounced volatility in world commodity prices. Despite the association of export restrictions with major food exporters, it is important to recall that twenty-four countries introduced these measures. This group was highly diverse and included many non-net-food-exporting countries such as China, India, Indonesia, Pakistan, Bangladesh, Guinea, and Bolivia (Demeke et al., 2008).

Other national responses included developing social safety nets, introducing consumer subsidies, and direct government purchases of food on international markets to increase domestic supply. Longer-term measures such as improving domestic agricultural production, extension services, and the use of novel technology/biotechnology are underway in many developing countries. Priority has been placed on food marketing and distribution to prevent post-harvest losses and spoilage. The global food price crises prompted the governments of many developing countries to increase their capacity to guarantee minimum levels of food security to their populations. This marks a significant departure from the past decades of mainstream development theories that emphasized trade liberalization and the corporatization of agriculture. The WTO, in conjunction with structural adjustments policies, provided an international framework for this a global project.

MULTILATERAL RESPONSES AND THE "NEW" GLOBAL FOOD SECURITY POLICY CONSENSUS

Multilateral responses to the global food crises have been numerous. Emergency food aid was a crucial short-term response. In 2008 alone, the UN World Food Programme (WFP), the agency responsible for administering international food aid, delivered more than US$5 billion worth of food assistance to 102 million people in 78 countries (WFP, 2009). The volume of international food aid in 2008 was unprecedented. In addition, the global food crises marked the entry of nontraditional donors for international food assistance such as Saudi Arabia, philanthropic organizations such as the Bill and Melinda Gates Foundation, Warren Buffett, and private individual donations in response to the WFP's fund-raising campaigns.

In addition to emergency food assistance, multilateral interventions also spanned several medium-term measures. These included financial assistance from the international financial institutions to assist countries with balance-of-payments problems resulting from high food prices. There was a major push to assist developing countries increase food production, and many of them received technical assistance, technology, and favorable access to food production inputs with assistance from bilateral donors, international institutions, and regional development banks.

From the start of the 2008 food crisis, international institutions and donors have cooperated to coordinate global food security interventions. Coordination was prompted by wide agreement among international institutions and key states about the severity of the food crisis and the urgent need for a global response. The focal point for international cooperation and coordination is the UN High Level Task Force on the Global Food Security Crisis (HLTF), established by the UN Secretary General in 2008 to coordinate across the UN system and Bretton Woods organizations.[3] The HLTF is comprised of more than twenty international institutions, including the WTO, and is networked to key global food security policy-making bodies such as the G8/G20, and the Committee for World Food Security, as well as global civil society, philanthropic organizations, and the private sector.

The WTO was among a handful of international institutions that actively participated in negotiating the Comprehensive Framework for Action (CFA). The CFA is the international policy document that best articulates the new global consensus on food security. The new consensus on global food security can be summarized as follows:[4]

- Increased food production/investment in developing country agriculture;
- Expanded social protection/assistance to increase the access to food;
- National ownership and accountability;
- Support for smallholder farmers, especially women;
- Recognition of the right to food as a central normative and operational basis for policy-making.

The new consensus on global food security policy is prominently visible at the level of ideas and discourse, for example, with the G8 declaration in 2008 on global food security and the World Bank's call for a new deal on agriculture.

The consensus is also backed by political and financial commitments at the international and national levels; the G20 pledged more than US$20 billion to support agriculture in developing countries, and developing countries have increased domestic spending on the agriculture sector.

Developments such as the HLTF and the new global security policy consensus are indicative of an emergent transnational policy space governing food security. The concept of a transnational policy space is different than the concept of policy space that is often used in the literature to refer to a country's flexibility in pursuing policies under its WTO commitments. According to Coleman (2005, pp. 94–98), the concept of a transnational policy space describes new forms of governance in response to globalizing processes – a space characterized by the lack of a fixed territoriality. Policy making occurs across territorial boundaries and involves communities of state and nonstate actors in which the identities of such individuals are shaped by self-aware engagement in global-scale problems as opposed to particular, national problems. A transnational policy space also displays significant political contestation and bids for power. As Coleman (2005, p. 98) reminds us, "In charting the contours of such a space, we must keep in mind that nodes of power congealed in institutions give structure to flows."

The WTO is a key institutional actor in this policy space. Not only is the WTO a member of the HLTF; its officials are active at this site. WTO officials are also participating in interagency collaboration projects such as developing policy recommendations on food price volatility for the G20, and are involved in policy deliberations at the recently reformed Committee for World Food Security. This newfound role of the WTO has been contested. According to the HLTF coordinator, Dr. David Nabarro, there was significant disagreement between the WTO and other key HLTF members about the role of trade policy during the interagency negotiations of the CFA.[5] The CFA's message on trade is balanced. It supports the conclusions of the Doha Round and envisages significant trade policy reform. This would include limiting the use of export taxes and restrictions, but also creating significant policy flexibility for developing countries. Yet global civil society organizations have been highly critical of the CFA for legitimizing the WTO, which many view as contrary to world food security.

To sum up, trade policy and the WTO featured prominently in responses to the global food crises. These crises provided the WTO with an opportunity to take on new governance roles as an autonomous, institutional actor at the HLTF and Committee for World Food Security. These roles are unprecedented for the WTO as it is an institution traditionally perceived as only an interstate negotiation and dispute settlement forum. The WTO's institutional design creates only a weak executive body. Yet the WTO and its officials now exercise types of decision- and policy-making capacities unparalleled in the GATT/WTO's history in the emergent transnational policy space for food security.

THE WTO AND FOOD SECURITY AFTER THE GLOBAL FOOD CRISES

The global food crises brought the global trade regime under greater international scrutiny. Although often underappreciated, the WTO plays a significant role in global food security policy. Food security–related provisions are found across all three pillars – domestic support, market access, and export competition – of the 1994 Agreement on Agriculture (AA). The WTO framework reserves a ministerial decision specific to food security and a built-in mechanism for international cooperation to address high food prices. Moreover, food security concerns have been a major source of tension between WTO members and have contributed to the present deadlock at the Doha Round.

THE ROLE OF INTERNATIONAL TRADE RULES AND FOOD SECURITY

The impacts of international trade rules on domestic food security have been a long-standing debate at the GATT/WTO since the establishment of the AA. During the Uruguay Round, the central concern was that agricultural trade liberalization would lead to higher world food prices. According to conventional economic theory of the time, it was assumed that reduced Northern farm subsidies would cease to depress world prices. This was significant because increasing agricultural prices was the primary objective of most GATT parties. However, it was acknowledged that higher food prices would adversely affect net-food-importing countries' and least-developed countries' food import bills and cause them serious balance-of-payments problems. The political compromise to the food security question was a ministerial decision, the Decision on Measures Concerning the Possible Negative Effects of the Reform Programme on Net-Food-Importing Countries, where donors pledged to assist developing countries facing rising food import bills resulting from the Uruguay Round reforms. Despite several mini-food-price crises following the implementation of the AA, in practice the decision proved very difficult to implement. This was in part attributable to the difficulty for developing countries of proving a direct causal relationship between reforms and higher food prices. There was also political resistance from donors and the international financial institutions to providing additional development and food assistance under this extraordinary mechanism. To this day developing countries regard the failure to implement the Net Food Importing Developing Countries (NFIDC) decision as evidence of bad faith on the part of developed countries.

The establishment of the WTO in 1995 prompted significant policy, academic, and political debates about whether free trade in food is compatible with achieving food security.[6] Although the WTO is only one link in the chain of the world food system, its legally binding framework and neoliberal orientation significantly structure the world food system. International trade rules not only constrain governmental action but have been crucial in creating an "enabling environment" for the deepening corporatization of food, seeds, and productive resources (such as genetic material) (McMichael, 2009). More specifically, the WTO exerts significant influence over developing countries' food policy through the AA. The AA defines what mix of public action and market-based solutions are available to states across a series of food security policy issues. The scope of WTO rules is demonstrated in Table 11.1.

Power also significantly influences the degree of policy flexibility developing countries enjoy. Even if developing countries have room to maneuver on paper, the power hierarchy at the WTO and the ability of powerful countries to exercise informal influence through persuasion and coercion have great bearing on their behavior. Furthermore, the WTO's legal culture marginalizes food security, thus encouraging conformity to the status quo. This stems from its tendency to undervalue the capacity and access of net-food-importing and least-developed countries, contributing to the already generalized uncertainty experienced by developing countries about where the fault line lies between policy innovation and deviation from the AA. This is not to suggest that other domestic and international constraints are insignificant. Clearly they are. But the role of power asymmetries and the chilling effect of the WTO's legal culture should not be underestimated.

Food security concerns were also visible in the Doha Round negotiations. Although concerns persisted among food importers about the potential of further reductions on Northern agricultural support to push food prices upward, these have been eclipsed by concerns about the impacts of Northern dumping of subsidized agricultural commodities on the livelihoods and food security of local producers. This is why at the Doha Round the Special Safeguard Mechanism and Special Products became contentious political issues, ultimately leading to its collapse (Wolfe, 2010).

TABLE 11.1. *Selected provisions in the AA and their relevance to food security policy*

Article	Description	Relevance
Article 5	*Special Safeguard Provisions*	Allows countries to limit the importation of the quantity of agricultural goods by imposing additional duties (to prevent dumping of goods)
Article 6	*Domestic Support Commitments*	Describes permissible forms of government assistance to agricultural and rural development, including investment subsidies and agricultural input subsidies to low-income or resource-poor producers in developing countries.
Article 10.4	*International Food Aid*	Establishes the criteria for differentiation between legitimate international food and disguised government export subsidies.
Article 12	*Disciplines on Export Prohibitions and Restrictions*	Sets out consultation process for implementation of export restriction or prohibitions permitted to relieve critical shortages of foodstuffs or essential products.
Article 15.2	*Special and Differential Treatment*	Establishes lesser obligations and longer implementation periods for developing countries. Exempts LDCs.
Article 16	*Least-Developed and Net Food-Importing Developing Countries*	Specifies obligations of WTO members to provide assistance to LDCs and NFIDCs in the event of higher food prices linked to trade liberalization.
Annex II, Paragraph 2	*General Government Services*	Specifies the types of government services to farmers (permissible and classified as non-trade-distorting).

Source: Author.

A MATTER OF TIMING

The official collapse of the Doha Round in July 2008 occurred just as the international community was being alerted to the first global food crisis. While the Doha Round negotiations were already in an advanced state of free fall, the global food crisis caught everyone by surprise. It had not been predicted by any of the major international organizations.

Doha remains on life support and the political conditions continue to be unfavorable for a resolution. Yet in Geneva the day-to-day consultations and negotiations at the official's level continues. The global food crises have been discussed at very informal levels of the WTO, such as the Sub-Committee on Least Developed Countries. It has been a prominent theme in the WTO's outreach activities such as its public forums. As discussed earlier, the WTO has been active in the emergent transnational policy space for food security. The global food crises have not significantly permeated the WTO's rulemaking work recently, with the notable exception of export restrictions, which are further discussed later in the chapter. The unresolved state of the Doha has seen most countries stick to their official position in the agriculture negotiations. This extends to their position on food security issues. Many WTO members have made statements that the global food crises only reinforces the need to lock in pro–food security provisions, such the Special Safeguard Mechanism, Special Products, and revisions to the Green Box.

Looking beyond WTO members' unwavering official positions, it is clear that the structural effects of the global food crises on the world food system, and how these structural effects impact the international trade regime, have not been recognized and appreciated. The new status quo of the world food economy involves higher food prices, increased global competition for agricultural resources for food, feed, and fuel, shifting global consumption patterns (i.e., the meatification of diets on a global scale), and intensified risks and vulnerability from two novel sources: financialization and climate change. This new global status quo differs in significant ways from the world that formed the basis of the current international trade regime for agriculture. The current international trade architecture is an edifice constructed on fundamental assumptions such as declining agricultural prices and oversupply, and with a corresponding ideational framework underlying an agenda of progressive trade liberalization and limited state intervention. If these assumptions no longer hold, what purpose does the current international trade system serve?

INTERSTATE DELIBERATIONS ON EXPORT RESTRICTIONS

One way the international community has sought to find new purpose for the international trade regime is by creating new rules on export restrictions. Export restrictions continue to receive significant attention in international debates about international trade and world food security. This debate is taking place on multiple fronts. Export restrictions are governed and permitted under conditions in Article XXII of the AA and Article XX of the GATT. WTO members are permitted to invoke export restrictions on a temporary

basis to ensure sufficient domestic availability of foodstuffs, but are required
to notify and consult trading partners. In 2008, Switzerland and Japan introduced a proposal at the WTO to tighten the rules around export restrictions
to ensure they are only used in extraordinary circumstances and that they
take into account the potential impacts on food importing countries. This
proposal has been included in the latest text of the draft agricultural modalities despite insistence from several developing-country net-food exporters that
this proposal goes beyond the Doha negotiating mandate, which specifically
excluded export restrictions (WTO, 2008). More recently at the 2011 WTO
Ministerial, members further agreed in principle to ensure that export restriction would not affect international food aid flows. Members were urged "to
commit to remove and not to impose in the future, food export restrictions
or extraordinary taxes for food purchased for non-commercial humanitarian
purposes by the World Food Programme" (WTO, 2011, p. 5).

The G8 have also called for food exporters to eliminate the use of export
restrictions, especially by countries such as Russia, Ukraine, and Argentina.
The discourse about export restriction in this forum has been framed to highlight that such policies are "irresponsible" and "exacerbating" global food insecurity. Export restrictions have certainly exacerbated the food price volatility,
but so too have biofuel mandates, which are policies of the North, yet these
have not received equivalent condemnation. This position has been echoed
by most international and regional organizations, especially the international
financial institutions. The CFA, for example, also calls for an end to export
restrictions. At the height of the 2008 global food price crisis, the Washington-
based International Food Policy Research Institute (IFPRI) called for an out-
right prohibition of export restrictions and suggested doing so outside the
WTO framework to develop new rules in isolation from the horse-trading that
drives multilateral trade negotiations.

REVISITING THE AA

The value of the existing international trade regime has been called into
question following the global food crises. This is of course a highly polarized
political struggle, one that goes far beyond the particulars of the WTO and
the AA or the disagreements between different groups of WTO members. At a
more technocratic level, one question that has been put forward is whether the
AA provides developing countries with sufficient "flexibility" to address food
security or whether the current DOHA draft modalities on agriculture are
a better option for WTO members (Karapinar and Häberli, 2010). Although

there is no consensus, most analysts suggest that the current draft modalities are a relative improvement on the AA.

The fact remains that the policy orientations between the AA and the post-global food crisis consensus diverge considerably: the AA seeks to limit state intervention in agriculture, whereas there is now recognition that certain aspects of agriculture and food policy require a more activist state. This situation introduces uncertainty to countries experimenting with new types of food security policies as to the WTO consistency of these policies. Many provisions in the AA are ambiguous and open to subjective interpretation. Achieving WTO consistency is more difficult in practice than commonly acknowledged. The following section examines three policy areas involving support for small-scale farmers and food reserves to highlight some of the tensions and uncertainties.

WTO RULES AND SUPPORT TO SMALL-SCALE FARMERS

The central pillar of the new consensus on global food security policy is increasing international support for small-scale farmers. Put simply, this means increasing the productive capacity of small-scale farmers. This group numbers 2–3 billion people who are generally poor, work small plots of land, and are highly vulnerable to food insecurity. Policies recommended by the new consensus include improving the access of small-scale farmers to productive inputs, extension services, and credit alongside public and private investments into basic infrastructure, storage, processing, and transportation. All these recommendations would translate into significant public investment and involvement in the agricultural sector.

Many of these recommendations fall under the scope of rules on domestic support in the AA. More specifically, policies fall either under: (1) the Green Box that includes policies and programs classified as non- or minimally trade-distorting support and thus not subject to spending limits; or (2) the Blue and Amber Boxes, trade- and production-distorting support, respectively, that are subject to spending limits. Of the two sets of boxes, most policies to support small-scale farmers fall under the Green Box. Green Box spending accounts for nearly 60 percent of developing countries' total agriculture spending. At first glance, having no spending limits for policies falling under the Green Box appears unproblematic. However, in the years preceding the Doha collapse and global food crises, developing countries negotiated for revisions of the Green Box. These included a new blanket provision to update and make common agrarian reform, rural development and poverty, and nutritional food security programs consistent with the Green Box. These policies were hardly earth-shattering but were a tough-fought win for developing countries.

It remains unclear if the new blanket provision on draft modalities in its current form ensures that all the possible permutations of post-crises national food security programs will be WTO-consistent. Under the WTO rules, unless a domestic policy meets specific criteria under the Green Box, regardless of whether the policy actually distorts trade, it is considered trade-distorting support and would thus fall under Blue or Amber Box.

This is the crux of the matter. The vast majority of WTO developing countries members do not have recourse to the Blue and Amber Boxes because most did not negotiate for them as they were undertaking structural reform during that period and massively disinvesting in their agricultural sectors. Many developing countries may unwittingly be adopting policies inconsistent with WTO protocols, even if these policies are fully consistent with the new global food security policy consensus. Even if developing countries were disciplined for deviating from the AA in the short term, the WTO's institutional power depends on everyone following the rules. Any gap between developing countries' commitments and food security policies would create serious and unresolved systematic issues.

WTO RULES AND FOOD RESERVES

The global food crises have renewed interest in national and international food reserves to address price volatility and facilitate emergency food distribution. In recent years, discussions at the UN and among the G8/G20 have examined how to improve food reserve policies at the national level and establish food reserves at the regional and international levels. As such, food reserves are a significant issue in the emergent transnational policy space for food security.

WTO rules are of significance to the global discussion on food reserves and their governance. The Green Box, for example, sets out criteria conditions under which states may maintain public food stockholding for food security that specify the following conditions: (1) the level of stocks must correspond to predetermined levels and these levels must also be explicitly set out in national legislation; (2) they must be financially transparent; and (3) food purchases by governments or their agencies must be made at prevailing market prices, and sales of food security stocks cannot be made at less than the prevailing market price for the product in question. Conditions (1) and (2) are fairly straightforward and serve to assure WTO members that stockholding programs are legitimate and transparent. Developing countries potentially have some extra policy flexibility here as they are permitted to acquire and release food stocks at administered prices instead of market prices. However, they must report any losses as part of their agricultural support spending. Developing countries have called for changes to these provisions to ensure that food stocks meet the standard of non- or minimally trade-distorting support in the Green Box when acquired from low-income or resource-poor producers for stockholding and that is later provided to the general population at subsidized prices. This potential change to the AA would be a significant deviation from existing rules and would provide a more enabling policy environment for food reserves.

A recent study by the Institute for Agriculture and Trade Policy identified several provisions in the AA and in other WTO agreements, which were significant impediments to making reserves operationally effective. These include those on state-trade enterprises (STEs), public procurement, and price bands. Issues may arise even if a food reserve program meets all the Green Box criteria (Murphy, 2010). The study highlighted that current WTO rules prohibit countries from establishing price bands that are central to the operation of a reserve system. Therefore, WTO rules prohibit one of the underlying objectives of food reserves – ensuring their responsiveness to swings in world food prices. Food reserves also face internal opposition at the WTO, making the probability of challenges to rules in the future low. Earlier in the Doha Round, WTO members considered several proposals to establish international food stockholding to respond to high food prices (Sharma and Konandreas, 2008). The United States, Canada, and Australia were vehemently opposed to this nonmarket mechanism, and the idea was dropped from negotiations despite many years of technical work by international institutions. The tide of global opinion is now clearly in favor of food reserves. Yet it is unlikely that if the issue were put back on the WTO agenda, it would produce a different outcome, because the positions of WTO members remain unchanged. Whether the WTO is a suitable forum for devising international trade rules more supportive of food reserves is doubtful.

THE HUMAN RIGHT TO FOOD AND THE WTO AFTER THE GLOBAL FOOD CRISES

A surprise outcome of the global food crises is the prominence of the human right to food as a normative anchor for the new consensus on global food security. This development is surprising because the human right to food has shifted from the periphery of the global food security debate to its center. This prominence is evident in the venerated place the human right to food has in the updated CFA, in all international declarations relating to the global food crisis, and in the incorporation of the right to food in national and multilateral food policy.[7] In addition, it is reflected in the significant role of the UN Special Rapporteur, Dr. Olivier De Schutter, and in the emergent transnational policy space for food security.[8] Following the global food crises, there has been renewed international support for the human right to food as a source of legitimacy and operational content for food security policy making.

Parallel to the rising prominence of the right to food in global food security policy has been a pattern of increasing interaction and contestation between the UN Special Rapporteur on the right to food and the WTO about international trade rules in agriculture. This interaction has become an important aspect of the emergent transnational policy space that has been partially constructed through repeated engagements between the UN Special Rapporteur on the Human Right to Food, Dr. Olivier De Schutter, and the WTO Director General Pascal Lamy. This section examines the highly personalized ideational contests at play in the transnational policy space for food security.

THE UN SPECIAL RAPPORTEUR ON THE RIGHT TO FOOD AND THE WTO

Despite the prominence of the right to food in the post-global food crises landscape, the idea of the human right to food remains controversial at the WTO. The general tension between international trade and human rights law is now decades old and widely acknowledged to be a continuing problem. Yet formal cooperation between the WTO and the UN human rights system is rare (Aaronson, 2007). Significant normative differences, as well as deep feelings of mistrust, remain strong among trade and human rights officials that continue to feed into this divide (Howse and Teitel, 2007). Such normative differences are evident in the interactions between De Schutter and Lamy. Yet these interactions are significant because they offer a rare case of repeated interaction between the UN human rights system and the WTO.

These interactions began with the De Schutter's mission to the WTO in 2008. This event marked the first official mission by any Special Rapporteur to an international organization. It also signaled a shift in the WTO's attitude to the UN human rights system, as the organization had refused to meet with the De Schutter's predecessor, Dr. Jean Ziegler.[9] De Schutter's mission to the WTO included consultations with WTO member states and the WTO secretariat, including Lamy. The mission was summarized in an official report presented to the Council and the UN General Assembly (De Schutter, 2008).

De Schutter's report observed conflicts between the WTO agreements and achieving world food security. Some of the issues he highlighted include increased food import dependency, the marginalization of small-scale farmers at the expense of transnational agribusiness, and supporting production and consumer practices that lead to negative ecological, health, and nutritional outcomes for populations (De Schutter, 2008, pp. 11–18). The report recommended WTO member states conduct a human rights impact assessment of trade agreements prior to their adoption to ensure that the human right to food is protected. In addition, the report stressed WTO members' obligations to protect the right and to maintain and/or increase policy flexibilities to protect food security.

De Schutter's report spurred greater dialogue about the right to food at the WTO. This included several initiatives, a video debate on the right to food, which the WTO posted on its website, the WTO's acceptance of a right-to-food panel at its public forum, and an invitation for De Schutter to present his report to the Committee on Agriculture. Outside the WTO, De Schutter and Lamy participated in a public debate hosted by Geneva in the spring of 2009 and have shared the stage on several panels on trade and human rights since. The global food crises have provided the backdrop for many of these interactions, with a consistent theme being the compatibility and coherence between the state's legal obligation to respect, protect, and fulfill the right to food and its international trade commitments.

De Schutter's position is consistent with most human rights advocates in that the right to food trumps trade agreements. As such, states should take steps to ensure food security for their population even if it means deviating from international trade commitments. In the context of repeated global food crises, De Schutter has urged the international community to break with the WTO's neoliberal orthodoxy, stating:

> Globalization creates big winners and big losers. But where food systems are concerned, losing out means sinking into poverty and hunger. A vision of food security that deepens the divide between food-surplus and food-deficit regions, between exporters and importers, and between winners and losers, simply cannot be accepted. (OHCHR, 2011)

Lamy has argued that international trade and the right to food are perfectly compatible, emphasizing that free trade, competition, and less distorted markets lead to lower food prices and reliable market conditions. According to Lamy (WTO, 2012), "International trade plays an important role in global food security. By fostering greater competition, trade allows food to be produced where this can be most efficiently done."

In addition, Lamy has gone on the record several times to declare to the international community that the WTO is the solution to global food crises. However, these claims are politically self-serving. The urgency of the world food insecurity problem and addressing food price volatility caused by export restrictions should not be treated lightly. Lamy's call to arms should be seen as one of many attempts to use of the idea of crisis to justify the resumption of trade talks. This discursive strategy is a well-established practice at the GATT/WTO. In addition to the global food crises, Lamy has evoked the global financial crises, and the specter of renewed protectionism, referencing the Great Depression, to resume the Doha Round.

The most recent development in the debate over the right to food and international trade occurred in December 2011 following the publication of a new document by De Schutter, *The World Trade Organization and the Post-Global Food Crisis Agenda*. This document was a follow-up to earlier statements by De Schutter about the incoherence between WTO trade rules and the new consensus on global food security. This document reiterates De Schutter's earlier recommendations but augments proposals for specific changes to the AA, for the establishment of an international protocol to monitor future impacts of trade liberalization on world food prices, and presents an idea of a food security waiver for developing countries to deviate from WTO rules when pursuing food security ends (De Schutter, 2011). The WTO was strongly critical of these recommendations. Lamy made a highly public response to De Schutter, publishing a letter emphasizing his disagreement with many of the latter's recommendations that states lessen their dependence on international trade. The letter was accompanied by more than seven pages of detailed critiques prepared by the WTO Secretariat, which signaled a significant effort by the WTO to attempt to counter De Schutter's political support from several developing-country WTO members and global civil society.

How might we interpret the repeated interactions and political contests between the UN Special Rapporteur on the right to food and the WTO? Firstly, repeated interactions between De Schutter and the WTO in general and Lamy in particular have been of substantive depth. They are beyond superficial sound bites or cynical political performance. This suggests the right to food is firmly part of the wider ideational contests that occur within a transnational policy space characterized by significant power asymmetries across its participants. Secondly, the emergent transnational policy space for food security is spurring a greater engagement of the UN human rights system and the international regime with each other. This can stimulate conflict but also cooperation.

Clearly, the WTO remains wary of human rights actors, but its recent actions point to a greater acceptance of human rights as a legitimate source of criticism of the international trade regime. The WTO no longer willfully ignores human rights actors. It engages them. Thirdly, and somewhat more speculatively, the prominence of the human right to food points to a possible shift in the trajectory of the food security–international trade debate. If the human right to food is successfully operationalized at the national and international levels as the post-crises food policies are consolidated, it will signal that the global food security landscape has significantly changed. Such changes may empower, or at least embolden and legitimate, a human rights–based approach to international trade. Over the medium term this may strengthen the position of advocates to greater public action for food security. The success of these actors will weaken support for the status quo of the AA, which in its current form is poorly suited for the present food security challenges facing developing countries.

CONCLUSION: NEW GLOBAL POLICY SPACES FOR FOOD SECURITY

The 2008 and 2011 global food crises have led to the emergence of a new global policy space for food security. The WTO has emerged as a key institutional actor in this new space alongside states, other international organizations, new transnational actors such as the UN Special Rapporteur on the right to food, and elements of global civil society. WTO rules, and their effects on world food security, have come under scrutiny and political contestation within this space. Yet such contestation is not a simple reproduction of the North-South conflicts surrounding existing WTO rules on domestic food security witnessed during the Doha Round. Instead, the new policy space is coalescing around novel ideas and governance practices in response to major structural changes in the global food economy, changes that themselves question the most basic assumptions underlying the WTO's agricultural trade regime. In the post-global food crises landscape, the interactions between the UN human rights system and the WTO suggest the continued relevance of current international trade rules for agriculture is highly contested in ways unimaginable just a few years ago. The current global food-trading order is highly contested, both inside and outside the WTO. All this suggests that the future of the international trade regime for agriculture may no longer be decided by state-based multilateral negotiations alone but also through political contests taking place through the transnational policy space for food security.

REFERENCES

Aaronson, S. A. 2007. Seeping in Slowly: How Human Rights Concerns are Penetrating the WTO. *World Trade Review* 6(3): 413–449.

Cohen, M. J. and Clapp, J., eds. 2009. *The Global Food Crisis: Governance Challenges and Opportunities*. Waterloo: Centre for International Governance Innovation and Wilfrid Laurier University Press.

Coleman, W. D. 2005. Globality and Transnational Policy-Making in Agriculture: Complexity, Contradictions, and Conflict. In *Reconstituting Political Authority: Complex Sovereignty and the Foundations of Global Governance*, edited by E. Grande and L. W. Pauly. Toronto: University of Toronto Press, pp. 93–119.

Demeke, M., Pangrazio, G., and Materne, M. 2008. *Country Responses to the Food Security Crisis: Nature and Preliminary Implications of the Policies Pursued*. Rome: FAO.

De Schutter, O. 2008. *Mission to the World Trade Organization*. Geneva: OHCHR.

De Schutter, O. 2011. *The World Trade Organization and the Post-Global Food Crisis Agenda*. Brussels: University of Louvaine.

FAO. 2008. *Soaring Food Prices: Facts, Perspectives, Impacts and Actions Required*. Rome: FAO.

Headey, D. and Fan, S. 2009. Anatomy of a Crisis: The Causes and Consequences of Surging Food Prices. *Agricultural Economics* (Supplement), 39, pp. 375–391.

Howse, R. and Teitel, R. G. 2007. Beyond the Divide: The Covenant on Economic, Social and Cultural Rights and the World Trade Organization. In *Dialogue on Globalization*. Geneva: Friedrich-Ebert-Stiftung. Retrieved March 12, 2013 from: http://library.fes.de/pdf-files/iez/global/04572.pdf.

Karapinar, B. and Häberli, C. 2010. *Food Crises and the WTO*. Cambridge: Cambridge University Press.

Margulis, M. 2009. Multilateral responses to the global food crisis, *Perspectives in Agriculture, Veterinary Science, Nutrition and Natural Resources* 4(12): 1–10.

McMichael, P. 2009. The World Food Crisis in Historical Perspective, *Monthly Review* (July). Retrieved September 8, 2013 from: http://monthlyreview.org/2009/07/01/the-world-food-crisis-in-historical-perspective.

Murphy, S. 2010. *Trade and Food Reserves: What Roles Does the WTO Play?* Minnesota: Institute for Agriculture and Trade Policy.

Office for the High Commissioner for Human Rights (OHCHR). 2011. Food Security Hostage to Trade in WTO Negotiations – UN Right to Food Expert. November 16. Available at: http://www.ohchr.org/en/NewsEvents/Pages/DisplayNews.aspx?NewsID=11608&LangID=E.

Ruel, M. T., Garrett, J. L., Hawkes, C., and Cohen, M. J. 2010. The Food, Fuel, and Financial Crises Affect the Urban and Rural Poor Disproportionately: A Review of the Evidence. *The Journal of Nutrition* 140(1): 170–176.

Sharma, R. and Konandreas, K. 2008. *WTO Provisions in the Context of Responding to Soaring Food Prices*, Commodity and Trade Policy Research Working Paper Series, 25. Rome: FAO.

Trostle, R. 2008. *Global Agricultural Supply and Demand: Factors Contributing to the Recent Increase in Food Commodity Prices*. Washington, DC: U.S. Department of Agriculture.

UN High Level Task Force on the Global Food Security Crisis. 2008. *Comprehensive Framework for Action*. New York: United Nations.

UN High Level Task Force on the Global Food Security Crisis 2009. *Updated Comprehensive Framework for Action*. New York: United Nations.

Wolfe, R. 2010. Sprinting During a Marathon: Why the WTO Ministerial Failed in July 2008. *Journal of World Trade* 44(1): 81–126.

World Food Program (WFP). 2009. Annual Report. New York: United Nations.

World Trade Organization. 2008. *Revised Draft Modalities for Agriculture*. Geneva: WTO.

World Trade Organization. 2011. *Eight Ministerial Conference: Chairman's Concluding Statement*. Geneva: WTO.

World Trade Organization. 2012. Pascal Lamy Speaks on the Challenge of Feeding 9 Billion People. February 12. Available at: http://www.wto.org/english/news_e/sppl_e/sppl216_e.htm.

PART V

Innovations in International Human Rights

12

"The space between us"*: Migrant Domestic Work as a Nexus between International Labor Standards and Trade Policy

Adelle Blackett

INTRODUCTION

In June 2011, the International Labor Organization (ILO) celebrated the adoption of the historic Decent Work for Domestic Workers Convention (No. 189) and Recommendation (No. 201) at the 100th Session of its annual International Labour Conference (ILC). I argue in this essay that the new ILO standard setting builds on and transcends the limits of framing labor rights as human rights, by infusing the elusive notion of "decent work"[1] with a strong normative core. In the new labor standards, decent work extends beyond a narrow but crucially prioritized set of fundamental principles and rights at work, to include a comprehensive normalization of working conditions and substantive social protections. In other words, decent work for domestic workers encompasses the core features of workplace citizenship.

This new ILO standard setting is most striking because it applies to a category deeply associated with histories of servitude and colonial subjugation. Domestic workers in the contemporary economy are also increasingly paradigmatic of the worst inequities of global South-North relations, epitomized in treacherous movements of persons across borders. Ironically, migrant domestic workers' trajectory provides market-enabling, "subsidized" but structurally undervalued "care." It is precisely the significant labor migration dimensions of domestic work in the new economy, and therefore in the new standard, that create space to consider labor and trade linkage. Few contest that the state laws and policies constraining the movement of migrant domestic workers

---

* "Bhima doesn't hear them. She is taking her orders from a different authority now, following the fluttering sound in her ears, the sound of her flapping wings, the sound of learning how to fly. Freedom." Thrity Umrigar, *The Space Between Us* (New York: Harper, 2007). Through fiction, Umrigar offers a poignant, incisive inquiry into the "relationship" between a domestic worker, the family for whom she works, and her own family.

259

across borders structure vulnerability and perpetuate some of the worst human rights abuses. Yet the market-enabling character of the "tertiary" and largely transnational paid care services is increasingly acknowledged. The new standard setting calls attention to this relationship.

This essay concludes with a preliminary sketch of the relationship between the notions of decent work, and the direction of reasonable labor market access. Rhetorically referred to as a "reverse social clause," it proposes to focus on the normative case for juxtaposing reasonable labor market access with decent work, to arrive at a renewed attention to "citizenship at work" within the home-workplace that is beyond national borders. It situates migrant domestic "service" work as the policy space between international labor standard setting and trade policy.

THE INTERNATIONAL LANDSCAPE

There are roughly 53 million domestic workers worldwide.[2] Women constitute almost half of all global migrants, and a significant majority of those women have become domestic workers.[3] The phenomenon is staggering, yet the transnational regulatory challenges have been underanalyzed. Domestic workers cross the jealously guarded borders of nation-states, to labor in "private" homes, to which state regulation has either explicitly not applied or implicitly not been implied. The regulatory gulf is mirrored in the disturbingly common stories of exploitation and abuse faced by domestic workers, particularly when they cross national borders.

The ILO's new standards address many of these challenges. The new international instruments map the occupational reality of domestic work in individual households. They emphasize the specificity of domestic work, with a view to identifying and rooting out historic patterns of discrimination that confine domestic workers to low-status, undervalued "dirty" work rather than socially valued, market- and society-sustaining care. They emphasize that domestic workers be treated as workers and human beings, whose human rights and personal autonomy need recognition and respect.

There is room for cautious optimism that the standards reflect a renewal in tripartite standard setting for the ILO. But it would be perilous to consider the subject of this standard setting as coincidental. Rather, I contend that the success of the standard setting reflects the ability to create convergence around the existence of a decent work deficit in the failure to meaningfully recognize and effectively protect the human rights of domestic workers.

The first pillar was to establish that this standard setting was a long time coming. Since 1948, the ILC had adopted a resolution on the conditions of employment of domestic workers, and in 1965 recalled the "urgent need" for standards on domestic work that would be "compatible with the self-respect and human dignity which are essential to social justice for domestic workers."[4] While the ILO had convened repeatedly to set robust standards on mostly male maritime workers, representing 1 million workers worldwide, the staggering numbers of mostly female and largely migrant workers were excluded from the decent work core.[5]

The new standards were adopted in a climate where there has been a pressing critique of the ILO's ability to sustain any significant standard setting, a virtual halt in new standard setting particularly on subject matter deemed sector specific,[6] and real resistance by some constituents to expanding the international corpus. The second pillar involved refocusing normative efforts on identifying and promoting "fundamental principles and rights at work" and a somewhat elusive, nonjuridical notion of "decent work," reflecting the broader shift away from labor standards toward "labor rights as human rights." The shifts to human rights language, immortalized by Virginia Leary as parallel tracks that rarely meet[7] and the normative restructuring through the lens of decent work, reflects for Vosko a "skilful effort at mediating escalating tensions inside the ILO between global capital, backed by a majority of industrialized states, and an increasingly vocal group of member states, trade unions, women's organizations and other NGOs concerned with improving the lives of marginalized workers."[8] Initiatives like this were considered by some to be deeply misguided.[9]

Skillful navigation could be witnessed in the interactions between advocates, architects, and negotiators of the new international labor norms. The instruments were cloaked in the "decent work" mandate from their first presentation to the Governing Body in its 301st Session in March 2008 as a potential (indeed the only potential) item for standard setting at the 99th ILC in June 2010. It was as if the very framing of the debate as to whether the ILO should take up standard setting on this category of workers at all asked, if the ILO's normative shift to decent work really does embrace all workers, then why had the ILO taken sixty-five years to act on this issue? The government of South Africa, supporting its inclusion, argued that it was "normal that the ILO, the custodian of labour standards, should be concerned with remedying the decent work deficit affecting that group and extending to domestic workers the whole range of protections that would enable them to exercise their rights in the workplace."[10] This decent-work framing pervaded the discussions at both the 99th and 100th session of the ILC.[11]

The language of human rights also surrounded the discussions at the ILC. For example, the government of Brazil reminded the conference committee on domestic workers that it "had a unique chance to negotiate a human rights treaty that would affect millions of workers. Domestic workers around the world were looking to the ILC to adopt a Convention that would help to overcome past injustices and give domestic workers a better future."[12] The government of Bangladesh urged that domestic workers' human rights should not simply be protected, but promoted, in the new instrument.[13] On the thorny issue of repatriation, the workers' vice chairperson urged that "[f]or migrant domestic workers, clarity in repatriation conditions was important from a human rights perspective."[14] And the government member of Peru, on behalf of the group of Latin American countries, "expressed satisfaction with the adopted instruments, which he was sure met the aspirations of millions of domestic workers around the world" and pledged that "Peru would work towards the implementation of both standards, based on the protection and promotion of human rights."[15] But perhaps most tellingly, the employer representatives – whose approach in the first year of negotiations at the ILC was decidedly oppositional during the 99th Session of the ILC in 2010, adopted an approach that showed a real recognition of the historic, human rights significance of the proposed instruments.[16]

The shift in the international labor standards to a language of human rights encapsulated in the decent work mandate did not translate, however, into a watered-down, hortatory framing devoid of strong substantive content. In fact, international labor standards are largely recognized to constitute "minimum standards" in that member states may – indeed are encouraged – to go beyond them.[17] Yet there is a distinct – albeit not unique – character to the ratifiable, treaty-based Convention No. 189[18] and its accompanying non-ratifiable, non-binding but guidance-based supplementary Recommendation No. 201. The standards aim to be comprehensive. They serve the role of bringing a historically marginalized category of workers who labor in the "informal" economy resolutely into a paradigm of workplace citizenship. Critically, the standards normalize domestic workers' time – time that has tended to be treated as boundariless by virtue of working and often living in the household, surrounded by never-ending care "need." The standards go further, to insist on equal treatment.

THE EQUALITY FRAME OF THE NEW INTERNATIONAL STANDARDS[19]

The equality lens in the new instruments is substantive and inclusive rather than abstract and undifferentiated. The latter lens is reflected in comparative practice through labor codes of general application that may "delete" formal exclusions of the "domestic workers" category found by the express mention of domestic workers as excluded categories in the definition of "employees" or otherwise excluded from the scope of application of all or part of the law. These textual "inclusions" have tended to mean that domestic workers are legally covered but extralegally excluded.[20] The standard embodies "specific regulation."

To secure domestic workers' human rights and to remedy historical exclusions of domestic work from much of labor law, the standards adapt a broad gamut of labor rights and social protections specifically to domestic work. In particular, international labor standards on decent work for domestic workers apply a specific regulatory model to ensure that features of the domestic work relationship that are different from many other workplace contexts are acknowledged and regulated in an equality-enhancing manner, rather than overlooked. It is important to add that they build on positive examples from national practice in a number of regions – including many developing countries – to establish a framework to regulate the domestic workers' conditions of employment, including when they migrate internationally. They complement the core human rights protections in the Convention on the Elimination of All Forms of Discrimination against Women, 1979 (entry into force 1981) and the 2008 CEDAW General Recommendation No. 26 on Women Migrant Workers, as well as Convention on Migrant Workers and the 2010 CMW General Comment No. 1 on Migrant Domestic Workers (2010).

A good example relates to living conditions, which must respect domestic workers' privacy (Art. 6). This formulation in an international instrument on work in the employer or client's household does not assume the traditional focus on the "sanctity of the home" and does not assume that neutrality means the status quo; rather it recognizes that domestic workers forced to live in the household need particular privacy protections to ensure that their living conditions are decent. This recalls the conceptualization proposed by Patricia Williams, in which the reliance on a rights based framework not

> discard rights but [see] through them or past them so that they reflect a larger definition of privacy and property: so that privacy is turned from exclusion based on self-regard into regard for another's fragile, mysterious autonomy.[21]

Convention No. 189 specifies that domestic workers who reside in the household where they work are not obliged to remain there, or remain with household members, during periods of daily and weekly rest or annual leave (Convention No. 189, Articles 9(b), 10). With a nod to prevalent practices that lend themselves to abuse in the sense that they overlook domestic workers' own autonomy, Article 13 of Recommendation No. 201 provides that "[t]ime spent by domestic workers accompanying the household members on holiday should not be counted as part of their paid annual leave." The expectation of a live-in relationship is interwoven, however, into most migrant domestic work schemes and reflects the unarticulated but at least implicit "customary" expectation of perpetual availability. It is not coincidental that data from

suggest that most domestic workers who are able to do so "self-
̣y trying hard to avoid living with their employer's household, as
a means to set boundaries around their working time and to preserve some
autonomy.[22]

Despite the complexity of multiple jurisdictions, the "customary" or pluralist law of the home-workplace[23] is troublingly consistent across space and
time. Expectations in domestic work feed into assumptions that migrant live-in
domestic workers will fill the spaces that female members of the family are
expected to occupy, and to do so endlessly. From a labor regulatory perspective, this is understood in translation, not as a labor of love, but as exploitative
working hours. One of the singular accomplishments in the new ILO standards, therefore, is to challenge the "boundarilessness" of domestic workers'
time that is associated with the customary expectation of domestic workers'
constant availability. In most states the pluralist law of the home-workplace is
at odds with formal state law, which, given its general scope, applies as a matter
of principle to domestic workers. State law is ignored, however, in part because
the shift from thinking of domestic work as other than servitude, and other
than family relations, has not been undertaken. Indeed, some contend that, as
work in the service sector, it should normatively be regulated differently than
other forms of work.[24]

Convention No. 189 calls for working time to be regulated in keeping with
the principle of equal treatment. This includes establishing normal working
hours and daily and weekly rest periods, while ensuring that wages are paid
at regular intervals and by legally recognized means. It strictly limits the
payment of wages in kind, which can be an important source of abuse (Art. 12).
Domestic workers are to be covered by minimum wage laws where they exist,
and that coverage should be without discrimination (Convention No. 189,
Article 11, Convention on the Elimination of All forms of Discrimination
Against Women, Article 11, paragraph d).

Regulations on working time – particularly as applied to live-in domestic
workers – therefore constitute one of the areas in which international standards
and even many contemporary national state laws diverge the most from the
"customary" or pluralist law of the home-workplace. They signal the transition
to a labor law framework in which hours are counted and remunerated and in
which domestic workers' own autonomy – including their own family life – is
to be respected.

Social protection needs are cardinal for domestic workers and their fam-
ilies across global care chains. A particularly noteworthy development in
Convention No. 189 is that all of the provisions of the Convention on
Migrant Workers apply to migrant domestic workers. Coupled with CEDAW's

General Recommendation No. 26 on women migrant workers and the C̶ mittee on Migrant Workers' General Comment No. 1 on migrant domc̶u̶c̶ workers, there emerges from the panoply of general and relevant labor standards a robust set of legal protections throughout the migration cycle. Regional initiatives, most recently the Council of Europe's recent Resolution 1811 of 2011, confirm a policy direction that favors regularization, transparency, and comprehensiveness in an approach to labor migration and development that emphasizes migrant workers' human rights.

The instrument takes pains to address some of the most vexing problems that face migrant domestic workers in particular, notably placement agencies operating transnationally.[25] Article 15 of Convention No. 189 requires states to "effectively protect domestic workers, including migrant domestic workers, recruited or placed by private employment agencies, against abusive practices."[26] Articles 7 & 8 of Convention No. 189 provide that domestic workers who are recruited in one country for domestic work in another must receive a written job offer, or contract of employment enforceable in the country in which the work is to be performed. The contract must contain a detailed list of terms and conditions of employment.[27] The possibility of establishing a model contract is also recommended.

Destination countries, like sending countries, are therefore called upon to treat domestic work like any other form of work, which is in keeping with Article 25 of the Convention on Migrant Workers. Human rights language – labor rights as human rights, and the "decent work for all" mandate – is invoked to argue that specific regulatory attention at the international level is necessary to ensure that domestic work is included into a workplace norm.

TRANSNATIONAL REGULATION OF THE MOVEMENT OF MIGRANT DOMESTIC WORKERS: THE LIMITS OF BILATERAL INITIATIVES

State regulatory approaches to the movement of migrant domestic workers have necessarily entailed a transnational component. Yet the transnational regulation has rarely been protective; rather, it has entailed managing migration, often through restrictive policies.[28] The comparative experiences to date leading to the adoption of the international standard illustrate the extent to which the often bilateral initiatives between sending and receiving countries have been inadequate. They require a fuller appreciation for the interaction across different governance levels.

Primarily there has been a significant effort to channel the movement of persons through bilateral agreements and memoranda of understanding

(MOU). Many member states treat those instruments as nonbinding, not attracting the same kind of scrutiny as international treaties. They nonetheless set out basic employment conditions in conformity with labor laws in the destination country.

One important example has been the agreement between the Philippines and Qatar, which also regulates the employment contract providing that any changes introduced subsequently by the employer are null unless they improve the workers' conditions of employment. The Agreement on Migration between Argentina and Peru expressly includes a nondiscrimination clause, providing for equal treatment between nationals of the host country and "immigrants" from the sending country.[29] Some other bilateral schemes outside of domestic work show signs of innovation, including alternative compensation arrangements and forms of social financing from destination to sending countries.[30] These types of agreements remain the exception, however. The predominant tendency has been to focus primarily on the management of migration, without addressing workers' rights. Agreements in this tradition may reflect rather than redress the power imbalances between some sending and receiving countries. International standards like Convention No. 189 and Recommendation No. 201 may in the future shift the onus of establishing comprehensive labor standards away from the realm of negotiation via bilateral agreements sought by sending countries, and onto destination countries.

Some countries combine an active strategy of negotiating bilateral agreements with a range of other regulatory options. A key example is the Philippines. The Philippines remains one of the most significant, coordinated migrant-sending countries, whose workers have tended to assume a "superior" market positioning vis-à-vis nationals of other regions in large measure because of the governmental engagement in setting the terms of their movement. The Philippines has been proactive through its Philippines Overseas Employment Administration (POEA), which sets out a comprehensive legislative framework that applies nationally and that stipulates the conditions under which a bilateral agreement may be concluded. Its legislative mandate includes industry regulation, notably licensing agencies and hearing complaints about them; employment facilitation, including entering into MOU, workers' protection, including pre-deployment information and seminars; and legal assistance and repatriation assistance, alongside general administration and support including research. Of particular interest in the industry regulation component is its insistence on establishing minimum labor standards. The main legislative vehicle for that has been the Migrant Workers and Overseas Filipinos Act of 1995, as amended. In Article 3 of the Act, the Philippines government requires that the receiving country must have existing labor and social laws protecting the rights of workers, including migrant workers; be signatory to and have ratified multilateral conventions, declarations, or resolutions relating to the protection of workers, including migrant workers; have concluded a bilateral agreement or arrangement with the government on the protection of the rights of overseas Filipino workers; and be taking "positive, concrete measures to protect the rights of migrant workers."[31]

The POEA and the government more generally have been criticized at key moments for both the underutilization of regulatory powers and the heavy-handed utilization of those powers. Most notable are the past bans on issuing visas for Philippine domestic worker migration to countries with stark records of abuse. Recently, and less than a month after the historic international labor standards were adopted, a targeted Philippines' initiative mandating application of a standard employment contract with a prescribed minimum wage met with determined regulatory backlash.[32] In anticipation of a deployment ban, and in response to a moratorium already in place in Indonesia, Saudi Arabia banned migrant domestic workers from these two Asian countries. The desired result was improved labor conditions in Saudi Arabia to facilitate the return of domestic workers from the Philippines and Indonesia. Largely, the ban led to a diversification of recruitment, facilitated by swift action on the part of private, largely unregulated transnational placement agencies. The result has been a sharp shift in the source of labor supply, notably to Kenya and Ethiopia.[33] Domestic workers from these countries and from other African countries have been shown in a number of studies to face labor market segmentation not only in the occupational sectors to which they have access, but also within those sectors. In domestic work, African migrant domestic workers reportedly are relegated to the most physically demanding and "dirty" forms of domestic work, and to the work with the lowest status and pay.[34] The troubling prospect is that a "hierarchy of abuse" in which domestic workers from particular regions – notably the African continent – are at the bottom may be accentuated in the globalization of migrant domestic work. The challenge to avoid a regulatory race to the bottom – so much a part of the fear and folklore surrounding claims for a "social clause" linking trade and labor standards in the literature of the early 1990s – resurfaces in what might be considered a "reverse" social clause claim. But if it is the reverse, it is largely rhetorical, as the sources of regulatory concern are more likely to be in the global North, than in the global South, or more precisely in the movement between regions from less "developed" to relatively more "developed" spaces.

It is important to acknowledge that certain states, like the Philippines, have been relatively successful at negotiating bilateral agreements with labor destination countries that have comparatively favorable migration terms – notably

268 Adelle Blackett

the possibility to obtain permanent resident status – and labor laws. This has been the case with Canada. The Philippines seeks to direct greater numbers of their migrant domestic workers toward those more favorable countries, in keeping with existing demand. Yet migrants' experiences are not linear either, and the movement from countries perceived to be less desirable to those perceived to be more desirable is increasingly documented.[35] Moreover, the geopolitical reasons surrounding decisions by migrants to move are complex, and not directly linked to poverty.[36] Supply continues to surpass demand. So in the constantly evolving example of Saudi Arabia, the Kingdom ultimately lifted its moratorium in October 2012 after conceding to apply the standard employment contract stipulations, although enforcement remains questionable and concerns remain that Filipino employment in the region will be reduced.[37] While reports in February 2013 suggest that the Philippine government will soon approve the recruitment of 2000 domestic workers to Saudi Arabia,[38] a new ban has been imposed this time by Sri Lanka, following the execution of domestic worker Rizana Nafeek. Saudi Arabia is expected to contract more than 45,000 Ethiopians to meet domestic worker demand.

TOWARD A DECENT WORK COMPLEMENT TO REASONABLE LABOR MARKET ACCESS? A PRELIMINARY SKETCH[39]

Experience with bilateral agreements regulating domestic work suggests that, despite some promise, they are woefully inadequate for regulating the conditions of work of marginalized workers. Workers entering under one agreement are too readily replaceable by workers made available under other bilateral agreements (or informal recruitment changes by agencies) from other states. Migration experts increasingly call for a mix of solutions, in which the multilateral features more prominently as a way to counteract the fluidity of networks organizing irregular migration.[40]

Increasingly, international and regional resolutions, declarations, comments, general observations, and now conventions and recommendations point in the direction of regularizing migration, and illustrate concern about distributive implications across borders. The movement of persons to provide care services as a domestic worker becomes an important part of the development strategy of sending countries, based on a logic of remittances. Migration in the care economy simultaneously relieves pressure on individual couples in society to rethink gender relations, on communities to reconsider patterns of continuous consumption, and on societies to reimagine the role of the state in providing care.[41] "Care work extraction" from developing countries creates care deficits.[42] Concretely, domestic workers' own international human rights to protection of their family by society and the state as recognized in Article 16(3) of the Universal Declaration of Human Rights and Article 44 of the Convention on Migrant Workers tend to be overlooked. Migration in the care economy entails looking at migrant domestic workers not only as workers, and not only as migrants, but also as human beings with care responsibilities and needs of their own.

Trade and development scholars such as Yong-Shik Lee make a case for a form of reasonable labor market access, under the General Agreement on Trade in Services (GATS) disciplines.[43] This essay does not seek to suggest that at a political level, the landscape has changed such that negotiation over a multilaterally negotiated liberalization of the movement of persons would permit such a development. Rather, the suggestion is that the policy landscape at the international level – and growing frustration with regulatory initiatives at the national and bilateral levels – may signal growing policy awareness of the need for alternative regulatory approaches. Important work on regularizing irregular migration – and policy makers' surprise over the extent of demand for regularization in countries such as Italy and Spain[44] – suggest that although the demand for migrant domestic workers is being met, the terms under which the labor is provided are profoundly unreasonable. The terms construct migrants' marginality through a failure to ensure respect for their fundamental human rights.

Part of reconstructing a notion of "reasonable" labor market access might be to weave a fulsome notion of a decent work complement into it. In other words, the reasonableness of the labor market access is based on the extent to which the fundamental human rights embodied in the comprehensive and specific regulatory device of Convention No. 189 and its accompanying recommendation are available to migrant domestic workers, wherever they work.[45]

A linkage proposal associated with this idea is decidedly rudimentary and preliminary. It is meant to galvanize thinking about a potential framework that is at least complementary – if not ultimately pareto superior – to the individually agreed-on temporary migration schemes prevalent in bilateral agreements, MOU, and regional trade agreements. The framework would in particular seek to displace the prevalence of treacherous clandestine movements that characterize asymmetrical, exclusionary mobility, wholly disconnected from an integrated labor rights framework and removed from any notion of citizenship at work. It would seek to challenge the labor market dislocations of "global care extraction" associated with this labor mobility,[46] by offering a degree of transnational labor regulatory coherence. In this regard, it would imagine a form of "social clause" that under carefully circumscribed conditions would aim to promote decent conditions for migrant workers. The counterbalance for reasonable labor market access – a reverse social clause – would require states, employers, and other business actors that avail themselves of migrant workers, particularly migrant domestic workers, to ensure that working conditions encourage states to protect and employers and business actors to respect[47] migrant domestic workers' human rights.

A fundamental principle of decency at work has been argued to underpin domestic labor standards legislation, and may be considered a counterhegemonic challenge to principles like market efficiency.[48] A decent work complement would build on the interplay between normative international starting points, national implementation through labor and human rights standards, the harnessing of domestic enforcement of remedies, and levels of international monitoring. A decent work complement in the form of a reverse social clause could be as simple as a requirement ensuring the "effective enforcement" of existing local labor law applicable to citizens and permanent residents who work in the domestic economy vis-à-vis migrant workers, with monitoring mechanisms (preferably engaging the ILO or decentralized in regional governance mechanisms) and reports that could be granted a degree of probative value in World Trade Organization (WTO) dispute settlement mechanisms. But it would not exclude direct challenge to the precariousness created by temporary labor migration schemes that tie workers to particular employers, and that provide solutions that reduce that precariousness, such as eliminating bonding to particular employers.[49] For example, the September 30, 2011 decision of the Hong Kong High Court, Court of First Instance, in *Banao* v. *Commissioner of Registration* essentially extended the equivalent of permanent resident status to a foreign domestic "helper" (FDH) of Philippine nationality. The applicant – the married mother of five children and property owner in the Philippines – worked in Hong Kong as a FDH since 1986, initially on a visa of less than a year. When she appeared before the court twenty-two years and a number of different visas later, it was forced to take notice of the fact that she "stayed and resided in her employers' respective residences," caring for Hong Kong families, despite returning to the Philippines upon the expiry of each FDH contract as was required by law. In a carefully reasoned decision that sets out the differential treatment she experienced and that draws on the International Covenant on Civil and Political Rights, the

Court adopted a purposive interpretation of Article 24(2)(4) of the Basic Law, concluding that immigration status is not conclusive of the parties' status as "ordinary residents."[50] Overturned on appeal, the landmark case was argued before the Hong Kong Court of Final Appeal on February 26, 2013.[51]

The decent work complement to reasonable labor market access would build on three insights. First, it refuses to retain as its implicit premise that developing countries face a decent work deficit unlike post-industrialized market economies. Rather, in its attention to global labor migration in a case such as the provision of domestic care, the notion of a decent work complement to reasonable labor market access acknowledges the structural causes of inequitable global labor market participation. It acknowledges, with Barry and Reddy, that "[a] system that imposes burdens on poor countries but does not require rich countries to share these burdens"[52] is deeply flawed.

Second, the approach builds on Barry and Reddy's affirmation that a constructive linkage "should be unimposed, transparent, and rule-based; involve adequate burden sharing; incorporate measures that ensure that appropriate account is taken of viewpoints within states; and be applied in a context-sensitive manner." Rather, it would build on the requirement in Article 16 that

> [e]ach Member shall take measures to ensure, in accordance with national laws, regulations and practice, that all domestic workers, either by themselves or through a representative, have effective access to courts, tribunals or other dispute resolution mechanisms under conditions that are not less favourable than those available to workers generally.

Clause 26 of Recommendation No. 201 not only encourages cooperation at bilateral, regional and global levels, but also provides that "[m]embers should take appropriate steps to assist one another in giving effect to the provisions of the Convention through enhanced international cooperation or assistance, or both, including support for social and economic development, poverty eradication programmes and universal education."[53]

Third, the decent work complement would seek to reconcile trade theory with state-centered assumptions about the appropriate locus for distributive justice. It insists on and problematizes the importance of the place of (re)production to the project of trade across borders. Focusing on migrant domestic work means considering the movement of persons to provide services in the tertiary economy within trade theory in as serious a manner from a nondiscrimination perspective as one would be forced to consider the conditions under which products enter national territory. If liberal trade is state-centered and interested in the conditions of trade not only at borders but within them, then an inquiry into labor market conditions when reasonable labor market access is advocated as a logical corollary of liberal economic policy making becomes essential.

The decent work complement would seek to operationalize multilaterally (if not [inter]regionally) what (most) labor-sending countries are inopportunely placed to accomplish bilaterally in (most) destination countries in the migration of domestic work. The focus in this work is not on the rigidity of a "clause" but rather on measures that seek regulatory complementarity, that recognize and promote reflective, counterhegemonic international deliberative spaces for interpretation,[54] and that promote policy coherence across governance levels for the social. In the process, it would not only operate multilaterally but more importantly would consider the interaction between governance levels.

The focus of further research on this topic is to identify how the decent work complement would harness reporting on the human rights conditions of migrant workers to monitoring and compliance institutions of international organizations including an ILO Committee of Experts and possibly special mandate holders of the United Nations Human Rights Council. While a decent work complement could ultimately engage with the ways of informing contextualized interpretation under the WTO dispute settlement body, the proposed linkage would harness a broad range of international informational, deliberative, and incentives-based opportunities – including the WTO's own Trade Policy Review Mechanisms – to consider how institutional linkages between international institutions can be engaged cooperatively to improve the South-North terms under which migrant domestic workers travel and work.

CONCLUSION

This essay has traced the broad contours of historic international labor standard setting on decent work for domestic workers. The framing of the standard setting as a human rights initiative to palliate the decent work deficit has led, perhaps paradoxically, to a robust labor rights norm, emblematic of what is required to bring domestic workers into a "citizenship at work" framework. The promise of the international standards – to extend decent work to all workers, as workers, irrespective of their territorial location – opens a significant new landscape for the governance of the movement of persons. This chapter has offered preliminary reflections on the contours of a decent work complement to reasonable labor market access. The direction would be to move the management of the transnationalization of global care work out from under the structured vulnerability created by the terms and collective action limits of bilateral agreements, toward multilevel governance responses anchored to the international. Of course, nothing about the current economic landscape suggests that there is political space to address global labor migration in care or in other sectors – nothing other than the sobering acknowledgment not only of infinitely permeable borders but also of the interdependence of receiving and sending economies on migrants' work. Migrant domestic care workers are no different. Decent work for domestic workers could begin a process of reimagining global landscapes, and the terms on which they are navigated.

13

Is There Policy Space for Human Rights Linkages in China's Trade and Investment Network?

Ljiljana Biuković*

INTRODUCTION: PREFERENTIAL TRADE DEALS ON THE NEXT FRONTIER

The July 2011 *World Trade Report* published by the World Trade Organization (WTO) reveals two important trends in the development of the landscape of international trade negotiations: the first is the continuing increase in the number of signed preferential trade agreements (PTAs); the second is that these PTAs are becoming broader in scope and deeper in regulatory detail (WTO Annual Report, 2011).

The Report finds that there are about 300 currently active PTAs and establishes that most of these agreements have moved away from simply avoiding relatively high most favored nations (MFN) tariffs established by the WTO toward the imposition of more stringent provisions (so-called WTO-Plus PTAs) and toward regulating areas beyond the scope of the existing WTO agreements. These new WTO provisions represent a new frontier for policy spaces; some of these are seen as positive steps whereas others are seen as invasive. For example, provisions related to government procurement, the protection of investment, the environment, and human rights standards are now often contained in PTAs signed by the European Union and the United States. The impact of international trade on human rights and vice versa has been the subject of scholarly debates since the establishment of the WTO (ECONOS, 2000 par. 15).

Scholars argue over the necessity to integrate the two subsystems of international law, and if such is indeed needed, how to conceptualize the integration. Developing countries often oppose initiatives that include references to human

* Stephen Rukavina (JD student) and Naayeli Ramirez (PhD candidate) provided research assistance for this work. The research is funded by a grant from Social Science and Humanities Research Canada ("Coordinated Compliance for International Trade and Human Rights," principal investigator Professor Pitman Potter, Faculty of Law, UBC).

TABLE 13.1. *Social policy vs. other policy areas in the WTO*

WTO Plus policy spaces		WTO enhanced policy spaces	
Social Policy	Other Policy Areas	Social Policy	Other Policy Areas
	PTA industrial goods	Environmental laws	Anti-corruption/money laundering-
	PTA agricultural goods	Labor market regulation	Competition policy
	Customs administration	Consumer protection;	Intellectual property
	Export taxes		Foreign investment policy
	SPS measures	Cultural cooperation	Movement of capital
	State trading enterprises	Education and training	Data protection/ information technology
	TBT	Health	Agriculture
	Countervailing measures	Human rights	Innovation policies /research and technology
	Anti-dumping	Immigration policy	Economic policy
	State aid	Illicit drugs	Public administration Dialogue
	Public procurement		Energy
	TRIMS measures		Antiterrorism
	GATS		
	TRIPS		Financial assistance Industrial cooperation Information technology Mining Nuclear safety Political dialogue Regional cooperation Taxation

Source: Adapted from *2011 WTO Report*, table 3.2; Horn et al., 2010.

rights in the text of WTO laws because they consider such references to be growth aversive and limiting to their national sovereignty, especially with respect to social policy.[1]

Table 13.1 identifies further attempts to impose limitations on national sovereignty, especially with respect to social policy.

According to the aforementioned *2011 WTO Report*, free trade agreements (FTAs) are still the most prevalent PTAs concluded among WTO members; they provide a means whereby governments both of developed and developing

TABLE 13.2. *Number of goods and services PTAs in force in 2010*

Parties	Goods	Goods and services	Services
Developed-Developed	13	9	1
Developed-Developing	36	40	0
Developing-Developing	145	41	1
Bilateral	104	64	0
Plurilateral	38	11	2
Plurilateral: at least 1 party is in PTA	52	15	0
Intraregional	110	33	2
Cross-regional	84	57	0

Source: 2011 WTO Report, table B.5.

countries implement WTO trade policy at the bilateral and the regional levels.[2] Moreover, regional and bilateral FTAs have increasingly become a vehicle for cooperation among developing countries (Baccini, 2011, p. 3).

Table 13.2 demonstrates the diversity of agreements that currently exist and their increased importance in developing countries.

Although economic integration through PTAs and FTAs initially gained precedence because they were favored by the EU and the United States, the principal actors in world trade, the current landscape of trade and investment agreements has been changing as a result of the increased economic power of emerging countries such as China, India, and Brazil. These emerging economies have started concluding trade and investment arrangements with other developing countries in order to ensure market access for their goods and services and to establish systems of protection for their growing overseas investments. This chapter focuses on the impact of the gravitational pull of China's priorities on its trade partners in Asia, Africa, and Latin America and the practical impact these trade agreements have had on innovative and diverse policy space among developing countries who find the need to remain competitive regionally and internationally. It also addresses different growth strategies relevant to living and working conditions.

THE SOUTH-SOUTH PATH TO DEVELOPMENT: THE HUMAN RIGHTS DILEMMA

Since the mid-1960s, developing countries have emphasized the need to "maintain, foster and strengthen their unity"[3] in order to increase their impact on the international trade regime and its organizations and thereby ensure their own enhanced development. Concern over the fact that the developing countries have not been able to "share [the] benefits of globalization on an equal footing with the developed countries" (UN General Assembly,

2000, par. 11) increased over the 1970s–1990s, and, under the auspice of the United Nations (UN) at the first South Summit (Havana, Cuba, 2000), a group of seventy-seven developing countries (G77) and China mobilized politically to promote South-South cooperation and the regional integration of the developing countries (*Ibid.*, paras. 40–42). The G77 emphasized that it would not allow the developing countries' right to economic development to be made conditional on their commitment to the protection of fundamental human rights and freedoms, labor standards, environmental protection, and so forth (*Ibid.* para 21).

The underlying argument for increasingly incorporating human rights norms into international trade law is that it will have a beneficial effect on the welfare of all of the WTO member states, particularly on all individuals living in these member states. Implied is the argument that the establishment of an institutional framework based on the rule of law (and thus limiting the role of the state in the regulation of markets and of private actors within them) is the foundation for achieving socioeconomic wealth in an open, liberalized market environment. Even though it is difficult to deny the attractiveness of normative propositions that emphasize the importance of human rights law over trade laws and that argue that human dignity is the underpinning norm of international law, it is necessary to understand that countries differ in their perception of what their human rights policies and priorities should be and that they might, accordingly, prefer different international treaty obligations with respect to the protection and promotion of those rights. Because of these reservations there is a sharp difference of opinion outside the developed world on how much trade agreements should emphasize social policies in FTAs (thus effectively reducing sovereign policy spaces).

In the two meetings subsequent to the first South Summit (2003 and 2005), the G77 and China reemphasized the need for enhanced coordination of developing countries' economic policies, endorsed trade and investment agreements (including bilateral treaties) among the participating states, and encouraged the members to establish a new institutional framework for sectoral cooperation (Marrakech Declaration on South-South Cooperation, 2003, par 8; Doha Declaration, 2005, pars 23, 47, 73). Although these accords acknowledged the importance of improving the conditions under which citizens in the participating countries lived – including the need to protect the environment and to promote health and cultural diversity – they did not directly address the parties' commitment to the protection of fundamental human rights. The agreements stressed rather the parties' respect for each country's "sovereign right to determine its own development priorities and strategies" (Doha Declaration, 2005, par 15(i)) and rejected any form of conditionality in their international treaties' provisions in their own development assistance; by doing so, the agreements allow for but *do not require* innovative and diverse policy development in human rights protection.

Although regional economic cooperation and integration among developing countries started in the 1960s,[4] it did not reach a level of deeper and broader integration until the 1990s.[5] It also notably did not include many references to fundamental rights until the late 1990s and the 2000s.[6] However, over those five decades, the developing countries of Africa and Latin America each developed a system of rules under which its regional human rights treaties and organizations were established; this could be interpreted as a sign of progress. However, as of yet, there exists no such *regional* system of human rights protection as is in place in East Asia.

CHINA'S PATH TO DEVELOPMENT: THE BIRTH OF A NEW HUB AND SPOKES

China, currently the world's second-biggest economy, has become a leading Asian "hub" of regional trade integration despite the fact that it joined the RTAs' bandwagon later than any other major economic powerhouse.[7] This integration has happened in parallel (though not necessarily in conjunction) with China's membership to the WTO. In 2001, ASEAN was the first of China's "spokes" to sign the Framework Agreement on Comprehensive Economic Cooperation (the Framework Agreement), and the free trade area between China and ASEAN came into effect in 2010.

After signing the Framework Agreement with ASEAN, China quickly expanded its FTA ties with other countries in Asia (in 2003 with Macau and Hong Kong,[8] in 2006 with Pakistan, and in 2008 with Singapore) and moved to build similar trade agreements across other continents. For example, in Latin America, China signed FTAs with Chile in 2005 and with Peru in 2009, as well as with New Zealand in 2008. China has also been negotiating FTAs with Australia since 2005 and with Norway and Iceland since 2008.[9] Note that China has not signed a single FTA in Africa, although it announced the launch of FTA negotiations with South Africa and the Southern African Customs Union (SACU)[10] in 2004. Table 13.3 presents a list of FTAs involving China that have been ratified or are currently under negotiation or under considerations.

CHINA'S FTA MODEL OF SOFT POWER AND MUTUAL RESPECT

China has opted for a framework model of FTA that provides for the gradual harmonization of markets, starting off with specific goods and subsequently

TABLE 13.3. *China's FTAs*

Ratified	Under negotiation	Under consideration
ASEAN	Gulf countries	India
Pakistan	Australia	Korea
Chile	Iceland	Switzerland
New Zealand	Norway	Japan
Singapore	SACU	
Peru		
Hong Kong		
Macau		
Costa Rica		

Source: Ministry of Foreign Commerce of China.

covering services and investments in separate agreements or memoranda of understanding.[11] In other words, the individual FTAs are narrow in scope. Early harvest programs are designed to accelerate the implementation of framework agreements with respect to specific goods.[12] The political and legal frameworks for China's involvement in various economic integration processes have been defined by the successive five-year plans for the country's economic and social development, its framework FTAs, early harvest programs, and memoranda of understanding. The Ninth Five-Year Plan (1996–2000) was the first one to promote "economic and trade cooperation with developing countries"; China accordingly commenced trade negotiations with ASEAN during that period.

The incentives for instituting the aforementioned FTAs are political as well as economic, for the FTAs have helped China build its reputation as an important regional partner and investor and as a peaceful but powerful neighbor. In other words, China has chosen the role of a "soft power" that promotes enhanced cooperation with developing countries on the basis of noninterference in their internal affairs and mutual respect for their political sovereignty.[13]

Some authors have remarked that, with the exception of Australia, all of China's FTAs are economically asymmetrical and are clearly politically driven. China is always one of the top five trading partners of the developing countries with which it has FTAs, yet those countries are not equally important to China as trade partners and their markets are not of a size that would be attractive to China.[14] However, their importance often comes from other reasons. For changing its policy toward Taiwan, for example, Costa Rica was rewarded in 2007 with a huge aid package that included an US$83 million soccer stadium, a US$1 billion joint venture to expand its main petroleum refinery, and preferential treatment in China for Costa Rican coffee.[15] Some FTA partners like Peru are simply a good source of the raw materials that China needs for its own economic growth;[16] others are important because of their membership in larger regional trading blocs to which China wants access.[17] All of China's FTA partners (including New Zealand, a developed country) have recognized China as a market economy, which could have implications for the further development of manufacturing industries in these countries.

BILATERAL INVESTMENT TREATIES (BITs): PROTECTING INVESTOR RIGHTS BEFORE TRIBUNALS

If FTAs have the potential to ensure trade liberalization and market access for China's goods and services (and, possibly, for its capital and labor) beyond general multilateral standards, China's bilateral investment treaties (BITs) *guarantee* the protection of foreign direct investments (FDIs) against regulatory acts of the host countries in an environment that lacks multilateral protection. There are about 3,000 active BITs in the world today, and their number is growing. They initially developed as agreements between developed and developing countries[18] under which private investors from the developed countries achieved substantive and procedural protection for their investments in developing countries and were ensured of dispute settlement before an international tribunal rather than before the courts of the host country. However, since the 1990s and the emergence of economically strong developing countries with their own outward investments, BITs have become a tool of trade policy of many developing countries as well. China has emerged as one of the most advanced developing countries and is second only to Germany in terms of number of BITs (more than 100, according to some reports[19]) that it has instituted.

BITs are the product of a climate that supports substantial and procedural protection for investments and liberalizations of the regulatory systems governing foreign investments in host countries.[20] In the 1970s and 1980s, when China was a target of Western FDIs, it generally opposed BIT provisions for international investment arbitration as a dispute settlement mechanism on the grounds that they favored foreign private investors by allowing them to bring claims before independent tribunals rather than before the Chinese courts.

However, since the mid-1990s, Chinese companies have started investing in projects around the world. Consequently, China has changed its policy on FDIs and is utilizing BITs in a manner similar to that presently practiced by the developed countries to provide a comprehensive protection mechanism for its massive investments in developing countries. China's BITs call for international investment arbitration on the basis of International Centre for Settlement of Investment Disputes (ICSID) or United Nations Commission on International Trade Law (UNCITRAL) rules[21] instead of relying on the host countries' court systems. However, China's first BITs that included investor-state arbitration provisions limited their application to disputes over the amount of compensation in case of expropriation and nationalization.

As the developed countries have done in their BITs, China insists on a broad definition of investment, thus ensuring that any kind of asset invested directly or indirectly by Chinese investors in a developing country is well protected (Berger, 2008, p. 8). Note also that the Memoranda of Understanding on environmental and labor standards that are included in China's BITs are not legally binding and never make reference to human rights protection. China justifies the approach on the basis of its commitment to nonintervention in the internal affairs of host countries.

According to the China's Ministry of Commerce (MOFCOM) November 2011 report, the country's foreign investments from January to September 2011 amounted to US$66.66 billion and the turnover of China's overseas projects was 12.4 percent higher than for the corresponding period in 2010; the value of new investment contracts increased by 13.6 percent to a total of US$93.12 billion.[22] The report explains that Chinese investors made direct investments in 2,418 enterprises in 129 countries during the first 6 months of 2011, and that the majority of these investments were made in emerging markets.

China has concluded more than 30 BITs with African countries, although it has not ratified a single FTA on that continent. In contrast, China has nine BITs and three ratified FTAs in Latin America. The Heritage Foundation reported that during 2010, China's FDIs totaled US$14.9 billion in Brazil, US$8.9 billion in Venezuela, about US$43.7 billion in Sub-Saharan Africa, and US$31.6 billion in East Asia (Heritage Foundation, 2011, p. 2).

THE CHINA EXIM BANK: PROTECTING CHINA'S INVESTORS

Where the Chinese-type FDIs and FTAs diverge from those traditionally used by Western developed countries is in their trade and investment arrangements; these are usually tied to or followed by financial agreements between the host country and the Chinese state financial institution – the China EXIM Bank.[23] EXIM Bank provides loans to developing countries under conditions that favor Chinese investors and exporters of goods and services. The arrangement is called aid for resources. EXIM loans are directed to host country projects that are essential for energy exploration and extraction. These projects facilitate both the operation of Chinese FDIs in the host countries as well as the transportation of imported Chinese goods within the host country. It is in the linkages of financial aid and loans to direct investment arrangements that China offers incentives of different kinds, ones that emphasize economic development and infrastructure building.

Over the past two years, China has lent developing countries more than US$110 billion to fund major infrastructure projects. That is more than the World Bank has lent those countries in the past three years (Gallagher, 2011). According to the 2009 U.S. Congressional Report on China Aid, infrastructure projects constituted 53 percent of aid distributed through China EXIM Bank, commercial loans constituted 42 percent, while grants and debt cancellation amounted to only 5 percent of the total amount of aid. More than 44 percent of investments went to natural resources and agriculture projects (U.S. Congress, 2009). The primary recipients of China EXIM Bank loans are countries in Africa and Latin America where China has massive investments in minerals and oil exploration projects.

The next sections of this chapter examine the impact of China's FTAs with other developing countries in Asia, Africa, and Latin America and further explore the "Hub and Spokes" analogy that has become standard metaphor when describing the emerging Chinese system.

CHINA'S AFRICAN POLICY GOAL: ESTABLISHING STRATEGIC PARTNERSHIPS

China's interest in building economic cooperation with Africa dates back to the 1950s and the Bandung Conference (Bandung I) where a group of African and Asian countries agreed to develop economic and cultural ties in order to "oppose colonialism and neocolonialism" by the United States and the Soviet Union.[24] Despite several attempts to establish strong economic ties with African countries in the 1950s and 1960s,[25] China had not developed a significant presence on the continent prior to the start of the South-South cooperation discourse in the first decade of this century. The 2005 Asia-Africa Summit defined the areas of trade and development that the participating states wished to prioritize and established that political solidarity and friendship would be the core principles of their cooperation.[26]

China's 2006 Africa Policy Paper called for the establishment of a strategic partnership with Africa on the basis of the five principles peaceful coexistence: sincerity, friendship, equality, mutual benefit, and reciprocity. The document also envisions the establishment of FTAs between China and the African countries. Over the past decade China has emerged as one of the top ten home countries with regards to FDI,[27] and, even without any FTAs with

African countries, China's exports to Africa have risen by 36 percent per year. At the same time, China's imports from Africa have risen by 81 percent, but the scope has narrowed so that imports are limited to oil and raw materials.

Most of the oil (approximately 85 percent) comes from Angola, Sudan, and the Congo, and the trade is conducted under contracts between China's oil companies, such as Sinopec, China National Petroleum Cooperation, the China National Offshore Oil Corporation, and Petrochina International, and their relevant African counterparts.[28] The trade deals are often followed by FDI projects that ensure China's access to the raw materials and oil for many years after the initial trade deal ends.

According to China's agenda for Africa, its investments there include US$10 billion in development aid and preferential loans, which themselves include building programs for "schools, hospitals, agricultural training facilities and malaria control centres."[29] In sum, Africa exports raw materials to China and receives manufactured goods from China, a traditional international division of labor of dependency. According to the IMF, it is expected that annual trade between China and Africa will have reached US$100 billion by 2010.

CHINA'S EXIM BARTER MODEL VERSUS THE OECD's FINANCIAL AID MODEL

China EXIM Bank has been involved in financing infrastructure projects in thirty-five African countries through aid and loans.[30] These arrangements are different from the standard financial aid and loans channeled from developed to developing countries under the Organization for Economic Cooperation and Development (OECD)[31] model and within the structure of international financial institutions such as the Paris Club and the IMF.

China EXIM long-term loans (usually with a maturity of twenty years and a three- to seven-year grace period) are based on contracts between an African state and EXIM Bank, which is essentially an extension of the Chinese state. Often loans are tied to concessions the recipients give to China to extract and export commodities from the host country, an arrangement that looks very much like barter.

Under the model China EXIM Bank developed in its agreement with Angola (and later applied to deals with other African countries), loans are given to a debtor country only if the contract for the project being financed has been awarded to a Chinese company (Sieber-Gasser, 2011, p. 4). In that way, loans are transferred as payment to a Chinese company employing mainly Chinese workers, which means that development assistance loans never actually get to the designated African states. Thus, under the Angola model, loan agreements include three parties and two contracts: one between China EXIM

Bank and the African state and the other between EXIM Bank and Chinese company doing the work that EXIM Bank is funding. Infrastructure projects have to be accepted and approved by the EXIM board, and it is EXIM, not the host country, that decides which Chinese company will be awarded the contract. This process is very different from the OECD-monitored ODA process of financial aid and grants for developing countries. It is perhaps more available than the latter, however, now that the budgets of the Western developed countries have been reduced by the global recession and Western countries themselves have lost investment interest in several places, particularly in politically unstable Africa.

LABOR RIGHTS: MISSING FROM CHINA'S AFRICAN POLICY

Concern over the impact of Chinese trade and investments is growing in Africa, especially in civil society and labor organizations. The continent has received loans and financial aid from China on very favorable financial terms but under agreements that have been criticized by local civil groups either as nontransparent or too open-ended and without a clear definition of the parties' rights and obligations. The critics usually advocate for a more thorough review of the agreements between Chinese companies and the African host states, with particular reference to the conditions attached to financial aid.

During the June 9–16, 2011 Annual World Bank Conference on Development sponsored by South Africa's Treasury Department, many participants were very critical of China's impact on labor and environmental standards in Africa, on its use of the African countries' natural resources, and on the lack of efficient regulation of investors' rights and obligations vis-à-vis those of the local communities (Mannak, 2011). It is also increasingly felt that Chinese loans and investments in Africa have not improved labor conditions or led to more jobs for African workers. New policy spaces with respect for human rights and democracy have remained largely underdeveloped. Two cases that follow illustrate this point.

In Zambia, there have been several mining accidents reported in Chinese-owned mines,[32] and in 2006, Chinese managers prevented several attempts by one Zambian cabinet minister to visit mines in Sinazongwe Southern Province. The riots in the Collum Coal Mine where two rioters died and twelve were injured after two Chinese managers fired into a crowd have been widely reported.[33] In 2010, operations at the mine were suspended because of unsafe working conditions after it was reported that local miners were working half-naked and without any protective gear. Since then, the working conditions have improved and salaries have doubled.[34] Without sufficient powers of supervision over Chinese investments, it is difficult for the Zambian government to improve labor conditions for their nationals even as the local labor laws provide for more labor rights than Chinese labor laws. Under Zambia's laws, miners have the right to protest poor conditions and to organize independent trade unions.

In Nigeria, China's second-largest export market in Africa and a major source of oil and gas, there are more than thirty Chinese companies operating trade investments of almost US$8 billion. China's main exports to Nigeria are machinery and equipment, auto parts, textiles and garments, footwear, chemicals, cement, etc. In addition to oil and gas, Nigeria exports agricultural products to China. Some reports state that Chinese investments have created over 30,000 jobs for Nigerians (Imhonlele and Momoh, 2010). The two countries have certainly concluded several trade and investment agreements and memoranda of understanding, not one of which includes provisions related to labour standards.

Recently, public concerns have been raised about Chinese disregard for local labor laws and the failure of China to fulfill its rather generous promises to build infrastructure in Nigeria.[35] Chinese investors use Chinese labor in their large industrial projects in Nigeria. This has effectively prevented any transfer of skills to the local population, even though training for African nationals is almost always a prominent feature of China-Africa bilateral trade agreements and memoranda of understanding (Nabine, 2009, p. 22). In addition, inexpensive textile products from China have led to shrinkage of the Nigerian textile industry.

In sum, although China has no FTAs in Africa, the combination of its BITs and EXIM Bank loans has had a tremendous impact on the level and direction of growth and long-term development in the region. Both BITs and loans facilitate the export of Chinese goods and services, and although they do contribute to the development of much needed infrastructure in Africa, their outcome has been to limit the continent's exports to China to natural resources and oil, to the exclusion of manufactured and agricultural goods, and also to reduce Africa's capacity to export those other products to countries other than China. Interestingly, some African scholars also argue that China has to do more to prevent corruption by keeping the local authorities that receive its loans accountable for the use of that money.[36]

CHINA'S ASIAN NEW SPHERE OF INFLUENCE

China is the largest trading partner of ASEAN in the region and it is the third-largest trading nation in the world. ASEAN is, in turn, the third-largest trading partner to China,[37] and the total cumulative trade volume of ASEAN-China agreement has been US$267 billion in the first three quarters of 2011.[38]

The ASEAN-China FTA, China's very first, was based on the 2001 Framework Agreement under which the two partners agreed to establish a free trade area within a ten-year period. It is important to analyze the ASEAN-China FTA against the background of the two partners' current practices in negotiating trade and investment agreements with other countries and in their human rights records both on the regional level and as individual states.

First, neither AFTA, the subsequent ASEAN agreements on the liberalization of trade on services and investments, ASEAN's FTAs with third countries,[39] nor China's FTAs with third countries[40] go beyond the trade disciplines established by the WTO for its members.[41] China and eight of the ten ASEAN countries are WTO members. Only Laos and Vietnam are still negotiating membership. Second, neither China's nor ASEAN's FTAs with third countries include human rights requirements as prerequisites for market access.[42] Third, neither the ASEAN member states nor ASEAN as a group have a good record in human rights promotion and protection.

Prior to its acceptance in the WTO, China's human rights record was the topic of numerous political and legal debates in the Western democracies. Interestingly, it has been in the plethora of bilateral trade and investment negotiations that followed China's acceptance into the WTO that most of the non-Western and developing countries' concerns regarding China's disrespect for human rights have started to emerge. Its trade and investment agreements in Africa have been criticized for having a harmful effect on the labor, health, and environmental rights of Africans (Li, 2009, pp. 28–31), but China often dismissed that criticism by pointing to the Western countries' colonization of Africa as a source of human rights problems and asserting that its own investments have actually served to improve the economic rights of Africans (Ruan, 2007).

It is not surprising then that China's and ASEAN's trade agreements make no reference to human rights standards. Consequently, the only mechanism for addressing any such problems lies in a provision of Art. 10 of the FTAs. Art. 10 is modeled directly on Art. XX of GATT 1994 and provides for exceptions to trade liberalization in order to protect public morals and human life. The Agreement on Trade in Goods of the Framework Agreement between ASEAN and China provides an additional exception with respect to the right of the parties to prevent the importation of goods that are the product of prison labor.[43]

THE HUMAN RIGHTS STANDARDS DEFICIT

It is noteworthy that ASEAN and China have agreed in general terms on eleven priority areas of cooperation: energy, transportation, culture, public health, tourism, agriculture, information technology, two-way investment, human resources development, the Mekong River Basin Development, and the environment (ASEAN-CHINA Dialogue Relations, 2011). However, dialogue between the parties rather than formal rule-making is the main mechanism that the FTA has stipulated for addressing these issues.

There is no empirical evidence so far that the ASEAN-China FTA is giving rise to conflict between trade and human rights norms, but the aforementioned criticism from ASEAN legal scholars and human rights activists points out potential areas of conflict. There is a concern that, because they have many of the same industries and because of China's far greater economic power and the strength of its manufacturing sector (particularly its lower labor costs), the FTA would undermine the competitive advantage of the ASEAN members' industries in their domestic markets as much as it would hurt the bloc's competitive advantage compared to the rest of the world (Yue, 2004). In addition, some health and environmental concerns are being raised in the ASEAN member states.[44] Because the FTA does not have any mediating provisions for balancing economic rules against human rights, the ASEAN governments are often called upon to modify their domestic environmental and health standards in order to protect their citizens against goods imported from China where the safety standards are lower.[45]

The dispute settlement mechanism[46] established to facilitate the ASEAN-China FTA and its surrounding agreements mandates that an arbitral tribunal be established solely to hear disputes that arise out of the application of the FTA[47] and the agreements that stem from it.[48] In other words, because the FTA itself does not deal with the relationship between the economic and the human rights aspects of the trade relationship, any balancing of the two has to be handled at the dispute settlement stage and ultimately rests on the final and binding arbitral decision.[49] Considering the context of the ASEAN-China FTA, and regarding especially the absence of a domestic human rights regime in China and of a regional one in the case of ASEAN, it is possible to hypothesize that this tribunal would take a similar course to dispute settlement tribunals of the WTO and prioritize the economic aspect of trade agreements.

Until 2010, most Chinese FDIs had been made under BITs with ASEAN countries: Hong Kong alone received 63 percent. Although the primary purpose of some BITs is to protect Chinese outward investments, they do provide another benefit – that of a dispute settlement mechanism in the form of international arbitration. Recently, a Malaysian investor filed an ICSID claim against China, the first ever to be brought against China on the basis of the two countries' BIT; however, this action was suspended before the tribunal had even been established.[50] China EXIM Bank financed a railway construction in Malaysia with a concession loan of US$500 million, and it also provided the Philippines with almost US$2 billion, primarily for mining projects expected to employ 3,000 people and secure for China mineral imports of US$300 million per year.[51]

CHINA'S LATIN AMERICAN TRADE POLICY: THE DRAGON IN THE ROOM?

China has FTA partnerships with three Latin American countries: Chile, Peru, and Costa Rica. These FTAs have established a modest institutional framework, including a dispute settlement tribunal. They do not contain any provisions covering investments but all of them have memoranda of understanding on social and security cooperation. Those with Chile and Costa Rica have memoranda of understanding on environmental standards, and the China-Peru FTA has a memorandum of understanding on labor cooperation. The memoranda are all nonbinding.

China has also concluded numerous bilateral trade and investment agreements with countries in the region and has emerged as one of their most important trading partners. It is one of the top five export markets for Argentina, Brazil, Chile, Cuba, and Peru; it is also one of the leading five sources of imports for Colombia, Mexico, Paraguay, and Uruguay.[52]

Interestingly, Latin America's FDIs in China have increased as well, although it has been argued that the true origins of those investments are unknown because the funds have come from tax havens like the Cayman Islands and the British Virgin Islands (Phillips, 2007, p. 8).[53] In November 2004, Chinese President Hu Jintao visited Argentina, Brazil, Chile, and Cuba and announced about US$30 billion in new Chinese investment in the region, primarily in gas and oil exploration and for building railways, communications satellites, and other major construction projects. Two-thirds of these investments were earmarked for Argentina.[54]

While trade and investments between China and Latin America have been growing since 2004, some countries, such as Colombia and Mexico, have been less successful than others, such as Brazil, Chile, Argentina, and Peru. Some authors, including Jenkins and Peters, suggest that this stems from differences in comparative advantage. Those countries rich in the natural resources sought by China have benefited more from trade with China than those (Mexico in particular) that export mainly manufactured goods like textiles and garments. Those countries are in direct competition with China's own manufacturing industries and they seem to be losing even their domestic markets to the cheaper Chinese goods.[55]

Philips, Jenkins, and Peters find anecdotal evidence that trade and investments between China and Latin America are gradually growing, but growing asymmetrically, and that the impact of imports from China on the region's economic development is increasing in complexity.[56] Even in the strongest Latin American economies, like Brazil, imports of Chinese manufactured goods, especially textiles, now pose a threat to domestic manufacturers. Phillips believes that the explanation for this situation lies in the facts that average wages in China are not much more than one-third of what they are in Brazil, thus allowing goods manufactured in China to be much cheaper than those manufactured in Brazil.[57] Jenkins and Peters report statistics from the Mexican textile industry trade association showing that illegal imports of Chinese manufactured goods account for 60 percent of the local garment market, and that this has caused local firms to shut down.[58] As has occurred in Africa, China has emerged as a threat not only in the Latin American countries' domestic markets but also in those countries' exports to third countries. It has already surpassed Mexico as the top exporter to the United States (*The Economist*, 2010).

In general, Latin America, like Africa, cannot anticipate much of a positive outcome from trade with China: exporting minerals is capital and labor intensive but will not lead to new employment opportunities for unskilled workers once the mines have been put into operation. Considering the facts that China's manufacturing industries have a competitive advantage over those of Latin America and that there is limited opportunity for agricultural exports to China, it is difficult to see that trade and investment arrangements between Latin American countries and China would in the long run lead to increased employment in Latin America.[59]

THE DOWNSIDE OF CHINA'S LATIN AMERICAN POLICY

Furthermore, China's trade and investment arrangements in Latin America have given rise to the same sort of labor and environmental issues examined in Africa and Asia. There have been tensions between local workers and communities and the Chinese mining project managers. The disputes over the Shougang Corporation's mining projects in Peru, which had started in the early 1990s because of low wages and environmental pollution, have been extensively reported (Chauvin, 2006; Romero, 2010).[60] The managers of the mine failed to respond to union grievances for more than four years. The most recent strike at Shougang Hierro, the only iron ore producer in Peru, ended in November 2011, and was also over low wages.

Another example of labor unrest is found at Chinalco investments, in what was once described as the "most productive copper mine anywhere on earth" (BBC, 2008). The project involved open-cast mining on Mount Toromocho, 140 km from the Peru's capital Lima. In order to mine the copper, Chinalco needed to displace the whole town of Morococha. The local population initially voted to accept compensation in the amount of US$2,000 plus a small house or an apartment in a new city built by Chinalco. Now local activists are questioning the company's resettlement policy in the light of the World Bank's resettlement standards.

As previously mentioned, China and Peru concluded a free trade agreement in 2009; the agreement, however, offers no guidelines for resolving the labor and environmental issues arising out of the current investment contracts. Article 161 states: "The Parties shall enhance communication and cooperation on labour, social security and environmental issues through the *Memorandum of Understanding on Labor Cooperation between the Government of the People's Republic of China and the Government of the Republic of Peru.*"[61] In other words, the FTA itself does not impose obligations on the parties; it simply invites them to cooperate.

EXIM BANK'S ASCENDANCY IN LATIN AMERICA AND THE EXPLOSION OF BITS

China's BITs with Latin American countries facilitate long-term investments by China in the excavation of raw materials, primarily minerals such as copper and iron, and in the exploration for oil in these countries. At present, BITs are in force between China and Argentina, Bolivia, Chile, Colombia, Costa Rica, Cuba, Ecuador, Mexico, Peru, and Uruguay. They are also in place in the Caribbean with Belize, Guyana, Jamaica, and Trinidad and Tobago. The minimum life of a BIT is ten years, except for those concluded with Cuba and Ecuador, which last for five years. None of these BITs has any provisions related to labor rights or the mobility of workers. Only the BIT with Colombia has a provision on environmental issues. All of the BITs have provisions allowing for dispute resolution under the UNCITRAL or the ICSID rules. These treaties ensure the protection of Chinese investments and limit the host countries' regulatory powers over long-term investments.

Gallagher (2010) reports that between 2000 and 2009, Chinese imports from Latin America reached US $41.5 billion. Chinese FDIs in Latin America are channeled into resources that China's fast-growing domestic manufacturing sector most needs: copper, oil, iron, and soybeans. Gallagher finds that China initially invested in Uruguay and Mexico as a springboard to access markets in countries such as Brazil and the United States.[62] Its investments later spread to Chile, Peru, Argentina, and Venezuela. China's more recent BITs in Latin America include an ICSID dispute settlement clause like that which had been recently activated in a dispute between a Chinese investor and Peru on the basis of the 1994 China-Peru BIT.[63] As previously mentioned, despite there being no FTA or BIT between China and Brazil, the two countries reached US$14.9 billion in trade in 2010. Indeed, Brazil has no BITs with any country in the world.[64]

Finally, China EXIM Bank has made it to Latin America. In 2009 it joined the Inter-American Development Bank (IDB) and in 2011 the Bank concluded a US$200 million two-year co-lending agreement with the IDB. This allows for financing of trade between China, Latin America and the Caribbean by funding public and private projects in the region.[65] The impact of this agreement is yet to be evaluated.

CHINA'S STATE-TO-STATE TRADE AND INVESTMENT POLICY SPACE

If the WTO path is considered to reduce their policy spaces, then WTO member states can use the FTA and BIT route to engage in negotiations of specialized trade and investment treaties that do not restrain government actions, particularly in policy areas that are outside of the WTO mandate. As previously argued, WTO Plus and further free trade agreements, regional FTAs, and BITs have been used not only by developed countries to coordinate their trade and investment policies with developing countries, but increasingly by developing countries seeking to emphasize rules relevant to their level of development, institutional capacity, and resource distribution priorities. Among developing countries, China has been very active in building its own network of trade and investment treaties with developing countries. In brief, China has relatively few FTAs (no FTAs in Africa and only four in Latin America), but it has numerous BITs (second only to Germany) concluded with developing countries. Finally, China has built its own model of financial aid to developing countries, primarily distributed through its state bank (EXIM), aiming to finance large infrastructure projects in Africa and Latin America.

The past decade has been one of unprecedented economic growth in China, some of it attributable to the expansion of trade with developing countries in Africa, Asia, Latin America, and the Caribbean. The structure of these agreements is rather simple, providing for modest institutional infrastructure, lowering tariffs for manufactured goods, and ensuring standard protection for foreign investments. In brief, the focus is on economic development while issues such as labor and environmental and social protection are either ignored or limited to nonbinding memoranda of understanding.

The mere structure of these arrangements and the patterns of export and import indicate that although China's aid has helped many regions grow, the developing countries need to do more to ensure that growth takes place in a more symmetrical way. For most countries on the other side of the treaties, economic growth based solely on increasing mineral exports is not sufficient to ensure that they achieve economic development; quite the contrary, by focusing on the export of unsophisticated raw materials, they are reducing their own development opportunities. These countries have to be able to obtain financial aid from China with no strings attached so that it can be utilized for sustainable development projects and to diversify their economies; developmental activities will have to be strictly monitored to guard against corruption and misuse of assets by local governments and officials.

HUMAN RIGHTS CLAUSES: THE GREY ZONE OF TRADE LIBERALIZATION

The EU and the United States – major proponents of trade integration – have used human rights clauses in their FTAs as a mechanism for coordinating the impact of trade arrangements with the protection of human rights in their numerous spokes: developing countries in Europe, Africa, and Latin America. Consequently, violations of democratic rights and labor standards could, at least in theory, result in the suspension of trade benefits for the developing countries. However, those EU and U.S. FTAs are often criticized as politically and economically asymmetrical from the outset because of the imbalance in power between developed and developing countries. They have also been criticized as unfair in outcome because developed countries that have more funds as well as advanced knowledge and technology are able to gain more benefits from trade liberalization than developing countries can. This, in turn, leads to an increasing wealth gap between the developed and developing worlds. In addition, human rights–related conditionality is criticized both as a harsh and inefficient means of promoting the human rights agenda and as a disguised barrier to trade.

Given the economic strength of China in the world market and its external policy with respect to the promotion and protection of international human rights laws and standards, it is almost certain that China will not compromise in its agreements with developing countries and somehow combine human rights norms with those of international trade. The attempts of ASEAN,

MERCOSUR, ECOWAS, and some other RTAs between developing countries to coordinate the performance of trade and human rights treaty obligations are just the beginnings of a slow evolutionary process to consolidate their
human rights agenda and to stabilize the regions. However, the fact that these
blocs have given themselves very limited institutional jurisdiction to deal with
the problem could make their protection of human rights more complex and
more difficult to achieve.

HUMAN RIGHTS: STILL THE ELEPHANT IN THE ROOM
FOR CHINA

It is also noteworthy that the WTO needs to be notified of PTAs concluded
between WTO members, including FTAs of any modality, and they need to be
scrutinized by the Committee on Regional Trade Agreements for consistency
with the WTO law; thus, those agreements are transparent and open to public
monitoring. On the other hand, BITs are not subject to a coherent body of
international treaty law; they are subject to rules of international customary
law and a patchwork of bilateral investment treaties. Thus, their structure and
impact on development and other policy areas are more open-ended than
those of PTAs.

Their focus is also primarily on protecting foreign investors from regulatory
actions of host states, so by their nature they are not the best tool for safeguarding a policy space. BIT rules and disciplines are usually open to public scrutiny
only when a dispute between a private foreign investor and a host state arises,
and only if a BIT that applies to the relationship between the parties provides
for ICSID arbitration as a forum for a dispute settlement. China has only
recently agreed to include a wider range of disputes under the ICSID arbitration, and the relations of Chinese companies with host developing countries
have rarely been publicly assessed.

The terms of China's financial aid to African and Latin American countries,
which never refer to human rights protection or good governance conditionality, are not subject to a standard OECD review performed by its Development
Assistance Committee (DAC) in order to ensure that financial aid is provided
in a manner that ensures economic development and the improvement of the
lives of people in the recipient countries. Although China has emerged as a
major donor of financial aid to developing countries, it has built trade relations using trade agreements that neither contain linkages to human rights nor
restrict developing countries from using their social policy spaces to advance
human rights.[66] In practice, however, the silence on human rights reflects
China's economic development priorities and the fact that it has not entered

into any regional human rights treaties. The genuine worry is that, given China's silence in its trade relations, developing countries that do have a genuine commitment to human rights (including labor standards and wages) will weaken that commitment in order to remain a competitive trading partner with China.

REFERENCES

ASEAN-China Dialogue Relations. (2011) para. 4. Retrieved March 14, 2013 from: http://www.aseansec.org/5874.htm.

Baccini, Leonardo. (2011) The Design of Preferential Trade Agreements: A New Dataset in Making. *WTO Staff Working Paper ERSD*, 3.

Berger, Alex. (2008) China's New Bilateral Investment Treaty Programme. *Presentation to SIEL 2008 Conference*, 4.

Chauvin, Lucien. (2006) Hierro Peru: China's Footprint in the Andes. *China Dialogue*. Online at http://www.chinadialogue.net/article/show/single/en/595-Hierro-Peru-China-s-footprint-in-the-Andes, March 12 2013.

Declaration of the First South Summit of the Group of 77 and China, April 12–14, 2000, United Nations General Assembly, A/55/74, at para. 11.

Djeri-wake, Nabine. (2009) Impact of Chinese Investment and Trade on Nigerian Economic Growth. *African Trade Policy Centre, Economic Commission for Africa*, 22.

Doha Declaration. (2005) *Action Plan of the Second South Summit, Doha, Qatar*, 23, 47, and 73.

ECONOS. (2000) The Realization of Economic, Social and Cultural Rights: Globalization and Its Impact on the Full Enjoyment of Human Rights, 15.

Gallagher, Kevin. (2011) The End of the "Washington consensus." *The Guardian*. March 7 2011. Retrieved September 9, 2013 from: http://www.theguardian.com/commentisfree/cifamerica/2011/mar/07/china-usa.

Gallagher, Mark. (2010) China and the Future of Latin American Industrialization. *The Frederich S. Pardee Center for the Study of the Longer-Range Future, no. 18.*

Imhonlele, Austin and Momoh, Siaka. (2010) Nigeria China Trade Hits 6 Billion. *Business Day Online*, June 24, 2010. Retrieved September 8, 2013 from: http://www.businessdayonline.com/NG/index.php/analysis/117-news/12108-nigeria-china-trade-hits-6-billion.

Mannak, Miriam. (2011) Africa: Concerns over Chinese Investment and Working Conditions, *IPS News*. Retrieved September 8, 2013 from: http://ipsnews.net/africa/nota.asp?idnews=42815.

Marrakech, Declaration on South-South Cooperation. (2003), 9.

Marrakech Framework of Implementation of South-South Cooperation. High-Level Conference on South-South Cooperation (2003). 8.

Mexico's Economy, Bringing NAFTA Back Home. (2010) in: *The Economist*.

Peru's Copper Mountain in Chinese Hands. (2008) in: *BBC News*.

Phillips, Nicola. (2007) Consequences of an Emerging China: Is Development Space Disappearing for Latin America and the Caribbean? *The Centre for International Governance Innovation Working Paper no. 14*, 8.

Romero, Simon. (2010) Tensions over Chinese Mining Venture in Peru. *The New York Times.* August 14, 2010. Retrieved September 7, 2013 from: http://www.nytimes.com/2010/08/15/world/americas/15chinaperu.html?pagewanted=all&_r=o.

Ruan, Wenjie. (2007) Lessons for the Controversy Surrounding WTO Social Clauses. *Group Economic Study.*

Sieber-Gasser, Charlotte. (2011) The Legal Character of Sino-African Tied Aid: Cunning Fox and Wise Dragon? NCCR *Trade Regulation, Working Paper No. 2011/47,* 4.

The Heritage Foundation. (2011) WebMemo no. 3133, 2. Retrieved September 8, 2013 from: http://www.academia.edu/1798405/Chinese_Investment_in_Africa_Checking_the_Facts_and_Figures.

Thomas Lum. (2009) China's Assistance and Government-Sponsored Investment Activities in Africa, Latin America, and Southeast Asia (Washington: Congressional Research Service, November 2009).

Times of China. (2006) Chinese Investors Prevent Minister from Visiting Coal Mine. Spiegel Online International, December 9, 2010. Retrieved September 8, 2013 from: http://www.spiegel.de/international/world/investment-with-strings-attached-cables-reveal-resentment-at-chinese-influence-in-africa-a-733870.html, September 8, 2013.

Wu, Mei and Yinging, Huang. (2009) Interpreting the Different Comments on Sino-African Relations, *Manager Journal* 11, 5–6.

Yue, Chia Siow. (2004) ASEAN-China Free Trade Area, *AEP Conference, Hong Kong.* April 12-13. Retrieved September 7, 2013 from: http://www.hiebs.hku.hk/aep/Chia.pdf.

Yunlong, Li. (2009) Sino-African Relations and Human Right Development in Africa, *Human Rights* 2, 28–31.

WTO Annual Report. (2011) Geneva: WTO. March 14 2013, Available at: http://www.wto.org/english/res_e/booksp_e/anrep_e/anrep11_e.pdf.

PART VI

China's Evolving State Policy and Practice

14

Human Rights and Social Justice in China*

Pitman B. Potter

INTRODUCTION: BUILDING SUSTAINABLE LABOR STANDARDS

Policy and regulatory systems for sustainability and social justice in China are still in development. In the area of labor relations, China faces considerable challenges related to labor conditions, which have led to social unrest and labor strife. While improvements have been pursued through such measures as the Labour Contract Law, international standards on rights to collective bargaining and independent unions continue to be rejected by the Party/State.

China's engagement with international labor standards reveals dynamics of selective adaptation as factors of perception, complementarity, and legitimacy affect processes of normative assimilation in China's traditional social policy spaces. China's ability to enforce both international and national regulatory standards is affected as well by forces of institutional capacity, revealed through factors of institutional purpose, location, orientation, and cohesion. The success of the PRC Party/State in managing these challenges will have a significant effect on its ability to secure social justice. China's friends abroad can support efforts to build sustainability in its labor management system, through professional and academic exchanges, technical cooperation, as well as through efforts to understand and respond to challenges of selective adaptation and institutional capacity.

ISSUES OF SOCIAL JUSTICE AND HUMAN WELL-BEING

China's approach to labor relations reflects challenges facing protection of social justice generally in the context of rapid economic development. The

---

* This paper is drawn from sections from my forthcoming book, *Law and Treaty Performance in China: Norms and Structures for Trade and Human Rights* (Vancouver: UBC Press, forthcoming 2014).

challenge to protect human well-being in China's fast-changing socioeconomic environment raises serious questions around sustainability of development and political stability. The general lack of institutions and processes for
the redress of socioeconomic grievances contributes to the problem (Cai, 2010).
China's official figures on popular demonstrations continue to rise,[1] indicating
the extent of popular dissatisfaction with current conditions. This has been
particularly so in rural areas where disputes are rampant over inequities in
land use, agricultural pricing and policy, and environmental conditions, both
social and natural.[2]

   The potential for sustainable development in China will depend on the
extent to which human well-being is protected through strong and expansive
policy spaces. However, China's pursuit of economic development has often
marginalized issues of political and civil rights, including labor rights. This
pattern has effectively reduced policy spaces for social justice, leading to policy
distortions that undermine protection of human well-being. The success of
China's development project may come to depend on whether the Chinese
people support the political and socioeconomic system on which development
is based, and this in turn will ultimately reflect whether people see their own
well-being served by China's policies. Labor relations are a key element in this
process.

   Labor relations policy also reflects approaches to poverty reduction. China's
economic development agenda has given significant attention to poverty
reduction as a condition for sustainability, in contrast with policies that
champion aggregate economic growth as a solution to poverty.[3] Yet the links
between poverty, income inequality, and development have been well documented throughout the post-Mao economic reform period (Lee and Selden,
200 Selden, 1993). Labor relations have been part and parcel of this process.
Regulatory structures and policies emphasizing elite-driven development work
to marginalize unskilled and even semiskilled workers who lack the education
and political associations to compete effectively in China's emerging market economy. Moreover, attempts to organize and control workers through
Party-led trade unions often has led to workers' interests being subordinated to
those of employers and their affiliates in the Party/State. While China's cities
and suburban areas (mostly but not exclusively along the eastern seacoast)
have in the main profited from the rapid economic growth of the past few
decades, interior provinces and rural areas have often been left out of the race
to development (Austrevicius and Boozman, 2006).

   China's academic and policy communities have given significant attention
to the problem of wealth disparity (Zhu, 2002). While attitudinal surveys suggest that many in China (as in Japan and the United States) attribute poverty
to laziness and lack of willpower among the poor (Leiserowitz et al., 2005),

historical conditions, resource (particularly land) scarcity, and inadequate opportunities for education are likely more important factors.[4] In the context of China's remarkable economic growth record, attitudes toward poverty may reflect disparities of wealth increasingly evident over the past two decades despite policies promoting economic development and poverty reduction. China's wealth gap between urban and rural communities is among the highest in the world[5] and is understood by Chinese leaders to be a major source of social instability (Ma, 2005). While sophisticated models already exist for achieving sustainability goals through the balancing of social and economic needs,[6] systemic implementation remains elusive. Labor relations are an important focus for policy intervention.

LABOR RELATIONS AND SOCIAL STABILITY: A SYSTEMIC TIPPING POINT

The area of labor relations offers particularly useful vectors for examination, each with its own significant implications for social sustainability. While labor contracts were made to favor principles of equal treatment of workers over contrary provisions such as absent market-driven mobility or wage supports (Jiang, 2009), workers are increasingly likely to be left at the mercy of efficiency-motivated employers. Even among state-owned enterprises, employment discrimination tends to distort merit-based systems for distribution of wages and benefits (Zhou, 2006). As a result, workers without the technical skills necessary to achieve a relative degree of bargaining parity with employers are unlikely to benefit from WTO-mandated legal reforms (Solinger, 2002).

As the expanded competition (local and international) brought on by the WTO makes controlling production costs an increasingly important element of business success, even those workers who are able to avoid layoffs see continued erosion in salaries and working conditions. China faces the prospect of becoming a "sweatshop of the world" as wages sink and working conditions deteriorate in the face of internal migration and international competition (Taylor, 2005). In the agricultural sector, efficiency and cost-cutting imperatives driven by WTO accession are likely to make profit margins thinner for peasants wholly in control of productive assets, and salaries lower for farm employees.

Policy initiatives aimed at the privatization of Chinese enterprises, along with greater attention to efficiency and reduced production costs, have contributed to declining labor conditions for industrial workers.[7] Increased worker unrest became a major challenge for Chinese labor policy early on in the post-Mao reform period. Between 1986 and 1994, 60,000 labor disputes were recorded (probably matched by a sizeable number of unreported disputes), and 3,000 labor disputes were noted during the first three months of 1994 alone.[8] In 1997, efforts to close or privatize inefficient state enterprises led to further unrest. In March, some 20,000 workers in Nanchong, Sichuan demonstrated and besieged city hall for more than thirty hours in one of the worst outbreaks of labor unrest in China since 1949.[9] In December, textile workers in Hefei, Anhui staged a sit-in to demand new jobs, following a similar protest in Yibin, Sichuan.[10] Public demonstrations have continued apace in subsequent years: the Public Security Bureau reported 87,000 public order disturbances in 2005, up from 74,000 in 2004 and 58,000 in 2003 (Ni, 2006). In 2006, some 94,000 disturbances were reported (Einhorn, 2008). The global economic crisis that erupted in late 2008 caused widespread plant closings and unemployment, especially for migrant workers (Han, 2009), raising the prospect of further social unrest: during 2008, some 170,000 demonstrations were recorded.[11] While combined efforts by legal institutions and public security forces to prevent social instability may continue to make worker-driven change difficult (Chan, 2001), worker demonstrations continue apace.

INTERNATIONAL STANDARDS: AN ESSENTIAL THRESHOLD FOR LABOR RELATIONS IN CHINA

China's capacity to build social well-being into its labor relations will depend to a considerable extent on greater acceptance of international standards. In a global context, local labor conditions reflect the influences of international economic conditions and tend to indicate for local people how China is faring in the international political economy. Labor also provides an essential dimension through which members of Chinese society derive specific economic returns from development. Hence, labor conditions offer a locus for determining costs and benefits of development for those on whose economic production development is based. Human rights in labor are provided in the International Covenant on Economic, Social, and Cultural Rights (ICSCR):

Article 6

1. The States Parties to the present Covenant recognize the right to work, which includes the right of everyone to the opportunity to gain his living by work which he freely chooses or accepts, and will take appropriate steps to safeguard this right.
2. The steps to be taken by a State Party to the present Covenant to achieve the full realization of this right shall include technical and vocational guidance and training programmes, policies and techniques to achieve steady economic, social and cultural development and full and

productive employment under conditions safeguarding fundamental political and economic freedoms to the individual.

Article 7

The States Parties to the present Covenant recognize the right of everyone to the enjoyment of just and favourable conditions of work which ensure, in particular:

(a) Remuneration which provides all workers, as a minimum, with:
    (i) Fair wages and equal remuneration for work of equal value without distinction of any kind, in particular women being guaranteed conditions of work not inferior to those enjoyed by men, with equal pay for equal work;
    (ii) A decent living for themselves and their families in accordance with the provisions of the present Covenant;
(b) Safe and healthy working conditions;
(c) Equal opportunity for everyone to be promoted in his employment to an appropriate higher level, subject to no considerations other than those of seniority and competence;
(d) Rest, leisure and reasonable limitation of working hours and periodic holidays with pay, as well as remuneration for public holidays.

Article 8

1. The States Parties to the present Covenant undertake to ensure:
    (a) The right of everyone to form trade unions and join the trade union of his choice, subject only to the rules of the organization concerned, for the promotion and protection of his economic and social interests. No restrictions may be placed on the exercise of this right other than those prescribed by law and which are necessary in a democratic society in the interests of national security or public order or for the protection of the rights and freedoms of others;
    (b) The right of trade unions to establish national federations or confederations and the right of the latter to form or join international trade-union organizations;
    (c) The right of trade unions to function freely subject to no limitations other than those prescribed by law and which are necessary in a democratic society in the interests of national security or public order or for the protection of the rights and freedoms of others;
    (d) The right to strike, provided that it is exercised in conformity with the laws of the particular country.
2. This article shall not prevent the imposition of lawful restrictions on the exercise of these rights by members of the armed forces or of the police or of the administration of the State.

3. Nothing in this article shall authorize States Parties to the International Labour Organisation Convention of 1948 concerning Freedom of Association and Protection of the Right to Organize to take legislative measures which would prejudice, or apply the law in such a manner as would prejudice, the guarantees provided for in that Convention.

China's ratification of the ICESCR brings with it obligations to comply with provisions on such matters as independent trade unions and the right to strike. The International Covenant on Civil and Political Rights (signed but not yet ratified by China) provides parallel provisions on freedom of association:[12]

Article 22

1. Everyone shall have the right to freedom of association with others, including the right to form and join trade unions for the protection of his interests.
2. No restrictions may be placed on the exercise of this right other than those which are prescribed by law and which are necessary in a democratic society in the interests of national security or public safety, public order (*ordre public*), the protection of public health or morals or the protection of the rights and freedoms of others. This article shall not prevent the imposition of lawful restrictions on members of the armed forces and of the police in their exercise of this right.
3. Nothing in this article shall authorize States Parties to the International Labour Organisation Convention of 1948 concerning Freedom of Association and Protection of the Right to Organize to take legislative measures which would prejudice, or to apply the law in such a manner as to prejudice, the guarantees provided for in that Convention.[13]

CHINA'S INTERNATIONAL OBLIGATIONS AND RESPONSIBILITIES: AN ABSENCE OF ENFORCEMENT

China's signature to the ICSCR, even absent formal ratification, carries at least the moral obligation if not legal responsibility to act consistently with these terms – obligations that are particularly forceful in light of their relationship with the labor provisions of the Covenant, which China has ratified.

The Declaration of the International Labour Organization on Fundamental Principles and Rights at Work expresses international standards on human rights in labor, focusing on four areas: labor organization and collective bargaining, freedom from forced labor, prohibitions against labor discrimination, and prohibitions against child labor.[14] Of these China has committed itself only to the prohibitions against child labor and against labor discrimination, ratifying international conventions against the two.[15]

China has engaged in international cooperation and development programs aimed at preventing trafficking for labor exploitation (Mulroney, 2010). However, China's government has remained largely indifferent to providing procedural guarantees for labor organizing and collective bargaining.[16] China has ratified neither the Freedom of Association and Protection of the Right to Organize Convention, 1948 (No. 87) (C. 87) nor the Right to Organize and Collective Bargaining Convention, 1949 (No. 98) (C. 98).[17] In addition, China has not ratified ILO conventions against forced and compulsory labor.[18]

On the other hand, China has ratified a broad range of international labor conventions on issues such as occupational health and safety, and labor administration.[19] China's Labour Law, Labour Contract Law, Trade Union Law, and related measures are broadly consistent with international standards on issues of time of work, working conditions, holidays and leaves, and pay rates.[20] Stronger protection for labor rights is in fact generally consistent with the official orthodoxy on the right to development.[21] However, the processes by which these substantive rights can be enforced effectively remains subject to the political purview of the Party/State. Enforcement of internationally recognized labor rights depends in part on provisions of the People's Republic of China (PRC) Constitution on freedoms of speech, of the press, of assembly, of association, of procession, and of demonstration, which are all conditional on supporting the Party/State and also lack concrete mechanisms for enforcement. Even in the area of gender rights, despite laudable efforts to educate women about their labor rights,[22] questions remain as to China's compliance with international standards on protection of women (Lee and Rudd, 2006).

LABOR REGULATION IN CHINA: ORTHODOXY AND ADAPTATION

Despite an elaborate regulatory regime under the Ministry of Labour for supervision and enforcement of labor protections (*Laodong he ji*, 2004), labor conditions in China have deteriorated steadily over the past two decades. Driven by the competitive pressures of local and global markets, employers have steadily reduced salaries and working conditions (Santoro, 2000). Institutional challenges include corruption and work to impede implementation of international standards on labor (Kumiko, 2010). Government agencies responsible for labor protection have been either complicit in such efforts or powerless to stop them (Barboza, 2008). The Labour Law of the PRC and its associated regulatory structures subject workers to significant political controls, both through Party-dominated unions and through weak negotiation and dispute settlement provisions (Potter and Li, 1996).

Orthodox doctrine distinguishes labor relations in China and purportedly serves to integrate labor power with other elements of production such as capital and materials (Yang and Lu, 2010). Thus labor relations are not the product of a market-based exchange of value but rather part of the broader integrated effort of production. This helps explain why the PRC Labour Law is emblematic of the tension between protecting workers' rights and maintaining their subservience to state control.[23] The integration perspective mandates state control over both the rights and interests of workers and the larger production effort of which they are a part. Thus, the statute extends a number of specific benefits to workers; these include various "guarantees" of equal opportunity in employment, job selection, compensation, rest, leave, safety and health care, vocational training, social security and welfare, and the right to submit disputes to arbitration.

Juxtaposed to these benefits are a number of obligations that workers must honor, including the duties to fulfill work requirements, the improvement of vocational skills, the carrying out of work safety and health regulations, and the observance of labor discipline and vocational ethics. Official reviews of the PRC Labour Law describe it as the complete articulation of the rights of workers,[24] such that workers' rights are only those articulated in the law and do not extend beyond the text of the legislation.[25] Alternative voices suggested that the provisions for labor contracts under the Labour Law allowed for more flexible arrangements determined by agreement between the employer and employee, albeit still subject to the general validity provisions of the Labour Law.[26] Thus, the Labour Law conditions the rights of workers on their submission to authority in a similar way as do the conditional grants of civil and political rights under the PRC Constitution.

The centrality of state power is protected more specifically in the Labour Law through provisions on labor unions, collective bargaining, and dispute resolution. Generally consistent with the PRC trade union regime,[27] the Labour Law entrenches the Party-dominated labor union system as the basic mechanism for enforcing workers' rights.[28] Some thirty-one provincial and ten national level industrial unions fall under the overall authority of the All China Federation of Trade Unions (ACFTU), a CPC United Front organization (Jiang, 2010). There is no legal sanction for the creation of independent labor unions that might challenge the Party's official policies.[29] The Trade

Union Law also grants CPC cadres close access to trade union leadership. The centrality of the state as the sole protector of workers' rights and interests has contributed to concerns about lax enforcement of the Labour Law's limited protections.[30]

CHINA'S LABOUR CONTRACT LAW: FORMALIZATION OF PRACTICE

During the late 1990s and early 2000s, China's booming economy was seen as evidence of the superiority of a Chinese model of development (Peerenboom, 2007), even while labor conditions in its factories remained largely unimproved. Yet the increase in number and severity of worker demonstrations over matters such as unpaid wages and working conditions revealed the extent to which the socialist market economy was apparently unable to protect workers' rights and interests.[31] China's Labour Contract Law (2008) formalized a number of significant principles including requirements for written contracts, compliance with labor law requirements on working hours, overtime requirements, and working conditions, as well as legal remedies.[32] Challenges remain in areas of contract interpretation on matters such as wages and working time, contract form and validity, the secondment of workers, the authority of state-controlled unions, and processes for dispute resolution (Dong, 2010). Despite these challenges however, the Labour Contract Law remains a powerful ideal for renewed commitment to enforcing labor rights. However, as indicated by foreign business groups concerned about the new measures, the prospect of discriminatory enforcement remains high (Dyer, 2007).

While the Labour Contract Law reflects a degree of commitment to harmonize orthodox policies on economic development with international human rights standards, potential problems of enforcement remain (Harris, 2008). Nonetheless, the new legislation offers the prospect of improving the enforcement mechanisms for protecting labor rights as it operates in conjunction with the Labour Disputes Mediation and Arbitration Law.[33] While the previous labor law regime extended to dispute resolution, most official guidance came in the form of administrative regulations and judicial directive, which generally were not effective across administrative and bureaucratic boundaries (Laodong, 2004b). The new legislation on labor disputes resolution aims to establish a national system for resolving labor disputes on the basis of the substantive provisions of the Labour Law and the Labour Contract Law. Increased worker awareness, assisted in part through self-help guides and public education, may help ensure more effective enforcement (Wang et al., 2010).

NORMATIVE AND OPERATIONAL DIMENSIONS OF LABOR RELATIONS IN CHINA

Normative dynamics of *selective adaptation* play an important role in China's state-centered labor system. The broad contours of selective adaptation emerge from the disparities between the normative framework of liberal capitalism – that tends to inform international labor standards – and local norms borne of China's socialist political economy. Disagreements over the relative weight to be accorded to the public and private economy (including property rights) continue in China as the transition to a post-socialist economy continues.

The labor standards articulated through the ILO tend to focus on labor relations between private capital and workers. Disparities of norms, however, are already present. For example, the ILO provisions on labor organizing, dispute resolution, and collective bargaining all presume that labor relations involve private capital. However, China's employers remain heavily state-centered, even among emerging "private" enterprises whose operations and regulations remain heavily dependent on personal relational networks between proprietors and the Party/State. This tension between international labor standards and China's labor system is augmented by factors such as perceptions, complementarity, and legitimacy.

Orthodox perceptions of international labor standards remain influenced by historical perspectives of resentment toward an international legal system from which China was excluded for many decades. Also important to note is that regime responses to efforts to establish independent labor unions in China reflect not only hostility toward the establishment of independent organizations over which the Party has little or no control, but also reveal conclusions about efforts to subvert the Chinese state by "hostile forces" (*didui shili*).

EMPIRICAL FINDINGS OF GOVERNMENT RESPONSIBILITY TO MANAGE THE LABOR MARKET

In contrast to such official perspectives, respondent professionals interviewed in Shanghai indicated a relatively high level of support for reliance on international standards in resolving labor conflict (63.9 percent). This is still significantly lower than in Canada, for example, where 86.4 percent of interviewees supported international standards (P1 HR/L QC43). Perceptions among respondents in Shanghai about the right to employment also revealed the legacy of the state-owned economy and the socialist ethos of permanent employment as 64.9 percent of respondents agreed that people should be guaranteed employment – in contrast with Canada's 20.1 percent (P1 HR/L QC54). Similar patterns are evident in responses on questions of who should be responsible for securing employment when people need it (P1 HR/L QC55):

	China	Canada
Government should provide employment	80.1%	48%
Government should support private firm employment	80.4%	61%
Individuals and family responsible	19.7%	39.6%

The role of trade unions in advocacy for employees was given high importance by 77.4 percent of respondents in Shanghai, in comparison with 55.9 percent in Toronto/Vancouver (P1 HR/L QC58). These elements of perception not only reveal differences between respondent groups in Canada and China but also show the extent to which perceptions of labor relations issues depart from the standards articulated in international human rights discourse. Interestingly, there is yet further discord between perceptions of interview subjects in Shanghai and the official perspective of regime orthodoxy, particularly in areas such as the role of trade unions, right to work, and the application of international law.

Orthodox views emerging from official documentation of the Party/State tend to diminish the role of trade unions as advocates for workers while also minimizing the right to permanent employment. They condition China's acceptance of international labor standards on local conditions. Responses from interview subjects in Shanghai indicate high support for each of these propositions. This suggests that the dynamics of selective adaptation operate not only at the international/national level but also at the national/subnational level.

Complementarity between international labor human rights standards and Chinese law is generally high, as China's legislative initiatives on labor rights have consciously incorporated international texts. Thus provisions in the labor law of China on times of work, working conditions, holidays and leave, and so on closely track those set forth in ILO conventions. However in process areas such as dispute resolution, China's continued resistance to independent labor arbitration and the continued insertion of Party officials into labor unions tend to depart from international standards.

THE GROWING GAP BETWEEN INTERNATIONAL LABOR STANDARDS AND CHINA'S STATE-RUN INDUSTRIAL RELATIONS SYSTEM

The disparities between international ILO standards and China's Party-centered labor system have important implications for the interpretation and implementation of international standards locally. Whereas substantive standards can be expressed through formal law and regulation, resistance to the process standards of the ILO often undermines their enforcement. Nonetheless, as part of the "united front" approach, Party leadership over trade unions in China is likely to remain a feature of the political economy for the foreseeable future. Even under circumstances where Party officials favor the rights of workers over employers, such as in the recent labor unrest at Foxconn and at Guangzhou Honda, this discretionary support underscores rather than diminishes the centrality of Party leadership. The continued absence of support for independent trade unions and independent labor arbitration will undermine China's compliance with international labor human rights standards.

The dimensions and boundaries of legitimacy possessed by China's labor system are evident most prominently in the range of strikes, demonstrations, and other labor unrest that has gripped China for the past decade or more. The episodes of worker suicides and labor stoppages at Foxconn Shenzhen and Honda Foshan demonstrate the extent of worker frustration about an ineffective trade union system that is seen to be in compliance with employers rather than effective as an advocate for workers' rights (Barboza and Tabuchi, 2011). An interpretation of the law issued in July 2008 by the Guangdong Higher Level Peoples Court and the Guangdong Labour Arbitration Committee acknowledged the need for enforcing labor contracts but also served to insulate the large Chinese electronics manufacturer Hawaii from costs and liability for a dispute with some 7,000 workers that had arisen prior to the law going into effect (Sun, 2008). While the new Labour Contract Law signals an important attempt by the government to secure better treatment for workers and in so doing to secure broader support from workers and society at large, implementation remains uncertain. Considerable fears that the new law will be directed primarily against foreign employers continue to emerge and have yet to be assuaged.

Legitimacy issues also arise in responses to interview questionnaires administered in Shanghai and Vancouver. Comparison studies showed that 59.1 percent of Chinese respondents indicated that deceit was of very high or highest importance as a cause of conflict in labor relations, in comparison with 24.6 percent of Canadian respondents (P1 HR/L QC31). Legitimacy dynamics are also evident in responses around options for resolving disputes over unfair labor treatment as only 13.3 percent of respondents in Shanghai considered negotiation to be most effective.

This qualified view on the relative utility of negotiation was evident not only in respondents' indications of what they personally would do in the event of a labor dispute but also in their general assessment of the effectiveness of negotiation in resolving labor disputes (China: 13 percent; Canada: 48.7 percent) (P1 HR/L QC33). Similar views were expressed around the fairness of negotiations (highest fairness; China: 9.8 percent, Canada: 34.4 percent) (P1 HR/L QC34). Paradoxically, as indicated in other responses, respondents in Shanghai indicated a high level of confidence (61.2 percent) in court litigation as having the highest level of fairness in resolving labor disputes (in contrast with Canadian respondents, of whom only 34.4 percent listed court litigation as having the highest fairness) (P1 HR/L QC34). Concerns about the legitimacy of trade unions were evident in responses about complaints over dangerous working conditions. Of respondents in Shanghai, only 17.9 percent consider the trade union to be of highest importance, in comparison with 46.1 percent of Canadian respondents (P1 HR/L QC40).

NORMATIVE IDEALS OF THE ILO AND THE CONSTRAINTS OF SOCIALIST DEVELOPMENT

Thus, factors of perception, complementarity, and legitimacy are evident in China's engagement with international labor standards. Perceptions of international standards are tempered by distinctions between the generally private market approach of the ILO and the socialist market policies of China's political economy. Complementarity tends to run relatively high on areas of substantive rights, but less so in the area of process for enforcing rights. Legitimacy factors are evident in orthodox responses to international labor standards but also in attitudes around the effectiveness of China's labor system.

While normative ideals in the areas of economic, social, and cultural rights may be broadly consonant with official norms of socialist development in China, achievement of these ideals has been constrained by factors of organizational structure and performance. *Institutional capacity* offers potential for understanding how regime ideals in areas of economic, social, and cultural rights will be fulfilled. Local conditions of rapid socioeconomic transformation also pose particular challenges for institutional capacity in protection of labor rights.

With official acceptance of the decline of class struggle, the regime turned its attention away from protecting social welfare and more toward supporting economic growth. The gradual loosening of social and economic restraints presented the regime with new challenges of maintaining political control while still presenting a broad image of tolerance aimed at building legitimacy. No longer did the conditions and presumptions of the state-planned economy justify state-controlled labor organizations to ensure that labor relations did not undermine state-centered policies and programs of development. Since the excess value of labor was formerly deployed (in theory at least) for the benefit of the state and society as a whole rather than to private interests, vigorous independent labor organizations and rights could be dismissed as unnecessary and unsuited to China's conditions.

However, with deepening economic reforms – particularly after China's accession to the WTO – that paved the way for the expansion of private capitalism, institutions of labor relations faced an environment of changing contexts and priorities. No longer could the government claim that restricting independent unions or the right to strike met the imperatives of revolutionary transformation. Rather labor controls were explained by reference to social stability and economic growth, but these claims rang increasingly hollow in the face of evident disparities in wealth and the emergence of an ultra-wealthy business elite whose profits depended on maintaining state control and coercion over low-paid workers. Labor institutions such as the All China Federation of Trade Unions and the Ministry of Labour insisted on maintaining firm control over labor relations, even as they struggled to maintain legitimacy and operational effectiveness.

Factors of institutional purpose are evident in the disparities over policy imperatives and purposes – particularly between the need to maintain stability and economic growth on the one hand and the need to protect workers' rights on the other. While labor rights have traditionally been a central feature of governmental programming in PRC – particularly during the state-planned/state-owned economy – in recent years, workers' rights have been given secondary importance over the need for stability and economic growth. Discrimination against migrant workers in particular has become a widely recognized problem that extends to issues of social exclusion, denial of political participation, and wage discrimination (Xie, 2009).

CHINA'S LOW-WAGE STRATEGY AND RISING LEVELS OF SOCIAL INSTABILITY

China's highly skilled manufacturing labor force has been the foundation on which China's export-led growth and impressive trade performance have been based. To a very considerable extent, it has been kept in place through the coercive power of the state. Indeed, questions arise as to whether China's artificially low wage system enforced through state security systems constitutes a trade subsidy to the extent that it artificially deflates wages for goods that are competing in the international market. The annual assessment process for local Party cadres once again revealed the relative importance given to matters of economic growth, investment, and employment, with significantly less attention paid to working conditions and labor rights. These conflicts over the purpose of labor administration have become particularly acute as China moves closer to full market status.

Factors of institutional location are also evident, as working conditions at productive facilities along China's seacoast remain better than they are in the interior. A major reason for this is the influence of China's accession to the WTO on human rights generally, as well as the relatively higher labor standards in foreign-invested firms that tend to dominate this area. Outside of the major cities and outside of the coastal areas, enforcement of labor rights tends to be more problematic.[34] Factors of institutional location are also evident in the discrimination imposed by local institutions against migrant workers seeking employment or social services (Xie, 2009). These factors of institutional location have begun to be addressed through China's rural development program.[35] However, as with China's current economic stimulus package, the rural development program is heavily dependent on state subsidies and capital investment of uncertain long-term sustainability.

Factors of institutional orientation arise particularly in the context of ideologies around labor organizing and the diminution of class struggle. China's All-China Federation of Trade Unions remains a product of the Party's united-front system, whose objectives are control and pacification of workers rather than their empowerment and advocacy. Hence ACFTU approaches toward collective bargaining and labor dispute resolution tend to focus primarily on processes of negotiation, with little attention paid to independent labor arbitration or litigation. Not surprisingly, survey respondents in Shanghai indicated a relatively low opinion of the effectiveness of the ACFTU's preferred methods of dispute resolution. Moreover, the ACFTU continues to pronounce the importance of Party leadership at a time when many workers have lost faith in the Party's capacity or willingness to protect their interests.

CHINA'S LABOR MARKET STRATEGY: A CONFLICTED POLICY SPACE

China's labor management regime has failed to keep pace with the increasingly capitalistic tendencies of China's socialist market economy. Factors of institutional cohesion are also present particularly in the ways in which employer preferences are validated by Party officials purportedly acting on behalf of trade unions. The role of Party officials as leaders in local trade unions while also being responsible for company profits and being evaluated on economic growth and capital investment puts local officials in a difficult conflict of interest, which tends to marginalize workers' rights. Corruption cases in which local officials have been induced to look the other way in the face of substandard working conditions, repeated failures to pay wages, and other exploitative practices are well known.[36] The emerging and increasingly intense conflicts between worker representatives and representatives from employers and the Party in local trade unions on one side and labor dispute tribunals on the other further indicate that the institutional framework for labor management in China is increasingly fractured. Yet without a meaningful and autonomous process for resolving these differences, institutional cohesion continues to suffer.

At the end of the day, however, China's participation in the changing global landscape linking trade and human rights will depend primarily on the willingness of the Party/State to accept meaningful empowerment of workers and independent civil organizations aimed at improving labor conditions in its industrial relations policy space. For China's new rulers to accept a diminution of their power in order to protect the rights and interests of the Chinese people is a priority at this time and in the future.

REFERENCES

(2004) *Laodong baozhang jiancha tiaoli ji xiangguan wenjian huibian* [Compilation of regulations and associated documents on investigation of labor protections]. Beijing: China Legal Publishers.

(2004b) *Laodong he ji laodong zhengyi chuli shiyong hexin fagui* [Applicable core laws and regulations on labor contracts and the resolution of labor disputes]. Beijing: Foursquare (Fangzhang) Press.

(2008) "Assessing the New Labor Contract Law," *Global Action*, January 11, available at http://globalaction4fairlabor.wordpress.com/2008/01/11/assessing-the-new-china-labor-contract-law-part-i/ (accessed June 25, 2013).

(2010) "Addressing social conflicts," *China Daily*, June 11.

Austrevicius, Petras and Boozman, John. (2006) "China's Development Challenge," *NATO Parliamentary Assembly*. 172 ESCTER 06 E, available at http://www.nato-pa.int/default.asp?SHORTCUT=1001 (accessed June 25, 2013).

Barboza, David. (2008) "Despite a Decade of Criticism, Worker Abuse Persists in China," *New York Times*, January 4, available at http://www.nytimes.com/2008/01/04/business/worldbusiness/04iht-sweatshop.4.9028448.html?pagewanted=2 (accessed June 25, 2013).

Barboza, David and Tabuchi, Hiroko. (2011) "Power Grows for Striking Chinese Workers," *New York Times*, June 8, available at http://www.nytimes.com/2010/06/09/business/global/09labor.html (accessed June 25, 2013).

Cai, Yongshun. (2010) *Collective Resistance in China: Why Popular Protests Succeed and Fail*. Stanford: Stanford University Press.

Chan, Anita. (2001) *China's Workers Under Assault: The Exploitation of Labor in a Globalizing Economy*. New York and London: Armonk and M.E. Sharpe.

Dong, Baohua. (2010) *Shishi laodong fa yinan wenti shendu toushi* [Deep perspectives on difficult issues of implementing labor law]. Beijing: Law Press.

Dyer, Geoff. (2007) "China's Labor Law Raises US Concerns," *Financial Times*, May 2, available at http://www.ft.com/cms/s/0/09d35e16-f8c4-11db-a940-000 b5df10621,dwp_uuid=9c33700c-4c86-11da-89df-0000779e2340.html (accessed June 25, 2013).

Einhorn, Bruce. (2008) "In China, a Winter of Discontent," *Bloomberg Business Week*, January 30.

Han, Jun, ed. (2009) *Zhongguo nongmingong zhanlue wenti yanjiu* [Research on strategic issues of migrant workers in China]. Shanghai: Shanghai Century Press.

Harris, Dan. (2008) "China's New Labor Contract Law. Harmonized Out of Existence?" China Law Blog (Harris and Moure pllc) (Dec. 8, 2008). Retrieved September 11, 2013 from: http://www.chinalawblog.com/2008/12/chinas_new_labor_contract_law_3.html.

Jiang, Guangping. (2010) "Zhongguo gonghui zai ying dui guoji jirong weiji zhong shili weihu gongren quanyi" [China's trade unions work to protect workers rights and interests during the international financial crisis], *Renquan* [Human rights], 1, 37–40.

Jiang, Yue ed. (2009) "Laodong zhe xiangyou pingdeng fuli daiyu" [Workers enjoy equal benefits and treatment], in *Laodong fa: Anli pingxi yu wenti yanjiu* [Labor law: Case analysis and study of issues]. Beijing: China Legal Publshing, pp. 290–296.

Kumiko, Julie K. (2010) *The Problems of Chinese Labor: Problems in the Implementation of Chinese Human rights Obligations*. Xlibris.

Lee, Ching Kwan and Selden, Mark. (2007) "China's Durable Inequality: Legacies of Revolution and Pitfalls of Reform," *Japan Focus*, http://faculty.washington.edu/stevehar/Lee%20and%20Selden.pdf (accessed June 23, 2011).

Lee, Leah and Rudd, Kevin M. (2006) *China's Labor Law Reforms and Its Compliance with ILO Conventions on the Protection of Women*. Canberra: Australian National University Press.

Leiserowitz, Anthony A., Kates, Robert W., and Parris, Thomas M. (2005) "Do Global Attitudes and Behaviours Support Sustainable Development?" *Environment*, 47(9), pp. 31, 33.

Ma, Josephine. (2005) "Wealth Gap Fuelling Instability, Studies Warn," *South China Morning Post*, December 22.

McGregor, Richard. (2006) "Data Show Social Unrest on the Rise in China," *Financial Times*, January 29.

Mulroney, David. (2010) "Speech to Launch Ceremony for Project to Prevent Trafficking for Labour Exploitation in China (CP-TING)," August 16, available at http://www.canadainternational.gc.ca/china-chine/highlights-faits/Labour ExploitationSpeechExploitationdiscours-March2010.aspx?lang=eng%26highlights_file=&left_menu_en=&left_menu_fr=&mission.

Ni, Ching-Ching. (2006) "Wave of Social Unrest Continues Across China," *Los Angeles Times*, August 10.

Peerenboom, Randall. (2007) *China Modernizes: Threat to the West or Model for the Rest?* Oxford: Oxford University Press.

Potter, Pitman B. and Li, Jianyong. (1996) "Regulating Labour Relations on China: The Challenge of Adapting to the Socialist Market Economy," *Les Cahiers de Droit Université Laval Law Review*, 37(3), pp. 753–775.

Santoro, Michael A. (2000) *Profits and Principles: Global Capitalism and Human Rights in China.* Ithaca and London: Cornell University Press.

Selden, Mark. (1993) *The Political Economy of Chinese Development.* New York and London: Armonk and M. E. Sharpe.

Solinger, Dorothy. (2002) "The Cost of China's Entry into WTO," *Asian Wall Street Journal*, January 4.

Sun, Yanbiao. (2008) "Huawei wan ren cizhi shijian yi chengwang shi 'wuxiao shou' bu chengli" [The event of 10,000 Huawei people resigning was a past event and so did not constitute "no point in talking"], *Caijing ribao* [Finance daily], July 22, C5.

Taylor, Andrew. (2005) "China Set to be World's Sweatshop, Report Warns," *Financial Times*, December 9.

Wang, Weiguo, Dai, Zhiqiang, and Zhu, Shaojuan, eds. (2008) *Laodong zhe quanyi baohu zidong shouce* [Voluntary handbook on protection of labor rights and interests]. Beijing: Tsinghua University Press.

Xie, Jianshe. (2009) *Zhongguo nongmingong quanli baozhang* [Safeguarding the rights of migrant workers in China]. Beijing: Social Sciences Academy Press.

Yang, Zhengxi and Lu Huiqin, eds. (2010) *Dangdai laodong fa lilun yu shiwu* [Theory and practice of contemporary labor law]. Guangzhou: Huanan Physics University Press.

Zhou, Wei. (2006) *Zhongguo de laodong jiuye qishi: Falu yu xianshi* [Employment discrimination in China: Law and Reality]. Beijing: Law Press.

Zhu, Guanglei. (2002) *Zhongguo de pin fu chuju yu zhengfu kongzhi* [Wealth disparity and government control in China]. Shanghai: Shanghai Union Press.

15

New Policy Space for Collective Bargaining in China

Sarah Biddulph

INTRODUCTION: CHINA'S INDUSTRIAL RELATIONS REGIME AND INTERNATIONAL LABOR STANDARS

The first decade following China's accession to the World Trade Organization (WTO) in 2001 has seen dramatic reforms to China's economy and increases in the breadth and depth of China's engagement with the international trading order. Many have commented positively on China's engagement with the international trading regime, citing its considerable responsiveness to the dispute resolution panel's rulings.

Yet in some areas, China seems to have resisted and even rebuffed international norms and conventions. Nowhere is this truer than in the regulation of labor rights in collective bargaining. Although China has been an active participant in the International Labour Organization (ILO), it has never shown any intention to ratify the conventions on collective bargaining and freedom of association. These conventions comprise two of the eight core conventions established by the 1998 Declaration on Fundamental Principles and Rights at Work. In her excellent study of China's process of engagement with, and socialization into, the international order, Ann Kent has noted that China's willingness to adopt reforms that would bring it into greater conformity with the international labor regime falters where doing so might be a "threat to the existing political system" (Kent, 2007). This has certainly been the case with the continuing prohibition on the establishment of independent trade unions and, by extension, collective bargaining.

China has been experimenting with the creation of novel industrial relations practices. It has created new domestic policy spaces for change. This model for regulating industrial relations has individualized both labor contracting and dispute resolution at the expense of collective interest representation. Its focus has been on articulating and enforcing legally mandated labor rights. What is missing is a system for the articulation and negotiation of interests, such as wages and work conditions. Collective consultation and contracting does not fulfill this role. The overall weakness of workers' position and accumulated grievances over low wages and the inability to obtain redress for abusive and unlawful employer conduct has inevitably fueled industrial unrest. Major legislative reforms were passed in 2007 and 2008 to address some of the main weaknesses in the existing legal regulatory regime and to provide better protections for workers' rights (Cooney et al., 2007). However, these reforms did not change the existing regulatory structure of industrial relations and so paid little attention to redressing weaknesses in systems of collective consultation and contracting.

This chapter develops the theme of domestic engagement with international trade and human rights norms, and the practical difficulties in creating links between these two bodies of rules. It does so by evaluating the tentative reforms to collective bargaining in China. Collective bargaining is emblematic both of the practical interconnectedness of international trade and rights regimes and China's failure to engage with international standards that are contrary to its fundamental political values. For this reason some argue that without drastic reform of China's political system, there can be no prospect of meaningful reforms to the structure and orientation of China's trade unions or its collective bargaining processes. The first section of the chapter also examines recent tentative reforms to systems of collective consultation over wages and conditions as one of China's policy responses to labor unrest. It considers the extent to which these debates and proposed reforms reveal some domestic policy spaces that might enable the adoption or consideration of reforms that are more consistent with international labor norms. The second section of this essay examines international norms of collective bargaining and the limits of China's engagement with the ILO on this topic. The third section examines China's economic and industrial background that has pushed this question to the forefront of industrial policy debates in the country. It examines the shape and motivation for the current focus on reforming existing Chinese models of collective consultation and contracting. It argues that the primary driver for reform is the state's urgent need to stem the growth of industrial unrest. Consequently, the primary objective of reforms is to promote stability. The final section of this chapter evaluates these reforms and reform proposals and concludes that while there is domestic policy space for reform, it is bounded within existing political orthodoxies about the position and role of China's unions and accepted modes of regulation, which favor approaches led by Party and government agencies. The likely outcome of these factors is that reform of collective consultation may improve mechanisms through which wages and conditions can be negotiated periodically, but they are unlikely to extend to promoting what the international community would consider industrial democracy.

LINKING TRADE AND LABOR AT THE INTERNATIONAL LEVEL: CHINA'S ENGAGEMENT WITH THE ILO ON COLLECTIVE BARGAINING

At a practical level, it is perfectly apparent that labor standards in any particular country have a direct impact on the terms of international trade. This is especially true for China, which has relied on exports as one of its primary mechanisms for economic growth. China's heavy reliance on low-cost exports to drive economic growth has been made possible in part by the low cost of domestic labor (Friedman and Lee, 2010, p. 507; Sharma, 2010). In fact, China has been identified as the economy against which many other economies of the global South compete for exports to countries of the global North, with the risk of precipitating a "race to the bottom" (Chan and Ross, 2003). Many countries have adopted a range of strategies to protect themselves against erosion of their export markets in the face of competition from China (Berik and van der Meulen Rodgers, 2008).

However, at the level of positive international rules, no such connection exists between labor standards and the terms of international trade. The countries of the South have been unwilling to link core labor standards with international trading rules, arguing that the inclusion of a social clause in the WTO agreements is inherently protectionist and designed to deprive low-wage countries of their comparative advantage (WTO Ministerial Conference, 2001). Instead of including a social clause in the WTO agreements, in 1996 the first WTO Ministerial Conference in Singapore affirmed the ILO as the primary agency responsible for promoting observance of "internationally recognized core labour standards."[1] These standards were articulated by the ILO in 1998 with the adoption of the Declaration on Fundamental Principles and Rights at Work (the "Declaration"). They comprise:

- freedom of association[2] and the effective recognition of the right to collective bargaining;[3]
- elimination of all forms of forced or compulsory labor;[4]
- effective abolition of child labor;[5]
- elimination of discrimination in respect of employment and occupation.[6]

The effective legal right to collective bargaining has been identified as a core means of promoting the common welfare and achieving social justice; the basic objective of the ILO. It is premised on "free discussion" and "democratic decision" between the representatives of workers and employers who enjoy equal status with governments.[7] The right of labor to associate freely and engage in collective bargaining has repeatedly been articulated as a core value of the ILO.[8] It is based on the idea that labor must have the power to organize freely and be able to take industrial action supporting bargaining over wages and conditions (Lieberwitz, 2006, pp. 641–653).

China has argued that it is not bound by the conventions on freedom of association and collective bargaining[9] as it has not ratified them.[10] However, the intention of the Declaration was to commit all ILO member states to this list of core labor standards regardless of whether or not they had ratified the relevant conventions (Alston, 2004, p. 460). The ILO's position is that members have agreed to "respect and promote" these core conventions even if they have not ratified them. It states that "the ILO *Declaration on Fundamental Principles and Rights at Work* is an expression of commitment by governments, employers' and workers' organizations to uphold basic human values – values that are vital to our social and economic lives."[11]

CHINA AND THE ILO: INTERNATIONAL LABOR STANDARDS AT BAY

One must also contextualize the debate about the binding nature of these conventions by understanding the ILO's lack of strong punitive mechanisms to enforce compliance.[12] It relies instead primarily on soft law mechanisms of supervision, peer pressure, and assistance to ensure compliance. China has in practice engaged with the ILO on the right to collective bargaining and freedom of association through a number of its mechanisms. The Follow-up mechanism to the Declaration, for example, has focused on encouraging progress toward ratification of these Conventions by asking countries to provide an annual report on domestic implementation of the rights contained in the Conventions that they have not yet ratified.[13] For instance, the ILO's Committee on Freedom of Association has effectively exercised jurisdiction to monitor all member states' compliance with freedom of association and collective bargaining conventions, including China. The Committee has heard a number of cases against China. Despite protestations that it was not bound by the Convention, ultimately China reluctantly agreed to provide information in response to complaints lodged against it.[14]

But, despite active engagement with the ILO in many other areas,[15] China has not indicated any willingness to change its fundamental stance on collective bargaining and freedom of association. In 2001, China ratified the

International Covenant on Economic, Social and Cultural Rights (ICESCR) but again refused to recognize the right of workers to join independent unions of their own choosing. While ratifying the ICESCR, China announced a reservation to the right to establish and join workers' organizations of one's own choosing under Article 8. China declared that the right to join a trade union would be implemented in accordance with Chinese law, more particularly the Constitution of the People's Republic of China, Trade Union Law of the People's Republic of China and Labour Law of the People's Republic of China. Both the Trade Union Law and the All China Federation of Trade Unions Charter emphasize the leadership of the Communist Party of China over the union movement.[16] Unions are required to "assist people's governments in conducting their work and shall uphold the socialist state political power of people's democratic dictatorship."[17]

In light of this international stance, it is important to examine domestic practices of collective contracting and recent debates arguing the need for significant changes both to the role and responsibilities of China's unions and to the system of collective contracting. To contextualize this discussion, this chapter briefly examines the current issues facing regulation of the labor market and the nature of collective contracting.

COLLECTIVE BARGAINING IN CHINA: ENTERPRISE UNIONS AND COLLECTIVE CONTRACTS

China's labor market has undergone dramatic transformation since the mid-1980s when the first steps were taken away from the previous administrative system of allocating urban workers to state-owned enterprises to a now more market-based labor contract system. The PRC Labour Law codified a regime of labor regulations governed primarily by individual labor contracts, supplemented by a system of collective contracts (Biddulph and Cooney, 1994, pp. 254–258). Collective contracts were to be negotiated and signed by the enterprise union and the employer. The All China Federation of Trade Unions has actively sought to expand coverage of collective contracts, even though this has required the assistance of a range of state and Party agencies to achieve this goal.[18] Moreover, China ratified ILO Convention 144 in 1990 and established a system of tripartite consultation.[19] Since the establishment of the tripartite meeting system in 2001, expanding the scope of collective contracts has been a main priority (Chen, 2010, p. 107; Clarke et al., 2004, p. 240). According to the press release issued after the 15th National Congress of Trade Unions held in October 2008, more than 140 million Chinese workers were then covered by a collective contract (M. Li, 2008; IHLO, 2009). Reports suggest that by the end of 2010, employees had entered into labor contracts in more than 97 percent of national-level enterprises and 65 percent of small-scale enterprises (Anonymous, 2010).

In terms of numbers, this looks like a very successful outcome. However, collective contracts have not been an effective vehicle for interest negotiations at the enterprise level. In practice, top-down administrative mechanisms such as quotas and instructions issued by the Party, government, and higher-level union organizations have been used to expand the reach of collective contracts.[20] As a result, many only reflect the minimum legal standards without the parties engaging in any form of bargaining over wages and conditions (Clarke et al., 2004, pp. 249–250). A fundamental problem rests with the enterprise union, with the union head often also being appointed by, and having a role in, enterprise management. These unions are neither able nor motivated to represent the interests of workers in negotiations, particularly if these interests conflict with the interests of the Party government policy or of the specific enterprise (Chen, 2010, pp. 107–108; Clarke et al., 2004, p. 242; Liu, 2010, pp. 35–36). In fact, many enterprise unions are the last to find out about strikes or other forms of industrial action. They then seek to mediate between the workers and management to secure a return to work. Seldom do they see their role as acting on behalf of workers and promoting their claims (Chen, 2010).

THE MAGNITUDE OF WORKER DISCONTENT

There is a huge distance between Chinese systems of collective consultation and a system of collective bargaining required by the ILO Conventions that speak of "free and voluntary negotiations" between independent representatives of both workers and employers to "set wages and conditions of work" and the "rules governing their relationship" (ILO, 2010). Part of the problem is that union representatives form elements of enterprise management, but the fundamental problem lies with the relationship between the union movement and the Chinese Communist Party. Rather than simply representing workers' interests, China's unions fulfill the important role of linking the Party and workers to obtain worker acceptance of Party programs (Harper, 1969, pp. 85–89; Howell, 2008, pp. 846–847).[21] All unions in China must be incorporated within the official federated union organization, the All China Federation of Trade Unions. It remains illegal to set up a union outside of the official union organization, and those who have attempted to do so have been severely punished (Walder and Gong, 1993; Chan, 1993; *China Labour Bulletin*, August 28, 2008).

The monopoly enjoyed by the All China Federation of Trade Unions over union organization comes at the cost of subordination to the Party in terms of both organization and policy (White et al., 1996, pp. 40–41). Unions thus owe a dual loyalty to "safeguard the concrete interests of the Chinese workers" but to do so while "safeguarding the overall interests of the people throughout the country . . . [and to] strive for the realization of China's socialist modernization" (All China Federation of Trade Unions, 2007). In the reform era, unions have been responsible for obtaining workers' cooperation in improving productivity and contributing positively to economic reform, often subordinating their responsibility to represent workers' interests.[22] Diversification and fragmentation of the workforce and the increasing power of enterprises and management have exacerbated this problem (White et al., 1996, pp. 45–46).

DOMESTIC PRESSURES FOR REFORM: LABOR UNREST AND THE 2008 FINANCIAL CRISIS

The onset of the Great Recession of 2008 not only challenged implementation of new models for regulating industrial relations, particularly between the first quarter of 2008 and the third quarter of 2009 (Yang, 2009); it also highlighted the extent to which China's economic growth had become reliant on exports and had become interdependent within global markets (Yu, 2010). A 4 trillion yuan stimulus package introduced in November 2008 for the years 2009 and 2010 alleviated the worst impacts of the crisis on China's domestic economy (Fu and Si, 2008). But it also highlighted the need to take further steps to reduce reliance on exports as the drivers of economic growth and the need to readjust China's economy to boost domestic consumption. Programs were put in place at the time to reduce the impact of the Great Recession on enterprises. These include: temporarily freezing the minimum wage (*Yang*, December 14, 2009; Friedman and Lee, 2010, p. 528; Liu, 2010, p. 49), strengthening the union's role in assisting enterprises in difficulty as a result of the Great Recession to forestall employee layoffs and preserve social stability (Pan, 2008), and transforming collective contracts into a device for increasing workplace flexibility and risk sharing.

Public attention was focused by a number of well-publicized violent mass protests in 2008 and 2009, such as the protest by workers in July 2009 against the takeover of the Tonghua Iron and Steel Group in Jilin, which ended in a senior manager being beaten to death (Canaves, 2009); a large-scale protest against job losses at the Baoding Yimian Cotton Mill and a subsequent march of more than 1,000 workers toward Beijing in April 2009 (IHLO, 2009); and the strike by taxi drivers in a number of cities in November 2008 (Branigan, 2008).

There were dramatic increases in strikes, street protests, mass petitions, and labor-related litigation, which in Guangdong accounted for 38 percent of all protests in 2008. In 2010, a spate of suicides at Foxconn and protracted strikes at several Hondaautoparts factories in Guangdong attracted worldwide attention (BBC News, March 28, 2010). The difficulty for China is that the increase in labor disputes, especially large public protests, not only signals systemic problems with China's industrial relations system, but also raises fears about the potential for this unrest to lead to broader social and political instability (Li, 1999; Chung et al., 2006).

The 2008 financial crisis did not usher in radical changes to industrial relations policy. It did help focus attention on the need to speed up economic readjustment and heightened political sensitivity to the impacts on social stability of industrial disruption. If anything, the protection of social stability has recently been raised to the highest administrative level. A central focus of the 2011 National People's Congress meeting was "stability protection" and "social management," with allocation of massive funding to support the establishment of the institutional infrastructure, including stability preservation committees, to support these programs (Lam, 2011).

The state has adopted a range of strategies to deal with the problems of increasing industrial unrest. These include law reform to deal with some of the worst failings of the current legal regulatory regime, improving the minimum wage, and reexamining the role that collective consultation and collective contracts might play in promoting industrial stability. The renewed focus on reinvigorating collective consultation must thus be understood in the context of this official preoccupation with controlling social and political instability.

REEXAMINING THE ROLE OF UNIONS AND COLLECTIVE CONSULTATION: SOME MODEST REFORMS

To cope with this ongoing unrest, China has encouraged unions to take a more active role in protecting workers' rights to prevent them from becoming completely irrelevant to workers. From the mid-2000s on, the All China Federation of Trade Unions has adopted a range of policies that advocate strengthening their representation and protection of workers' rights (Howell, 2008, p. 847; Zhu et al., 2011; China Labour Bulletin, 2008) issuing the Blue Paper on the Role of Chinese Trade Unions in Safeguarding the Legitimate Rights and Interests of the Workers (the "Blue Paper") in 2007 and amending the All China Federation of Trade Unions Constitution in 2008.[23] The Blue Paper emphasized expanding collective contracts and improving the processes of collective consultation, particularly with respect to wages, as a way of protecting the rights of workers. The All China Federation of Trade Unions' interpretation of rights protection is inextricably linked to maintaining stability as rights protection is understood as being protection of the right to participate in the benefits of economic reform and development for the purpose of promoting stable labor relations.[24]

The Party and union focus on industrial stability, and their understandings of how this stability might be achieved establishes the outer boundaries within which collective contracting reforms are taking place. The focus is on preventing disputes entirely, or resolving them in the early stages of bargaining. Stability understood as an absence of disputes imposes limits on the extent to which industrial action taken in pursuit of collective bargaining can be tolerated or accepted. While the ILO advocates collective bargaining as a way of "stabilizing industrial relations" (ILO, 2010), many in China have argued that collective bargaining would lead to more strikes and other forms of industrial disruption.

Contrarily, there are those who acknowledge that there is presently no regularized mechanism for negotiation of interest-based claims. With the possible exception of a small number of individuals with very strong bargaining power, individual labor contracts generally do not provide an adequate mechanism for negotiating periodic pay increases or other periodic improvements in working conditions. Since the Ministry of Human Resources and Social Security issued the Minimum Wage Regulations in 2004, increasing the minimum wage has been one mechanism used to improve the conditions of China's lowest-paid workers. In recent years many provincial governments have significantly increased the minimum wage.

The Communist Party of China's 12th Five Year Economic and Social Development Plan launched in March 2011.[25] However, there is doubt over whether raising the minimum wage can effectively address the problem of labor instability (Su, 2011). It certainly cannot substitute for negotiating interest-based claims, a function that in theory may be served by collective bargaining. A constrained policy space has developed to tackle this issue and prevent industrial unrest by exploring ways collective consultation and collective contracts may be reformed.

REINVIGORATING COLLECTIVE CONSULTATION AND CONTRACTING: NEW INITIATIVES

The system of collective contracts has been in place for a number of years, with trade unions authorized to conclude collective contracts with the employer at enterprise level in the 1992 Trade Union Law.[26] The system of collective contracts was formally established in articles 33–35 of the PRC Labour Law in 1994,[27] but it was not until 2004 that detailed provisions governing collective contracts were passed in the Provisions on Collective Contracts.[28] These provisions are effective to the extent they are not superseded by provisions of the 2007 Labour Contract Law, which sketches a regulatory system for collective contracts. While the primary model of collective consultation and contracting is at enterprise level, Article 53 authorizes industry- and regional-level collective contracts to be concluded at the county level. This provision provides legislative authorization for an experimental policy mandating the conclusion of industry-level collective contracts primarily in Zhenjiang. This type of collective contract has been used primarily to fix wage rates and to provide for periodic wage increases. This type of collective contracting has been concentrated in sectors such as construction, mining, textiles, food, security, service, and the taxi industry, where there are many small or medium-sized privately owned enterprises without enterprise unions in a particular district (Xinhua Web, June 4, 2010). In these situations, regional unions have organized trade-based union associations to represent workers in the same industry and to negotiate with local employers' associations to fix common wage standards and working conditions (Liu, 2010, pp. 44–47).

CHALLENGING THE ENTERPRISE UNION MODEL

One of the best-known illustrations of this form of collective negotiation is the Wenling model of tripartite collective bargaining in the woollen knitwear industry in Xinhe township, Wenling. The industry comprises a large number of mostly small-scale local family-run enterprises. Because of the seasonal nature of the work, employers took a range of draconian measures, including non-payment of wages, to ensure workers did not leave during the busy season. This resulted in widespread industrial disruptions including strikes, work slowdowns, and mass petitioning to higher levels. Collective consultation was initiated as a way of responding to this unrest. A collective agreement was ultimately concluded between the Changyu knitwear industry union and the Xinhe town industry association 2002 (Wen, 2011, pp. 116–117). The successful conclusion of this agreement depended very much on active support by the Xinhe Party Committee and the local government. This type of industry-level agreement has been embraced by top political levels as a model to be adopted nationwide.[29] Such forms of collective agreement are expanding, with reports that in January 2010, 200,000 industrial or regional collective contracts and 417,000 collective contracts involving wage collective bargaining had been concluded, covering 51.1 million employees (Juan, 2010).

This type of agreement has the advantage of bypassing the enterprise union, or enabling negotiations to take place where there are a large number of nonunionized workplaces. One major attraction of this model for China is that it was seen as effectively resolving serious problems of labor unrest, including strikes and petitioning. Despite the positive evaluation of this form of collective wage negotiations, there is some evidence that the outcomes for participants have not been as good as claimed. Eli Friedman's extensive work on sector-level collective contracts in nearby Rui'an suggests that neither workers nor individual enterprises had input during the negotiations and that the labor disputes had not been resolved despite the collective agreement. He also concluded that to the extent industry agreements in Zhejiang have been effective, this success has been heavily dependent on the specific provincial mode of development. This calls into question the capacity of extending this model of collective contracting nationwide (Friedman, 2011).

FROM COLLECTIVE CONSULTATION TO AUTONOMOUS COLLECTIVE BARGAINING: SOME GREEN SHOOTS

In Shenzhen and Guangdong, senior government officials have been more willing to use the language of collective bargaining occasionally instead of the more commonly employed term "collective consultation." In 2008, the Shenzhen Congress Standing Committee issued the Shenzhen Measures on Implementing the PRC Trade Union Law, which provided that collective bargaining rather than collective consultation would be the core focus of union work. In a speech at the promulgation of the Measures, the head of the legal department of the municipal union, Zhang Youquan, asserted that the use of the term "collective bargaining" reflected the objective reality that there is a conflict of interest between labor and capital in Shenzhen. He maintained that such a provision better reflects the actual labor environment in Shenzhen, which has a high proportion of foreign investment enterprises and small and medium-sized privately owned enterprises (Li et al., 2008, p. 5). This language was taken up at the central level when Song Xiaowu, the head of the National Economic Reform Research Committee and member of the Chinese Communist Party Central Committee, stated in March 2010 that a system of collective bargaining should be introduced into state-owned enterprises and that the equal status of the unions in the bargaining process should be guaranteed (Anonymous, 2010).

What are we to make of these calls to institute a system of collective bargaining? At the moment it is difficult to determine whether the government is just being patronizing (Zheng, 2010, p. 27). There are signs of willingness in some regions to reform the existing system of negotiating collective contracts toward permitting more vigorous forms of collective consultation to take place, particularly in Shenzhen and Guangdong. There are also signs of resistance to more radical reforms.

In the absence of a more comprehensive national law on collective consultation, some tentative steps have been taken at the local level to legislate for measures that strengthen union responsiveness to the workers they are supposed to represent and to facilitate collective negotiations.[30] In the Shenzhen regulations, for example, these include setting up a system of direct election of union leadership[31] and prohibiting the enterprise management personnel from occupying leadership positions in the union. Such personnel include the legal representative, general and deputy general manager, cadres with equivalent positions, responsible people in the personnel department, or any relatives of these categories of person working in the same enterprise (article 11(3)). These provisions are a significant departure from the weak provisions in the Trade Union Law on management representation in the enterprise union.[32]

Draft local regulations in both Shenzhen and Guangdong, such as the Shenzhen Labour Relations Collective Consultation Regulations and the Guangdong Regulations on the Democratic Management of Enterprises, propose to go even further to facilitate a more robust form of collective negotiation. The draft Guangdong regulations even suggest that there may be some circumstances where strikes and other forms of industrial action would be permissible in the process of negotiating a collective contract if the employer delays or obstructs wage negotiations (draft 3, article 51). Still, the draft regulations themselves contain provisions indicating that implementation will continue to be dependent on support and enforcement by local government agencies. These reform proposals have faced intense opposition and lobbying from Hong Kong and from international industry representatives. As a result, the regulations have not yet been passed (Chen, 2010).

THE POSSIBILITY FOR POLICY SPACE INNOVATION: WHAT TYPE? HOW MEANINGFUL?

These proposed reforms indicate a willingness of local governments to facilitate more robust forms of collective negotiation. That being said, without fundamental changes to China's unions, or reforms that enable the enterprise unions to be bypassed in the process of collective bargaining, the impact of these proposals will be limited. Those advocating reform from within the existing system discuss ways of strengthening union accountability to workers and the centrality of union rights protection work. However, these cannot be seen as radical policy proposals for reforming the system, as unions would merely be performing the role allocated to them by the Party.

Reforms to collective contracting remain bounded by prohibitions on independent labor organizations. As a result, calls to strengthen collective consultation and collective contracting will continue to rely heavily on the support and participation of local governments and Party organizations.[33] Rather than introduce reforms that bring Chinese models of collective consultation closer to the international standards, ongoing reforms have sought to bypass or minimize impediments in the existing industrial landscape. These hardly constitute radical changes to China's traditional policies. Such reforms draw on established regulatory patterns to achieve their objectives. These include coordinated action by the Party, government, labor departments courts, and the union hierarchy. An examination of the recent innovations in collective contracting such as the Wenling model of industry-wide collective consultation reveals that their success depended very much on the initiative and support of the local Party and government.

The tentative steps toward strengthening the processes of collective consultation, although framed as "rights protection," are most readily understood as a way of reducing labor disputes and achieving the more modest goal of enabling workers to participate in the benefits of economic and social development to the extent and in the ways determined by Party policy. The willingness to use collective contracts during the financial crisis of 2008 to shore up the profitability of enterprises through temporarily freezing wage increases and introducing risk-sharing measures, demonstrates that collective contracts are not inevitably understood as a mechanism for improving worker's wages and conditions. Policy space remains embryonic. Although there are some green shoots, much more needs to be done. Collective bargaining in modern China may be harnessed for other purposes when considered necessary. It reveals a particular state-centered view of social justice, one that is provided by the state, in contrast to the more decentered view of social justice advocated by the ILO, which emphasizes the priority of workers' agency in negotiating and securing decent working conditions.

REFERENCES

All China Federation of Trade Unions (2007) "A Brief Introduction of the All-China Federation of Trade Unions."

Alston, Philip (2004) "Core Labour Standards and the Transformation of the International Labour Rights Regime," *European Journal of International Law* 15: 457–521.

Anonymous (2010a) "Perfect the System of Collective Bargaining: Give Full Play to the Role of the Unions," *China County Economic News*, March 15, 4, available at http://www.xyshjj.cn/bz/xyjj/sib/201003/40260.html, accessed September 11, 2013.

Anonymous (2010b) "Yuji Nianmo Quanguo Guo Guomo Yishang Qiye Laodong Hetong Qianding Lv da 97%" ["It Is Expected That by the End of the Year Over 97% of National Scale Enterprises Will Have Signed Labor Contracts"] available at http://finance.sina.com.cn/g/20101230/12219187021.shtml, accessed September 11, 2013.

BBC News (2010) "Foxconn Suicides: Workers Feel Quite Lonely," March 28. http://www.bbc.co.uk/news/10182824, accessed September 8, 2013.

Berik, Gunseli and van der Meulen Rodgers, Yana (2008) "The Debate on Labour Standards and International Trade: Lessons from Cambodia and Bangladesh." Working Paper No 2007–03, *Department of Economics Working Paper Series University of Utah*, January.

Biddulph, Sarah and Cooney, Sean (1994) "Regulation of Trade Unions in the People's Republic of China," *Melbourne University Law Review* 19: 253–292.

Branigan, Tania (2008) "China Taxi Drivers Strike as Economic Unrest Spreads," *The Guardian*, November 24, available at www.theguardian.com/world/2008/nov/24/china-taxis, accessed September 10, 2013.

Canaves, Sky (2009) "Chinese Steelworkers Fight Privatization Effort," *Wall Street Journal*, July 27, available at http://online.wsj.com/article/SB124863589915981859.html, accessed September 10, 2013.

Chan, Anita (1993) "Revolution or Corporatism: China's Workers and Trade Unions in Post-Mao China," *The Australian Journal of Chinese Affairs* 29: 31–61.

Chan, Anita and Ross, Robert (2003) "Racing to the Bottom: International Trade without a Social Clause," *Third World Quarterly* 24: 1011–1128.

Chang, Gansheng (2004) "Zuzhi Qilai, Qieshi Weiquan" ["Get Organized, Conscientiously Protect Rights"], *Gonghui Bolan [Labor Union Expo]* 11: 6–7.

Chen, Feng (2010) "Trade Unions and the Quadripartite Interactions in Strike Settlement in China," *The China Quarterly* 102: 104–124.

Chen, Xiaowei (2010) "The Draft Shenzhen Collective Consultation Regulations: Stop the Minimum Wage Standard Becoming the Highest," East Money, available at http://finance.eastmoney.com/news/ 1350,2010092797798072.html, accessed September 11, 2013.

China Labor News Translations (2008) "Collective Wage Consultation: A Breakthrough for Resolving Labor Disputes in Wenling Zhejiang," *China Business Report*, October 10.

China Labour Bulletin (2008) "Founder of Independent Trade Union Released from Prison." Available at http://www.clb.org.hk/en/content/founder-independent-trade-union-released-prison, accessed September 10, 2013.

China Labour Bulletin (2008) "The Case of China: The Challenge of Labour Unrest in a Communist-Run Capitalist Economy," available at http://www.clb.org.hk/en, accessed September 6, 2013.

Chung, Jae Ho, Lai, Hongyi, and Xia, Ming (2006) "Mounting Challenges to Governance in China: Surveying Collective Protestors, Religions Sects and Criminal Organizations," *The China Journal* 56: 1–31.

Clarke, Simon, Lee, Chang-Hee, and Li, Qi (2004) "Collective Consultation and Industrial Relations in China," *British Journal of Industrial Relations* 42: 235–254.

Cooney, Sean (1999) "Testing Times for the ILO: Institutional Reform for the New International Political Economy," *Comparative Labor Law and Policy Journal* 20: 365–399.

Cooney, Sean, Biddulph, Sarah, Li, Kungang, and Zhu, Ying (2007) "China's New Labour Contract Law: Responding to the Growing Complexity of Labour Relations in the PRC," *University of New South Wales Law Journal* 30: 786–801.

Elliott, Kimberley (2000) "The ILO and Enforcement of Core Labor Standards," International Economics Policy Briefs, available at http://www.iie.com/publications/pb/pb00-6.pdf, accessed September 10, 2013.

Friedman, Eli (2011) "Economic Development and Sectoral Unions in China: The Cases of Guangdong and Zhejiang," *Comparative Chinese Labour Studies Conference*, 1–51.

Friedman, Eli and Lee, Ching Kwan (2010) "Remaking the World of Chinese Labour: A 30 Year Retrospective," *British Journal of Industrial Relations* 48: 507–533.

Fu, Jing and Si, Tingting (2008) "NDRC Reveals Details of Stimulus Package," China Daily, November 27, available at www.chinadaily.com.cn/business/2008-11/27/content_72467, accessed September 7, 2013.

Harper, Paul (1969) "The Party and Unions in Communist China," *The China Quarterly* 37: 84–119.

Howell, Jude (2008) "The All-China Federation of Trade Unions Beyond Reform? Slow March of Direct Elections," *The China Quarterly* 196: 845–863.

IHLO (2009) "Baoding Workers' Rally: Harbinger of a Long March?" available at http://www.ihlo.org/LRC/WC/210409f.html, accessed September 11, 2013.

IHLO (2009) "Updates to Collective Bargaining and Collective Contracts: New Laws – Same Deal?"available at http://www.ihlo.org/LRC/ACFTU/040309.html, accessed September 12, 2013.

International Labour Organization (2010) "Collective Bargaining," available at http://www.ilo.org/public/english/dialogue/themes/cb.htm, accessed September 19, 2013.

Juan, Shen (ed.) (2010) "The Majority of Enterprises of Provincial Level and Above Scale Have a Labor Contract Signing Rate of over 90%," *The National People's Congress of the People's Republic of China*, 16–17, available at www.npc.gov.cn/npc/zt/qt/ldhtfsslzn/2010-03/02/content_1546872.htm, accessed September 11, 2013.

Kent, Ann (2007) *Beyond Compliance: China, International Organizations, and Global Security*. Stanford, CA: Stanford University Press.

Lam, Willy (2011) "Beijing's Blueprint for Tackling Mass Incidents and Social Management," *China Brief* 11: 3–5.

Li, Ma (ed.) (2008) "1.091 Million Collective Contracts Signed Nationally; 140 Million People Covered," China Network, October 7, http://www.china.com.cn/gonghui/2008-10/07/content_16577631.html, accessed September 11, 2013.

Li, Wei (1999) "Ruhe Yufang he Kongzhi Qunzong Jiti Shangfang" ["How to Prevent and Control the Masses Engaging in Collective Petitioning"], *Mishu zhi You [The Secretary's Friend]*, 34–35.

Li, Wei, Chen, Xiaowei, Shi, Xisheng, and Liu, Yan (2008) "Gonghui Jiang Daibiao Zhigong Jiti Tanpan" ["The Union to Represent Workers in Collective Bargaining"], *Shenzhen Shangbao [Shenzhen Business News]*, July 31, 5.

Lieberwitz, Risa (2006) "Linking Trade and Labour Standards: Prioritizing the Right of Association," *Cornell International Law Journal* 38: 641–653.

Liu, Mingwei (2010) "Union Organizing in China: Still a Monolithic Labor Movement?" *Industrial and Labor Relations Review* 64: 30–52.

No author (2010) "Guangzhou: Disputes between Labour and Capital Have Become the Primary Factor Affecting Social Stability," available at http://acftu.people.com .cn/GB/11177287.html, accessed September 11, 2013.

Pan, Yue (2008) "Vigorously Implement the 'Mutually Agreed Action' between Trade Unions, Enterprises and Employees to Promote Unity and to Mobilize the Broad Masses of Workers to Contribute to Stable and Rapid Economic Development," The National People's Congress of the People's Republic of China, available at http://www.npc.gov.cn/npc/xinwen/syxw/2008-12/30/content_1465498.htm, accessed September 11, 2013.

Sharma, Ruchir (2010) "The Post-China World: The End of the Boom Is Now in Sight, and the Ripple Effects of Slower Growth Will Span the Globe." Newsweek, June 20. Available at http://www.thedailybeast.com/newsweek/2010/06/20/the-post-chin, accessed September 10, 2013.

Su, Zhenhua (2011) "Tigao Zuidi Gongzi Bushi 'Wengong' Hao Banfa" ["Raising the Minimum Wage Is Not a Good Way to 'Stabilize the Workforce'"]. Xinwen Zaobao [Morning News], available at http://finance.ifeng.com/job/xshq/20110121/3269954. shtml, accessed September 13, 2013.

Walder, Andrew and Gong, Xiaoxia (1993) "Workers in the Tiananmen Protests: The Politics of the Beijing Workers' Autonomous Federation," *The Australian Journal of Chinese Affairs* 29: 1–29.

Wang, Min (2008) "China's Unions Revise Their Constitution to Expand Their Protection of the Rights and Interests of Migrant Workers," Xinhua Web, available at http://news.xinhuanet.com/newscenter/2008-10/21/content_10229720.htm, accessed September 11, 2013.

Wang, Quanbao (2011) "Chuanguo Zongonghui 'Yi Wequan Lai Weiwen'" ["All China Federation of Trade Unions : Protecting Stability by Protecting Rights"]. *China Newsweek* 4: 20–21.

Wen, Xiaoyi (2011) "Jiti Tanpan de Neibu Guojia Jizhi: Yi Wenling Yangmaoshan Hangye Gongjia Jiti Tanpan Weili" ["The Internal State Mechanisms in Collective Bargaining: Evidence from the Collective Bargaining by Wenling Sweater Industry"], *Shehui [Society]* 1: 112–130.

White, Gordon, Howell, Jude, and Shang, Xiaoyuan (1996) *In Search of Civil Society: Market Reform and Social Change in Contemporary China*. Oxford: Clarendon Press.

WTO Ministerial Conference (2001) "Doha WTO Ministerial 2001: Briefing Notes."

Xinhua Web (2010) "The All China Federation of Trade Unions Responds to This Reporter's Questions on Implementation of the Rainbow Programme," Xinhua News Agency, June 4, available at http://news.xinhuanet.com/politics/2010-06/04/c_ 12181248.htm, accessed September 11, 2013.

Yang, Lin (2009a) "2009 Background to Conflicts Between Labour and Capital: The Global Financial Crisis," Sina. available at http://news.sina.com.cn/c/sd/2009-12-14/094219255581_2.shtml, accessed September 11, 2013.

Yang, Lin (2009b) "Zhuazhu Zhongxin Shen shi Laozi Geju, Xiaochu Laozi Mao-dunZhe Yinchong, Tiaozheng Laogong Zhengci de Jihui" ["Seize the Opportunity to Reevaluate Labor Relations, Eliminate Potential Labor Problems, and Reformulate Labor Policy"], Liaowang, available at http://www.gmsh.org.cn/news/view.asp?id=19701, accessed September 11, 2013.

Yu, Yongding (2010) "China's Response to the Global Financial Crisis," East Asia Forum, available at http://www.eastasiaforum.org/2010/01/24/chinas-response-to-the-global-financial-crisis/, accessed September 11, 2013.

Zhang, Wuchang (2010) "Gongzi jiti xieshang geng rongyi daozhì bagong shi yanzhong huohai" ["Collective wage negotiations are more likely to lead to strikes – it will be a serious disaster"], available at http://expert.bossline.com/1551/viewspace-%2019226, September 11, 2013.

Zheng, Guanghuai (2010) "Laogong Quanyi yu Anfuxing Guojia – Yi ZhuJiang San-jjiao Zhou Nongmingong Weili" ["Workers' Rights and Interests and the Appeasing State – Migrant Workers in the Pearl River Delta Region as an Example"], *Kaifang Shidai* [*Open Times*], pp 27–38. Available http://caod.oriprobe.com/articles/23927631/The_Rights_of_Labor_and_the_Propitiatory_State.htm, accessed September 12, 2013.

Zhu, Ying, Warner, Malcolm, and Feng, Tongqing (2011) "Employment Relations 'with Chinese Characteristics': The Role of Trade Unions in China," *International Labour Review* 150: 127–143.

16

Industrial Relations in Post-Transition China: The Challenges of Inequality and Social Conflict

Chang-Hee Lee

INTRODUCTION: A NEW ERA FOR EMPLOYMENT RELATIONS?

In China, the 2000s have witnessed rapid building of institutions of industrial relations – particularly trade union memberships, collective bargaining coverage and tripartite consultation mechanisms – as part of the Party-state's concerted response to the social crisis arising from the painful transition of employment relations in the 1990s. The Party-state's political imperative of maintaining social harmony and stability has driven these initiatives. Although trade unions generally remain ineffective, there is evidence that unions with better governance structures designed to channel workers' collective voices (e.g., workers' congress and collective bargaining) are likely to produce positive effects on working conditions. However, the "collective voice" face of unions is likely to be limited or altered by the "Party" face of unions at the enterprise level and beyond.

Employment relations and industrial relations in China have undergone a tremendous transformation as part of the transition to a market economy. The year 2008 marked the thirtieth anniversary of economic reform (1978–2008). That year China introduced a series of high-profile pieces of labor and social legislation; these included the Labour Contract Law, the Employment Promotion Law, and the Labour Dispute Mediation and Arbitration Law, which was later followed by Social Insurance Law in 2010. The introduction of these laws signals that China is entering a new phase of economic and social development.

Changes in the 2000s are not confined to the labor law regime. China has accelerated the building of industrial relations institutions, a unique policy space for the workplace. Developments include the creation of tripartite consultation bodies from central down to district levels, the promotion of collectives, and union organizing campaigns. As a result, China has seen an unusual growth of collective agreements of various kinds during the last decade, although there are serious doubts about their quality and process. Considering that the concept of collective bargaining was virtually unknown in China until the early 1990s, this is still an impressive development.

At the same time, however, labor conflicts of various forms (whether formal complaints to the arbitration councils, wildcat strikes, or street protests) both within and outside the formal labor relations system also have seen an explosive growth since the 1990s. The fact that labor protests have grown alongside collective agreements indicates that the institution-building exercise undertaken by the official industrial relations actors may not necessarily lead to the institutionalization of the workers' collective voice and thus fail at producing the desired effects of social harmony.

This chapter attempts to offer an overview of industrial relations and collective bargaining developments since the early 1990s. In the following section this essay describes the political, economic, and social context of these industrial relations developments. In the third section key features of the emerging industrial relations regime in China are analyzed, including the political imperatives behind industrial relations developments, the new legal framework of industrial relations, tripartism, employers' organizations, and finally recent union organizing campaigns. The fourth section offers an overview of collective bargaining and analysis of a new attempt to develop coordinated bargaining in interaction with the government policy framework. This section also contains a preliminary attempt to examine the effectiveness of union governance and collective bargaining in improving working conditions at the workplace. The concluding section summarizes major findings.

INDUSTRIAL RELATIONS AND COLLECTIVE BARGAINING IN CHINA: A TIME OF TESTING

The 2000s have witnessed a sudden surge of concerted efforts to introduce and expand new industrial relations practices. This move can be understood properly against the social upheavals caused by China's move to a market economy on an unprecedented scale and at an unprecedented pace for the last thirty years. The economic reforms have turned China, once in complete isolation from the global trading system, into the third-largest economy in the world. The economic growth of the past thirty years enabled China to reduce poverty on the largest scale and at the fastest pace in world history. The economic transformation has also brought sweeping changes to social and economic structures:

1. While the urbanization rate was only 17.8 percent in 1978, it surpassed the 50 percent mark in 2011. In 1978, 71 percent of the total work-force worked in the agricultural sector. This number had decreased to less than 50 percent in 2005, and secondary and tertiary industry accounted for around 20 percent and 30 percent of the workforce, respectively.

2. In 1978, virtually all workers worked in the public sector, whether in urban state-owned enterprises (SOEs) or on rural collective farms. In 2005, more than 80 percent of workers worked in a nonpublic sector, including household farmers who made up 47 percent of the total work-force.

In the 1980s, economic reforms produced benefits for the entire population, reviving rural economies, narrowing urban-rural gaps, and lifting the majority of the population out of poverty without producing clear losers in the process (Naughton, 2007). However, as China's economic growth became increasingly dependent on the urban export sectors during the 1990s, the economic reforms reached the crucial stage of affecting public enterprises in urban areas. It was here that the economic reforms began to produce clear winners and losers in Chinese society, generating high social tensions.

GROWING INEQUALITY AND DECLINING WAGE SHARE OF GDP FOR CHINESE WORKERS

Over the last thirty years, China has become one of the most unequal societies from being one of the most equal (albeit equally poor) societies. In 2005, China's Gini coefficient reached 0.46, surpassing India and the Philippines, which were known for their extreme degree of unequal distribution of incomes.

After a brief period of rural economic revival in the early years of the economic reforms in the 1980s, the rural economy lagged far behind the urban economy. As a result, the urban-rural per capita income ratio has become 3.33 to 1 in 2007, worse than 2.6 to 1 in 1978. The ratio of GDP per capita of the richest to the poorest province grew from 7.3 to 1 in 1990 to 13 to 1 in 2003.

Overall, it is believed that real wage growth for workers – particularly those with low skills – lagged behind overall productivity gains and GDP growth. As a result, the wage share of GDP has declined from 52 percent in 1999 to 40 percent in 2007, while the private consumption declined from 47 percent to 37 percent of the GDP during the same period.

A host of factors are at work in the widening of income gaps and the declining wage share of GDP. These include government policy initiatives favoring urban industrialization geared toward export-oriented economic development at the expense of the rural population; a decentralized fiscal policy regime that penalizes underdeveloped localities; artificial barriers between rural and urban labor markets, which put rural workers in a disadvantaged position to urban workers; and unbalanced bargaining power between employers and workers.

The growing income/wage gaps and the rapidly declining wage share of GDP have become one of top concerns of the country's political leadership and policy makers for two reasons. First, the declining wage share lies at the heart of the country's economic imbalance. The slow wage growth has led to much slower private consumption growth relative to the overall economic expansion in China, causing a continuous decline in the share of consumption in GDP, which in turn has led to a rising dependence on export and investment as drivers for the country's growth. A consequence of this is the possibility of global trade conflicts with major trading partners. Second, the widening income/wage gaps, if unchecked, can threaten social cohesion and stability.

THE RECENT EXPLOSION OF SOCIAL CONFLICTS AND LABOR DISPUTES POST-FINANCIAL CRISIS

Along with greater disparity undermining sustainable economic development, China has witnessed an explosive growth in social conflicts – labor disputes in particular – over the last two decades. The incidences of "collective protests" of various natures rose to 60,000 in 2003 from around 10,000 in 1993.[1] The fact that labor-related protests accounted for 46.9 percent of all collective protests in 2003 clearly demonstrates that labor issues have become a major source for social tension and conflict in China. The number of labor disputes referred to local arbitration councils across China has also grown dramatically, as shown in Table 16.1. The growth rate of labor disputes was somewhere between 30 percent and 50 percent a year in the 1990s.

The explosive growth of various forms of labor conflicts in the 1990s and early 2000s is closely associated with the transformation of China's economy from centrally planned to market oriented, resulting in an upheaval of the employment regime in both state and nonstate sectors. The market reforms challenged rural-urban divisions[2] as well as stable employment relations in SOEs. Millions from the rural population moved to coastal cities in search for urban jobs created by nonstate enterprises in those coastal areas where special economic zones were established. In spite of some recent improvements, rural migrant workers did not enjoy the same legal rights and social benefits, such as

TABLE 16.1. *Labor Disputes in China*

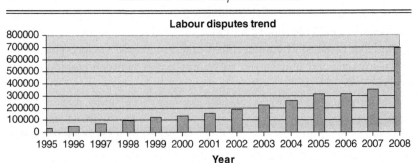

Note: This is the number of labor disputes referred to China's labor arbitration councils. This is not the number of strikes. There is no official statistics on strikes, which are believed to also take place in a considerable number.
Source: China Labour Statistics Yearbook (various years), State Statistics Bureau, and Ministry of Human Resources and Social Security ed., Beijing, China, China Statistics Press.

medical insurance and pension, as their urban counterparts did. The second-class citizen status allowed employers to exploit migrant workers through all kinds of abuses, particularly forced overtime for excessively long hours in hazardous working conditions and often the nonpayment of wages.

The restructuring of public enterprises – SOEs, collectives, and township/village enterprises (TVE) – entered a decisive phase in the 1990s with large-scale layoffs. From the mid-1990s to the early 2000s, 30 million workers lost their jobs in the SOE sector alone as some SOEs went bankrupt while others made drastic reductions in their workforce in order to survive. Workers who were laid off or in danger of being laid off took protest actions against SOEs' failure to honor their liability in terms of pension, medical, and housing benefits.

SOE workers in China's rust belt undertook "protest out of desperation" over the unfulfilled government commitment to provide "goods of collective consumption," while migrant workers in the sun belt of China undertook "protest against discrimination over wages and working conditions" in newly emerging nonstate sectors (Lee, 2007). In restructuring the economy, the state has discarded the old social contract, but a new social contract was yet to emerge. This situation led to the explosive growth in labor conflicts in both sun belt and the rust belt throughout the 1990s and into the early 2000s.

If unchecked, widening income gaps of all sorts and explosive growth of labor conflicts can threaten social stability. Yet China lacked labor market institutions and labor politics that could address the aforementioned problems of achieving "equity through voice mechanism" in the 1990s, when protests of workers in the rust and sun belts converged to produce social tensions.

INDUSTRIAL RELATIONS DEVELOPMENTS IN THE 1990s

In hindsight, it is fair to say that the 1990s was a crucial period for laying basic legal foundations for market-based employment relations and industrial relations in China, as important first steps of introducing various legal regulations were taken. These included the very first Trade Union (1992) and Labour Laws (1992 and 1994, respectively). Since the Cultural Revolution in 1960s, China's employment and labor relations had been administered without national laws.[3]

The Labour Law was an attempt to create new legal norms governing contract-based employment relations while introducing legal provisions for collective bargaining[4] and labor dispute settlement. However, the legal provisions of the Labour Law were far too ambiguous or abstract to provide any meaningful protection to workers exposed to entirely new market-based employment relations; more effectively, they offered convenient legal grounds to convert state-sector jobs (known as iron-bowl job or lifetime employment) into contract-based ones.

The adoption of the Labour Law was significant for the evolution of modern industrial relations in China because it laid down legal foundations for collective agreement and a formal mechanism of dispute settlement for the first time since the mid-1950s.[5] With the new legal provisions, All China Federation of Trade Unions (ACFTU) made its first nationwide attempt to introduce collective agreement in the mid-1990s.

Actual progress on the ground, however, was very limited during the 1990s, for a number of reasons. The Party-state's goal was firmly set on economic development, to be achieved at any cost. The "race to the bottom" of lowering labor standards was underway between provinces in their fierce competition to attract more investment while struggling to deal with the legacy of a socialist economy in their efforts to restructure the public enterprises. In this atmosphere, enforcement of labor laws was often conveniently ignored. Since local governments did not regard rural migrant workers as citizens deserving legal protection, labor law meant little for hundreds of millions them.

Trade unions were not ready to cope with the new reality of market-based employment relations. In fact, ACFTU was facing its own crisis. Between 1995 and 1999, it lost 17 million members as a result of the large-scale restructuring of SOEs. At the same time, ACFTU struggled to adjust its functions and to find its place in a rapidly expanding nonstate sector, with little success. Collective bargaining campaigns were largely formalistic exercises, resulting in collective agreements that were no more than the mere legal-minimum conditions. With the Party-state's policy priority firmly on economic growth at whatever costs, trade unions under the control of the Party-state had neither the political motive nor the organizational incentive to push for the representation of workers.

INDUSTRIAL RELATIONS DEVELOPMENT UNDER THE POLICY PARADIGM SHIFT OF 2000s

The agenda of "building a harmonious society" espoused by the new leadership of Hu Jintao since the early 2000s was a response to the looming social crisis described in the previous section. The new political leadership set ambitious goals for redirecting China's economic and social development strategies toward a more balanced development. They sought to balance rural and urban development through support for rural development, create sustainable development through better environmental protection, establish a balance between export and domestic sector development, and reach a balance between economic efficiency and social equity. These goals have become not only the social but also the economic imperative after the outbreak of the global economic crisis in 2008, although it is yet to be seen whether the proclaimed goals can be achieved as the political masters of the country desire. This is because, in spite of the pronounced shift of policy priorities at the central level, there is a deeply embedded development bias, embodied in the collusion between the party-government apparatus and business interests at decentralized levels.

The Party-state soon discovered a new value of trade unions as key pillars of social management to stabilize the "core social relations" – in other words, labor relations. Thus the harmonious-society agenda encouraged and directed industrial relations actors to build and spread new practices and institutions of industrial relations. Under the goal of building harmonious labor relations, the promotion of collective agreements and institutionalization of tripartite consultation gained a new importance.

In recent years, particularly after the global economic crisis, the state has attached even more importance to labor relations institutions not just as a social safety valve but also as an economic mechanism to boost domestic consumption by boosting workers' incomes. As a result, the local Party apparatus and governments have become more supportive of industrial relations institution building.[6] Trade unions and the work of building an all-encompassing industrial relations system have become crucial parts of the Party-state's corporatist strategy that aims to preempt social conflicts by expanding the sphere of the union monopoly and incorporating workers into official systems of industrial relations (Lee, 2006).

MAJOR DEVELOPMENTS OF LABOR LAWS AND INDUSTRIAL
RELATIONS IN THE 2000s

- 2000: Implementation decree on collective wage negotiation, issued by MOLSS
- 2001: Revision of Trade Union Law
- 2001: Establishment of national tripartite consultation committee for coordination of industrial relations
- 2001: National Tripartite Committee issued Joint Notification for Promotion of Collective Bargaining and Collective Agreements
- 2003: At the 14th National Congress, ACFTU announced its new policy of actively organizing rural migrant workers
- 2003: ACFTU began its experiment of direct election of enterprise union leaders in some localities
- 2004: Revision of Provisions on Collective Agreements by the Ministry of Labour and Social Security (MOLSS)
- 2006: National Tripartite Committee issued Common Views on Promoting Regional/Sectorial Collective Bargaining
- 2006: ACFTU made a breakthrough in organizing Wal-Mart branches
- 2007: National People's Congress (Chinese legislature) adopted Labour Contract Law, Employment Promotion Law, and Labour Disputes Mediation and Arbitration Law, all of which came into effect in 2008

Source: Chang Lee (2012)

CREATING NEW POLICY SPACES FOR INDUSTRIAL
RELATIONS IN THE 2000s

The legislative reform of China's industrial relations in the 2000s started with seemingly trivial changes made to the 1992 Trade Union Law in 2001. The revision of the Trade Union Law in 2001 neither altered the political environment for union operation nor addressed the representational deficiency of the trade unions at the workplace. However, it did open up several new and significant institutional opportunities for the ACFTU.

First, the revised Trade Union Law put "safeguarding the legitimate rights and interests of workers" as the basic duties and functions of trade unions. This was given predominance over protecting the "overall interests of the entire Chinese people." The 1992 law made the safeguarding of workers' rights an additional obligation in the interest of the entire Chinese people.[7]

Second, the revision opened policy spaces to establish unions in small enterprises. The revisions now stipulated that a joint trade union could be set up if enterprises are employing less than twenty-five workers – the threshold for setting up an enterprise union. This seemingly small change opened a policy space for Chinese trade unions to experiment with various forms of organization (such as street-level unions or joint unions) in small and medium enterprises (SMEs), which had been traditionally difficult to organize. This change allowed Chinese trade unions not only to penetrate into SMEs but also to open a space for collective labor relations beyond enterprise level.

Third, Articles 33 and 34 of the revised Law provide a legal basis for union participation at the government policy level on a wide range of labor and social policy issues. This includes tripartite consultation at various levels on major issues of labor relations. Based on these provisions, tripartite actors in China have begun to establish tripartite consultation committees (TCCs), opening a space for trade unions at various levels to mobilize support from the government and employers' organizations in pursuing their agenda.

In the early 2000s, China also adopted a number of national-level regulations aimed at promoting collective bargaining and wage negotiation. In the early 2000s, MOLSS adopted an Implementation Decree on Collective Wage Negotiation (2000) designed to set procedural rules on wage negotiation as a way of fixing wage increases. As most collective agreements were little more than replications of legal minimum conditions, they often failed to address wage increase and distribution issues. With the adoption of the aforementioned decree, ACFTU began to promote wage negotiation in particular in addition to promotion of collective bargaining in general. Similarly, the revision of the Provisional Regulation on Collective Agreement in 2004 also helped spread the new practices of collective agreements by making further elaboration of procedural rules on collective bargaining, expanding the scope of the collective bargaining agenda, and introducing the concept of "bargaining in good faith."

NEW WORKPLACE NORMS AND SHORTCOMINGS

Also noteworthy is the increased use of a tripartite joint communiqué in pushing for new practices of industrial relations after the tripartite consultation mechanism was officially launched in 2001. For example, Common Views on Promoting Regional/Sectoral Collective Bargaining issued by the tripartite actors at national level in 2006 gave a great impetus to the spread of the regional/sectorial collective agreements. Until the Labour Contract Law gave legal recognition to regional/sectorial agreements (articles 53 and 54) in 2007, there was no legal foundation for collective bargaining beyond the enterprise level. Chinese labor laws in 1990s supposed that industrial relations existed only at the enterprise level.

Although the Labour Contract Law (2007) is primarily about legal norms on individual employment relations, it is likely to have both a direct and an indirect impact on collective industrial relations. Firstly, the Labour Contract Law requires employers to have consultation with trade unions or workers' representatives in making decisions on such matters as dismissal and redundancy, and also in drafting or revising work rules. Secondly, the entire chapter 5 of the law codifies what has been already been in practice, including wage negotiation and regional/sectorial bargaining, reaffirming the legal foundations for those practices. Thirdly, there are likely to be indirect effects through the law's better protection of individual workers' rights such as improved rules for nonfixed contracts. With better job security and improved legal rights, workers are more likely to seek improvement of their working conditions through the "voice" mechanism (i.e., collective bargaining) rather than the "exit" mechanism.

In addition, it is to be noted that local regulations play a significant role in shaping local industrial relations developments. In a number of provinces, the provincial people's congresses (provincial legislature) adopted local regulations that tend to offer more favorable legal environments for trade union and collective bargaining developments. For example, twenty-two provinces (out of thirty-one) have so far adopted their own regulations on collective bargaining. Contents of local regulations vary, but many of them make subtle readjustments to the relations between workers and unions at enterprise and local levels; some of them also attempt to define procedural rules on strike actions, which are absent in any national laws and regulations.

In spite of these new legal initiatives, China's legal framework for industrial relations remains problematic. Many of the regulations mentioned earlier are not national laws and therefore carry much less authority for enforcement. But more fundamentally, all legal initiatives taken so far do not recognize either the freedom of association or the right to strike. In the absence of freedom of association, the ACFTU, which is given an official monopoly of workers' representation, does not face credible challenges that could trigger genuine union development. The absence of official recognition of the right to strike makes it hard for unions to exert collective pressure on employers in the hope of breaking deadlocked negotiation.

The absence of freedom of association and the right to collective action is likely to invite more government intervention as the government intends to achieve social harmony in the form of more equitable labor market outcomes. The freedom of association and the right to strike are fundamental conditions for industrial relations to produce equitable labor market outcomes through voluntary interaction between two parties. In the absence of those rights, whether it wants or not, the government would have to intervene every step of the way toward achieving social policy goals, as an industrial relations system without those rights is not likely to produce social equilibrium through the "voice" mechanism.

INSTITUTIONAL CLONING OF TRIPARTITE CONSULTATION SYSTEMS IN CHINA

As described in the preceding section, the Revision of the Trade Union Law created a legal foundation for tripartite and bipartite (government-union) consultations at various levels. Based on these provisions, tripartite actors in China have begun to establish tripartite consultation conferences (TCCs), starting with the creation of the National TCC in 2001.[8] The national TCC is headed by the vice-minister of the Ministry of Human Resources and Social Security (MOHRSS), the vice-chairperson of the ACFTU, and the vice-president of the China Enterprise Confederation (CEC). The TCC has been established to improve coordination among the three parties in their efforts to develop harmonious labor relations, reflecting the overriding concern of the Party-state to maintain social stability through better labor relations (Lee and Clarke, 2003).

By 2004, TCCs had been established in all provinces and most municipalities. Now tripartite joint efforts are being made to set up TCCs at district level. The pace at which TCCs have spread down to the lower levels of administration clearly indicates that this "institutional cloning" of tripartite mechanisms was apparently conducted in a top-down manner. Even though there is a degree of local variations in terms of scope of agenda for TCCs, the TCC's mandate is mostly limited to narrowly defined labor relations issues such as the promotion of collective bargaining, joint inspection of labor law enforcement, and (sometimes) new local regulations on industrial relations. In spite of its inherent limits described earlier, the institutionalization of TCCs has been a catalyst of a recent industrial relations evolution in China. TCCs have become a major vehicle for spreading new practices of collective agreements across localities and sectors, as discussed later in the chapter.

There has been skepticism about the nature of tripartism in China, including questions as to the value of tripartism in the absence of independence of the parties involved. For this reason, some have called it the "multi-headed monologue" (Brown, 2006). It certainly appears that the TCCs at local levels are more about implementing joint decisions made at the national level than about consulting for joint decision making, and that each actor's policy choice is constrained by the Party-state's political and policy imperatives.

However, there is a growing divergence among the three parties in the TCC at various levels, as the highly contested process of legislative debate on the Labour Contract Law has demonstrated. ACFTU represented voices for better legal protection of workers' rights and interests against both local and foreign business positions. The recent adoption of a series of pro-worker legislation appears to have become a wake-up call for business communities in China to strengthen their ability to influence law and policy making. In turn, this is likely to cause each party to sharpen their positions, leading to further divergence among the parties involved.

EMPLOYERS' ORGANIZATION AND THE TRIPARTITE CONSULTATION MECHANISM

A particularly tricky problem has arisen in the process of institutional cloning of TCCs at lower levels of the government administration: the representation of employers at decentralized levels. The CEC is the only officially designated organization of employers in China. However, it does not have its branch at lower levels of administration such as some cities and most districts where TCC have been set up. At the lower level of administration where the CEC has no branches, representatives of employers are sometimes "elected" from influential employers of the localities as an interim measure or from the local branches of the State Economic and Trade Commission (SETC), which is the government agency supervising the CEC.

Another problem with employers' representation is the CEC's state-owned enterprise origin. The CEC was established by the SETC as China began to experiment with the decentralization of the management of SOEs in the late 1970s. Its purpose was to maintain links between SETC and the SOEs that had formerly been under the direction of the State Planning Commission. In 1998, the SETC authorized the CEC to act as the representative of all enterprises in industrial relations matters; in 1999, it issued instructions to all provincial governments requiring them to delegate this authority to CEC (Lee and Clarke, 2003). Because of its origin being linked to SOEs, the CEC is yet to develop an organizational capacity to represent all types of employers.

Among other business associations, *Gongshanglian* (All China Federation of Industry and Commerce, the organization of domestic private businesses) is believed to be the most powerful organization, representing Chinese private businesses (not foreign or public enterprises). The top leaders of *Gongshanglian* concurrently hold senior positions within the National People's Congress and the China People's Political Consultative Committee. At the

TABLE 16.2. *Trade union membership in China*

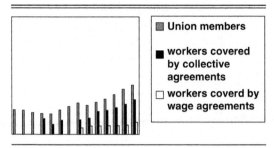

Source: Chinese trade unions statistics yearbook, Research
Department of All China Federation of Trade Unions ed.,
Beijing, China, China Statistics Press, various years.

same time, *Gongshanglian* has thousands of local sectorial employers' associations at decentralized levels, allowing it to participate in the TCC at these
levels and engage in regional/sectorial bargaining together with ACFTUs
local branches (Lee et al., 2011). After succeeding in gaining their seats in
most provincial TCCs under the so-called 3+1 formula, the *Gongshanglian*
has been formally accepted in the national TCC as of late 2010. The *Gongshanglian's* participation is likely to make the tripartite system a more real
forum of contested decision making.

RAPID GROWTH OF UNION MEMBERSHIP AND DIVERSE
FORMS OF TRADE UNIONS

In the early 2000s, the unionization drive gained momentum. In fact, the
13th National Congress of ACFTU was a crucial turning point as it adopted
a resolution for organizing campaigns under the slogan of 'Set up unions
wherever workers work.' Table 16.2 shows that trade union membership has
expanded rapidly since 2001, reversing the decline in the 1990s.

The rapid increase in trade union membership is closely associated with the
revision of the Trade Union Law and the 2003 decision for organizing migrant
workers.[9] First of all, as noted earlier, the revision of Trade Union Law opened
new ways to set up unions in small enterprises. Different forms of trade unions
(such as street unions, joint unions, or regional/sectorial unions) had already
been tried on an experimental basis in a limited number of localities before
the revision. But the revision accelerated the spread of various forms of unions
beyond the enterprise level, enabling local trade unions to "cover" many
workers who were previously out of reach of trade unions.

Secondly, the decision at the 14th National Congress of ACFTU in 2003 to formally accept rural migrant workers as a part of "working class" and therefore a legitimate part of trade unions accelerated the unionization drive. As of the end of 2006, 40.9 million rural migrant workers were claimed to be covered by unions, indicating a 24.1 percent annual increase from 2005, which is higher than the overall growth rate of union membership (13.1 percent). The ACFTU decision to cover rural migrant workers was a part of the overall Party-state policy of gradually integrating rural and urban labor markets.

Finally, ACFTU's successful organizing campaign against the Wal-Mart stores[10] in 2006 displayed a new approach. Traditionally local union officials approached employers, without even contacting workers, to get their permission to set up trade unions. If employers agree to unionization, trade unions at higher levels often let employers decide how to set up enterprise unions, leading to many of these unions being controlled by employers. In the face of Wal-Mart employers' resistance, however, ACFTU approached rank-and-file workers, instructing them of advantages of union membership. After gaining support from twenty-five workers, ACFTU declared unionization of a Wal-Mart branch and demanded recognition of the union branch by employers. However, this approach is an exception rather than the rule.

The aforementioned changes are significant for they enabled the unusually rapid expansion of union membership since the early 2000s. However, the officially reported number of trade union members in China is most likely to have a statistical "bubble," exaggerating real bargaining power of Chinese unions. The number is more likely to be a result of local union cadres' competition to report the achievement of the target numbers rather than genuine trade union organizing. The fact that fee-paying members' ratio to total membership has constantly declined in recent years may be indirect evidence that the quantitative outcome of the union organizing campaign has only loose relations with the genuine process of unionization and therefore to the strength of workers' organizations at the workplace.

Most enterprise unions are thus independent from workers and dependent on employers. Factors that contribute to this are the lack of freedom both of association in terms of workers' choice for alternative unions and of workers' right to elect their leaders. When these are combined with the still predominant approach to union setup that allows employers to dominate the process of establishing and managing unions, the result is hardly surprising.

Nevertheless, the numerical expansion of trade union memberships with diverse organizational forms, even after considering the statistical inflation, is likely to create a new environment for Chinese trade unions to expand their sphere of influence. It will be particularly so when trade unions can operate in the workplace where institutional channels for collective voices of workers are installed in an increasingly greater number, as the following sections show.

COLLECTIVE BARGAINING DEVELOPMENTS IN 2000s: AN ENLARGED POLICY SPACE?

Developments in collective bargaining have contributed to the importance of workers in previously restricted policy spaces. Collective bargaining development gained a crucial momentum in the 2000s. First of all, collective bargaining coverage has expanded at an unusually rapid pace. Particularly the number of collective agreements and workers covered by those agreements has surged since 2001. In 1999, 42.7 million workers were covered by collective agreements; this number increased to 61.6 million, 97.7 million, and 128 million in 2002, 2004, and 2007, respectively. Second, the number of workers covered specifically by wage agreements has shown modest but steady growth. In 2002, 27.4 million workers were covered by wage agreements.[11] The number has recorded modest growth: 35.3 million in 2004 and 39.6 million in 2007. Third, collective bargaining has begun to take place at multiple levels of the economy, not just at the enterprise level. This new development was closely associated with the experiment of diverse forms of trade union organizations (such as street union, joint unions, and regional/sectorial unions). The revised Trade Union Law paved the way for these developments and the tripartite Common Views on Promoting Regional/Sectorial Bargaining facilitated their implementation. In 2007, 45.6 million workers were reported to be covered by these agreements.

Many observers – both foreign and domestic, including some officials of the government and ACFTU – agree that there are serious deficiencies in the current collective bargaining system in terms of both the quality of the agreements and of the bargaining process. In this respect, a sudden increase in collective agreements can be more easily explained by bureaucratic competition to meet targets than by a real increase in collective bargaining (as it is the case with union membership). Indeed, many collective agreements tend again to be little more than a replication of the legal minimum conditions with minor modifications, while the collective bargaining process tends to be a ritualistic preparation of joint documents with little or no formalistic involvement of workers and without a genuine process of negotiation (Lee, Clarke and Li), 2004.

Nevertheless, collective agreements, including wage agreements, are becoming more substantial in a growing number of enterprises, even though they are still a minority. In a new labor market environment where serious labor shortages give better bargaining position to workers, the recent emphasis on wage negotiation appears to have triggered interests of workers in the bargaining. The author's field research confirms this pattern: wage negotiation increases interests and participation of union members in the union affairs, and in turn enterprise unions come under greater pressure to become more accountable to their members (Lee, 2006).

The rapid spread of regional/sectorial agreements over policy spaces also deserves special attention. Chinese trade union officials and academic observers attach increasingly high importance to this development, as regional/sectorial union organizations can be independent from individual employers' influences in theory and in practice. Indeed, a recent empirical study (Liu, 2007) found that regional/sectorial unions were generally more capable of articulating workers' demands in a same sector concentrated in the same locality, acting independently from individual employers. Some regional/sectorial agreements succeeded in negotiating higher minimum wages for various occupations over the mandatory local minimum wages set by the government.

Labor shortages since the mid-2000s created an enabling environment for sectorial bargaining. During this period, employers were struggling with unusually high turnover, which damaged their production and increased the frequency of labor disputes. Therefore, employers had a collective self-interest in fixing wages and working conditions at the sectorial level. The regional/sectorial agreements are far more advanced geographically in provinces around Yangtze River delta (Zhejiang and Jiangsu), than in the Pearl River delta, Southern China. They also tend to be more advanced in localities where small and medium-sized Chinese enterprises are concentrated, rather than in localities where foreign or joint ventures are the dominant players (Lee et al., 2011). This pattern appears to be associated with the domestic employers' dense organizational network (and forward/backward industrial links among them), which enable the aggregation of their individual interests into collective ones. This type of regional/sectorial bargaining has a great potential of creating a negotiated wage floor, in addition to local minimum wages, in domestic SMEs where low-paid migrant workers are concentrated.

EFFECTS OF TRADE UNIONS AND COLLECTIVE BARGAINING IN THE WORKPLACE AND BEYOND

We described a decade-long process of institution building of China's fledgling industrial relations, largely engineered by the Party-state and the official trade unions. As the result of concerted efforts by the Party-state and the ACFTU,

collective agreements have spread across China and have come to cover a
majority of the workers – as far as the official number is concerned. The
question then is: Can China's new industrial relations arrangements produce
the desired labor market outcomes, as they do in other developed economies?

Trade unions in developed economies demonstrated, admittedly until the
neoliberal globalization took hold, that trade unions could contribute to more
equitable labor market outcomes in terms of narrower wage gaps and standard-
ization of wages across firms and sectors, primarily through collective bargaining. Also, the existence of trade unions tends to lower turnover of employees,
as workers would choose to improve their working conditions through "voice"
rather than "exit" (Freeman and Medoff, 1986). All of these outcomes are
closely associated with trade unions as democratic and representative organizations where majority rank-and-file workers can have a bigger say in the
formulation of bargaining strategies. The well-functioning voice mechanism
is likely to produce more equitable outcomes. However, data about unions
and collective bargaining's effects on labor market outcomes in China are still
incomplete or inconclusive.

THE IMPACT OF POLITICAL INCORPORATION OF TRADE UNIONS: A DOUBLE-EDGED SWORD

At the political level of decision making, Chinese trade unions have recently
shown their effectiveness in pursuing their agenda. Of course, the political
support of the Party-state was crucial for pro-worker legislation such as the
Labour Contract Law and other initiatives. Throughout the legislative process,
the ACFTU has shown its political and technical capacity as well as its political
savvy to overcome mounting oppositions from both domestic and foreign
capital. ACFTU has also successfully put its agenda into the provincial and
municipal legislative bodies to create a more favorable regulatory environment
for unions' work at local levels. In this respect, the newly created tripartite
consultation committee was also a useful vehicle for local trade unions to
translate those new regulations into practice by mobilizing the support of the
local government and employers' organizations for the spread of collective
agreements and other initiatives.

The enhanced political influence of trade unions is closely related to a
significant elevation of the ACFTU leadership's political profile within the
political structure of China. In 1995, there were only five provincial trade
union federation chairpersons who were also vice-presidents of the provincial legislatures (out of thirty-one provinces), and six chairpersons who were
members of the provincial party's standing committees. These numbers have

increased to nine and seven, respectively in 2001, and twelve and eleven in 2006 (Feng, 2008).

However, the concurrent appointment of union leadership to senior party/political posts is a double-edged sword. It can certainly enhance trade unions' political influence over the legislative and decision-making processes, particularly when they need to overcome the opposition of the increasingly powerful lobby of the business community in China. In a sense, therefore, the union's link to the Party may help unions bring a balance to their relations with employers in the absence of right to strike. At the same time, a deeper incorporation of trade unions into the formal state structure allows the Party-state to exercise more direct control over the trade unions. Under this arrangement, it is likely that unions be more accountable to the Party-state than to workers.

CHANGING UNION GOVERNANCE AND COLLECTIVE BARGAINING AT THE ENTERPRISE AND LOCAL LEVEL: WHAT ROLE FOR UNIONS?

Understanding workplace labor relations in China is an intellectual challenge. Labor relations at the enterprise level display a great degree of diversity by locality and ownerships, and have undergone changes at an extraordinary pace.

Generally speaking, trade unions at the enterprise level are mostly seen as ineffective. The ineffectiveness of trade unions at the workplace is well reflected in various surveys that show over and again that workers' satisfaction with trade unions is usually very low.

But there is newly emerging evidence that some trade unions might become more effective at the workplace in offering some benefits such as higher wages, shorter working hours, and better social insurance coverage in some localities. A Zhejiang University research group undertook a survey of 3,700 workers at 205 enterprises in 6 cities in Zhejiang province to measure unions' effects, to see whether Chinese unions could produce similar effects as Freeman and Medoff's (1984) study found in the United States.

The researchers grouped workers into four types: union members whose union leaders are elected; union members whose union leaders are not elected; non-union workers of a company where union leaders are elected and; non-union workers of a company where union leaders are not elected. After controlling all other factors such as ownership, sector, and size, the study found that union members whose union leaders are elected were more likely to have higher wages, shorter working hours, and better social insurance coverage, among other things (Yao et al., 2008).

Lee and Liu (2011) have taken this research one step further through their survey of 600 enterprises in 4 major cities in China: Shenzen in Southern China, Shanghai and Hangzhou in East China, and Changchun in Northern China. Their study tries to see the effects of union-related independent variables. Among these are union structure (whether enterprise unions have well-established delegation structure down to workshop or team level); the existence of channels for workers' collective voice such as collective bargaining and workers' congress; and the election of enterprise union leaders – on various human resource management practices and working conditions such as layoff, job security, training, intrafirm wage inequality, and additional social benefits (such as supplementary pensions and medical insurance schemes). The preliminary results show, not surprisingly, that the existence of enterprise unions alone makes little differences in most aspects of working conditions and performance.

What the survey did find was that those unions having better governance structures[12] could actually produce some positive effects such as less intrafirm wage inequalities, better law compliance, and supplementary benefits. Also, when unions actively participate in managerial decision making either through workers' congress or collective bargaining, workers' voluntary turnover rates and frequency of collective redundancy is likely to be lower than in enterprises lacking such participation. In addition, the practice of unions' participation in the management decision making is closely associated with less use of short-term contracts and more use of open-ended contracts, even after controlling all other factors (Lee and Lie, 2010).

This may imply that the recent quantitative expansion of industrial relations institutions such as trade unions, collective bargaining, and workers' congresses cannot be discarded just as a matter of formalistic and bureaucratic exercise. The evidence suggests that unions at a workplace with various labor relations institutions (such as collective bargaining and workers' congress) are closely associated with better labor compliance and some supplementary benefits, such as supplementary pension or medical benefits. Their effects on wages and other key working conditions are still rather limited, however.

MULTIPLE IDENTITIES AND ROLES OF UNIONS AT THE ENTERPRISE LEVEL

There is another force at work in defining the degree of collective voice face of enterprise unions in China: the Party face of the trade unions. According to a survey of 1,811 enterprise union leaders, 90.3 percent are members of the Communist Party. The so-called election of union leaders at the enterprise level is heavily influenced by the Party committee. More than 72 percent of SOEs, 71.9 percent of foreign invested enterprises, and 41 percent of domestic private enterprises have party committees in their enterprises (Qiao, 2010). Combined with the fact that enterprise unions are under influence (or dominance) of employers in the nonstate sector, the Party face of trade unions limits and alters the collective voice functions of trade union institutions in the workplace and beyond. As Qiao (2010) puts it, trade unions find themselves in a new situation where they have to play multiple roles, with multiple identities between workers, managers, and the party apparatus.

It is to be noted that there has recently been a growing recognition among trade union officials at political levels that employers' dominance of enterprise unions is a hindrance to the functioning of trade unions. This recognition of the problems with enterprise unions has led to a number of experiments such as regulatory provisions requiring rank-and-file workers to be represented proportionately in workers' congress and enterprise union committees, and cautious promotion of direct election of enterprise union leadership. In a similar context, unions place greater importance on building unions and labor relations institutions at local and/or sectorial levels where they can be relatively autonomous from the influence of individual employers. At the same time, it also reflects that unions at the regional level can mobilize their authority as quasi-state agencies to put pressure on recalcitrant employers, while enterprise unions are subordinate to managerial authority at the enterprise level.

CONCLUSION: CONTESTED POLICY SPACE AND
THE FUTURE OF INDUSTRIAL RELATIONS

The previous sections described China's significant industrial relations system. This system has seen many changes since the early 2000s, not only in its regulatory framework but also in institutional arrangements. These include the nationwide introduction of tripartite consultation mechanisms, the expansion of union organizations and collective bargaining coverage, and experiments of different forms of unions and collective agreements beyond the enterprise level. The sudden surge of various initiatives designed to build new institutions of industrial relations reflects the state's concern on social instability and their priority of building harmonious labor relations at the time of social crisis (triggered by the social and economic transformation of the last three decades). However, it is yet to be seen whether the state's project of building harmonious labor relations will achieve its goals.

Some empirical research indicates that many well-known cases of innovations turned out to be short-lived, failing to survive in a meaningful manner.

Unions at the Wal-Mart branches in China, which attracted high attention at home and abroad for their democratic, bottom-up approach to organizing, are reported to have lost their initial dynamism and become as uninspiring as traditional enterprise unions with Chinese style. The wool industry bargaining in Wenling city, Zhejiang province, which was praised by Prime Minister Wen Jiabao for its innovative approach, has ceased to function as a meaningful mechanism for joint wage fixing at the sectorial level. It appears that the institutional environment lacks freedom of association needed for workers to organize or join unions of their own choosing, and to elect their leaders and manage unions independently from management's interference. Many such noble experiments soon lose their dynamism.

It may not be surprising then to see simultaneous growth of collective agreements and other industrial relations institutions built by the official actors and of labor disputes of various natures. While the official system of industrial relations may have become more, albeit marginally, effective in influencing wages and working conditions, the system may not have become a mechanism to channel workers' voices and inspiration based on representational democracy at the workplace and beyond. This may explain, as we showed, why union workplaces with various kinds of official labor relations institutions in place are still not capable of having significant effects on wages and why those same workplaces are able to enhance legal compliance and to bring some marginal benefits.

In the meantime, Chinese workers, who have so far been missing from the official industrial relations system, have begun to take collective actions to defend their rights and to improve wages and working conditions outside the official industrial relations system; this was witnessed during the wave of wildcat strikes in 2010. There are a host of factors that are likely to stimulate, sustain, and spread collective actions by Chinese workers. One is labor shortage, which gives better bargaining position to workers; another is the emergence of a new generation of workers who are better educated. A third is a favorable political and legal environment.

Workers are demanding a fairer distribution of the wealth they contributed to creating as well, as human dignity in the workplace. If the state wants to achieve the goal of harmonious labor relations, it would have to bring changes to the representational foundation of China's labor relations to be more in line with the ILO's principles on freedom of association and the right to bargain collectively enshrined in its Conventions 87 and 98.

This is not just an issue of preserving and building harmony in the workplace. It is also closely related to modifying China's growth model and rebalancing the global economy. With the recent global economic crisis, it has become clear that China can no longer sustain its export-driven growth model; it therefore has to boost domestic consumption and to do so it needs to boost workers' incomes. This is why the 12th five-year development plan of the Chinese government (2011–2015), which aims to transform China's development model into one based more on domestic consumption, makes the promotion of wage negotiation as one of the key priorities in its labor and social policy framework, exactly because it hopes that wage negotiation can boost wages of low-paid workers and ensure fairer distribution. Should autonomous wage negotiation begin to occur on a large scale, the workplace policy space may become the most important site for innovation in terms of compensation and working conditions. The question of industrial relations reform, particularly democratic reform of representational foundation, is no longer just a question of social stability; it is also a question about the sustainability of China's economic growth.

REFERENCES

All China Federation of Trade Unions, 2007, *Chinese Trade Union Statistical Yearbook*, Beijing: China Statistics Press.

Brown, Ronald, 2006, "China's Collective Contract Provisions: Can Collective Negotiation Embody Collective Bargaining?" *Duke Journal of Comparative & International Law*, 16, no. 35, 35–77.

Feng, Chen, 2008, "Union Power in China: Source, Operation and Constraints." Unpublished paper, presented at Seminar on Chinese trade unions and labor relations, organized by China Industrial Relations Institute, Beijing.

Freeman, Richard and Medoff, James, 1986, *What Do Unions Do?* New York: Basic Books.

Gallagher, Mary Elizabeth, 2005, *Contagious Capitalism: Globalization and the Politics of Labor in China*. Princeton, NJ: Princeton University Press.

Lee, Changlee, 2013. A New Face of China: Dialogue with Leading Intellectuals of Modern China. Seoul, Korea: Changbi.

Lee, Changhee, and Liu, Mingwei, 2011, "Collective bargaining in transition: measuring the effects of collective voice in China," in Susan Hayter (ed.), *The Role of Collective Bargaining in the Global Economy – Negotiating for Social Justice*. Cheltenham, UK: Edward Elger.

Lee, Changhee, 2006, "Transformation of Industrial Relations in East Asian Transition Economies: Review of Industrial Relations Changes in China and Viet Nam," *Journal of Industrial Relations*, 48, no. 2, 415–429.

Lee, Changhee, 2008, *Emerging Chinese Model of Industrial Relations? – An analysis of Recent Transformation of Industrial Relations at National, Local and Enterprise Level in China*. Seoul: Korea Labor Institute.

Lee, Changhee and Clarke, Simon, 2003, "Towards a System of Tripartite Consultation in China," in Malcolm Warner (eds.), *The Future of Chinese Management: Studies in Asia Pacific Business*. London: Routledge.

Lee, Changhee, Clarke, Simon, and Li, Qi, 2004, "Collective Consultation and Industrial Relations in China," *British Journal of Industrial Relations*, 42, no. 2, 235–254.

Lee, Changhee and Liu, Mingwei, 2011, "What Do Unions Do in China?" In Susan
Hayter (ed.), *The Role of Collective Bargaining in the Global Economy: Negotiating
for Social Justice*. Geneva: International Labour Organization.

Lee, Chingkwan, 2007, *Against the Law: Labor Protests in China's Rustbelt and Sunbelt*.
Berkeley, Los Angeles, and London: University of California Press.

Liu, Mingwei, 2007, "Bottom-up Change? Reforms in Chinese Regional Unions."
Working Paper, School of Industrial and Labor Relations, Cornell University.

Naughton, Barry, 2007, *The Chinese Economy: Transitions and Growth*. Boston, MA:
The MIT Press.

Qiao, Jian, 2010, "Between the Party-State, Employers and Workers: Multiple Roles of
the Chinese Trade Union during Market Transition – A Survey of 1,811 Enterprise
Union Chairpersons," in Masaharu Hishida, Kazuko Kojima, Tomoaki Ishii, and
Jian Qiao (eds.), *China's Trade Unions – How Autonomous Are They*. New York:
Routledge.

Taylor, Bill, Chang, Kai, and Li, Qi, 2004, *Industrial Relations in China*. London:
Edward Elgar Publishing.

Taylor, Bill and Li, Qi, 2007, "Is the ACFTU a Union and Does It Matter?" *Journal of
Industrial Relations*, 49, no. 5, pp. 701–715.

Yao, Xianguo, Li, Min, and Han, Hui, 2008, "Effects of Trade Unions in Labor Relations: Empirical Analysis of Zhejiang Province Case." Unpublished paper, presented
at Seminar on Chinese Trade Unions and Labor Relations, organized by China
Industrial Relations Institute, Beijing.

Notes

CHAPTER 1

1. Only states and international organizations are regarded as subjects of international law, so binding rules must be created as obligations on states to regulate corporations; the adequacy of state implementation of such obligations is generally monitored through procedures such as the evaluation of self-reporting, or peer review (favoured, e.g., by the Organisation for Economic Co-Operation and Development [OECD]). A few international human rights regimes provide for rights of individual petition, but these are also aimed at ensuring state compliance.

2. See Picciotto (2011, ch. 5.2.2.2).

3. For documentation of Israel's violations of human rights, see Human Rights Watch, http://www.hrw.org/middle-eastn-africa/israel-and-occupied-territories. The extension of Israeli settlements into the West Bank has been repeatedly denounced as illegal (see, e.g., 'Council Conclusions on the Middle East Peace Process', 3166th EU Foreign Affairs Council meeting, 14 May 2012, para. 6), yet products from such settlements have been routinely granted certificates of origin by the Israeli authorities, thus benefiting from preferential market access, until a challenge by the German customs administration was upheld by the European Court of Justice (*Brita Gmbh v Hauptzollamt Hamburg Hafen*, Case C-386/08, Judgment of the Court, 25 Feb. 2010).

4. These are not the discrete bargains of classical contract law, but administrative agreements governing long-term relationships, better understood as 'relational' or 'regulatory' contracts (Campbell, 1999; Collins, 1999; Freeman, 2000), and indeed the role of regulatory agencies often complements such contracts (Vincent-Jones, 1999; Stern, 2012).

5. In other leading capitalist countries the state played a more direct role in that period. In Germany this took place within a formalized framework which included state-supervised cartels, whereas in the United Kingdom the longer history of the centralized state and the greater homogeneity of ruling elites permitted much more informal supervision of business and industry.

6. This and the next section draw substantially on Picciotto (2011), especially his final chapter.

7. Thus, the work of Joerges and Neyer on the role of expert and scientific committees in regulatory decision making in the EU (Joerges and Neyer, 1997; Joerges 1999) characterized them as "deliberative," in the sense that the participants approach issues open-mindedly rather than from pre-formed positions (in particular in favour of national interests), seeking to reach consensus through evaluation of valid knowledge (Joerges, 1999, p. 320). However, they had reservations, especially about the management of the interaction between various types of committee, so that it was still questionable whether the EC committee system 'gives proper expression to the plurality of practical and ethical views which should be included within risk assessment procedures'. The conclusion seemed to be that the system is certainly not a closed or homogeneous epistemic complex, but its openness is limited or haphazard, if not selective (Ibid., p. 321). Others have been more explicitly critical of the ways in which the European Commission's restriction of public consultation and involvement, through its management of the committee system, has undermined the legitimacy of some decision making in the EU regulatory networks (Landfried, 1999; Vos, 1999).

CHAPTER 2

1. See, e.g., the MERCOSUR arbitral award of 6 September 2006 in the "Bridges case" between Argentina and Uruguay (cf. Lixinski, 2010, p. 351 ff).
2. See, e.g., the UNCITRAL Arbitral Decision on Liability of 30 July 2010 in *AWG v Argentina* (i.e., one of the more than forty arbitration proceedings against Argentina's restrictions in response to its financial crisis in 2001), at para. 262: "In the circumstances of these cases, Argentina's human rights obligations and its investment treaty obligations are not inconsistent, contradictory, or mutually exclusive."
3. Cf. UN document A/HRC/RES/17/4 of 6 July 2011.
4. See UN Resolution 63/116 on the 60th Anniversary of the UDHR adopted on 10 December 2008.
5. In Cases C-402/05P and C-415/05P, *Kadi*, ECR 2008 I-6351, the EU Court confirmed its jurisprudence that respect for human rights is a condition of the lawfulness of EU measures: "[T]he obligations imposed by an international agreement cannot have the effect of prejudicing the constitutional principles of the EC Treaty, which include the principle that the Community acts must respect fundamental rights, that respect constituting a condition of their lawfulness which it is for the Court to review." Even though "the European Community must respect international law in the exercise of its powers," including "observance of the undertakings given in the context of the United Nations," it is "not a consequence of the principles governing the international legal order under the United Nations that any judicial review of the internal lawfulness of the contested regulation in the light of fundamental freedoms is excluded."
6. Cf., e.g., *Phoenix Action Ltd v Czech Republic*, ICSID Arbitration Award of 15 April 2009 (Case No ARB/06/5), para. 78 (finding that investment protection "should not be granted to investments made in violation of the most fundamental rules of protection of human rights").
7. Cf. Cases C-402/05P and C-415/05P, *Kadi* (n. 13).
8. Cf. Thomas (2009, p. 257 ff).

9. Cf. Article 9 ECHR. For different limitation clauses, see, e.g., Articles 8, 10, or 11 ECHR. Some human rights guarantees (like the prohibition of torture in Article 3 ECHR) do not provide for any governmental limitation.

10. On the "capabilities approach" in human rights law and philosophy see, e.g., Nussbaum (2006, p. 69 ff). The German Constitutional Court, for example, recognizes a human right to respect and protection of human dignity based "on an understanding of the human being as an intellectual and moral creature capable of freely determining and developing itself. The Basic Law conceives of this freedom not as that of an isolated and autonomous individual, but as that of an individual related and bound to society" (BVerfGE Vol. 45, 187, at 227). The Constitutional Court derives from the human right to dignity individual social rights of access to the resources necessary for a life in dignity, cf. Merten and Papier (2006), specifically §40 (Leistungsrechte) and §44 (Schutzpflichten).

11. Cf. Allan (1993, pp. 135–143). Cass (2005, pp. 168, 176, 191) claims that in "mature constitutional systems, for example in the United States, Canada and Australia," neither individual economic freedom nor other individual rights are "a matter considered essential to constitutionalization in the received tradition of constitutionalization"; yet, Cass ignores comparative constitutional law beyond common law countries.

CHAPTER 3

1. In fact, Chile's transition to democracy coincided with the end of the Cold War; the presidential elections that opened the doors to the new dispensation took place a scarce four weeks after the fall of the Berlin Wall. Thus there is a neat overlap between the emergence of the post–Cold War international system and that of Chile's new democracy. This also coincides with the rise of complex interdependence and globalization.

CHAPTER 4

1. Necessarily stylized, because it is certainly too early to say what the true nature, let alone real impact, of social protest still under way might be (with reference to the well-known 1970s quote [or misquote] by Chinese premier Zhou Enlai regarding the French Revolution; see Richard McGregor, "Zhou's Cryptic Cautions Lost in Translation," *Financial Times*, June 10, 2011, at http://www.ft.com/cms/s/0/74916db6-938d-11e0-922e-00144feab49a.html#axzz1rYVdlsoC).

2. While the negotiations in the Doha Round launched in 2001 are in a state of suspended animation and their agenda is outdated (see Cho Sungjoon, "The Demise of Development in the Doha Round Negotiations," 45 *Texas International Law Review* 573 [2010]), and regional trade agreements increasingly proliferate, the WTO – and in particular its dispute settlement system – continue to function as the principal forum for international trade regulation.

3. The "Battle in Seattle" refers to the disruptive protests and violent clashes that took place during the WTO's Third Ministerial Conference, held in Seattle, Washington, in November–December 1999; for one account related to the trade and human rights debate, see Clyde Summers, "The Battle in Seattle: Free Trade, Labor Rights

and Societal Values," 22 *University of Pennsylvania Journal of International Economic Law* 61 (2001); and with respect to the nature of social protest at that event, see Mary Kaldor, "'Civilising Globalisation': The Implications of the 'Battle in Seattle'." 29(1) *Millennium: Journal of International Studies* 105 (2000).

4. In reference to the so-called Occupy Movement, most strongly associated with the protest camp in Zuccotti Park off Broadway in New York City, kicked off in the fall of 2012 (see, e.g., Verena Dobnik, "Wall Street Protesters: We're in for the Long Haul," The Associated Press, *Bloomberg Businessweek*, October 2, 2011, available at http://www.businessweek.com/ap/financialnews/D9Q4CNR81.htm), but short-hand for the much broader wave of social protest that has swept many parts of the world since the summer of 2011.

5. The May 1985 G7 summit in Bonn "attracted 30,000 demonstrators demanding global justice"; see John Keane, "Monitoring Democracy?" in *The Future of Representative Democracy*, edited by Sonia Alonso, John Keane and Wolfgang Merkel (Cambridge: Cambridge University Press, 2011), 212 at 226.

6. This summit reportedly attracted "up to 80,000 well-briefed and well-organised protesters" (*ibid.*). For one narrative, from the perspective of the demonstrators, see www.daysofdissent.org.uk/berlin.html.

7. See www.nadir.org/nadir/initiativ/agp/en.

8. "Ultimately, the WTO meeting fell victim not to protests *outside* in the streets, but rather to serious substantive disagreements *inside* the convention center between developing and developed countries over the prospective agenda new trade-talks"; see Jeffrey J. Schott, "The WTO after Seattle," in Jeffrey J. Schott, *The WTO after Seattle* (Washington, DC: Institute for International Economics, 2000), 3 at 5.

9. "The protests in Seattle brought attention not only to the WTO and its policies, but also to the widespread organized opposition to those policies"; see Lynne Owens and L. Kendall Palmer, "Making the News: Anarchist Counter-Public Relations on the World Wide Web," 20(4) *Critical Studies in Media Communication* 335 (2003), at 349.

10. Ibid.

11. For an interesting analysis of the role Genoa and other anti-globalist demonstrations played in attracting media attention to anti-globalist agendas, see Johan F. M. Swinnen and Nathalie Franken, "Summits, Riots and Media Attention: The Political Economy of Information on Trade and Globalisation," 29(5) *The World Economy* 637 (2006).

12. Available at http://www.citizen.org/trade/article_redirect.cfm?ID=1569. For an earlier discussion, see Tomer Broude, *International Governance in the WTO: Judicial Boundaries and Political Capitulation* (London: Cameron May, 2004), p. 54.

13. Ibid.

14. See http://www.iatp.org/documents/cochabamba-manifesto.

15. Paradoxically, protest organization was itself based on transnational cooperation, leading to global policing responses; see Kate O'Neill, "Transnational Protest: Sates, Circuses and Conflict at the Frontline of Global Politics," 6(2) *International Studies Review* 233 (2004).

16. General Agreement on Tariffs and Trade, October 30, 1947, 61 Stat. A-11, T.I.A.S. 1700, 55 U.N.T.S. 194.

17. *WTO Agreement: Marrakesh Agreement Establishing the World Trade Organization*, April 15, 1994, Legal Instruments – Results of the Uruguay Round 4 (1994) 33 I.L.M. 1144 (1994).
18. For an example, see Neil McCulloch, L. Alan Winters, and Xavier Cirera (eds.), *Trade Liberalization and Poverty: A Handbook* (London: Centre for Economic Policy Research, 2001), in which a series of studies demonstrates that the effects of trade liberalization on poverty vary among states, sectors, and areas of regulation, and are sometimes positive, sometimes negative.
19. For a general survey of the literature on this aspect, see Andrew T. F. Lang, "The Role of the Human Rights Movement in Trade-Policy Making: Human Rights as a Trigger for Policy Learning," 5 *New Zealand Journal of Public and International Law* 77 (2007). For an analysis aimed especially at economic, social, and cultural rights, see Robert Howse and Ruti G. Teitel, "Beyond the Divide: The Covenant on Economic, Social and Cultural Rights and the WTO," Friedrich Ebert Stiftung, Occasional Paper No. 30, April, 2007. For a useful graphic depiction of the diverging views of the effects of economic liberalization on human rights, see M. Rodwan Abouharb and David Cingranelli, *Human Rights and Structural Adjustment* (2007), p. 68.
20. Agreement on Trade-Related Aspects of Intellectual Property Rights, April 15, 1994, Marrakesh Agreement Establishing the World Trade Organization, Annex 1C, Legal Instruments – Results of the Uruguay Round, 33 I.L.M. 1125 (1994).
21. See Article 12 of the International Covenant on Economic, Social and Cultural Rights (ICECSR) [CITE].
22. For a series of case studies of trade law's relations with particular human rights in specific contexts, see Thomas Cottier, Joost Pauwelyn, and Elisabeth Bürgi Bonanomi (eds.), *Human Rights and International Trade* (Oxford: Oxford University Press, 2005).
23. See Walden Bello, "From Melbourne to Prague: The Struggle for a Deglobalized World," Talk delivered at a series of engagements on the occasion of demonstrations against the World Economic Forum (Davos) in Melbourne, Australia, 6–10 September 2000, available at http://www.ratical.org/co-globalize/WB0900.html.
24. This was from a speech by Pascal Lamy, "Globalization and Trade Opening can Promote Human Rights," at Dies Academicus Ceremony of Award of Doctor Honoris Causa – Geneva, 5 June 2009, at http://www.wto.org/english/news_e/sppl_e/sppl128_e.htm.
25. The literature on human rights conditionality is extensive. Important milestones in this literature are Philip Alston, "International Trade as an Instrument of Positive Human Rights Policy," 4 *Human Rights Quarterly* 155 (1982); and Lorand Bartels, *Human Rights Conditionality in the EU's International Agreements* (Oxford: Oxford University Press, 2005).
26. For a detailed discussion, see, e.g., Part II of Deborah Cass, *The Constitutionalization of the World Trade Organization* (Oxford: Oxford University Press, 2005).
27. For a central exposition of this thesis, see Ernst-Ulrich Petersmann, "Time for a United Nations 'Global Compact' for Integrating Human Rights into the Law of Worldwide Organizations: Lessons from European Integration," 13(3) *European Journal of International Law* 621 (2002); for a discussion, see Robert Howse, "Human Rights in the WTO: Whose Rights, What Humanity? Comment on Petersmann," 13(3) *European Journal of International Law* 651 (2002); Philip Alston, "Resisting

the Merger and Acquisition of Human Rights by Trade Law: A Reply to Peters-mann," 13(4) *European Journal of International Law* 815 (2002); and Ernst-Ulrich Petersmann, "Taking Human Dignity, Poverty and Empowerment of Individuals More Seriously: A Rejoinder to Alston," 13(4) *European Journal of International Law* 845 (2002).

28. For one expression of such an approach, see UN, ECOSOC, *Mainstreaming the Right to Development into International Trade Law and Policy at the World Trade Organization* (Study by Prof. Robert L. Howse), UN Doc. E/CN.4/Sub.2/2004/17 (June 9, 2004).

29. http://www.time.com/time/person-of-the-year/2011/.

30. See "New Age of Rebellion and Riot Stalks Europe," *Times Online*, 22 January 2009, at http://web.archive.org/web/20090227034720/http://www.timesonline.co.uk/tol/news/world/europe/article5563020.ece.

31. For a list of U.S. cities in which Occupy protests reportedly have taken place, see http://en.wikipedia.org/wiki/List_of_Occupy_movement_protest_locations_in_the_United_States.

32. For example, one popular account of the evolution of the Occupy movement includes a "Timeline of a Movement on the Move," beginning on January 25, 2011 – the beginning of the Tahrir Square demonstrations in Egypt; see Writers for the 99%, *Occupy Wall Street: The Inside Story of the Action that Changed America* (Melbourne: Scribe, 2012), at 202.

33. Ibid. at 51 et seq.

34. Such as David Graeber; for a profile, see Drake Bennett, "Who's behind the Mask," *Bloomberg Businessweek*, 31 October 2011, at 64 et seq.

35. For example, Dafni Leef, a figurehead activist of the Israeli Rothschild Boulevard protests in 2011–2012, has entirely dismissed any claims by the recently elected leader of the centrist Kadima Party, Shaul Mofaz, that he will lead the social protests in the summer of 2012; see Natasha Mozgovaya, "Israeli Social Protest Leader: A New Movement is Underway," *Haaretz*, 1 April 2012, at http://www.haaretz.com/news/national/israeli-social-protest-leader-a-new-movement-is-underway-1.421962: "In general all of these declarations about leadership – 'I will do, I will lead, I will protest with the people' – they are all empty statements. This protest is a civil protest."

36. For example, Israeli popular protest leaders in the summer of 2011 consistently downplayed any links between problems of social justice in Israel and the continued occupation of Palestinian Territories by Israel; for a critique, see Lev Greenberg, "This Time, The Social Protest Must be Political," *Haaretz* (in Hebrew), 9 April 2012, at http://www.haaretz.co.il/opinions/1.1682328. The Occupy movement emphasized inclusion of racial minorities; see Writers for the 99%, *supra* note 48, at 112–122.

37. See http://www.democraciarealya.es/manifiesto-comun/manifiesto-english/.

38. See *Markerweek*, special issue, 22 December 2011 (in Hebrew), with a comparative survey of social policies in Denmark, Finland, Germany, and Sweden.

39. See http://www.nycga.net/resources/declaration/.

40. See Robert Howse, "The End of the Globalization Debate: Continued," in Meredith Kolsky Lewis and Susy Frankel (eds.), *International Economic Law and National Autonomy* (Cambridge: Cambridge University Press, 2010).

41. Howse at 11.

CHAPTER 5

1. The Canadian model is complex and deceptively legalistic. It is an "opt in" model where, factory by factory, each group of workers is required to join by signing a card. The card is supposedly like a vote that is not universal and is subject to an expensive and cumbersome sign-up drives, which gives employers the right to participate in the factory floor campaign under a free-speech provision; it makes a mockery of any resemblance to a universal franchise. It is a limited franchise protected and restricted by the courts. The right to strike by European standards is heavily curtailed and controlled by the courts and provincial legislation. Companies can and do operate during a strike and can and do call on local police to protect "replacement" workers (Fudge, 2010). Legally, workers have a restrictive right to picket that does not allow them to shut down the plant but only provide the public with information about the lockout or strike. Even the grievance procedure has been taken over by lawyers and quasi-judicial labor boards and far removed from the rank-and-file (Tucker, 2009). The mainstay of the industrial relations practice is that workers cannot be fired arbitrarily and the employer must give just cause for dismissal. This important mainstay of the Canadian model has not protected hundreds of thousands of workers who lost their jobs in the fallout from the 2008 global financial meltdown. With respect to human rights violations, Ontario has created parallel system to protect workers from discriminatory practices in the workplace and offers the citizenry an alternative grievance based system. Still Canada's model of industrial relations has not collapsed or succumbed to the drive for continental integration. It is in slow decline, and the numbers of workers bargaining collectively has dropped relatively and absolutely (Arthurs, 2007).

CHAPTER 7

1. See, for example, Bhagwati, 1993.
2. See Kohli, 1989; Harriss, 1987 for greater details.
3. Many commentators believe that the reforms had begun during the second stint of Prime Minister Indira Gandhi, beginning in 1980, followed by her successor in 1985–1986. The slowness of the introduction of early reforms and the sudden nature of policy change in 1991 has induced scholars like Bhagwati (1993, p. 3) to classify the three periods as those of "reform by stealth," "reform with reluctance," and "reform by storm."
4. http://www.indlawnews.com/38015ad8fc90dc27e781af47f5446e2d.
5. The Commission was set up under government of India notification F. No. 1/7/2004-FIU. Details are drawn from its website, http://www.investmentcommission.in/.
6. http://www.maxindia.com.
7. http://www.jubl.com.
8. http://www.niit.com.
9. *Times of India*, November 28, 2009.
10. Italics added.
11. http://timesofindia.indiatimes.com/India/IAS_officers_find_greener_pastures_without_quitting/articleshow/2413135.cms.

12. Arun Maira is reported to have been entrusted with the task of making suggestions for reinventing the role of Planning Commission and making it more effective. http://www.livemint.com/2010/01/04223753/Planning-Commission-evaluates.html?d=1.
13. Rs. 1 crore is equal to Rs. 10 million.
14. http://nationalelectionwatch.org/files/new/pdfs/Lok%20Sabha%20high%20level%20analysis.pdf.
15. http://www.ficci.com/.
16. Rajiv Gandhi was the first prime minister who invited businessmen to accompany him on his foreign trips. On hearing of such inclusion in PM's entourage, the Indian ambassador to the USSR is reported to have telegraphed his displeasure. Rajiv Gandhi told the foreign ministry officials to throw the telegram in the dustbin and proceed with his plans (Sinha, 2005, p. 12).
17. For an elaboration of this argument, see Panagriya, 2008.
18. In fact, the World Bank conducts a worldwide survey assessing the business environment and the speed with which a government responds to an application to set up an enterprise. In a survey carried over 183 countries, World Bank has ranked India at 132 in 2009, with Singapore, New Zealand, United States, Hong Kong, Denmark, and United Kingdom being at the top in that order (World Bank, 2009).
19. These networks have also had tendency to convert into partnerships for illegal gratification. Corruption has become a major issue and currently anti-corruption social movements are gathering steam.
20. New Delhi government has announced partial privatization of water management in New Delhi. A project on the PPP model will begin with private companies. This will ensure efficiency of water distribution network and reduce non-revenue water (*Times of India*, November 29, 2011).
21. The reform period has seen a fall in levels of poverty, but Brazil boasts of much better performance where the population living in extreme poverty has come down to around 9% in comparison of India's 34%. Figures for infant mortality rate are 18 per 1,000 and 50 per 1,000, respectively; for underweight children 2.0 per 1,000 and 46 per 1,000, and for female literacy 99 and 74. World Bank characterizes India Growth with Disappointing Outcomes for the Poor; see World Bank Policy Research Paper (2009).
22. Speech available at http://pmindia.nic.in/speech/content.asp?id=53.
23. Various central and state governments have also demonstrated the willingness to lobby for individual companies, particularly in the international realm, and this is best exemplified by the Indian government's efforts during Mittal Steel's takeover of Arcelor in 2006 and Tata Steel's acquisition of the Anglo-Dutch giant Corus (Murali, 2006. p. 97). More recently, the Chief Minister of Orissa has lobbied for mining giants Vedanta and POSCO with the prime minister.

CHAPTER 8

1. This section heavily draws on Ray (2005).
2. It is interesting to observe that many of the advanced industrial nations had a weak patent regime even as late as the 1960s.
3. See Bhaduri and Ray (2006) for details.

4. Other elements of the structural adjustments program followed by India include industrial reforms leading to abolition of industrial licensing, virtual elimination of MRTP regulations, divestment of public sector units, and de-reservation and reduction of benefits of the small-scale sector.
5. A firm may, however, circumvent the lack of domestic demand by developing second-generation non-conventional delivery systems only for the export markets.
6. Biology has been neglected in India, perhaps because of its tradition of process patent regime encouraging analytical chemistry in the pharmaceutical and other chemical industries.
7. Although the cost of clinical trial depends also on the availability of diseased population, where Indian holds a comparative advantage insofar as the infectious diseases are concerned, high cost of testing equipment still puts up deterring cost.
8. This is not to suggest that the challenges to the small-scale units are any less severe or less important, but an analysis of the small-scale sector would constitutes a separate program of research study.
9. See, for instance, Reich (1994) for a discussion of Bangladesh.

CHAPTER 9

1. *Economist* magazine, November 14–20, 2009.
2. Brazil has imposed temporary taxes as high as 6% since 2009 in an attempt to control a flood of speculative capital into the country, which has driven up its exchange rate to overvalued levels.
3. The studies were led by Ricardo Barros. This account is based on the summaries in Lopez-Calvo and Lustig (2009: 12–15).
4. The pension transfers are the largest of the non-*labor* income sources. They bring the weight of transfer payments to 8.6% of GDP in 2008, having risen from 6.9% in 2002 (Barbosa 2010, p. 2). Pension spending is generally regressive and thus is not included in the following discussion.
5. Interview with official at the Brazilian National Development Bank, Rio de Janeiro, July 1, 2011.
6. http://www.plataformabndes.org.br/site/. The umbrella organization RedeBrasil, formed in 1995 to resist the policies of the multilateral development banks, shifted its focus to the BNDES in the mid-2000s, out of recognition that it was now the source of financing for most of the projects they opposed. Interview with two leaders of RedeBrasil, Brasilia, June 18, 2009.
7. Telephone interview with a BNDES official, Rio de Janeiro, July 4, 2011.

CHAPTER 10

1. Three such measures include raising tariffs up to WTO bound levels rather than customary applied levels, which are often much lower, using export restrictions on food or other commodities of particular importance to the domestic economy (such as China's restrictions on exports of rare earth elements), and imposing local sourcing requirements for public stimulus or green technology investments. Some of these measures, however, have provoked trade challenges.

2. "Jobs, jobs, jobs" – a proposition rebuked by a recent study, which argues that "there is as yet no credible, socially just, ecologically sustainable scenario of continually growing incomes for a world of nine billion people" (Sustainable Development Commission, 2009, p. 8).

3. In 2009, and later in 2011, the EU reached a compromise with the two major complainant countries (the United States and Canada, respectively), whereby retaliatory sanctions would be reduced or eliminated in exchange for an increased import quota of "quality" (non-hormone-treated) beef (http://trade.ec.europa.eu/doclib/press/index.cfm?id=685).

4. Austria, Belgium, Denmark, Finland, France, Germany, Greece, Ireland, Italy, Luxembourg, Netherlands, Portugal, Spain, Sweden, and United Kingdom.

5. Eurodad.org.

6. Unless otherwise cited, references for the information that follows can be found in the recent open access article by Labonté, Mohindra and Lencucha (2011). For the sake of brevity, only tobacco and food trade are discussed in this section. In brief: alcohol trade disputes have generally centered on discriminatory taxation on imports, and it remains unclear whether taxation by alcohol content (a public health objective) will be trade-permissible. Changes in physical activity have more to do with urbanization than trade, although trade-related globalization is an oft-cited dynamic underpinning rapid urbanization in the developing world.

7. Brazil, Russia, India, China.

CHAPTER 11

1. The author acknowledges his active role in these global policy debates. Parts of this chapter draw from a briefing note prepared by the author under the auspice of the UN Special Rapporteur on the Human Right to Food, *The World Trade Organization and the Post-Global Food Crisis Agenda*, available at: http://www.srfood.org/images/stories/pdf/otherdocuments/20111116_briefing_note_05_en.pdf.

2. There is a significant body of literature; for examples, see FAO (2008); Trostle (2008); Heady and Fan (2009); Cohen and Clapp (2009).

3. For background information on the HLTF, see http://un-foodsecurity.org/.

4. This summary is based on both the original 2008 CFA and its updated version in 2009.

5. Interview with David Nabarro, June 5, 2009.

6. There is a substantial literature exploring this dimension of policy space.

7. According to the FAO, more than twenty-three recognize the right to food explicitly as a human right, including Brazil, India, and Mexico.

8. Special Rapporteurs are part of the special procedural mechanisms of the UN Human Rights Council (formerly Council for Human Rights) to permit the Council to monitor and debate human rights practices at the country and global levels. Mandate holders elected by the Council are often prominent human rights experts and/or individuals of high moral standing. Mandates fall under various titles (e.g., Special Rapporteur, Independent Expert, Representative of the Secretary-General, etc.) but all encompass the same basic duties and responsibilities: analyzing the human rights situation of a thematic issue or country situation, undertaking country missions, and alerting the UN and the international community to specific human

rights situations. The Special Rapporteur on the Human Right to Food is a thematic mandate in existence since 2000. De Schutter was elected in 2008. He was preceded by Jean Ziegler who served as the Special Rapporteur between 2000 and 2008.

9. This fact is confirmed by official correspondence between the WTO and Jean Ziegler, obtained by the author.

CHAPTER 12

1. Director-General of the International Labour Office, Decent Work Report of the Director General of the ILO to the International Labour Conference, 87th Session, Geneva, 1999.

2. See ILO, *Domestic Workers across the World: Global and Regional Statistics and the Extent of Legal Protection* (Geneva: ILO, 2013). Methodological challenges abound in determining who counts as a domestic worker. See Martha Alter Chen, "Recognizing Domestic Workers, Regulating Domestic Work: Conceptual, Measurement, and Regulatory Challenges" (2011) 23 CAN. J. WOMEN & L. 167.

3. UN Development Programme, *Overcoming Barriers: Human Mobility and Development* 25 (2009), at http://hrd.undp.org/en/reports/global/hrd2009/; UN Department of Economic and Social Affairs, *United Nations Population Facts*, November 2010, at 3 (adding that the proportion varies with age), at http://www.un.org/esa/population/publications/popfacts/popfacts_2010-6.pdf; ILO, *Women and Men Migrant Workers: Moving Towards Equal Rights and Opportunities* (n.d.), at http://www.ilo.org/wcmsp5/groups/public/@dgreports/@gender/documents/publication/wems_10118.pdf.

4. Official Bulletin (Geneva) Vol. XLVIII, No. 3, July 1965, Supplement I, 20–1.

5. See the government representative of Australia, to the June 2011 session of the International Labour Conference – International Labour Conference, Provisional Record No. 15, 100th Session, Geneva, June 2011, at paragraph 37.

6. The 2006 Maritime Labour Convention reflected an industry-driven consolidation of existing ILS. See Cleopatra Doumbia Henry, "The Consolidated Maritime Labour Conventions: A Marriage of the Traditional and the New," in Jean-Claude Javillier and Bernard Gernigon, eds., *Les normes internationales du travail: Un patrimoine pour l'avenir: Mélanges en l'honneur de Nicolas Valticos* 319 (Geneva: ILO, 2004). The new standards on domestic workers built on some of the insights and regulatory innovations in the maritime labor standard. See also Adelle Blackett, "Introduction: Regulating Decent Work for Domestic Workers" 23 *Canadian Journal of Women and the Law* 1 (2011).

7. Virginia A. Leary, "The Paradox of Labor Rights as Human Rights," in Lance A. Compa and Stephen F. Diamond, eds., *Human Rights, Labor Rights and International Trade* (2003).

8. Leah F. Vosko, "'Decent Work': The Shifting Role of the ILO and the Struggle for Global Social Justice" 2 *Global Social Policy* 19 (2002).

9. See, e.g., William Simpson, "Standard Setting and Supervision: A System in Difficulty," in Javillier and Gernigon, *Les normes internationales du travail: un patrimoine pour l'avenir* (2007); Laurence R. Helfer, "Understanding Change in International Organizations: Globalization and Innovation in the ILO," 59 *Vand. L. Rev.* 649 (2006); Brian Langille, "Imagining Post 'Geneva Consensus' Labor Law for Post

'Washington Consensus' Development," 31 *Comp. Lab. L. & Pol'y J.* 523 (2010); Anne Trebilcock, "Putting the Record Straight About International Labor Standard Setting," 31 *Comp. Lab. L. & Pol'y J.* 553 (2010); Kevin Kolben, "Labor Rights as Human Rights," 50 *Virginia International L.J.* 449 (2010).

10. Minutes of the 301st Session of the Governing Body of the International Labour Office, March 2008, paragraph 18, adopted as amended at the 302nd Session, June 2008, by GB 302/2.
11. International Labour Conference, Provisional Record No. 15, 100th Session, Geneva, June 2011, at paragraph 12779.
12. Ibid. at paragraph 21.
13. Ibid. at paragraph 187.
14. Ibid. at paragraph 440.
15. Ibid. at paragraph 1275.
16. Ibid. at paragraph 1278. For a discussion, see Adelle Blackett, "The Decent Work for Domestic Workers Convention and Recommendation, 2011" (2012) A.J.I.L. 778 at 792–793.
17. Article 19 clarifies that the Convention does not affect more favorable provisions applicable to domestic workers under other international labor Conventions.
18. As of January 22, 2013, Convention No. 189 has been ratified by Uruguay, the Philippines, Mauritius, and Italy. It was set to enter into force on September 5, 2013, twelve months after the date that it was first ratified by two ILO member states.
19. This discussion draws on reflections in Adelle Blackett, "Domestic Workers at the Interface of Migration and Development," Background Paper prepared for UN-Women, the MacArthur Foundation, and the Swiss Global Foundation on Migration and Development, African Domestic Care Workers at the Interface of Migration and Development, Accra, Ghana, September 21–22, 2011.
20. See the articles in the special issue of the *Canadian Journal of Women and the Law*, Vol 23:1, 2011 on regulating decent work for domestic workers.
21. Patricia J. Williams, *The Alchemy of Race And Rights* (Cambridge, MA: Harvard University Press, 1993) at 164–165.
22. See Shireen Ally, *From Servants to Workers: South African Domestic Workers and the Democratic State* (Ithaca, NY: Cornell University Press, 2010); see also Alana Erickson Coble, *Cleaning Up: The Transformation of Domestic Service in Twentieth Century New York City* (New York: Taylor and Francis, 2006).
23. Adelle Blackett and Dzodzi Tsikata, "Vulnerable Workers," in Frédéric Mégret et al., eds., *Dignity: A Special Focus on Vulnerable Groups*, Swiss Initiative to Commemorate the Sixtieth Anniversary of the Universal Declaration of Human Rights, June 2009, at 59. Available at http://www.udhr60.ch/report/HumanDignity_Megret0609.pdf.
24. See Einat Albin, "From 'Domestic Servant' to Domestic Worker," in Judy Fudge et al., eds., *Blurring Legal Boundaries: Regulating for Decent Work* (Oxford: Hart Publishing, 2012) 231.
25. CMW General Comment No. 1, paragraph 9. It is worth noting that The Council of Europe, in Resolution 1534 of 2007 on the situation of migrant workers in temporary employment agencies, has called for member states to establish international cooperation between labor inspectors, police and border guards.

26. See also CMW General Comment No. 1, paragraph 34, which adds at paragraph 35 that only those agencies observing the criteria and codes should continue to operate.

27. Article 7, paragraph 2.

28. Adelle Blackett, "Promoting Domestic Workers' Human Dignity through Specific Regulation" in Antoinette Fauve-Chamoux, ed., *Domestic Service and the Formation of European Identity: Understanding the Globalization of Domestic Work: 16th–21st Centuries* (Bern: Peter Lang, 2004).

29. ILO, Law and Practice Report, op. cit.

30. See Yeates, op. cit. at 436.

31. See also Domestic Helper Deployment Ban to Saudi Arabia Sought, *Business World*, Manila, February 9, 2011. Available at http://www.bworldonline.com/content.php?title=Domestic%20helper%20deployment%20ban%20to%20Saudi%20Arabia%20sought&id=26069. It took a significant time before the ban was ultimately lifted, and renewed threats persist.

32. See Migrant Rights, "Avoiding Reform, GCC States Seek Alternative Sources of Labor," February 11, 2013, available at http://www.migrant-rights.org/2013/02/11/avoiding-reform-gcc-states-seek-alternative-sources-of-labor/.

33. Reports indicate that approximately 3,000 Kenyan migrant workers are registered with the Embassy in Riyadh, but the actual numbers are likely much higher. See Joyce J. Wangui, "Pursuit of Greener Pastures in Saudi Arabia Spells Doom for Kenyan Immigrants," July 10, 2011. Available at http://www.thewip.net/contributors/2011/07/pursuit_of_greener_pastures_in.html. See also Migrant Rights, *ibid.* (noting that recruitment is coming also from Morocco, and explicitly stating that the recruitment of Ethiopian domestic workers is considered a "good alternative" because the domestic workers are less expensive and Ethiopia has lax labor requirements).

34. See, e.g., Marina de Regt, "Employing Migrant Domestic Workers in Urban Yemen: A New Form of Social Distinction," 6 *Journal of Women of the Middle East and the Islamic World* 154 (2008); JoAnn McGregor, "Joining the BBC (British Bottom Cleaners): Zimbabwean Migrants and the UK Care Industry," 33 *Journal of Ethnic and Migration Studies* 801 (2007); Francie Lund, "Hierarchies of Care Work in South Africa: Nurses, Social Workers and Home Based Care Workers," 149 *International Labour Review* 495 (2010); Sarah van Walsum, "Regulating Migrant Domestic Work in the Netherlands: Opportunities and Pitfalls," *Canadian Journal of Women & Law* 141 (2011).

35. See Chantal Thomas, "Migrant Domestic Workers in Egypt: A Case Study of the Economic Family in Global Context," 58 *American Journal of Comparative Law* 987 (2010).

36. See Rhacel Salazar Parrenas, *Children of Global Migration: Transnational Families and Gendered Woes* (Stanford, CA: Stanford University Press, 2005).

37. Migrant Rights, *ibid.* The article raises the prospect of an informal or illegal economy of domestic workers from the Philippines, noting that " [i]n the past, state attempts to force alternatives have aggravated citizens, who often turn to illegal markets to secure their preferences."

38. "After Lifting of Deployment Ban, Saudi Arabia Expects 2000 Domestic Workers from the Philippines," InterAksyon, February 3, 2013, available at

http://www.interaksyon.com/article/54219/after-lifting-of-deployment-ban-saudi-arabia-expects-2000-domestic-workers-from-philippines.

39. The discussion in this section draws on the more extensive discussion in Adelle Blackett, "Development, the Movement of Persons and Labour Law: Reasonable Labour Market Access and Its Decent Work Complement" in Tonia Novitz and David Mangan, eds., *The Role of Labour Standards in Sustainable Development: Theory in Practice* (Oxford: Oxford University Press, 2012).

40. Aderanti Adepoju, Migration in Sub-Saharan Africa: A background paper commissioned by the Nordic Africa Institute for the Swedish Government White Paper on Africa. Lagos, September 14, 2007. Available at http://www.sweden.gov.se/content/1/c6/08/88/66/730473a9.pdf at 45.

41. See Lourdes Beneria and Gita Sen, "Class and Gender Inequalities and Women's Role in Economic Development – Theoretical and Practical Implications," 8 *Feminist Studies* 157 (1982).

42. Parrenas, op. cit. at 14 ("first . . . the exhaustion of state care resources by structural adjustment policies that mandate the servicing of the foreign debt and second via the depletion of the labor supply of care workers").

43. Yong Shik Lee, *Trade and Development* (2006); discussed in *Trade, Labour Law and Development: A Contextualization* (2010).

44. See Kitty Calavita, *Immigrants at the Margins: Law, Race and Exclusion in Southern Europe* (Cambridge: Cambridge University Press, 2005).

45. In my opinion, the frequent presumption that the liberalization of the trade in services is necessarily temporary warrants close critical scrutiny. See the position taken by the Quebec Human Rights and Youth Rights Commission on permanent resident status, and second-best policy alternatives, as they relate to human rights legislation: CDPDJ, La discrimination systémique à l'égard des travailleuses et les travailleurs migrants, December 2011, available at http://www.cdpdj.qc.ca/publications/Documents/Avis_travailleurs_immigrants.pdf.

46. See Parrenas, op. cit.

47. See Human Rights Council, Report of the Special Representative of the Secretary-General on the issue of human rights and transnational corporations and other business enterprises, John Ruggie Guiding Principles on Business and Human Rights: Implementing the United Nations "Protect, Respect and Remedy" Framework, Seventeenth Session, March 21, 2011.

48. See Federal Labour Standards Commission, "Fairness at Work: Federal Labour Standards for the 21st Century (Harry Arthurs Report)," Ottawa, 2006, available at http://www.rhdcc-hrsdc.gc.ca/eng/labour/employment_standards/fls/pdf/final_report.pdf.

49. See ILO, Report IV: 1 Decent Work for Domestic Workers, International Labour Conference 2010 (1999).

50. *Ibid.* at para. 171.

51. Vallejos Evangeline Banao v. Comm'r of Registration, Case No. HCAL 124/2010 (C.F.I. Sept. 30, 2011); Vallejos Evangeline Banao v. Comm'r of Registration, Case No. CACV 204/2011 (C.A. Mar. 28, 2012). Both decisions are available at http://legalref.judiciary.gov.hk/. See also "Filipino Maid's HK Residency Case in Top Court," *Boston Herald*, February 26, 2013.

52. Barry and Reddy, op. cit. at 25.

53. *Ibid.* at 79.
54. See Ian Johnstone, *The Power of Deliberation: International Law, Politics and Organizations* (Oxford: Oxford University Press, 2011); Jutta Brunnée and Stephen Toope, *Legitimacy and Legality in International Law* (Cambridge: Cambridge University Press, 2010); Iris Marion Young, *Inclusion and Democracy* (Oxford: Oxford University Press, 2000).

CHAPTER 13

1. See Joel P. Trachtman, "Unilateralism and Multilateralism in U.S. Human Rights Laws Affecting International Trade" in Frederick M. Abbot, Christine Breining-Kaufmann, and Thomas Cottier (eds.), *International Trade and Human Rights* (Ann Arbor: The University of Michigan Press, 2006), 357–383, at 360–366, and Sisule Frederick Musungu, "International Trade and Human Rights in Africa: A Comment on Conceptual Linkages" in Frederick M. Abbot, Christine Breining-Kaufmann, and Thomas Cottier (eds.), *International Trade and Human Rights* (Ann Arbor: The University of Michigan Press, 2006), 321.
2. *WTO Trade Report, supra* note 1, at 18. According to the Report, 44.1 percent of all PTAs in force in 2010 are FTAs. See figure B.4., 62.
3. *Joint Declaration of the Seventy-Seven Developing Countries* made at the conclusion of the United Nations Conference on Trade and Development (UNCTAD), Part V. 9, Geneva, June 15, 1964, online at http://www.g77org/doc/Joint%20Declaration .html.
4. For example, the Organization of African Unity (OAU) was established in 1963; the South East Asian Nations (ASEAN) created their own association, the first and so far the only RTA in Asia in 1967; the Andean countries Bolivia, Columbia, Ecuador, and Peru in Latin America created an economic community (the Andean Community) and the first of three RTAs in Latin America in 1965.
5. For example, the birth of MERCOSUR in Latin America brought together the biggest and economically strongest Latin American countries (Brazil and Argentina joining markets with Uruguay and Paraguay and allowing Chile to become an associate in 1991); SADC and COMESA in Africa revitalized the old forms of integration in 1992 and 1994, respectively; and the ASEAN established the free trade area in 1992.
6. In 1998, MERCOSUR adopted the Protocol of Ushuaia and included a "democracy clause" in its treaty system requiring that all of its members and associates to maintain domestic democratic institutions. Also in 1998, the Council of Ministers of the MERCOSUR adopted the Social and Labour Declaration. ASEAN has added to its legal framework the Declaration on the Inauguration of the ASEAN Intergovernmental Commission on Human Rights in 2009.
7. Henry Gao indicates that China was slow to join the trend toward regionalization for several political and economic reasons, such as the country's long ignorance of the importance of bilateral and regional trade initiatives because of its focus on internal economic reforms, its focus on GATT participation, the 1997 financial crisis in Asia, and then the importance of the WTO membership negotiations. See Henry Gao, "China's Strategy for FTAs: Political Battle in the Name of Trade"

in Ross P. Buckley et al. (eds.), *East Asian Economic Integration: Law, Trade and Finance* (Cheltenham, UK: Edward Elgar, 2011), 104-T 120.

8. The agreements with Hong Kong and Macao are called the Closer Economic Partnership Arrangements (CEPAs).

9. The list of all signed FTAs is available online at http://fta.mofcom.gov.cn.

10. The Southern African Customs Union (SACU) was established in 1910 and it is the world's oldest customs union. The members of SACU are Botswana, Lesotho, Namibia, South Africa, and Swaziland.

11. See, for example, the FTA negotiation process with ASEAN. See also Henry Gao, *supra* note 42.

12. On the Early Harvest Program related to the China-ASEAN FTA, see http://big5 .fmprc.gov.cn/gate/big5/ph.china-embassy.org/eng/sgdt/t171568.htm.

13. Evan Ellis, "Chinese Soft Power in Latin America: A Case Study," 60 JFQ 85 (2011), at 85. Ellis borrowed the term "soft power" from Joseph Nye who referred to it as "a dynamic created by a nation whereby other nations seek to imitate that nation, become close to that nation, and align their interests accordingly."

14. See H. Gao, *supra* note 42. See also Rhys Jenkins and Enrique Dussel Peters, "The Impact of China on Latin America and the Caribbean," IDS Working Paper 21, May 2007, at 8. Jenkins and Peters argue that China is one of the top five export markets for Argentina, Brazil, Chile, Cuba, and Peru and also one of their five leading sources of imports.

15. See E. Ellis, *supra* note 48, at 89.

16. Jenkins and Peters claim that more than three-quarters of China's import from Argentina and Chile are soya and copper, respectively, two-thirds of imports from Brazil are soya, iron, and steel, and two-thirds of imports from Peru are copper and fishmeal. *Supra* note 49, at 10.

17. Gao cites the FTA with Norway as China's gateway to the European Economic Area, the one with Chile as a door to Latin American market and in particular to the markets of MERCOSUR and the Andean Community, and the one with Singapore as a potential link to that country's FTA partners such as Japan, South Korea, or the United States. *Supra* note 42.

18. Alex Berger, "China's new bilateral investment treaty programme" (on file with the author), presentation to SIEL 2008 Conference, p. 4. Berger claims that since the early 1990s only large developing countries such as China, India, and Brazil were able to refrain from signing BITs under the terms of developed countries.

19. Berger reports that in June 2007, China already had 120 concluded BITs. *Ibid*, at 7. But see UNCTAD website that reports only 88 BITs concluded by China.

20. For a comprehensive analysis of the impact of BITs and, in particular, on the impact of investment arbitrations on public law, see Gus Van Harten, *Investment Treaty Arbitration and Public Law* (Oxford: Oxford University Press, 2007).

21. China has ratified the *ICSID Convention on the Settlement of Investment Disputes between States and Nationals of Other State* in 1994 and has embraced the Convention's dispute settlement mechanism in its recent BITs with developing countries.

22. http://english.mofcom.gov.cn/index.shtml.

23. http://english.eximbank.gov.cn/. According to the website, "founded in 1994, the Export-Import Bank of China is a state bank solely owned by the Chinese government.... The Bank is headquartered in Beijing. By the end of 2010, the Bank has eighteen domestic business branches, and three overseas representative offices, namely the Representative Office for Southern & Eastern Africa, Paris Representative Office and St. Petersburg Representative Office. At present, it has established correspondent relationship with more than 500 banks."

24. For a history of China-Africa trade relation, see Uche Ewelukwa Ofodile, "Trade, Empires and Subjects – China-Africa Trade: A New Fair Trade Arrangement, or the Third Scramble for Africa?" 41 *Vanderbilt Journal of Transnational Law* 505 (2008).

25. Ofodile cites the early trade agreement with Egypt (1955) and a series of agreements in the 1960s (with Congo Ghana, Mali, Somalia, Zaire, Burundi, Kenya, Benin, Central Africa, Tunisia, Tanzania, and Zambia). *Ibid*, at 515.

26. *Ibid*, at 520.

27. *Ibid*, at 519.

28. *Ibid*, at 527.

29. See "Foreign Minister Yang Reviews Three-Year Achievements of the Forum on China-Africa Co-operation," China, Ministry of Foreign Affairs (MOFA), at http://www.fmprc.gov.cn, accessed March 4, 2010.

30. Institute of Developing Economics, Japan External Trade Organization (IDE-JETRO), African Growing Enterprises file, Part 10. China's Infrastructure Footprint in Africa, available at http://www.ide.go.jp/English/Data/Africa_file/Manualreport/cia_10.html.

31. In brief, the OECD model requires lenders to transfer aid to developing countries through the OECD official Overseas Development Assistance (ODA) program and under the supervision of the OECD Development Assistance Committee (DAC). This program was established to ensure that grants and loans really constitute overseas development assistance – that is, that loans are undertaken by "government or government bodies, with the promotion of economic development and welfare as their main objectives," and are made on concessionary terms.

32. For reports on some accidents and protests in Zambia, see http://www.ihlo.org/CINTW/Zambia.html.

33. See the recent report on the Collum Coal mine online at http://www.theworld.org/2011/10/mining-in-zambia-one-year-after-collum-coal-incident/.

34. *Ibid*.

35. Emeka Umejei, "Nigeria: Another Look at China's Trade Investment in the Country," *Daily Independent* (Lagos), June 25, 2011. This author reports that Chinese companies pay incredibly low wages to Nigerian workers. The same report argues that some of the promised oil investments never materialized: a $6 billion oil refinery in Lagos or four other promised oil refineries worth $23 billion. *Ibid*.

36. See, for example, Stephen Muyakwa, an agricultural economist from Zambia and the chairperson of the Zambia Civil Society Trade Network. See Miriam Mannak, *supra* note 72.

37. Note that trade volume between China and ASEAN in 2010 was thirty-six times what it was in 1991. See China-ASEAN Expo, available online at http://eng.caexpo.org/news/t20111220_98741.html. Sarah Y. Tong and Catharine Chong, "China-ASEAN

Free Trade Area in 2010: A Regional Perspective," EAI Background Paper no. 519, April 12, 2010, report that China was the fourth-largest trading partner of ASEAN in 2010.

38. See China-ASEAN Expo, *ibid.*
39. See the website of ASEAN for a complete list of FTAs that the bloc concluded with third countries.
40. For the list of China's FTAs, see http://fta.mofcom.gov.cn/english/fta_quinshu .shtml. Not all FTAs texts are available in English.
41. The agreements on trade in goods concluded between ASEAN and Korea includes a provision that the justified exceptions to trade liberalization, in addition to those mentioned in Art. XX GATT, are those related to prohibition of import of goods produced by prison labor (Art. 11(e) in the *ASEAN-Korea Agreement*.
42. But see the *Agreement on Trade in Goods under the Framework Agreement on Comprehensive Economic Cooperation between ASEAN and the Republic of Korea*.
43. The provisions of Art. 12(e) of ASEAN-China agreement on trade in goods are identical to these of Art. 11(e) of ASEAN-Korea agreement on trade in goods.
44. Iman Prihandono, "Human Rights and the ASEAN-China FTA," *The Jakarta Post*, January 12, 2010. Lowering prices in the agriculture and the fisheries sectors by liberalizing markets to allow the Chinese agricultural and fisheries industries access to the ASEAN market could lower prices of domestic products and could then further impact negatively on the living standard of local fishermen.
45. *Ibid.*
46. *Agreement on Dispute Settlement Mechanism of the Framework Agreement on Comprehensive Economic Co-Operation Between the Association of Southeast Asian Nations and the People's Republic of China*, November 4, 2002, came into force in 2005, online at http://www.aseansec.org/16635.htm.
47. Art. 6: three-member panel of arbitrators to be appointed if the parties could not resolve their controversies by consultation (Art. 4), conciliation and mediation (Art. 5).
48. Art. 2(3)(4).
49. Art. 2 explicitly excludes the concurrent jurisdiction of any other tribunal once the parties have activated the process under this agreement.
50. ICSID Case No. ARB 11/15.
51. The NYU Wagner research of China's loans and other economic assistance during the 2002–2007 period, as published in 2008 under the title "Understanding Chinese Foreign Aid."
52. Jenkins and Peters, *supra* note 49.
53. Philips argues that the British Virgin Islands are the second most important source of FDI in China.
54. Phillips, *ibid.*
55. Jenkins and Peters, *supra* note 49, at 11.
56. Phillips, *supra* note 103, at 10; Jenkins and Peters, *supra* note 49, at 13.
57. Phillips, *supra* note 103, at 10.
58. Jenkins and Peters, *supra* note 49, at 13.
59. Jenkins and Peters, *supra* note 49, at 25. The authors said that in 2004, more than 3 million farm workers lost their jobs in Mexico. CANAINTEX 2005 reports that

some businesses in Mexican garment industry have relocated production to China. *Ibid*, at 25.

60. See Lucien Chauvin, "Hierro Peru: China's Footprint in the Andes," *China Dialogue Net*, December 1, 2006. The author reports a special congressional commission investigation on the sale agreement and the Chougang's failure to meet its commitments on the basis of the sale contracts, but the investigation made no impact on working conditions or protection of the environment.

61. China-Peru FTA text in English is available online at http://fta.mofcom.gov.cn/topic/enperu.shtml.

62. *Ibid*, at 3.

63. The 2009 ICSID tribunal decided in *Tza Yap Shum v. Peru*, the first case brought before ICSID on the basis of a BIT concluded by China.

64. Chile, for example, has more than forty BITs and more than fifty FTAs, Peru has more than thirty BITs, and Argentina has more than fifty BITs.

65. See the IDB website at www.iadb.org/en/news/news-releases/2011-03-28/.

66. Note that some of the emerging countries are already members of OECD: Chile, Turkey, and Mexico. For the DAC membership, see http://webnet.oecd.org/OECDGROUPS/Bodies/ListByIndexView.aspx?book=true.

CHAPTER 14

1. "Risk of social turmoil as number of jobless grows, researcher warns," *South China Morning Post*, December 6, 2008; Liang, Jing "The CPC's crisis and China's lease on life," *Zhengming* (Hong Kong), November 2008; Dyer, Geoff, "Top Chinese official warns of downturn," *Financial Times*, November 27, 2008 http://www.ft s/s/0/621foec4-bca1-11dd-9efc-0000779fd18c.html (accessed June 25, 2013); Cha, Ariana Eunjung, "As China's Jobless Numbers Mount, Protests Grow Bolder: Economic Woes Shining a Light on Social Issues," *Washington Post*, January 13, 2009, p. A7.

2. Li, Fan, "Unrest in China's Countryside," *China Development Brief*, Vol. 6, No. 2 (2006), pp. 6–8; McGregor, Richard, "Data show social unrest on the rise in China," *Financial Times*, January 19, 2006. For an unconfirmed report that some 180,000 protests occurred in 2010, see Sun, Liping, "Lingui qianzhan: Chui shixu shi dangxia de yanjue tiaozhan" [Looking ahead to the two meetings: Social disorder is an immediate serious challenge], *Jingji guancha wang* [Economic Observer Net] July 30, 2011, http://www.eeo.com.cn/Politics/by_region/2011/02/28/194539.shtml (accessed July 29, 2011).

3. Mestrum, Francine, "Poverty Reduction and Sustainable Development," *Environment, Development, and Sustainability*, Vol. 5 (2003), pp. 41–61.

4. For details, see World Bank Poverty Reduction and Economic Management Department, "China: From Poor Areas to Poor People – China's Evolving Poverty Reduction Agenda," available at http://siteresources.worldbank.org/CHINAEXTN/Resources/318949-1239096143906/China_PA_Report_March_2009_eng.pdf (accessed June 25, 2013).

5. UN Development Programme, "China: Human Development Report 2009/10," available at http://www.undp.org.cn/pubs/nhdr/nhdr2010e.pdf (accessed June 25, 2013).

6. For a detailed discussion of these, see Shi, Tian and Gill, Roderic, "Developing effective policies for sustainable development of ecological agriculture in China: The case study of Jinshan County with a systems dynamics model," *Ecological Economics*, Vol. 53 (2005), pp. 223–246.

7. For more detailed discussions, see Gao, Mobo C. F., "On the sharp end of China's economic boom – migrant workers," *China Rights Forum* (Spring 1994), pp. 12–13, 27; Ping, Liu, "Dying for Development," *China Rights Forum* (Fall 1994), pp. 14–15, 27. For a discussion of privatization policies, see Walder, Andrew G., "China's Transitional Economy: Interpreting Its Significance," *China's Transitional Economy*, The China Quarterly Special Issue (December 1995), pp. 963–979.

8. For details, see "Labour Minister: Strikes 'inevitable' with reform," Hong Kong, AFP, July 15, 1994, in *FBIS Daily Report-China*, July 15, 1994, pp. 12–13.

9. For details, see Forney, Matt, "We Want to Eat," in *Far Eastern Economic Review*, June 26, 1997.

10. For details, see "China dissidents call on workers to form unions," *Reuters*, December 23, 1997.

11. For details, see "Risk of social turmoil as number of jobless grows, researcher warns," *South China Morning Post*, December 6, 2008; Liang, Jing, "The CPC's crisis and China's lease on life," *Zhengming* (Hong Kong), November 2008; Dyer, Geoff, "Top Chinese official warns of downturn," *Financial Times*, November 27, 2008, http://www.ft.com/cms/s/0/621f0ec4-bca1-11dd-9efc-0000779fd18c.html (accessed June 24, 2013); Cha, Ariana Eunjung, "As China's Jobless Numbers Mount, Protests Grow Bolder: Economic Woes Shining a Light on Social Issues," *Washington Post*, January 13, 2009, p. A7.

12. See "International Covenant on Civil and Political Rights," available at http://www.ohchr.org/EN/ProfessionalInterest/Pages/CCPR.aspx (accessed June 25, 2013).

13. See "International Covenant on Economic, Social and Cultural Rights," available at http://www.ohchr.org/EN/ProfessionalInterest/Pages/CESCR.aspx (accessed June 25, 2013).

14. ILO Programme on the Promotion of the ILO Declaration on Fundamental Principles and Rights at Work: The Declaration, available at http://www.ilo.org/declaration/thedeclaration/lang-en/index.htm (accessed June 25, 2013).

15. See "ILO Programme on the Promotion of the ILO Declaration on Fundamental Principles and Rights at Work: Status by Country," available at http://www.ilo.org/declaration/follow-up/annualreview/ratificationstatus/lang-en/index.htm (accessed June 25, 2013).

16. Merchant, Toby, "Recognizing ILO Rights to Organize and Bargain Collectively: Grease in China's Transition to a Socialist Market Economy," *Case Western Journal of International Law*, Vol. 36 (2004), pp. 223–253; Yang, Qiu, "ILO Fundamental Conventions and Chinese Labor Law: From a Comparative Perspective," *Chinese Law and Policy Review*, Vol. 2 (2006–2007), pp. 18–43.

17. International Labor Organization, "Country Baselines Under the 1998 ILO Declaration – China," available at http://www.ilo.org/wcmsp5/groups/public/-ed_norm/-declaration/documents/publication/wcms_decl_facb_chn.pdf (accessed June 25, 2013). For texts of conventions, see "Convention 87: Convention on Freedom of Association and Protection of the Rights to Organise, 1948," available at http://www.ilo.org/ilolex/cgi-lex/convde.pl?C087 (accessed June 25, 2013); "Convention

98: Convention on the Application of the Principles of the Right to Organise and to Bargain Collectively, 1949," available at http://www.ilo.org/ilolex/cgi-lex/convde .pl?Co98 (accessed June 25, 2013).

18. See International Labor Organization, "Country Baselines Under the 1998 ILO Declaration – China," available at http://www.ilo.org/wcmsp5/groups/ public/---ed_norm/---declaration/documents/publication/wcms_decl_facb_chn. pdf (accessed June 25, 2013). For texts of conventions, see "Convention 29: Convention on Forced or Compulsory Labour 1930," available at http://www. ilo.org/ilolex/cgi-lex/convde.pl?Co29 (accessed June 25, 2013); "Convention 105: Convention on Abolition of Forced Labour 1957," available at http://www.ilo.org/ ilolex/cgi-lex/convde.pl?C105 (accessed June 25, 2013).

19. See International Labor Organization, "International Labor Standards Database: Ratifications," available at http://www.ilo.org/ilolex/english/newratframeE.htm (accessed June 25, 2013); Guthrie, Robert, "The Development of Workers' Compensation in China: Emerging International and Internal Challenges," *Journal of Asian Law*, Vol. 10 (2008), pp. 133–158.

20. For a comprehensive set of PRC laws and regulations, see Yang, Yunzhou and Huang, Xinfa, eds., *Laodong: Falu zhengce shiyong zhinan* [Labor: Practical guide to law and policy]. Beijing: China Law Press, 2009. Also see Yang, Zhengxi and Lu, Huiqin, eds., *Dangdai laodong fa lilun yu shiwu* [Theory and practice of contemporary labor law] Guangzhou: Huanan Physics University Press, 2010.

21. See, e.g., Ma, Hongguo and Li, Xianbo, "Guoji maoyi zhong do renquan wenti: Yi fazhanquan wei shijiao" [Human rights in international trade: From the standpoint of the right to development], *China foreign law network*, available at http://www. shewai.com/news_info.asp?classcode=0&keyno=0&prono=494 (accessed June 25, 2013).

22. See Beijing University Law School Women's Legal Research and Service Centre, ed., *Laodong quanyi yinan baiwen* [One hundred difficult questions on labor rights and interests]. Beijing: Labor Press, 2001.

23. See, generally, Potter, Pitman B. and Li, Jianyong, "Regulating Labour Relations on China: The Challenge of Adopting to the Socialist Market Economy," *Cahiers du Droit*. Université Laval, 1996.

24. See, e.g., Ji, Yanxiang, "Weihu laodongzhe hefa quanyi de jiben falu" [A basic law for safeguarding the legitimate rights and interests of workers], in *Jingji jingwei* [Economic transit] (Zhengzhou), June 1994, pp. 30–32, 69; Guo, Xiang, "Laodong fa: Weihu zhigong hefa quanyi de jiben fa" [The Labour Law: A basic law for protecting the lawful rights of staff and workers], in *Gongren ribao* [Worker's Daily], January 5, 1995, p. 5.

25. See Guo, Xiang, "Laodong fa: Weihu zhigong hefa quanyi de jiben fa" [The Labour Law: A basic law for protecting the lawful rights of staff and workers], in *Gongren ribao* [Worker's Daily], January 5, 1995, p. 5. While China claims adherence to international treaties on the rights of workers, it claims that, as a developing country, some international labor standards are inapplicable to China. See Zhang, Zuoyi, "Zhongguo laodong lifa" [China's labor legislation], in *Zhengfa luntan* [Theory and discussion on politics and law], no. 6 (1994), pp. 1–4 at pp. 1 and 4.

26. Compare: Dong, Baohua and Lu, Yu, "Lun shiji luxing yuanze: Tiaozheng gebie laodong guanxi de jiben yuanze" [On the principle of specific performance: Adjusting basic principles of various labor relations] with Lu, Yu and Tang, Chanfeng, "Lun laodong hetong uxiao" [On invalid labor contracts], in Dong Baohua, ed., *Laodong hetong yanjiu* [Research on labor contracts]. Beijing: China Labor and Social Protection Press, 2005, pp. 26–53 at pp. 45–53, and pp. 202–224, respectively.

27. Under the 1992 Trade Union Law, trade unions once again receive the authority to represent staff and workers in concluding collective contracts with enterprises and institutions. Article 26 of the 1983 Charter of China's Trade Unions, passed by the Tenth National Congress of China's Trade Unions, authorized basic-level trade union committees to represent staff and workers to sign collective labor contracts. See "Zhongguo gonghui zhangcheng," in *Gonghui fa shouce* [Handbook of trade union law]. Beijing: Democracy and Legal System Press, 1994, pp. 63 and 380.

28. See: "Laodong fa jiaqiangle gonghui de weihu zhineng" [The Labour Law has strengthened the safeguarding capacity of the unions], in *Gongren ribao* [Workers Daily], January 5, 1995, p. 4; "Jiaqiang gonghui gaige he jianshe de qiaoji" [A useful scheme for strengthening reform and construction of the unions], in *Gongren ribao* [Workers Daily], January 23, 1995, p. 1; Guo Xiang, "Laodong fa: Weihu zhigong hefa quanyi de jiben fa" [The Labour Law: A basic law for protecting the lawful rights of staff and workers], in *Gongren ribao* [Worker's Daily], January 5, 1995, p. 5.

29. See, generally, Biddulph, Sarah and Cooney, Sean, "Regulation of Trade Unions in the People's Republic of China," *Melbourne University Law Review*, Vol. 19 (December 1993), pp. 255–292.

30. Cooney, Sean, "Making Chinese Labor Law Work: The Prospects for Regulatory Innovation in the People's Republic of China," *Fordham International Law Journal*, Vol. 30 (2006–2007), pp. 1050–1097; "Laodong fa zhi jianshe de lichengbei" [The milestone established by the Labour Law system], in *Gongren ribao* [Workers Daily], January 9, 1995, p. 1; "Qixin xieli tuijin laodong fa zhi jianshe" [Make consolidated efforts to promote the establishment of the labor law system], in *Gongren ribao* [Workers Daily], January 27, 1995, p. 1; Cao, Min, "State vows to protect interests of laborers," *China Daily*, July 8, 1994, p. 1, in *FBIS Daily Report-China*, July 8, 1994, pp. 17–18.

31. See U.S. Department of State Bureau of Democracy, Human Rights, and Labor, "2004 Country Report on Human Rights Practices – China," available at http://www.state.gov/g/drl/rls/hrrpt/2004/ (accessed June 25, 2013).

32. See *Hetong fa, Laodong: Xiao quan shu* [Labor law: Small compendium]. Beijing: Law Press, 2010.

33. See *Laodong zhengyu: Zhuce ban fagui zhuanji* [Labor disputes: Annotated collection of laws and regulations]. Beijing: Law Press, 2010; Ho, Virginia Harper, "From Contracts to Compliance? An Early Look at Implementation Under China's New Labor Legislation," *Columbia Journal of Asian Law*, Vol. 23, no. 1 (2009), pp. 35–107; Zhu, Xiao, "Laodong zhengyi tiaojie zhongcai fa zhong laodong zhengyui chuli tizhi de shiyong wenti yanjiu" [A study of issues of application of the structure for resolving labor disputes in the Labor disputes mediation

and arbitration law], *Zhengfa lungong* [Politics and law discourse], No. 2 (2009), pp. 55–59.

34. See, e.g., Zhou, Wei, "Zhongguo difang jiuye lifa li de hefaxing yanjiu" [Study of the legality of local unemployment legislation in China], in Zhou, Wei, *Zhongguo de laodong jiuye qishi: Falu yu xianshi* [Employment discrimination in China: Law and Reality]. Beijing: Law Press, 2006, pp. 213–295.

35. See "Zhonggong zhongyang guanyu tuijin nongcun fazhan ruogan zhongda wenti de jueding" [Decision on Major Issues Concerning the Advancement of Rural Reform and Development], *Xinhua*, October 19, 2008.

36. See literary accounts in Zhan, Peng, *Zheng fa wei shuji* [Secretary of the Political Legal Committee]. Kunming: Yunnan People's Press, 2009.

CHAPTER 15

1. Ministerial Declaration of the first WTO Ministerial Conference, available at http://www.ilo.org/declaration/lang-en/index.htm.

2. Convention 87: the Convention on Freedom of Association and Protection of the Right to Organise, ILO, 1948, available at http://www.ilo.org/ilolex/cgi-lex/convde .pl?Co87.

3. Convention 98: the Convention on the Application of the Principles of the Right to Organise and to Bargain Collectively, ILO, 1949, available at http://www.ilo.org/ ilolex/cgi-lex/convde.pl?Co98.

4. Convention 29: the Convention on Forced or Compulsory Labour, ILO, 1930, available at http://www.ilo.org/ilolex/cgi-lex/convde.pl?Co29; Convention 105: the Convention on Abolition of Forced Labour, ILO, 1957, available at http://www.ilo .org/ilolex/cgi-lex/convde.pl?C105.

5. Convention 138: the Convention on the Minimum Age for Admission to Employment, ILO, available at http://www.ilo.org/ilolex/cgi-lex/convde.pl?C138 ratified by China in 1999; Convention 182: the Convention on the Prohibition and Immediate Action for the Elimination of the Worst Forms of Child Labour, ILO, 1999, available at http://www.ilo.org/ilolex/cgi-lex/convde.pl?C182 ratified by China in 2002.

6. Convention 100: the Convention on Equal Remuneration for Men and Women Workers for Work of Equal Value, ILO, 1951, available at http://www.ilo.org/ilolex/ cgi-lex/convde.pl?C100 ratified by China in 1990; Convention 111: Convention on Discrimination in Respect of Employment and Occupation, ILO, 1958, available at http://www.ilo.org/ilolex/cgi-lex/convde.pl?C111 ratified by China in 2006. Dates of ratification are available at http://www.ilo.org/declaration/follow-up/annualreview/ ratificationstatus/lang-en/index.htm.

7. Declaration of Philadelphia 1944 Paragraph I(d): "fundamental principles on which the Organization is based."

8. ILO Declaration of Fundamental Principles and Rights at Work 1998, ILO Declaration on Social Justice for a Fair Globalization 2008.

9. Country baselines under the ILO Declaration Annual Review (2000–2010): Freedom of Association and the Right to Collective Bargaining (FACB), available at http://www.ilo.org/wcmsp5/groups/public/-ed_norm/-declaration/documents/ publication/wcms_091262.pdf.

10. Nor has it ratified the conventions on elimination of all forms of forced or compulsory labor: Conventions 29 and 105. Country baselines under the ILO Declaration Annual Review (2000–2010): the Elimination of All Forms of Forced or Compulsory Labour (FL), available at http://www.ilo.org/wcmsp5/groups/public/-ed_norm/-declaration/documents/publication/wcms_091264.pdf.

11. http://www.ilo.org/declaration/lang-en/index.htm. Another argument is that China is bound to these principles through being a party to the UDHR, which in article 23 provides for core labor protections: "(1) Everyone has the right to work, to free choice of employment, to just and favourable conditions of work and to protection against unemployment. (2) Everyone, without any discrimination, has the right to equal pay for equal work. (3) Everyone who works has the right to just and favourable remuneration ensuring for himself and his family an existence worthy of human dignity, and supplemented, if necessary, by other means of social protection. (4) Everyone has the right to form and to join trade unions for the protection of his interests." Available at http://www.un.org/en/documents/udhr/.

12. Apart from the reporting and review mechanisms, the ILO supervises compliance through its processes for responding to complaints: ILO Constitution article 22 and 19 in respect of reporting and article 24 in respect of complaints. Countries are required to report on their actions to promote compliance with the core labor conventions that they have not ratified; Elliott, 2000, available at http://www.iie.com/publications/pb/pb00-6.pdf. Where a convention has been ratified, monitoring of compliance by the ILO's Committee of Experts on the Application of Conventions and Recommendations goes only so far as to consider whether the legal system complies with the convention; Cooney, 1999, p. 377. A complaint made under ILO Constitution article 26 about gross violations of a convention to which the country has acceded may, if the country refuses to act on recommendations to rectify the problem, fall under article 33, which provides that the "Governing Body may recommend to the Conference such action as it may deem wise and expedient to secure compliance therewith."

13. "ILO, The Declaration," available at http://www.ilo.org/declaration/thedeclaration/lang-en/index.htm.

14. Kent, 2007, pp. 185, 190–192, discussing China's responses to cases brought by the ICFTU against China, Cases 1500 and 1652, after the crackdown on independent unions during and after the 1989 Tiananmen Square massacre.

15. In December 2010, China had ratified twenty-five Conventions with twenty-two of those in force, including four of the eight Fundamental Conventions. It has submitted all of the requested reports on application of the ratified conventions. International Labour Conference 100th Session 2011, *Information Document on Ratifications and Standards Related Activities*, available at http://www.ilo.org/wcmsp5/groups/public/-ed_norm/-relconf/documents/meeting-document/wcms_151865.pdf.

16. The *Trade Union Law* article 4 reiterates, among other things, leadership of the Communist Party and union focus on economic construction.

17. *Trade Union Law* article 5.

18. Clarke et al., 2004, p. 239. For example, in 2001, the Joint Circular on Promoting Collective Consultation and Collective Contracts mandated the involvement of a range of interested state agencies and enterprise associations in

implementing the system of collective contracts throughout the country; *Trade Union Law*, article 5.

19. Tripartite Consultation (International Labour Standards) Convention, signed June 21, 1976, ILO Convention No. 144 (entered into force May 16, 1978), available at http://www.ilo.org/ilolex/cgi-lex/convde.pl?C144.

20. See, e.g., Shanghai Municipal Human Resources and Social Security Bureau 2008 Notice on Promoting the Work of Collective Wage Consultation, April 1, 2008.

21. The dual obligations of the unions are embodied in the Trade Union Law of the People's Republic of China (1992) (People's Republic of China) National People's Congress ("Trade Union Law 1992") articles 4, 5, and 6, and replicated in the Trade Union Law of the People's Republic of China (People's Republic of China) National People's Congress ("Trade Union Law 2001") articles 4, 5, and 6.

22. *Trade Union Law* 2001 Article 7.

23. In 2004, Wang Zhaoguo, member of the Political Bureau of the CCP Central Committee, Vice Chairman of the National People's Congress (NPC) Standing Committee, and Chairman of the All China Federation of Trade Unions, announced the program: "Get Organized and Conscientiously Protect Rights" (Chang, 2004). At the All China Federation of Trade Unions' 15th Congress, the following provision was added to article 28: "Adhere to the path of developing socialist trade unions with Chinese characteristics, adhere to the 'Get Organized and Conscientiously Protect Rights' work plan, put workers first, take the initiative in protecting rights in a scientific way and according to law." See Wang, 2008 and Yang, 2009. Trade Union Law 2001, Article 7.

24. Wang, 2011, p. 20. Linking rights protection to the primary objective of stability maintenance in this way was articulated in the Harmonious Society policy, which was formally adopted at the close of the Sixth Plenary session of the 16th CPC Central Committee meeting on October 11, 2006 in the Resolution on Major Issues Regarding the Building of a Harmonious Socialist Society, available at http://www.china.org.cn/english/report/189591.htm.

25. Chapter 32 section 1, available at http://news.sina.com.cn/c/2011-03-17/055622129864.shtml.

26. Trade Union Law, Art. 20: "Trade unions shall assist and guide workers and staff members in signing labour contracts with enterprises or institutions managed as enterprises. Trade unions shall, on behalf of the workers and staff members, make equal consultations and sign collective contracts with enterprises or institutions under enterprise-style management. The draft collective contracts shall be submitted to the congresses of the workers and staff members or all the workers and staff members for deliberation and approval. When trade unions sign collective contracts, trade unions at higher levels shall afford support and assistance to them. If an enterprise infringes upon labor rights and interests of the workers and staff members in violation of the collective contract, the trade union may, according to law, demand the enterprise to assume the responsibilities for its acts; if the disputes arising from the performance of the collective contract fail to be settled through consultations, the trade union may submit them to the labor dispute arbitration bodies for arbitration; if the arbitration bodies refuse to accept the case or the trade union is not satisfied with the arbitral ruling, the trade union may bring the case before a People's Court."

27. Labour Law article 33 provides: "The staff and workers of an enterprise as one party may conclude a collective contract with the enterprise on matters relating to labour remuneration, working hours, rest and vacations, occupational safety and health, and insurance and welfare. The draft collective contract shall be submitted to the congress of the staff and workers, or to all the staff and workers for discussion and adoption. A collective contract shall be concluded by the trade union on behalf of the staff and workers with the enterprise; in an enterprise where the trade union has not yet been set up, such contract shall be also concluded by the representatives elected by the staff and workers with the enterprise."

28. Passed on May 1, 2004 by the Ministry of Labour and Social Security (MOLSS) (now Ministry of Human Resources and Social Security [MOHRSS]). These provisions supersede the 1994 Provisions on Collective Contracts and provide the current legal framework for concluding collective contracts.

29. In 2007, Wen Jiabao noted that the "Wenling model can be studied and promoted" (China Labor News Translations, October 10, 2008). In 2006, the All China Federation of Trade Unions, MOHRSS, the Chinese Enterprises' Federation, and the Chinese Entrepreneurs' Association jointly issued the Opinion on Developing Regional and Industry Level Collective Consultation Work, available at http://www/gd.lss.gov.cn/ldtzw/zc/flfg/zxfg/t20061025_12690.htm.

30. Examples are: Shenzhen Regulations on the Promotion of Harmonious Labour Relations, which took effect on November 1, 2008; the 2007 Shanghai Collective Contracts Provisions; 2009 Hainan Collective Contracts Provisions; the Guangdong Guidelines on Enterprise Collective Consultation on Wages passed on August 5, 2010; and the Zhejiang Province Collective Contracts Provisions passed by the Zhejiang Provincial Peoples' Congress, which were scheduled to take effect on January 1, 2011.

31. Shenzhen Measures on Implementing the PRC Trade Union Law, Art 11(1), which provides that candidates for the positions of union chair and vice chair and standing committee members shall be nominated by union members, approved by the higher-level union, and subject to direct election by the union general assembly.

32. Trade Union Law 2001, Art 9 merely prohibits close relatives of main management personnel of enterprises from membership in grassroots trade union committees. It does not expressly prohibit managers themselves from membership in the enterprise union committee.

33. For example, the Zhejiang Collective Contracts Provisions, the draft Guangdong Regulations on the Democratic Management of Enterprises, and the Shanghai Provisions on Employee Representative Councils.

CHAPTER 16

1. "Collective protest" (*quntixing shijian*) refers to various collective actions, often outside China's legal procedures. The collective protest can take place over a variety of issues, including labor, land, environment, and others. The data is collected by the Public Security Bureau, which is seldom made public. China does not produce data on strike action, as the right to strike is not mentioned in any of Chinese legislation. Instead, the Ministry of Human Resources and Social Security collects

data on labor dispute cases referred to local arbitration council. When this essay refers to statistics on labor disputes, it means the number of cases officially referred to the arbitration council.

2. As Naughton noted, China was a dualistic egalitarian society before the economic reform (Naughton, 2007). Under the planned economy, China maintained a dualistic society where urban residents enjoyed far better living conditions at the expense of a vast rural population. But within rural and urban sectors, there was a high degree of egalitarianism.

3. During the Cultural Revolution period, even the operation of the ACFTU was suspended until Deng Xiaoping decided to rehabilitate the national union as a part of his reform programs in late 1970s.

4. In all legal documents, China uses the term *jitixieshang* (collective consultation) instead of *jititanpan* (collective bargaining). Though industrial relations practitioners increasingly use *jititanpan* in recent years, the official term for collective bargaining in China is still *jitixieshang* as it does not have a connotation of conflict or confrontation. Considering that the right to strike is still not officially recognized, the term *jitixieshang* may better describe the current situation of collective bargaining in today's China, as collective bargaining can function fully under *shadow of a possibility* of industrial actions.

5. Collective bargaining was actively promoted in the early years of the People's Republic of China. But as Mao declared China's transition toward the socialist stage in mid-1950s, the unitarist labor relations system of socialist economy emerged where there was supposed to be no separation of interests between workers and "enterprises." Until the 1990s, collective bargaining did not take place at all (except a very few experiments in the 1980s, mostly in foreign joint ventures).

6. In many localities, the vice-mayors of the municipalities act as the head of tripartite industrial relations task force responsible for promotion of orderly collective bargaining and other labor relations priorities.

7. The article 6 of the 1992 Trade Union Law stipulated that "*in addition* to safeguarding the overall interests of the people of the whole nation, trade unions should safeguard the legal rights and interests of staff members and workers." But the revised Trade Union Law says that "the basic duties and functions of trade unions are to safeguard the legitimate rights and interests of workers and staff members. While protecting the overall interests of the entire Chinese people, trade unions shall represent and safeguard the legitimate rights and interests of workers and staff members."

8. It is to be noted, however, that the tripartite consultation mechanism was established in a number of municipalities (such as Nanjing and Dalian) on an experimental basis in the late 1990s, before the establishment of the national TCC.

9. Until 2003, rural migrant workers were not regarded as part of the working class. Therefore, rural migrant workers employed in urban labor markets were in principle outside the unions' organizing targets.

10. While organizing unions in MNCs has been a priority since the late 1990s, it was President Hu Jintao's urge in March 2006 to set up trade unions and party organizations in foreign invested enterprises that prompted the ACFTU to take a prompt action.

11. Before 2002, there was no official statistics on wage agreements and regional/sectoral agreements, as there was no nationwide policy of promoting wage negotiations and regional/sectoral agreements.
12. Better governance structure includes elements such as elections and a well-established union organization down to shop floor level, supported by workplace institutions of workers' collective voice (such as workers' congress and collective bargaining).

Index

CPSIA information can be obtained at www.ICGtesting.com
Printed in the USA
LVOW04s0514270815

451532LV00003B/12/P